Advance Praise

T0379675

"This book is a unique and glorious blend of science and practice! Kudos to Ana Gómez for gifting clinicians with this substantive, state-of-the-art, integrative, trauma-informed approach. Her discussion of trauma is comprehensive and considers a range of contemporary issues such as neuroscience, attachment, trauma defenses, and implicit and explicit memories (to name a few), offering guidance on how to approach trauma recovery in a thoughtful, safe, and precise manner. I am particularly impressed with the ample suggested language, phrasing, and questions that clinicians often struggle to develop. Trauma-informed concerns are described succinctly, alongside a range of possible verbal and nonverbal (nondirective and directive) interventions, making this book immediately useful and relevant for clinicians supporting children and families through the trauma recovery process."

—**Eliana Gil, PhD,** senior clinical director, Gil Institute for Trauma Recovery and Education, Fairfax, VA

"Many of our clients, because of their powerful defenses, trauma-based fears, and dissociative tendencies, struggle to make use of all that EMDR has to offer. In this well-written book, infused with compassion, wisdom, and creativity, Ana Gómez provides a comprehensive guide to integrating EMDR therapy with sandtray therapies in the service of reaching and treating those with deep wounds but limited access to their own stories and emotions. It is an informative and inspiring read!"

—**Deborah L. Korn, PsyD,** faculty, EMDR Institute and Trauma Research Foundation, coauthor, *Every Memory Deserves Respect: EMDR, the Proven Trauma Therapy with the Power to Heal*

"Ana Gómez masterfully describes how her EMDR-sandtray-based therapy integrates various theories and modalities with her extensive clinical experience. She artfully articulates the deep understanding and insights sandtray provides, which are valuable and informative even to non-EMDR practitioners. Gómez also encourages clinicians to use the tray to expand their awareness, explore their own mind, and develop their 'therapeutic home.' Her profound comprehension and artful description of this integrative method is truly exceptional."

—**Linda E. Homeyer, PhD, LPC-S, RPT-STM, RST-CT,** coauthor of *Advanced Sandtray Therapy: Digging Deeper in Clinical Practice*

"Through the masterful stewardship of Ana Gómez, learn to guide your clients with compassion and clarity in working through their complex issues and situations. Written in a clear and practical way, this book addresses how to assist your clients with the complexities of working with trauma and dissociation, and deepen your therapeutic relationship within the framework of Gómez's multimodal EMDR-sandtray-based framework. This nuanced and culturally responsive approach empowers you to understand trauma in a new and effective way that supports your work with your clients and their experience in the world. Overlooked topics such as addictions, attachment to the perpetrator, neurodiversity, and intersectionality of identities are addressed."

—**Marilyn Luber, PhD,** editor of the *EMDR Scripted Protocol* books and coauthor of *Treating Depression with EMDR Therapy: Techniques and Interventions*

EMDR-Sandtray-based Therapy

EMDR-SANDTRAY-BASED THERAPY

Healing Complex Trauma and Dissociation
Across the Lifespan

ANA M. GÓMEZ

Norton Professional Books
*An Imprint of W. W. Norton & Company
Independent Publishers Since 1923*

This book is intended as a general information resource for professionals practicing in the field of psychotherapy and mental health. It is not a substitute for appropriate training or clinical supervision. Standards of clinical practice and protocol vary in different practice settings and change over time. No technique or recommendation is guaranteed to be safe or effective in all circumstances, and neither the publisher nor the author can guarantee the complete accuracy, efficacy, or appropriateness of any particular recommendation in every respect or in all settings or circumstances.

All patients described in the book and all session transcripts are composites. The author is not a lawyer, and nothing contained in this book should be construed as legal advice. For advice about how to prepare legally appropriate informed consent documents, or for any other legal advice or legal questions related to your therapy practice, please consult an attorney with relevant expertise.

Any URLs displayed in this book link or refer to websites that existed as of press time. The publisher is not responsible for, and should not be deemed to endorse or recommend, any website other than its own or any content that it did not create. The author, also, is not responsible for any third-party material.

Foreword © 2025 by Marshall Lyles
Copyright © 2025 by Ana Gómez

All rights reserved
Printed in the United States of America
First Edition

For information about permission to reproduce selections from this book, write to Permissions, W. W. Norton & Company, Inc., 500 Fifth Avenue, New York, NY 10110

For information about special discounts for bulk purchases, please contact
W. W. Norton Special Sales at specialsales@wwnorton.com or 800-233-4830

Manufacturing by Versa Press
Production manager: Gwen Cullen

ISBN: 978-1-324-05365-1

W. W. Norton & Company, Inc., 500 Fifth Avenue, New York, NY 10110
www.wwnorton.com

W. W. Norton & Company Ltd., 15 Carlisle Street, London W1D 3BS

1 2 3 4 5 6 7 8 9 0

To my mother, Elizabeth, whose love remains the foundation of my being, guiding me even beyond this world.

To Jim, my life companion and constant source of strength, who provides a safe space for me to embrace life in all its forms.

To my sister, Oderay, who reflects and nurtures my truest self.

To my furry children, who have taught me the true essence of unconditional love.

To the clients who allowed me to join them in the depths of existence.

CONTENTS

Acknowledgments ix

Foreword xi

Introduction xiii

CHAPTER 1

A Multimodal Approach to EMDR-Sandtray-based Therapy: Defining Complex Trauma and Dissociation

1

CHAPTER 2

Phase 1: Foundational and Advanced Skills

25

CHAPTER 3

Phase 2: Preparation

67

CHAPTER 4

Phase 2: Advanced Capacity Building and Strategies to Work With Complex Trauma and Dissociation

112

CHAPTER 5

Systemic Work With Parents and Children

143

CHAPTER 6

Phase 3: Assessment

180

CHAPTER 7

Phase 4: Desensitization

207

CHAPTER 8

Phases 5–8: Installation, Body Scan, Closure, Reevaluation, and Future Template

248

CHAPTER 9

Advanced Strategies During Reprocessing Phases With Complex Clients

263

CHAPTER 10

The Therapeutic Relationship and the Intersubjective Field

292

CHAPTER 11

Group EMDR-Sandtray-based Therapy

309

CHAPTER 12

Special Populations and Considerations in the Application of EMDR-Sandtray-based Therapy

337

Appendices:

Appendix 1   379

Appendix 2   383

Appendix 3   386

Appendix 4   387

References   389

Index   401

ACKNOWLEDGMENTS

I extend my deepest gratitude to Francine Shapiro, a mentor and teacher whose vision and brilliance showed us the transformative gift of EMDR therapy. Her pioneering work has shaped a path that countless others, myself included, continue to follow and expand.

To the trailblazers of EMDR therapy, sandtray and sand-based therapies, whose groundbreaking contributions laid the foundation upon which I now humbly stand. Their ingenuity and dedication have paved the way for us to carry this profound work into new frontiers of healing.

To the storytellers—children, adolescents, and adults—who entrusted me with the privilege of being their companion and witness on their sacred journeys of self-discovery. Your courage to explore the depths of your being has not only illuminated my understanding of the human mind but also inspired me in ways words cannot fully convey.

To Deborah Malmud, for believing in my work and steadfastly supporting my efforts. To my initial companion and editor, Emily Bradley, whose guidance and early partnership helped shape the original manuscript. I am immensely grateful to the exceptional Norton team, whose thoughtful feedback and unwavering support have been invaluable: Julie HawkOwl, Olivia Guarnieri, and McKenna Tanner.

To the countless clinicians who have sought my consultation and supervision over the years and those who have attended my trainings—your questions, cases, and curiosity have continuously challenged and expanded the boundaries of my awareness, sharpening my understanding of both therapy and humanity.

To my husband, Jim Mason, whose enduring love, constant support, and countless sacrifices gave me the time and space to dedicate myself fully to writing and editing this book. Your patience, love, and sense of humor sustained me through the challenges of this journey.

To my family—my parents and siblings—who provided the foundation of love, encouragement, and space that nurtured my innate desire to think deeply, explore boldly, and embrace the complexity of life from an early age.

I especially dedicate this book to my mother, Elizabeth, whose love, safety, and consistent reciprocity I carry in my heart. Thank you for creating the space for my wings to grow.

To my sister Oderay, a life companion who reflects my mind with such love and insight—you are a profound source of strength and inspiration.

To all my furry companions who were often on my lap or near my computer, offering their genuine love and support as I worked countless hours to write this manuscript—and a special thanks to Lady and Candy. Your comforting presence has been an important part of this journey, and I am deeply grateful for the solace and joy you bring to my life.

To the spiritual companions who have walked with me on this journey, whispering words of wisdom as I poured my heart and soul into these pages. I recognize that I am but a vessel through which the infinite wisdom that surrounds us flows. Thank you for guiding me to the still, sacred place where ideas take root and insights are born.

Finally, I honor my journey for the wisdom and growth it has imparted, allowing me to traverse the vast spectrum of human experience. Within these profound contrasts—light and shadow, joy, and sorrow—I have found the richness of life and the inspiration for this work.

FOREWORD

Many years ago, I was a new EMDR clinician who was won over by the potential healing this approach could offer people who are hurting, but I was perplexed about how to reach my particular clientele with it. Back then, I was primarily serving children and families impacted by complex trauma and had been trained in the world of expressive and play therapies; there were few bridges from EMDR to those populations and approaches. That's when I discovered the writing of Ana Gómez. She became a bridge for me. She offered possibilities for moving through these liminal spaces with care, creativity, and fidelity.

Since that time, I have read everything Ana has written, have attended multiple workshops she has taught, and have had the good fortune of spending many hours in deep dialogue with her about all manner of topics. Regardless of the context, spending time with Ana changes you. She is a generous leader in the field of EMDR and her reach feels impossible to quantify. Even with all of her previous positive impacts, this book, *EMDR-Sandtray-based Therapy: Healing Complex Trauma and Dissociation Across the Lifespan,* might be her most valuable offering yet. You can feel her authenticity and passion. Her years of cultivated wisdom come through as approachable and inspirational.

In this book, Ana manages to be pragmatic without being formulaic, hope-giving without over-promising, and honoring of the wisdom of past thinkers without hindering the possibility for future inspiration and adaptation. The following chapters are structured around EMDR's phases, while pausing in moments to welcome background knowledge about sandtray therapy, complex trauma, and systemic thought. These concepts are beautifully integrated and Ana makes a compelling case for how combining EMDR and sandtray from a systemic perspective can impact lives of all ages impacted by complex trauma.

In the first chapter, Ana sets a tone for the book that is both scholarly and humanizing. Taking time to offer a contextual overview of the ideas that will be deeply explored later, the reader feels conceptually grounded and prepared to move into the chapters that focus more on application. Chapters 2, 3, and 4 kindly spend a generous amount of time honoring how

xi

to more deeply know the stories and capacities of clients with complex trauma without pressuring or rushing their progress.

Chapter 5 invites the reader to consider how to keep the family system in mind. Complex trauma ripples through relational networks, and healing can be amplified when the therapist is prepared to work with the attachment energy held in these networks. This chapter offers a space for theoretical weaving to occur as well as ideas for how to create a welcoming environment for all clients in the sand tray.

Chapters 6, 7, 8, and 9 equip sandtray clinicians to move further into EMDR treatment planning and service provision by presenting thoughtful methods of titration into the compassionate reprocessing of painful memories. Continuing with the style of earlier chapters, Ana discusses the *why* and *how* of these EMDR phases while illustrating application through examples of what a clinician might say to make the transitions feel safe and intentional. There are also ample case examples that bring the material to life.

I am particularly delighted about Chapter 10 on "The Therapeutic Relationship and the Intersubjective Field." Sometimes, an unintentional side effect that comes from a therapeutic approach deepening into evidence-based territory is a pull away from a focus on the therapeutic relationship. Ana highlights the necessity of monitoring this relationship in the cocreated healing spaces for complex trauma. Once again bringing in relational neuroscience and modern attachment theory, this chapter sharpens the reader's conviction to contemplate self-of-the-therapist as an integral part of developing into a responsible EMDR clinician.

The final two chapters focus on special applications, populations, and considerations. Including resources for group work and addressing often overlooked needs, these closing pieces address important issues and leave room for future works. The book closes in a manner that helps a clinician to feel satiated and prepared.

I feel lucky to have been given access to a book that will soon become an often-cited, seminal resource in both the EMDR and sandtray therapy communities. This read is worth the time investment and I can imagine therapists dog-earing pages and consulting sections over and over. They will carry Ana as part of their inner treatment team as they provide hope to families doing the brave work of addressing complex trauma. Thank you, Ana, for lighting a way into shadowy places. We can all move more surefooted because of what you bring into the world.

—**Marshall Lyles, LMFT-S, LPC-S, RPT-S,** EMDRIA-approved
consultant, and coauthor of *Advanced Sandtray Therapy:
Digging Deeper into Clinical Practice*

INTRODUCTION

Many children, adolescents, and adults live in fear, carrying stories from their past that trap them in anguish, shame, and a sense of defectiveness and unworthiness. The weight of these unspoken experiences can be isolating, leaving them struggling with the burden of their untold truths. The torment left by trauma has molded their identity and their ways of relating to the world, themselves, and others. Despite these challenges, individuals exposed to chronic traumatization also possess deep-seated strengths, capacities, and ancestral resources. Resilience in this population does not speak to their capacity to bounce back; it is about the ongoing, arduous process of reclaiming their wholeness and returning to themselves.

For many of our clients, trauma left them in a constant state of physiological activation, unable to verbally tell their life accounts. When the psychotherapeutic encounter relies solely on verbal capacities, parts of our clients' stories may never be known or recognized. As Siegel (2020) eloquently stated, "We must keep in mind that only a part of memory can be translated into the language-based packets of information people use to tell their life stories to others. Learning to be open to many layers of communication is a fundamental part of getting to know another person's life" (p. 143). The brain's bihemispheric structure imposes the challenge of therapeutically relating and strategically embracing the full biology of the human mind. Sometimes, the client's stories exist only in body-based memory or hidden implicit images that are not organized cohesively or coherently, and the client lacks explicit awareness and temporal orientation to them.

In my many years of working with clients touched by adversity and hardship, I have observed the multiple adaptations they have had to make to live with the daily reminders of their painful stories. I always wondered how we, as therapeutic companions, can support their healing when their voices have been silenced by trauma. How do we accompany them as they embrace the, often painful, journey toward realizing their wholeness and attaining integration? Their suffering is frequently multifaceted and complex, requiring clinicians to provide multiple roads and possibilities, as clients of all ages embrace their life histories and their connection to themselves.

Being a therapeutic companion to hundreds of children, adolescents, and adults has profoundly changed me. It has touched deep layers of my own existence. For years, I struggled with cases that were extremely demanding and complex, often encountering stagnation in the therapeutic process. After my training in EMDR therapy in 2000, I reached into what I knew from my training in play therapy and sandtray therapy. I integrated it into the framework of EMDR with clients of all ages, especially the ones who were not responding to treatment—mostly due to their deep wounds, strong defenses, trauma-related phobias, and dissociative tendencies. I wondered what would happen if my clients could utilize images and symbols instead of working verbally on resources or even memories of trauma.

To my surprise, I witnessed incredible movement in places where immobility and inertia had once existed. I observed stories unfolding and clients dialoguing with what was once hidden in implicit memory and behind rigid defensive walls. The symbols and avatars in the sandtray began to penetrate old barricades built in the service of survival. Emotions and somatic states that were held prisoner emerged, embedded in the protective forces of metaphors and symbols. For clients who did not have a voice, the sand tray and the sand characters became theirs. This experience led me to develop the union of EMDR therapy with sand-based therapies. EMDR-sandtray-based therapy became the portal to access some of the deepest wounds, which are often cognitively invisible yet somatically felt. Over the years, as I expanded my understanding of the human mind, I began to weave a multimodal and transtheoretical approach to EMDR therapy for complex trauma. In addition to the adaptive information processing (AIP) model, I incorporated other theoretical models for case conceptualization addressing attachment, dissociation, emotion regulation, the Polyvagal Theory, and interpersonal neurobiology (IPNB).

EMDR-Sandtray-based Therapy: Its Roots and Origins

The origins of EMDR therapy began in 1987 when Dr. Francine Shapiro encountered her own adversity and found the central elements of what is now a comprehensive psychotherapeutic approach. Her first randomized study was conducted in 1989 with individuals experiencing the debilitating symptoms of post-traumatic stress disorder (PTSD). Through arduous work and trials, Shapiro created the principles, model, methodology, and standardized procedures of EMDR therapy, layer by layer. I have witnessed the transformative nature of this psychotherapeutic method. Clients who had once lived their lives burdened by the belief that they were damaged and unworthy became able to see themselves as valuable and good enough after EMDR treatment. They were able to convert and transmute their shame and fear into self-acceptance and self-compassion. Through this therapeutic process, they finally completed and somatically recalibrated their trapped bodily states and truncated responses.

I had the great honor of being trained by Dr. Shapiro as an EMDR trainer and of coauthoring and collaborating with her on various projects. I learned from her brilliant, inquisitive mind and her tireless, courageous spirit. Today, EMDR therapy is a psychotherapeutic approach that has the support of reputable worldwide organizations and robust research across multiple populations.

Sandtray therapy, on the other hand, has a history deeply rooted in over 100 years of healing practices. Thirty years ago, when I embarked on my journey as a psychotherapist, I found myself instinctively drawn to play and dance. Both have always been fundamental parts of my life. Play is a powerful, innate motivational system (Liotti, 2017; Panksepp & Biven, 2012) that fosters learning, discovery, curiosity, and social bonds. I stand on the shoulders of numerous pioneers and authors in the fields of EMDR therapy, play therapy, sand-based therapies, and neuroscience who have laid the foundation for those who follow.

This book provides EMDR and sandtray clinicians—experts and novices—with the theory, research, and guidelines for intentional decision-making in utilizing EMDR-sandtray-based therapy with clients across the lifespan. This volume presents a multimodal approach to the use of EMDR and sandtray therapy, offering diverse pathways to bridge the AIP model (F. Shapiro, 2001, 2018; Shapiro, 2007) with other seminal theories. The delivery of EMDR–sandtray therapy is anchored in theories of attachment that provide the framework to understand and therapeutically address the profound influence of early relationships on the development of the self and the role of disrupted attachment in complex trauma. The multimodal approach to EMDR–sandtray therapy draws insights from dissociation theories as well as from pioneers and contemporary scholars in the field, providing a critical framework for addressing dissociation in its multiple manifestations and its spectrum of symptoms. Concepts and constructs from IPNB are incorporated into the AIP model, addressing multiple levels of integration and emphasizing the interconnectedness of the mind, embodied brain, and relationships. Additionally, polyvagal-based interventions using the sandtray and miniatures collection, parts work, play therapy, gestalt therapy, and systemic work are masterfully incorporated to enhance the power of EMDR and sandtray therapies in the treatment of complex trauma and dissociation.

Each chapter provides decision-making markers, step-by-step procedural steps, practical strategies with composite case examples, and pictures inspired by real cases that address various dimensions of complex trauma. Clinicians will also have access to EMDR-sandtray-based protocols that titrate the entrance into traumagenic memory networks to accommodate various degrees of affect tolerance and gradually adjust the work to each client's integrative capacities and readiness to do trauma work. This book also provides multiple delivery formats for EMDR and sandtray therapy, including individual, group, family, and dyadic practice. EMDR-sandtray-based group and family therapy not only represents a unique feature of this book but also provides powerful avenues for healing. Systemic EMDR-sandtray-based therapy for children and their parents provides a portal into the healing of generational wounds and the integration and repatterning of the child's and parent's embodied minds as well as their relational bond.

The chapters of this book are organized around the eight phases of EMDR therapy (Chapters 1, 2, 3, 6, 7, and 8) while incorporating EMDR–sandtray theory, principles, and procedures. Additional chapters (4 and 9) address advanced case conceptualization, decision-making markers, and strategies for working with clients who present with greater complexity and dissociative tendencies. Chapter 5 addresses intergenerational, systemic, and dyadic work with children and their caregivers, while Chapter 10 delves into the clinician's embodied mind in the therapeutic relationship and the intersubjective field in EMDR–sandtray work. Chapter 11 explores the applications of EMDR-sandtray-based therapy with groups and families and Chapter 12 addresses its use with various populations and issues, including grief and loss, abuse, neurodiversity, addictions, cultural identities and telehealth.

Undeniably, inhabiting my own existence has shaped the fabric of this book. My healing and search for congruence within myself have profoundly influenced my work as a consultant, teacher, author, and companion to others. My journey of self-discovery is woven into the fabric of this book, and the process of writing it has somewhat altered my inner landscape and human voyage. It has certainly been a bidirectional and transformative relationship!

EMDR-Sandtray-based Therapy

CHAPTER 1

A Multimodal Approach to EMDR-Sandtray-based Therapy

Defining Complex Trauma and Dissociation

Since individuals exposed to repetitive experiences of trauma present with many diagnoses besides PTSD, the term *complex trauma* better encompasses the extensive effect that overlaps with multiple forms of symptomatology. Herman (1992/2022) suggests that complex post-traumatic stress disorder (cPTSD) is a syndrome resulting from chronic exposure to trauma, especially interpersonal trauma. Individuals who have experienced complex trauma often present with substantial disturbances in affect regulation and self-organization as well as with dissociation and somatization. According to Courtois and Ford (2013), complex trauma occurs chronically, repetitively, cumulatively, and interpersonally during critical periods of development. This trauma hinders the individual's neurodevelopment, integrative capacities, regulatory systems, and identity formation, resulting in dissociative processes and long-lasting and multidimensional consequences. Dissociation leads to disturbances in the integration of consciousness, memory, identity, emotions, perception, body representation, motor control, and behavior (American Psychiatric Association, 2022). The polytraumatization that typifies these experiences generally transpires within significant relationships during the client's formative years, resulting in pervasive disruptions in regulatory capacities that manifest in relational deficits; attentional challenges; and reduced capacities for information processing, impulse and behavioral control, somatization, and physical and identity development (Ford, 2021).

Due to the multifaceted nature of trauma, it has no unified definition across institutions, authors, or disciplines. According to the *Diagnostic and Statistical Manual of Mental Disorders,* Fifth Edition (American Psychiatric Association, 2022), trauma encompasses "actual or threatened death, serious injury, or sexual violence" (p. 271), excluding any stressful events that do not involve an immediate threat to life. Contrary to this perspective, Lyons-Ruth and Jacobvitz (2008) contend that children are not equipped to assess danger the way adults do and may perceive separation or emotional distance from a caregiver as endangering. Complex trauma carries the repercussions of unfulfilled and missed developmental milestones due to a relational environment that did not furnish the child with what they needed to form a healthy sense of agency, integrity, and identity. Exposure to chronic relational misattunement has been called "invisible complex trauma" (Schore, 2019) and "hidden trauma" (Lyons-Ruth et al., 2006). These repetitive macro- and microruptures—occurring in all forms of insecure attachment, especially disorganized—may constitute attachment trauma. The wounding relational terrain in early attachment experiences impacts neurodevelopment, manifesting in pervasive patterns of affect dysregulation or dissociation (Hill, 2015; Schore, 2019).

There is a critical need for a more nuanced and inclusive definition of complex trauma that expands the parameters and that reframes our current understandings. While a sole theory and definition of complex trauma may remain elusive, we must acknowledge how our field has reached a much greater understanding of the intricate interplay of systemic, societal, cultural, relational, and individual factors that influence its impact.

Sandplay, Sandtray, and Sand-Based Therapies

History points to Margaret Lowenfeld, in the 1920s, as one of the pioneers of sandtray–based therapies. Her work was inspired by H. G. Wells's 1911 novel *Floor Games.* In Lowenfeld's attempts to help children impacted by the First World War, she created the World Technique. Children were invited to take items from "the wonder box" and place them inside a sandtray to represent their inner world and self (Turner, 2017). Lowenfeld believed that play was a healing experience. For Lowenfeld, the sandtray provided a bridge between the child's inner and outer worlds, allowing her to understand the feelings, thoughts, and ideas they could not express with words. As she continued to develop the World Technique, she used sand trays with wet and dry sand and a cabinet with various figures. She introduced her work in London in 1928. Since then, clinicians worldwide have been using her techniques.

Dora Maria Kalff later integrated elements of Lowenfeld's work and Carl Jung's (1934–1955/1969) personality theory to create "sandplay." According to Turner (2017), sandplay "is a non-verbal [*sic*] play therapy that intentionally creates a space for the unconscious to manifest" (p. 159). In sandplay, therapists hold the unknown and the material emerging from the unconscious in the tray without trying to interpret it. When the mind receives the space, the psyche can work with the symbols that emerge in the tray on its own time and rhythm (Turner, 2017). This is what Kalff called "the free and protected space." According to Kalff (1980/2003), "When a child feels that he is not alone—not only in his distress but also in his happiness—he then feels free, but still protected, in all his expressions" (p. 30). The therapist provides a safeguarded therapeutic atmosphere that gives the unconscious mind space to express itself and move toward healing and alignment with the self. Jung claimed that images, symbols, and stories were the language of the unconscious, while words and rational reasoning were those of the conscious mind (Turner, 2017). In sandplay, the child makes up for the missed developmental stages (Kalff, 1980/2003).

According to Kalff (1980/2003), individuation (the process of the psyche integrating material from the unconscious with the conscious personality) of the self occurs spontaneously in children due to sandplay work. For adults, sandplay will commence at the age when the trauma began or took place. According to Turner (2017), "The tray of an adult can easily appear to be the sandplay of a five-year-old, if there was wounding that happened at age five" (p. 8). From a different approach, Shapiro (2018) states that memory networks containing traumagenic material—implicit and explicit— remain frozen in time with the same worldview and perspective of the age in which the trauma occurred. When the memory becomes activated in the present, the thoughts, emotions, and bodily states are evocative and reflective of the much younger mind that encoded the experience.

Multiple non-Jungian therapeutic methodologies have been developed that utilize the sandtray and miniature figure collection. Sandtray therapy encompasses a variety of approaches beyond Jungian psychology. Homeyer and Sweeney (2017) define sandtray therapy as:

> An expressive and projective mode of psychotherapy involving the unfolding and processing of intra- and inter-personal issues through the use of specific Sandtray [*sic*] materials as a nonverbal medium of communication, led by the client or therapist and facilitated by a trained therapist. It is a process that seeks to promote safety and control for the client so that emotionally charged issues can be addressed through the medium. (p. 1)

According to Homeyer and Sweeney (2017), sandtray therapy is a flexible cross-theoretical intervention that can be adapted to multiple therapeutic models. In his afterword, Martin M. Kalff (Dora Kalff's son) (2020) discusses colleagues integrating sandplay therapy with EMDR therapy and encourages further exploration of incorporating methods from beyond analytical psychology into sandplay practice.

Sand-based work can be infused with language and verbal expressions, and at the same time, it may be verbally discreet. The sandtray work becomes a vehicle for the verbally vigorous explicit mind and the symbol-based, emotionally active, implicit mind. It may depict rambunctious data and the whispers of silenced and unspoken material. Clinicians can move from nondirective and client-driven occurrences to directive and clinician-guided interventions. Sand-based strategies work with individuals who have rich verbal capacities and with those who possess none.

The field of sand-based therapies is experiencing a remarkable expansion, with contributions and blends from multiple approaches and disciplines. Each method adds to the palette and offerings of sand-based approaches. A vast array of pathways—ranging from classic Lowenfeld method and Jungian psychology to gestalt, cognitive–behavioral frameworks, somatic methodologies, and now EMDR therapy—provide a nuanced and ever-evolving therapeutic landscape.

Scientific Support

Multiple studies present quantitative and qualitative data that support the effectiveness of sand-based therapies in children, adolescents, and adults with histories of trauma, behavioral challenges, and more.

Sandplay meta-analysis, including 40 studies and 1,284 participants (Wiersma et al., 2022), suggests that sandplay is an effective treatment for children and adults with wide-ranging mental health challenges.

In a longitudinal and qualitative study using sandplay and sandtray therapy with children ages 7–10 with a history of sexual abuse, Angeles Tornero and Capella (2017) collected data from observations and video recordings of children's therapeutic work. As treatment progressed, there was a movement toward organization, positive outcomes in the tray, and the reconfiguration of meaning assigned to the traumatic events.

In a group of preadolescents, sandtray therapy was effective in reducing internalizing and externalizing behaviors as rated by their teachers (Flahive & Ray, 2007).

Jang et al. (2019) utilized sandplay therapy with children who had a history of homelessness and were living in a welfare facility in Uganda. Quantitative and qualitative data were collected, showing improvements in PTSD symptoms and resilience.

In a phenomenological study, a neurointegrative approach to sandtray therapy to process combat trauma in military members was effective (Kern Popejoy et al., 2020).

A recent sandplay meta-analysis including 40 studies (Wiersma et al., 2021) showed a significant effect size, suggesting that sandplay therapy is an effective treatment for children and adults with a wide range of mental health issues.

The effect of sandplay therapy on mother–child attachment security and communication was assessed in children aged five and six who had low grades at school (Oh et al., 2013). The findings show that joint sandplay work improved the parent–child relationship and functional communication and reduced dysfunctional communication after 12 weeks of treatment.

EMDR Therapy and the Adaptive Information Processing System Model (AIP)

EMDR therapy was developed in the late 1980s by Francine Shapiro (2001, 2018). EMDR is organized around eight phases of treatment, as follows:

TABLE 1.1			
Eight Phases of EMDR Therapy			
Phase 1: Client History and Treatment Planning	**Phase 2:** Preparation	**Phase 3:** Assessment	**Phase 4:** Desensitization
Information gathering and psychosocial history. The clinician begins to study the client's clinical landscape, creating a baseline containing trauma and attachment history and the presence of capacities.	Aims to increase emotional equilibrium, scaffolding capacities for the presence and regulation of affect, and the crafting of a solid foundation for the safe accessing and processing of distressing trauma memories. Establishing the therapeutic alliance and cocreating safety.	Activating the selected memory and the associated cognition, emotions, and bodily states. Use of baseline measuring scales.	When the client meets markers for readiness, memory systems are accessed and reprocessed until the client attains greater levels of integration and moves to adaptive resolution. The clinician uses dual attention stimulation, such as eye movement and tactile or auditory stimulation.
Phase 5: Installation	**Phase 6:** Body Scan	**Phase 7:** Closure	**Phase 8:** Reevaluation
Strengthening of adaptive memory networks and positive cognitions that are embodied and highly charged in affect.	Accessing, assimilating, and reprocessing embodied sensations and manifestations.	Ensuring the client returns to balance and safety after every session and at the end of treatment.	Evaluating the effectiveness of treatment and adjusting accordingly.

The AIP model serves as the theoretical framework that guides EMDR clinical practice. According to F. Shapiro (2001, 2007, 2018), an AIP system exists in the brain that is capable of assimilating incoming information and moving it to an adaptive resolution. However, trauma creates imbalances that prevent the AIP system from operating optimally. Trauma ruptures homeostasis and neural coherence (Cozolino, 2014), inhibiting the brain circuitry that is biologically organized to process and assimilate trauma-induced cognitive, emotional, somatic, and behavioral states. Furthermore, these memories, which contain images, sounds, affect, and physical sensations from the event, exist frozen in a state-dependent form that can be reactivated by current stimuli (F. Shapiro, 2018). Memories of hardship and adversity are not past narratives but biological imprints that coexist moment-to-moment in the traumatized mind, shaping its present reality. F. Shapiro (2018) stated that these unintegrated traumagenic systems become the lenses the traumatized mind uses to perceive and give meaning to the present. When present stimuli activate traumatic memory systems, their original schemas flood the individual's mind and field of consciousness, becoming the lens the mind uses to see, feel, and perceive the present reality. F. Shapiro (2018) described it as the "past becoming present." Temporal orientation becomes rigid as the client fuses with the past or the future or continues to see the past in every particle brought into their present reality. As a result, the person responds to the present as if the past were still occurring. They become a prisoner of their life stories and trauma-formed embodied narratives. Their present is inevitably altered by the experiences that have not been assimilated and integrated into their mind.

The AIP model posits that clinical symptoms manifest and emerge from the activation of unintegrated synaptic systems (F. Shapiro, 2018; Hensley, 2021) that hold traumagenic explicit and implicit schemas which contain somatic, emotional, behavioral, motor, and cognitive realities.

Memory networks containing primitive, maladaptive encodings from the early trauma coexist with adaptive information. The perceptions of the adult, or "bigger self," cohabit with the views and perspectives of the wounded "younger self" without appropriately linking. The memory networks that conform to the wounded younger self maintain the sense of self and the view of others and the world from when the trauma occurred. These cognitive, emotional, and sensorimotor states live in the background, frozen in time, as a constant reminder of the painful stories.

For some individuals, especially those with developmentally early chronic trauma, adaptive information is scarce and often limited or absent due to missing developmental experiences. F. Shapiro (2018) highlighted the importance of adaptive memory integrating with traumatic circuits during reprocessing sessions. Even though EMDR therapy focuses on memory assimilation and synthesis, identity and state integration are at its core. A byproduct of EMDR work is a renewed connection to oneself and a reorganization of the embodied mind's relationship with its life stories.

6   EMDR-Sandtray-based Therapy

EMDR therapy stimulates innate processing and healing mechanisms so these memory-held structures can finally be moved to integration and resolution. As a result, the individual is free to embrace the present with a renewed sense of self and identity. As integration occurs through multiple domains, the cocreation of new meanings emerges. Clients can develop a new relationship with themselves, their stories, and their past with self-compassion, empowerment, and self-determination.

A distinctive element of EMDR therapy is its use of bilateral stimulation (BLS), or dual attention stimuli (DAS), and the eight phases of treatment. According to F. Shapiro (2018), BLS/DAS activates the information processing system. This allows the assimilation, detoxification, integration, and recalibration of emotions, of rigid bodily, motor, and behavioral states, and of memories that are frozen in time and filled with trauma-formed belief systems. The clinician accompanies the client as they birth new realities, new understandings and realizations, and new and more expansive ways of relating to their stories and to themselves.

Scientific Support

EMDR therapy has been found to accelerate information processing and is recognized as an evidence-based approach for the treatment of trauma and trauma-related symptomatology (Maxfield, 2019). It has robust scientific support, with over 44 randomized control trials evaluating its effectiveness with PTSD, major depressive disorder, bipolar disorder, psychosis, anxiety disorders, obsessive–compulsive disorder, substance use disorder, and pain in adults (Maxfield, 2019). EMDR therapy has been shown to be effective with complex clinical presentations; symptoms of anxiety, phobia, panic and depression in adults (Yunitri et al., 2020, van der Kolk et al., 2007); borderline personality disorder (Wilhelmus et al., 2023); and psychotic disorders (van den Berg et al., 2015). Yunitri et al. (2023) found that EMDR and cognitive processing therapy achieved the most robust long-term outcomes based on a comprehensive meta-analysis evaluating 18,897 studies and the short- and long-term effects of treatments for PTSD.

Randomized control trials and systematic reviews have found EMDR therapy to be effective with children and adolescents (Barron et al., 2019; Karadag et al., 2019; Manzoni et al., 2021; Rodenburg et al., 2009; Teke & Avşaroğlu, 2021). It has also been found to be a promising treatment for children and adults impacted by chronic traumatization (Chen et al., 2018; Olivier et al., 2022; Karadag et al., 2019).

Organizations such as the World Health Organization (2013), the National Institute for Health and Care Excellence (2018), the California Evidence-Based Clearinghouse for Child Welfare (2006), the International Society for the Study of Dissociation (in press), and the U.S. Department of Veterans Affairs and Department of Defense (2023) have recommended EMDR therapy for the treatment of post-traumatic stress disorder (PTSD).

However, research and literature on the effectiveness of the standard use of EMDR therapy versus adapted versions are not currently available. Despite the lack of research on the union of EMDR and sandtray therapy, there is abundant clinical support, from my experience treating hundreds of clients exposed to chronic traumatization across the lifespan in the last 25 years and from numerous consultees and EMDR–sandtray training participants who have reported on its extensive effectiveness. This is the first book to fully address the complexities and procedures of merging these two modalities, and one that I hope stimulates investigation in this domain.

Bringing Together EMDR and Sandtray Therapies

Given the nonlinear nature of complex trauma and its fragmented and unpredictable recall, therapists must provide a variety of portals and access routes into the inner experience. EMDR therapy is a potent, evidenced-based approach with significant therapeutic benefits for individuals impacted by trauma. Sandtray and sand-based therapies offer a powerful symbol, image, and metaphor-based pathway that quiets hardened, defensive tactics, thereby supporting homeostasis and wholeness. This book does not propose to change the essence of EMDR therapy but to enrich each of its phases as we accompany clients with complex clinical terrains and unique developmental needs.

The union and integration of these two models and philosophies requires careful contemplation and theoretical and practical congruency and alignment. Much care has been placed in fostering regard for each methodology and honoring their qualities and perspectives while bringing modifications that can support the healing of individuals exposed to complex traumatization and dissociation across the lifespan.

In EMDR-sandtray-based therapy, the therapist is the *active companion* who provides a safe and trusting space for stories to unfold. This companionship enables the *storyteller* (client) to travel into the deepest layers of the wounded self. The client can finally find an environment where accrued life burdens can be safely embraced and healed.

According to Kalff (1980/2003), the work in the tray is a pathway to the psyche and the unconscious, which uses the ancient language of symbols. From a different approach, and utilizing the AIP model, EMDR–sandtray becomes the road into traumagenic memories and their cognitive, emotional, and sensorimotor schemas at the core of the client's sense of self and their symptoms. The tray becomes the safe space for the mind to dialogue with itself, to be witnessed by the other, and to be explored in joint curiosity and amusement. In EMDR and sandtray therapy, there is a recognition of the inner capacities and organic movement of the mind toward healing, wholeness, and integration.

In EMDR–sandtray, the clinician carries the theoretical constructs of the two approaches and their procedures in fullness. At the same time, they bring space to hold the client's embodied mind and their moment-to-moment shifting states and reality. The clinician makes microadjustments to meet the client's demands for safety and regulation (Schore, 2019) as the client engages in a transformative journey of renegotiating their relationship with their life story through sandtray and the framework and model offered by EMDR therapy. In EMDR-sandtray-based therapy, the therapeutic relationship offers attuned companionship, where the clinician mentalizes and holds in mind the client and their story, which opens the space for shared coherence and the cocreation of new meanings and self-organizing processes.

The sand tray and the miniatures accompany the mind as it travels through multiple layers of the self. They grant the distance that the mind requires to explore and embrace what would otherwise be overwhelming and, at times, terrifying. Sandtray-based techniques within EMDR therapy provide an entrance into the unspoken world that lies beneath the aware and conscious mind. The characters in the tray become the mind's avatar through which dilemmas, conflicts, trauma, and predicaments are seen, felt, and acknowledged. These embodiments allow the client to express, experience, complete, and execute new actions that could not be performed during the traumatic event. Through the tray and the characters, the mind can reconfigure its self-betraying narratives into those of empowerment, hope, and self-compassion. These new opportunities expand and elevate the embodied and relational mind into new dimensions of self-discovery.

In real life and in the tray, a specific figure, a person with certain attributes, a relational dynamic, or an animal and its characteristics all hold the potential to awaken parts of an individual's story and an opportunity to find the self. An individual's actions, movements, choices, tendencies, polarities, likes, and dislikes tell their story. The mind is drawn to the segments of itself that the reality around it contains. EMDR–sandtray therapeutic work is a portal to the story within; it holds the potential to awaken the lost and fragmented slivers of the self.

In EMDR–sandtray therapy, we engage with multiple levels of information processing, encompassing cognitive, emotional, and sensorimotor domains. This approach facilitates both bottom-up and top-down information processing. The information generated from the right brain is accessed, and verbal material from the left brain is invited to expand awareness. The process may be wordless, leaving the client free to access images and embodied information.

During the work with the sandtray and the miniature figures, the clinician remains synchronized and attuned to the verbal and nonverbal ascending and descending information. The body is an active participant and storyteller in the process. The clinician remains observant and curious, witnessing any shifts in the client's state and in their own.

Physicalization (Gómez, 2019) of what is emerging in the moment is invited into the tray. What exists and is unfolding in the inner world is represented—if ready—in the physical world through the symbols and images of sandtray work. The clinician delivers invitations and gives permission for the client's story to surface as it pleases. For instance, if fear manifested in the sand world, the clinician would invite this emotion to materialize in the tray in a way that best resonates with the client. Options may be offered, such as:

> ❝ I wonder if we can invite this feeling to show up in the tray in any way it wants to be seen/witnessed. It may be visible and open to being heard and known, partially visible, or hiding under the sand or a tray covering. In any case, it is okay."

The client and their avatars can show up and exist in the tray how they want to be seen and witnessed. Movement, color, and sound may also accompany the flow of the emotional experience, giving the individual a titrated and systematic unveiling of affective states.

Each phase uses the sandtray and figures in unique ways. During the initial phases of EMDR therapy, sand tray techniques support the client in expressing what cannot be articulated with words. Cognitive, emotional, and sensorimotor stories that exist below the conscious mind, or the memories that overwhelm the client's system, can now be brought into the physical world. Sandtray work actively supports gathering psychosocial history, giving support, or challenging verbal narratives offered by clients during the initial phases of treatment.

Through the preparation phase, the symbols and images in the tray can awaken internal and external resources. They can support the client in connecting with their inner strengths, powers, and assets. Adaptive memory networks may spontaneously emerge or be actively invited into the sand. Clients may bring hidden treasures, resources, and assets into their creation. The calm-safe or "okay" place can be *physicalized* and visible to the client so that the tangible representations associated with feeling calm, safe, and grounded are internally experienced and externally observed.

The images and the language of symbols (with unique and personal meanings for each client) can stimulate the emergence of new resources that were absent when the traumatic events occurred.

As the client and clinician move into the reprocessing phases, accessing traumagenic information occurs at a distance that honors the client's capacities and developmental needs. The sand work offers multiple levels of distance and portals into trauma-formed synaptic networks.

In EMDR-sandtray-based therapy, the clinician utilizes various levels of directiveness. A continuum from directive to nondirective tactics provides many possibilities through moment-to-moment decision-making in each therapeutic encounter. A nondirective stand may best serve the client's mind to freely travel to the places it longs to go and be. Other times, a directive approach can provide the client with the support, guidance, and direction they need to find repair, correction, and healing.

EMDR-Sandtray-based Therapy With Children

Children generally do not have the language, cognitive capacities, and skills to construct and tell their life stories. Moreover, they do not have the capabilities to understand the complexities of the injuring dynamics that traumatized them in the first place. When working with children exposed to trauma early in life, the reemergence of traumagenic data often does not surface verbally but through embodied states, and reenactments. How can a child cognitively understand a parent who is loving in one moment and belligerent and abusive the next? Yet, during play moments in the sand tray, the child creates stories using figures that encompass the heart of their suffering and inner conflicts. Further, the child may reenact the dynamic with the therapist.

Andrew, a 13-year-old, witnessed his siblings being abused. He was the silent witness, unable to fight against an overpowering father. In his therapy session, he created a world where a mean farmer abused the animals. The only witness was a bull that quietly, powerlessly, and angrily watched the abuse. Andrew stated that although the bull wanted to defend the animals, it felt powerless. Over several sessions, he created stories depicting similar conflicts. Yet, he did not acknowledge these occurrences in his life nor connect the stories in the tray with those of his own life. His therapist observed only a teenager who often stated that his life was "great" and that nothing bothered him, even though he regularly engaged his classmates with violence and hostility. Andrew was frequently called to the principal's office and had significant difficulties with sleep and food intake. His verbal narratives did not match his life history, current circumstances, or present symptoms and struggles. In his relationship with the clinician, he

FIGURE 1.1 A sand world of a mean farmer who keeps animals trapped in cages and abuses them. Near the farmer is a bull—an angry, silent bystander—witnessing the abuse. The bull is immobilized and unable to help his fellow animals.

FIGURE 1.2 A closer look at the mean farmer and the bull, witnessing the abuse of his friends and family, in the sand world.

frequently reenacted the antagonizing strategies and avoidance that helped him survive his past and his family of origin's wounding dynamics.

Depending on their development, children may use deeper symbolism and metaphorical elements or literal representations. Young children may engage in concrete and simple narratives in the tray, while older children may pursue in more elaborate storytelling. Youngsters often create sand worlds with greater movement and are more likely to step in and out of the sand tray. Sandtray work may be challenging for very young children, who may put the sand and figures into their mouths, and thus sandtray therapy may not be the recommended form of treatment (Rae, 2013). Overall, sandtray creations furnish clinicians and children across developmental stages with a rich and dynamic window into their inner worlds and life stories.

EMDR-Sandtray-based Therapy With Adolescents

Given the time and opportunity, most adolescents will embrace sandtray therapeutic work. However, some resistance and questions about the developmental appropriateness of sandtray work with this age group often surface. Adolescents may perceive EMDR procedures (especially BLS/DAS) as unconventional and strange. They may also consider the playfulness occurring in the tray and with the miniatures as immature and unworthy of their time. They may say, "That is for children, and I am not a child." However, with invitations to play in the tray and reassurance that this form of therapy is for all ages, the teenager will eventually embrace this therapeutic work.

Individuals with internalized social expectations and cultural beliefs, especially in fast-paced societies prioritizing productivity, may perceive play as fruitless and a "waste of time" that is unlikely to help them achieve their intended therapeutic goals. Also, growing up in a traumatizing, rigid, or chaotic environment may have impacted the development and maturation of the adolescent's play system, inhibiting its expression. The play system may have deeply rooted associations with shame and trauma, resulting in play deprivation and a complete refusal to engage in therapeutic play.

The clinician's consistent presence, flexibility, and respect for the adolescent's autonomy and agency in the therapeutic process will create an environment of safety. Leave invitations to use the sandtray open, without creating any pressure; instead, begin with a small and gradual introduction to the tray. This may be just representing the adolescent's relationship with a friend, emotion, or future goal. Using a directive approach, such as asking the teen to sequence events chronologically while inviting them to look at the chain of thoughts, emotions, actions, and responses from others, may present a more linear approach to the initial work in the tray that the hesitant teen may be more willing to perform.

For the undecided adolescent, a titrated approach is often necessary and welcomed. The teen may create a sand world or represent in the sand a situation occurring with peers for just a few minutes. Adolescents may depict triggers and concerns that often occur as they begin the journey into adulthood.

Building trust, providing choices and a sense of control, and using a titrated and gradual approach while normalizing their hesitancy will support the adolescent in making informed decisions about embracing EMDR-sandtray-based treatment.

EMDR-Sandtray-based Therapy With Adults

The sandtray apparatus combined with EMDR is effective and efficient in helping adults increase self-awareness and self-understanding and to process trauma. As with adolescents, adults may hesitate to engage in play due to cultural biases toward linear, left-brain thinking and a lack of familiarity with EMDR and sandtray. However, when the clinician offers sufficient information about the benefits of EMDR–sandtray, adults may be open to trying it.

Physical limitations or discomfort may play a role in preventing the client from fully embracing the therapeutic work in the tray. For instance, a person with a disability may struggle to walk around to select the miniatures. Actively explore the barriers, ensure the sandtray setup is accessible, and adapt to accommodate the individual's needs.

EMDR–sandtray may be an initial offering or suggested when the client is stranded or showing signs of stagnation in the therapeutic process. Sometimes, a combination of both standard EMDR treatment and EMDR-sandtray-based therapy may occur with some clients as the clinician pendulates between the two.

Adults more often will engage in explicit explorations and processing of memory compared to children, who more openly and actively work with implicit portals into memory systems and self. However, because of the symbolic nature of sand work, adults who work in the tray can more easily access the memories in the nonverbal and implicit domain of the mind that lacks conscious recognition and that occurred in prelinguistic periods of their development. Through the EMDR–sandtray work, implicit and nonverbal traumatic accounts can move gently and gradually into awareness and consciousness throughout the eight phases of treatment.

For the adult who relies on intellectualization and higher cognitive capacities, the work in the sand may circumvent defenses (Homeyer & Sweeney, 2023). Adult trays may not possess the fluid movement common in children, and they may be used within the context of verbal therapies with adults (Rae, 2013). The tray can hold the space for relational dynamics and conflicts so the adult can examine the sequential links within an event or multiple events in the tray. The adult can study and gain insight into the complex interplay of cognitive, emotional, somatic, and behavioral states during the initial phases of treatment. Timelines, life events, and resources may be invited to the tray through the symbols offered by the miniature collection. Visual representations of the adult's life and their experiences of trauma support the identification of memories, triggers, and future life visions. During the reprocessing phases, the tray also provides clients with space for processing, integrating memories, and reconnecting and reorganizing their relationship with themselves.

Trauma-Related Defensive Strategies

For many traumatized individuals, the sand becomes the vehicle to transport painful stories and a pathway into life accounts that are unrecognized and rejected by the conscious mind. Sandtray work provides multiple levels of distance from the memory and its accompanying affect which dim the client's activation and modulate mechanisms of adaptation that emerged to ensure survival. Not all memories make themselves known verbally and overtly. Encounters with early relational trauma form rigid defenses and hardened patterns of activation. for some clients, overt targets for EMDR reprocessing may surface in a verbal form with the participation of higher cognitive capacities. Explicit, conscious encoding may be verbalized and acknowledged, while mechanisms of adaptations allow for the conscious expression of such events. However, the conscious mind may not easily access implicit, nonconscious memories that exist below awareness in nonverbal, affective, and sensory forms. Mechanisms of self-protection and self-defense override and block the recollection or expression of these events. Instead, they may emerge in reenactments in the sand tray, in the relationship with the therapist and with others, and in the client's play themes.

Functional adaptations and defenses developed for survival often emerge in the tray, such as control, pleasing, overdoing, perfectionism, dissociation, and especially avoidance. Consistently positive sand worlds may depict defensive and self-protective tendencies, and strictly organized worlds may reveal rigidity and perfectionism. Frequent themes of vacant worlds with many unknowns and empty spaces may represent multiple forms of self-protection, including dissociation and avoidance. However, the symbol-based approach of sandtray work softens the rooted and trauma-formed defense system, allowing a titrated entrance into traumagenic networks.

Dissociation in EMDR-Sandtray-based Therapy

For individuals who grew up in environments that did not provide what they needed to attain an integrated sense of self, dissociative parts can be represented in the tray. According to Putnam (1997), babies are born with discrete behavioral states that become more complex, interconnected, and amplified as they come in contact with their relational world. Infants are not born with a unified sense of identity. Instead, they follow a path toward developing an integrated or a fragmented sense of identity, depending on the relational experiences that surround them.

According to Putnam's (1997) theory of discrete behavioral states, trauma creates discrete states of consciousness that alter associative pathways. When chronic and repetitive, the states of consciousness evolve into personality traits that become increasingly segregated, resulting in dissociative alterations in identity, where there is a differential accessibility to autobiographical memory and a state-dependent sense of self. The worlds of individuals with a dissociative inner structure are often colored by polarization and fragmentation. Dissociative parts often enter the sand tray hidden in stories and avatars. The clinician honors the paths chosen by the compartmentalized inner system. These stories and internal structures may surface gradually or rapidly. Often, they show up with high internal conflicts and radical polarization. However, the sandtray and avatars become a haven where the dissociative inner formations can emerge anonymously and without naming themselves until it is safe.

Sandtray work creates space for multiple sensory modalities to participate and integrate. Tactile exploration, visual stimulation, movement, and kinesthetic awareness offer a multidimensional experience. The rich sensory stimulation and engagement inherent to the sandtray work create conditions in which clients challenged by dissociative tendencies and short attention spans can cultivate presence.

I approach dissociation in EMDR–sandtray not as a pathology but as an accommodation adopted to deal with trauma and a deeply wounding relational environment that failed to provide the individual with what was needed to attain an integrated and unified sense of self. I conceptualized dissociation as a spectrum of experiences and adaptations made in the service of survival. EMDR-sandtray-based therapy approaches dissociation with a depathologizing and deshaming lens. It recognizes and highlights the mind's best attempts to find a space to exist despite its frequent exposure to incongruent and disorganizing experiences. To preserve the relationship with wounding attachment figures and create space for memories of unbearable pain, the mind had no choice but to compartmentalize its existence and live in a fragmented world of identities. This internal organization and structure provided shelter to the wounded mind. Recognizing and acknowledging the individual's suffering and internal organization as well as the division that allowed them to exist are paramount. In EMDR–sandtray, the sand figures and the clinician bring recognition to the diverse aspects of the self. At the same time, they surround the client with compassion and respect without becoming lost in the system of parts, connecting with them as if they were separate people.

The sand tray allows ego states and dissociative parts to unblend into sand figures. In the tray, parts may dialogue and reduce conflicting dynamics, resulting in greater coconsciousness and system stability. The client can create individual (for each part) or collective resources (the entire dissociative system) in the tray. Additionally, the client does not have to rely on the capacity to visualize and imagine, as the sand tray and the miniatures collection provide a symbol-based and visually rich experience.

Explicit and Implicit Access

Explicit memories may enter the tray as well as implicit stories that carry the essence of the client's inner conflicts—hardships that may be unknown to their conscious minds. Through EMDR's eight phases, the symbolic nature of sandtray work deepen the process for the client and clinician. Sandtray work provides multiple levels of distance that form a continuum that extends from multiple variations of implicit and explicit access to memory systems. Implicit access is characterized by creating and reprocessing "worlds" depicting characters that can tell the client's untold stories. In implicit access, the avatars in the tray provide the space for the client's mind to express what would otherwise be intolerable, to experiment with actions they could not execute during the traumatic events and to contact wounded layers of the self in need of expression, recognition, and healing. However, the client's mind is free to refuse conscious ownership and recognition.

Belinda, a 6-year-old who experienced abuse and bullying, created a story in the tray in which a "kitty is being hurt by a big lion, and it feels really scared and powerless." If the child shows signs of readiness for processing, the story of the kitty may become a target the child can work with without having to own and acknowledge the story or its accompanying affect. Interweaves (see Chapter 7) that bring resources to the world created in the sand tray can assist the client in completing defensive responses and meeting unmet developmental needs. Reprocessing the story can allow the client to experience the acts of triumph they were deprived of while the traumatic event unfolded. This time, the character serves as the voice, the avatar, and the actor who delivers the client's story and allows them to experience the world from a different perspective.

Eventually, buried wounds reach consciousness when the individual is prepared and equipped to confront their inner shadows. In time, the elements of the traumatic event stand in front of the client's conscious mind as it moves into explicit access. Face-to-face, the client can now fully or partially own these stories, surrounded by the safety and companionship provided by the therapist and other helpers that may exist in the tray. The active accompaniment given to the client during the reprocessing of painful events serves as a reparative experience. The companionship allows the client to safely restore homeostasis, repair previously disrupted autonomic states, reassign new meanings, reshape self-identity, and reclaim agency and authorship over their life stories.

Throughout the eight phases of EMDR–sandtray work, and especially during Phase 5, clients can create, allocate, and enhance meanings and embodied beliefs while using symbols and images to represent them. This may occur implicitly or explicitly. The new emerging belief system is not only a cognitive experience but one that is physicalized, embodied, and represented in the world of images and symbols. In EMDR–sandtray, the companion (therapist) and the storyteller (client) can shift the attention from the symbols to the embodied narratives emerging moment-to-moment, particularly during Phase 6. Embodied trauma and somatic holding patterns can be released through the stories unfolding in the tray and the engaged involvement of body–mind systems.

A Multimodal Approach to EMDR-Sandtray-based Therapy

Although EMDR therapy is a unifying theory and model (F. Shapiro, 2018), it is also integrative and encompasses aspects of multiple approaches. According to F. Shapiro (2018), "As a clinical approach, the EMDR paradigm opens up new therapeutic possibilities by supporting an integration of key treatment elements from the major psychological modalities" (p. 49). F. Shapiro, from the inception of EMDR therapy, reached into other therapeutic methods to enrich the model, methodology, and procedures. Due to the complexity of its symptoms and the ways trauma impacts neurodevelopment, some authors advocate for a multimodal approach to its treatment (Amaya-Jackson & DeRosa, 2007) and the delivery of EMDR therapy (Gómez, 2013, 2021a). The movement in psychology toward integrative practices encompassing multiple approaches is increasingly evident. Neuroscience has expanded our awareness of the depth of the therapeutic work required to promote healing. It challenges us to practice from an integrated way of understanding the human mind. Badenoch (2008) calls for a humble stance, "Today's discoveries amend and expand yesterday's" (p. 307).

Maintaining an open and flexible mentality that can integrate previous and current findings in psychotherapy can move us to an increasingly cohesive and integrated way of practicing.

EMDR-sandtray-based therapy brings an integrative-multimodal and transtheoretical approach to using EMDR and sandtray therapy, with multiple theories and adjunct approaches that enrich our understanding and treatment delivery. The human mind is complex, especially when it carries the wounds, intricacies, ambiguities, and distortions left by exposure to pervasive trauma. Clinicians often need an arsenal of tools to navigate the complexities of treating chronically injured clients.

EMDR–sandtray offers a blended path into the human mind, with multiple contributions from other approaches. The eight phases of EMDR and the AIP model, alongside sandtray theory and practices, continue to guide clinical practice. However, concepts and constructs from interpersonal neurobiology, the Polyvagal Theory, attachment theory, dissociation theory, somatic paradigms, mindfulness, and the understanding of the neurobiological substrate of human existence enrich case conceptualization and treatment delivery. All to bring greater insight and awareness into how the mind is injured and finds healing, homeostasis, and realizes wholeness.

Interpersonal Neurobiology (IPNB)

Interpersonal neurobiology (IPNB) is a pillar that, combined with the AIP model, supports the therapeutic work of EMDR–sandtray. Siegel (2020) brings from IPNB multiple constructs that contribute to the healing of the wounded mind: resonance, trust, engagement, genuine curiosity, openness, and acceptance. According to Siegel (2017), this is how individuals feel felt and two become "we." Corrective experiences with the therapists, wherein clients enter into the "we-space," form in the client new neural firing patterns and challenge old internal working models, memory systems, and metaperceptions based on self-betrayal and self-abandonment. Interpersonal and relational neurobiology posit that systems are innately self-organized to differentiate and link while moving toward integration and wholeness (Siegel, 2010).

Are the self and the mind merely emergent properties of brain functioning and neural activity? Considering that the AIP model in EMDR does not offer a clear perspective of the mind, consciousness, and the self, I draw insight from IPNB and Siegel's definition of the mind. According to Siegel (2020), the "mind is the emergent, self-organizing, embodied, and relational process that regulates the flow of energy and information. . . . A core aspect of the mind is an embodied and relational process that regulates the flow of energy and information" (pp. 4–5).

Vertical and Horizontal Integration in EMDR–Sandtray: Recognizing the Divided Brain

EMDR–sandtray provides the mind with creative ways of capturing the material emerging from the right and lower brain while continuing to engage higher cognitive and left-brain verbal capacities. This accessing of trauma in EMDR-sandtray-based therapy is titrated to accommodate various degrees of affect tolerance. The process gradually adjusts to the client's integrative capacities and readiness to realize and assimilate such material. In EMDR therapy, especially during its reprocessing phases, vertical and horizontal integration are promoted as memories are assimilated and linked into a larger and more complex system of networks.

According to Siegel (2020), vertical integration is "the integration of the 'lower' functions of the brainstem and limbic regions with the 'higher' operations of the frontal neocortex, such as cognitive and motor planning" (p. 415). Studies using cerebral blood flow (CBF; single photon emission computed tomography [SPECT]) that look at neurobiological changes during EMDR therapy have shown an activation pattern shift during memory processing from emotional and limbic to cognitive–cortical (Pagani et al., 2012). This may represent the reorganization of the story within that moves from highly charged physiological and affective states to congruent and coherent narratives held by greater awareness and mentalizing capabilities.

Trauma can interfere with and inhibit the brain's capacity to vertically and horizontally synchronize. It has been proposed that vertical and horizontal integration is at the core of the development of separate self-states and structural dissociation (Lanius & Paulsen, 2014). EMDR–sandtray strategies and procedures aim to support clients in accessing, reprocessing, and integrating material generated by the lower and higher circuits of the brain in addition to right/left brain representations and ways of interacting with the world. To honor the client, we must have the space to hold the whole person and their ways of knowing and experiencing the world. This requires that the psychotherapeutic process not rely solely on verbal communication but be open to multiple inter- and intrapersonal forms of expression.

Gestalt Therapy

EMDR–sandtray also brings theoretical constructs and therapeutic strategies from methodologies, such as gestalt therapy, that support clinicians in comprehending the phenomena emerging in the tray (Perls et al., 1951), helping them recognize and navigate polarities within the client's experience. Buried and unseen inner divergences not recognized by the conscious mind may emerge in the tray during EMDR work. Trauma creates binary states and rigid divisions in the psyche. Characters in the tray may represent powerlessness, submission, and a lack of agency, while others exude infinite power. Strong dichotomous and binary states emerging in the tray point to areas of division in need of recognition, a process aligned with gestalt therapy's focus on integrating polarities and fostering awareness of conflicting aspects of the self. These contrasting inner forces long for their opposite and for the linking of the differentiated reality (Siegel, 2023).

The Polyvagal Theory

The union of EMDR therapy and sandtray therapy weaves other theories and approaches into an integrated whole. Among those is the Polyvagal Theory (Porges, 2011), which is incorporated throughout the eight phases of treatment as a matrix that supports the recognition of autonomic patterns of activation that are often nonconscious and involuntary. Porges helped us understand that the nervous system has multiple defense mechanisms. The vagus, a primary sensory nerve of the parasympathetic nervous system, is a bidirectional pathway between the brain and the visceral organs. Of its fibers, 80% transport information from the viscera to the brain, while the remaining 20% consist of motor fibers that enable the brain to modulate our physiology (Porges, 2011). Porges uses evolution as an organizing principle of his theory and shows how the autonomic nervous system is hierarchically organized to respond to and interact with the environment the organism encounters. These autonomic subsystems are as follows:

1. The **unmyelinated vagal pathway** (parasympathetic dorsal nervous system) provides primary regulation to the organs below the diaphragm. According to Porges (2021), when this system is recruited for safety, it supports homeostasis. However, when it is enlisted for defense, it moves the organism to immobility and collapse.
2. The **myelinated vagal system** (parasympathetic ventral vagal) regulates the organs above the diaphragm. This extends the labor of the autonomic nervous system to support growth, restoration, connection, and the down-regulation of defenses.
3. The **system of mobilization and fight/flight defensive response** (sympathetic nervous system).

Traumatogenic memory systems are intricately connected to patterns of autonomic activation that have become deeply rooted and sensitized. Often, these disrupted autonomic patterns become visible in the tray, represented in worlds and stories that show the high activation and presence of sympathetic forces. The dorsal vagal system may materialize in sandtray worlds as avatars and surroundings that come into view as shutdown or immobile. The ventral vagal is also visible in characters and tray embodiments that show appreciation for or actively seek play, connection, and collaboration. They may manifest as characters depicting empowerment, support, kindness, and so forth. These systems are also visible in the client's verbal and nonverbal expressions, which cue the attuned clinician to the physiological states that inhabit the client's mind.

Attachment Theory

Attachment theory (Bowlby, 1988) is also central in EMDR-sandtray-based treatment. Early attachment experiences mold the mind and set the foundation for representational structures that influence the individual's relationship with themselves, others, and the world. It is an essential theory and body of knowledge that is foundational in using EMDR and sandtray. Adults' states of mind regarding attachment experiences often surface in the tray. Preoccupation and dismissiveness will show their voices through implicit and explicit worlds. Dyadic trays created by parents and children can depict relational patterns of safety and connection or disengagement and enmeshment.

Children with avoidant attachment patterns and adults with dismissing states of mind may create emotionally detached and lonely or superficially positive trays. Before they could communicate verbally, these individuals hid their true feelings from attachment figures and, later on, from themselves. To coexist with their caregiver's insufficiencies, they had to edit the self to maintain a relationship with their distant, disengaged, rejecting, and neglectful caregiver (Cundy, 2019). They had to hide their needs to protect their relationship with the caregiver. Often, the sand worlds are nuanced by their primary mechanisms of adaptation: avoidance.

The child with disorganized attachment and the adult with unresolved states of mind battle an internal conflict defending against the person they want connection with. Their sand creations expose the chaos, confusion, and lack of coherence in their internal working models, memory systems, and self-narratives, which mirror the disorganized minds of their caregivers, resulting in metaperceptions of defectiveness and the belief that there is something wrong with them and their bodies, which then results in the development of a confused self (Fonagy et al., 2002, 2019). They may create scenes in the tray that symbolize a lack of interconnected and unified structure in their internal world. Miniatures and stories in the tray mirror their internal fragmentation and disintegrated memories. Their sand worlds are nuanced by contradictions and polarizations that reflect internal ambivalence and conflicts.

Models of Multiplicity of the Mind

The multimodal approach to EMDR–sandtray brings methodologies that embrace the multiplicity of the human psyche and the ways consciousness may exist in parts that cohabit within an individual (van der Kolk, 2014). Therapeutic models such as ego states therapy (Watkins & Watkins, 1997) and internal family systems (R. Schwartz, 1995, 2021; Schwartz & Sweezy, 2020) point to the notion that multiple states or parts coexist within one mind. Parts, according to Holmes and Holmes (2007), "refer to the experience of having shifting states of mind that have unique sets of thoughts, feelings, and behaviors" (pp. 1–2). Depending on the internal and external environment, a particular state of mind will arise, and when these conditions change, that part will go back into consciousness (Holmes & Holmes, 2007, p. 104). The structural dissociation theory addresses the division in the personality that occurs as a result of trauma. Multiple levels of dissociation are formulated, from primary structural dissociation, observed in PTSD, to tertiary structural dissociation, which presents in dissociative identity disorder (DID; van der Hart et al., 2006). The AIP model (F. Shapiro, 2001, 2007, 2018) addresses these multiplicities by presenting a model of memory systems containing cognitive, emotional, sensorimotor, and behavioral trauma–based states that remain segregated and frozen in time. While parts work may not be necessary for all clients, highly dissociative clients would benefit from this level of work within the framework of EMDR-sandtray-based treatment.

Somatic Therapies

F. Shapiro (2018) recognized the importance of supporting body-based processing and interventions. Phases and procedural steps of EMDR therapy actively endorse the body as a site of experience and expression. EMDR–sandtray expands the body–mind connection by dynamically inviting bodily involvement through the eight phases. Tenets and strategies from somatic experiencing (Levine, 2015) and sensorimotor psychotherapy (Ogden et al., 2006) especially are used during the preparation and reprocessing phases of EMDR-sandtray-based treatment. The sandtray work can kindle sensations and truncated responses, awakening somatic consciousness and sensory storytelling. This is an opportunity to foster a deeper connection to bodily experiences, exploring the interplay between embodied states and the stories they evoke in the tray. Sandtray work gives the body a tapestry of opportunities for embodiment practices that recalibrate and integrate felt experiences and sensorimotor imprints manifested from trauma.

Intersectionality and Cultural Sensitivity

Intersectionality and culturally affirming and sensitive practices are important elements in EMDR-sandtray-based treatment. Clinicians support the expression, exploration, and identification of multiple dimensions of the client's cultural identities in the tray and throughout the eight phases of treatment. The EMDR–sandtray clinician should ensure that interventions are culturally affirming, flexible, and appropriate for clients from multiple backgrounds. Experiences of systemic oppression and power imbalances as well as historical trauma and marginalization are explored and invited into the tray when there is sufficient trust and safety within the therapeutic space. The creation of an inclusive physical space along with the provision of inclusive miniatures create the foundation for culturally affirming practices of inclusivity.

Conclusion

This chapter has outlined essential aspects of the union of EMDR and sandtray therapies that will be expanded on in further chapters. It presented a multimodal approach to EMDR–sandtray that encompasses multiple theories and modalities that synergistically complement the delivery of EMDR treatment. This is not eclecticism but a masterful integration of multiple ways of understanding and working with the mind to promote healing and integration. The EMDR model and methodology act as the guiding force and road map, while sandtray theory and clinical work synergistically and complementarily join in to mitigate the enduring consequences of chronic exposure to trauma.

The human mind is complex. None of the current models, theories, or therapeutic approaches fully address these complexities. Recognizing and accepting these limitations as well as the subjectivities and biases of the therapeutic work give the clinician the power of choice. Otherwise, we may become prisoners of our predispositions, theories, paradigms, and preconceptions. I remain committed to approaching existence from a humble and open mind that recognizes the expansion and shifts occurring in our understanding of reality, the formation of the self, and the multiple roads toward healing that exist.

24   EMDR-Sandtray-based Therapy

CHAPTER 2

Phase 1: Foundational and Advanced Skills

To incorporate sandtray strategies into the initial phase of EMDR therapy, clinicians need to develop the skills and competencies to utilize them both. Likewise, they need the figures, tools, and materials that accompany this sacred work. This chapter will introduce the foundational skills, equipment, and tools needed to utilize EMDR–sandtray in your practice. Sandtray-specific skills will be presented, starting with how to get your own sandtray and build your miniature collection. I will address world exploration and sandtray foundational skills based on and inspired by the work of sand-based therapy pioneers (Lowenfeld, 1993; Kalff, 1980/2003; Homeyer & Sweeney, 2017, 2023; Smith, 2012; Rae, 2013; Turner, 2017) as well as new ways of embracing the work in the tray using a multimodal approach to the EMDR methodology.

We will address two main portals into the client's embodied mind: implicit and explicit. Synchronicity, attunement, reciprocity, mentalization (Fonagy et al., 2002), and reflective communication are essential in the EMDR–sandtray process. Mentalization and the capacity to hold the other's mind in mind (Fonagy et al., 2002) results in contingent responses that promote a state of safety. The witness/companion (therapist) fosters corrective and reparative experiences wherein the client is felt, seen, recognized, and validated. In this chapter we will explore how to use the tray, the miniatures, and the sandtray methods to support the client in developing a relationship with themself and their life stories. This chapter also addresses how sandtray strategies and protocols enhance and expand the possibilities and richness of history collection and treatment plan development during Phase 1.

Phase 1 of EMDR–Sandtray Therapy: History and Treatment Planning

EMDR treatment follows the unique, phase approach, which fits into the phase-oriented model introduced by Pierre Janet in the 1900s. This approach is now recognized by the International Society for the Study of Dissociation (2004) as the gold standard for treating complex trauma. Although a linear methodology has been proposed in EMDR, especially in cases of a single trauma event, a circular approach is often needed for individuals with complex trauma (Courtois, 2004; Gómez, 2023a). This rotation, that moves clinicians around the eight phases of treatment based on the client's rhythm, requires a strong understanding of each phase and attunement to the client's pace and tempo.

During Phase 1, the clinician gathers relevant history organized around the three prongs proposed by F. Shapiro (2001, 2018): past, present, and future. Clinicians collect information on attachment history, relational dynamics, trauma history, capacities, resources, and nervous system tendencies, among others. Considering the complexities of these clients' stories and their relationships with their autobiographical memories, history collection may be highly convoluted. Defenses and self-protective strategies emerging from chronic traumatization, trauma-related phobias, and the presence of fragmentation and an inner dissociative organization make the creation of a clinical landscape intricate. Children and individuals exposed to chronic traumatization tell their life accounts through relational and play-based reenactments (Gil, 2017). For this purpose, sandtray offers a fertile ground where life accounts can emerge, especially in their implicit form. The stories and sandtray worlds can provide support, validation, and confirmation to the verbal narratives offered during history taking, or they may challenge and even contradict the verbal narratives provided during intake. This chapter offers multiple portals into the client's life story through sand worlds that optimize and enrich history gathering and treatment planning.

Creating Your Own Sandtray Equipment and Collection

The Sandtray

The sandtray represents a sacred space where the mind can dialogue with itself. In Jungian psychology, the tray is the space that holds the psyche (Kalff, 1980/2003). In EMDR–sandtray work, the tray is the vehicle the embodied mind uses to bring stories and life events into the physical world, allowing the mind to reshape its relationships with these autobiographical stories and with itself. The characters are the mind's avatars, through which the mind can experiment, execute, complete, and experience actions and urges that could not be experienced during the traumatic life event(s).

The trays may be of multiple shapes and sizes, which differs from sandplay, where strict adherence to a particular tray measurement is recommended. According to Homeyer and Sweeney (2017), the standard tray in

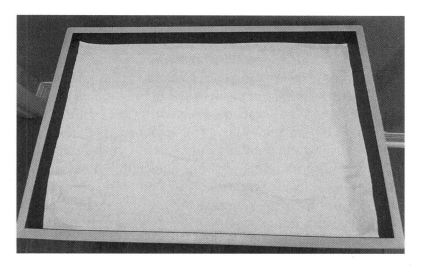

FIGURE 2.1 **A typical, rectangular sandtray with a bed of white play sand on a blue (not shown) bottom.**

FIGURE 2.2 **An octagonal sandtray.**

sandtray therapy is close to Kalff's recommendations. It is rectangular, around 30 inches by 20 inches, and 3 inches deep. However, round, octagonal, and square trays may be used, as they give clients multiple opportunities for expression.

Having at least three to four trays is recommended. Different sizes and shapes provide the client with a variety of experiential possibilities. Some clients will find comfortable containment in a small tray, while others will experience constriction. A large tray may provide freedom and amplitude to one client while making another feel exposed. You may make your own tray or purchase one. Deeper trays are recommended for young children, since they might be more likely to spill the sand outside the tray.

The tray can be made of wood or plastic. Starting with Lowenfeld (1993), trays were made to be waterproof to allow for the use of water in the tray. In addition, the bottom was painted blue so the client could engage in multiple activities and forms of self-expression involving the representation of water, rivers, and oceans. When using a wet sandbox, the possibilities for sensory and kinesthetic stimulation grow as the client creates multiple landscapes that provide a wealth of embodied encounters. The client may sink their hands into the sand or touch the surface, feeling its texture and weight. Children, especially, experiment and interact with the sand through movements such as smoothing, shaping, pushing, squeezing, pressing, lifting, moving, pinching, and drawing patterns. The client can create roads, tunnels, and channels that open possibilities for movement in areas of the body left frozen by trauma. Water also offers sensory stimulation as it enters the tray and mixes with the sand, transforming its consistency. Clients may feel the resistance of the hard sand or the softness of moist sand. The clinician accompanies and witnesses the felt and embodied encounters while the client immerses themself in these sensory experiences. The clinician mirrors, reflects, and supports interoceptive, exteroceptive, and mindful awareness of what unfolds from moment to moment.

> ❮ I am just noticing how your hands and arms move with, inside, and out of the tray and the sand. I also notice your face changing as you move. Can we be curious together and see what is happening for you?"

If the client reports feeling regulated or shares comfortable emotions, invite them to connect to their feelings and how their body communicates the arrival of those feelings. You may use slow and short sets of BLS/DAS if the client is already familiar with EMDR forms of BLS/DAS.

Containers of various shapes and sizes can be placed inside the tray to hold water or sand. Besides water representing rivers, oceans, and lakes, it may also symbolize magical elements or special powers.

A 7-year-old child who suffered physical abuse from her mother used water to symbolize her special powers and strength. When she "visited" her life stories, she often sprinkled warm water in the tray, especially in areas where strength and courage were needed. These special powers allowed her to escape from her abuser while using her voice in the tray and restructuring her relationship with her life story.

A stand or table with wheels may allow the tray to be brought to an accessible location where clients can easily reach it from different angles without obstruction. Ideally, the tray's height should be adjustable so clients can access it regardless of height, mobility needs, or desires. Ideally, a room should be dedicated to the sandtray work, but this may be an unattainable luxury for some clinicians.

28   EMDR-Sandtray-based Therapy

The Sand

Having at least three colors of sand for clients to explore and use at different times during the eight phases of treatment is recommended. That said, at least one should be a neutral-colored sand. Ensuring the sand is sterile and does not contain materials that can harm clients is essential. You may add glitter to the sand to add shimmer. The sand's texture is important as well (Rae, 2013). Sand that is too thin may become powdery and bothersome, and sand that is too thick might be too rough for some clients. The goal is to have multiple sand options so the client's mind has a palette of color possibilities to express itself with. Rice, beans, lentils, and other small grains can add unique sensory experiences and textures to the tray. Clinicians should offer clients access to versatile and engaging sensory encounters.

The Miniatures Collection

This is one of the most enjoyable parts of building your sandtray practice. The search for figures is a lifelong pursuit. After close to three decades of using sandtray therapy, I have accumulated an extensive collection. However, I still look for figures wherever I go. The miniature collection provides language, symbols, and images so the self can find possibilities for expression. A comprehensive collection of miniatures will support your clients in accessing the light and the shadows within. The miniatures must be able to walk with clients through rowdy and rambunctious, tender, laborious, and tranquil moments. The exact number of figures needed is difficult to calculate. Some authors recommend 300 (Homeyer & Sweeney, 2017), while others recommend up to 1,000. Clients must have access to a rich collection that brings sufficient possibilities without being overwhelming. Clients may take too long to select figures if the collection has grown too large. If it is too small, it may fall short of providing sufficient possibilities for expression.

For a comprehensive list and selection of miniatures, see Appendix 1. In addition to the items commonly listed in the literature, individuals with complex trauma using EMDR–sandtray may require access to an extended miniature inventory, such as:

1. Containers of various sizes and shapes to titrate access to traumatic data
2. Small bottles filled with colored sand (to potentially represent personal powers, fairy dust, etc.)
3. Small sticky notes to write notes, beliefs, and affirmations
4. Figures representing diverse identities and inner divisions, such as figures with multiple heads, wings, bodies, or human puzzles
5. Cloth coverings in various sizes and transparencies to suit different needs and provide multiple titration levels when accessing disturbing material

Phase 1: Foundational and Advanced Skills   **29**

FIGURE 2.3 **Multiple figures showcasing multiplicity.**

6. Addiction items
7. Light-up wands to provide BLS/DAS
8. Binoculars to expand and contract the sandtray view, access various perspectives, and expand or contract the sand world's scope
9. Brushes for BLS/DAS and to move the sand
10. Objects that make sounds, such as bells, chimes, and musical boxes; these add an auditory dimension to the client's sensory experience
11. Textured miniatures, such as rough, smooth, bumpy, or poky objects, fabrics, and stones, provide the client with embodiment and somatic connection possibilities; the client may explore the textures of a sensation or emotion
12. When creating your sandtray collection, it is essential to prioritize safety, particularly with younger clients. Select durable, nonbreakable materials such as wood, plastic, or fabrics

Bring culturally affirming and inclusive representational objects and figures when acquiring your collection. Do not buy just the figures you like. Expand to the ones that repel you, and even disgust you, as well as neutral ones. It is also recommended to have various miniature sizes (Rae, 2013). Some may be big, while others may be tiny. The size of the figure serves as a means of expression. A strong emotion of fear may be depicted by using a giant figure. Figures do not need to be perfectly put together. Some broken figures with missing parts may add richness to the collection and depict how many clients experience themselves (Homeyer & Sweeney, 2017, 2023).

Once you have figures, the next step is to consider the best way to organize them in your office or playroom. There are three methods of organizing your collection in the sandtray and sandplay literature (Rae, 2013;

Homeyer & Sweeney, 2017; Smith, 2012) that trace back to Margaret Lowen-feld (1993) and Dora Kalff (2003/1980).

1. **Open display:** You need shelves to display all your figures. This is the best way, as the figures, symbols, and images are readily available and visible.
2. **Organized in plastic bins:** Figures must be organized into categories and the bins must be labeled to make it easier for the client to find what they are looking for.
3. **Partially displayed:** Some figures are displayed, and others are stored in plastic bins, such as those that may be developmentally specific or too activating for some clients.
4. **Portable display:** If you provide home-based psychotherapy, you will need a portable collection and sand tray.

Keep in mind the population you serve. If you work primarily with children, ensure the shelves are low enough or that you have a safe stool available.

The Therapeutic Spaces

Therapeutic work occurs within various spaces; some tangible, visible, and observable, and others intangible, felt, implicit, and, at times, below awareness. However, both contact the client's nervous system and activate a neuroception of danger or safety. The intangible spaces fall into the inter-subjective field where the client and clinician's embodied and relational minds join. How is the clinician's nervous system contacting the client's system? How is the clinician's inner space organized to support the client's healing? Does the clinician have enough space, flexibility, and tolerance for diversity? Can the clinician hold space for various needs, nervous system tendencies, and rhythms?

The tangible and physical spaces, including the therapeutic room and the miniature collection, also touch and hold space for the client's embodied mind. For individuals with deep attachment injuries and acts of omission, the corrective experience of validation, mirroring, and acknowledgment begins with a room and a collection that provides recognition, validation, containment, and safety—whispering, "You exist here. There is space for you here. You matter here."

There are multiple ways of organizing your sandtray space. A dedicated room for the sandt ray, the miniatures, and the therapeutic work is ideal. Clinicians with only a portion of a room for sandtray work should have trays on wheels to move the tray when needed. Ensure you and the client have access to all tray sides to observe and access the tray from multiple angles.

Lyles (2021) recommends making the room flexible to accommodate clients with varied and diverse needs. Lyles emphasizes the importance of being truthful about what we can offer considering the available space. Creating mobility in the room may mean moving chairs to create adequate space for diverse clients. A clinician may not be able to accommodate every disability, but remaining open, flexible, and willing to converse with clients about their needs will cultivate safety. Each therapeutic moment requires a unique adaptation to the client's needs for safety and regulation. Keep in mind that neither the physical room nor the interpersonal space will be flawless, as imperfections are inevitable. According to Lyles (personal communication, March 27, 2023), a powerful question is: "What do you need me to do differently for you to feel considered and for your needs to be accommodated?"

Levels of Distance and Levels of Reprocessing in EMDR–Sandtray Work

The goal of EMDR therapy is to promote the assimilation of memory, which results in integration across multiple dimensions of physiological states, consciousness, and identity. When delivering a comprehensive approach to EMDR-sandtray-based therapy, the client often navigates from memory integration into more profound understandings and connections to their most authentic self. EMDR phases are organized to safely access and reprocess the biological imprints left by trauma and the cognitive, emotional, behavioral, and somatic legacies that lie at the core of the current symptoms. One of the most significant assets and gifts offered by sandtray therapy is its use of symbols and metaphors, which offers the conscious mind distance and a refuge from what may otherwise be overwhelming. Symbols allow information to gradually enter the conscious mind without setting self-protective and defensive strategies in motion or causing activation that exceeds the client's tolerance capacities. Sandtray strategies uniquely accompany each phase of EMDR while aligning with their specific goals and objectives.

Individuals affected by chronic traumatization may be prone to dissociative processes and alterations in consciousness, which challenge their capacity to stay present and engaged. These clients may be prone to immersion, zoning out, absorption, daydreaming, and general disengagement from the present. The sandtray process includes standing up; walking; approaching the sand; collecting and touching, moving, relocating, removing, and burying figures; interacting with the miniatures collection—fostering presence, engagement, and connection to the body. Reprocessing and exploring traumatic states will inevitably challenge the client's sense of safety and move the individual into either mobilization and hyperarousal or dorsal vagal hyperarousal. Movement and play in the tray stimulate social engagement while in the hybrid connection and convergence of the biological systems, such as the sympathetic or parasympathetic systems. Coupling these states with sufficient participation of the ventral system constitutes a neuro-exercise that repairs previously ruptured autonomic states (Porges, 2017). In EMDR–sandtray, the sympathetic nervous system is sometimes recruited as the client's painful stories emerge in the tray while contained and modulated by the social engagement system. At other times, immobility occurs as the client experiences the forces of the dorsal vagal system while in the safety of the space created by the clinician and a companion, such as a parent. The clinician's prosodic voice and presence create a safe space for the client to witness the movement and slow dance of the dorsal system. The reconfiguration of autonomic patterns closely accompanies the assimilation and integration of memory pursued in EMDR–sandtray.

The Sandtray Protocol and Procedural Steps

Homeyer and Sweeney (2023, pp. 51–43) propose a six-step protocol when using sandtray therapy. This is a good standard that clinicians can modify based on their orientations and approaches: (1) preparation; (2) introduction to the client; (3) creation in the sandtray; (4) postcreation; (5) sandtray cleanup; (6) documenting the session.

Rae (2013) recommends an extended format that contains ten aspects of the sandtray sessions: (1) introducing the sandtray process; (2) world creation; (3) silent reverie; (4) reflecting/directing; (5) entering the world; (6) exploring from inside the sand world; (7) leaving the world; (8) summarizing; (9) forming a plan; (10) photographing and clearing.

The following procedural steps and protocol are inspired by these two proposed models while infusing novel elements to fit the unique characteristics of EMDR-sandtray-based therapy. Remember that the steps are modified and flexibly used depending on the phase of EMDR treatment in which they are used. These steps are (1) introduction and invitation; (2) world creation; (3) embracing the world: being with and sitting with; (4) world exploration; (5) resource identification; (6) closure; (7) note-taking and case conceptualization.

Introduction and Invitation

How each client responds to the initial invitation to engage in sandtray work is largely diverse. Some clients will initiate the creation of worlds and stories almost immediately, while others may show hesitation or fear (Rae, 2013). The clinician adapts to each client's needs and provides as little or as much information as required and requested. Allow the knowledge, theory, and procedural steps that often fill your intellectual and cognitive mind to support you while keeping space to hold the data emerging from your client. Staying humble, open, and flexible to accommodate the uniqueness of each client will support you in providing a corrective relational environment to the client that has experienced a multitude of relational ruptures. Remember that the phrases, sentences, and narratives offered throughout this book are intended only as examples and possibilities. As you accompany your clients, you simultaneously hold theoretical constructs, procedural steps, and emerging information from the intersubjective field. Different words, prompts, invitations, and introductions may be necessary. The steps and examples are intended not to constrict you nor mandate a specific response, but to support you in discerning and responding to the evolving nuances of the moment.

When working with children, you might begin by introducing the three storytellers: the mind, the heart, and the body. Each of the storytellers communicates with a distinctive voice. The mind speaks through words and images, the heart through feelings and emotions, and the body through sensations. This metaphor lays the foundation for increasing self-awareness, interoceptive recognition, and mindful observation of cognitive, emotional, and somatic material. It also supports the client in maintaining consciousness of their own embodied mind.

The next step is introducing the tray, the sand, and the miniatures. The invitation to play and touch the sand may begin a long relationship between the client, the sand, and the sand tray (Homeyer & Lyles, 2022). The figures are usually introduced as the companions and voices of the storytellers and the child as a whole. They assist the mind, heart, and body in telling their stories.

For some children, less is better. Very few explanations are needed before inviting the child to pick figures to place inside the tray. Like in EMDR, there is no right or wrong way to play or work with the sand and the sand tray. The companion honors and accepts whatever unfolds. The main message given to the storyteller is that anything can happen in the tray that they want to witness or see happening: "Let whatever happens happen" or "This is your world to do with as you please" (Rae, 2013, p. 76). So, the first encounter with the sand, the tray, and the miniatures collection can be casual and may consist of just playing with the sand. Some clients place figures in the tray immediately, and some move on to create a complete world or story (Smith, 2012). Let the client know they are welcome to pick whichever figures they are drawn to and place them in the tray. They do not need a clear understanding of why they are drawn to a specific figure Remind the client that some storytellers may not know the why, but they know the what. The heart and body may know what they want, even if the underlying reason is unclear.

34   EMDR-Sandtray-based Therapy

Adult and adolescent clients may have the most questions and hesitation because they see this work as something for children. For some clients, the experience of being a child is colored by shame and powerlessness. Engaging in activities often associated with children may activate traumagenic memory systems. Trauma occurring early and chronically in life impacts the development of inborn motivational systems (Steele, 2021). Some of these motivational systems, such as the play, fear, and panic systems, may become dysregulated, overactive, or inhibited because of trauma (Liotti, 2017). According to Panksepp and Biven (2012), when the fear and the panic systems are chronically activated, the play system becomes inhibited, giving rise to diminished opportunities to exercise play urges. Play may become a source of distress and negative affect for many clients and an implicit reminder of the trauma and the relational insufficiencies they endured. Using a compassionate and empathic approach, the clinician extends invitations that the client can accept or refuse. Invitations remain open even if the client initially refuses or rejects the idea of doing sandtray work (Smith, 2012).

Many children may initially show no interest in working or playing with the sand tray but actively engage later. Openness and freedom to choose are conveyed early on in treatment. Adults and adolescents need reassurance that these practices have been used for many years with clients of all ages. This is an ancient language, just like the language of dreams. Ask them if they dream in sentences or metaphors and symbols. Reiterate that when we are in a deep state, we communicate with ourselves through symbols and stories. The mind is already equipped to respond and work with symbolic means of communication. Speaking about the two ways of knowing the world may help a skeptical client: Let them discern the right and left ways of knowing and interacting with the world. Remind the clients that the symbol-based brain is most closely connected to the body and emotions and can see the whole. The right brain can access life accounts encoded early and in implicit memory (Schore, 2019) and thus, working closely with it can give the client a route into traumas that may lack conscious and explicit recollection.

Once the client has been acquainted with the sand, the tray, and the figures, the next step is to ask the client to visit the miniature collection and pick those they are drawn to:

> ❝ I invite you to look at all the figures and companions and pick the ones you like. You don't need to have a reason for liking them; you only need to *feel* inside the pull to select them. I am giving you a basket, so you can put the figures inside. You can pick whichever figures you want and as many or as few as you wish. I can sit here in silence

or walk with you (or accompany you) while talking if that is what you want."

Some clients are comfortable with silence, which most sandtray therapists recommend. However, silence may be an activating stimulus for some clients, especially those injured by relational disconnection, neglect, and loneliness. We are therapeutic partners, so clients should be included in the decision-making process. Where they want us to be, whether they want us to talk, if they want us to sit or walk with them during the figure selection . . . all these issues will be decided with the client.

World Creation

Once the client has finished collecting miniatures, they are invited to place the figures in the tray however they want. Anything can happen in the tray, and there is no right or wrong in anything they create. The clinician conveys that they will be there waiting, in silence, unless the client wants to connect verbally. If silence is uncomfortable, the clinician should use description and reflective communication. For instance:

- I see you just found a spot for this figure.
- I see you are looking at these two figures and trying to decide between them.

The goal is to create verbal "contact" and provide verbal companionship, not to direct what the client is doing.

Some authors believe that inviting the client to "create a story" may yield a linear world, highly influenced by the left brain (Rae, 2013). In my experience, using the word "story" sometimes excites clients who are ready to tell a story but places a burden on those who may see this as a task they have to accomplish. Some clients may feel ill-equipped to form a story or worry it will not be good enough. The term "world" seems to give greater freedom to create without expectations. However, the language used by the clinician should be individualized to each client.

Clinicians must be aware of the client's space. According to Rae (2013), the area inside and above the tray is the domain of the sandtray creator (storyteller), so leaning, reaching over, and touching the tray or the miniatures is discouraged. Clinicians should not cross these boundaries unless the client invites it, in which case it is recommended to seek the client's guidance.

Invite the client to connect with the miniatures, welcoming the mind, the mind, heart, and body to participate:

" Let your mind, heart, and body guide you in choosing the figures."

Curiosity is one of the most significant therapeutic assets. Noticing the cognitive, emotional, and sensorimotor states that arise, moment-to-moment, with curiosity instead of judgment offers a portal and an entrance into the client's embodied mind. What patterns of autonomic activation are emerging in the sand world and within the client's body? What relational patterns unfold between characters? Are tendencies of dismissiveness, avoidance, and disconnection emerging, or are there, instead, symbiotic and anxious relational patterns between characters? The clinician provides an active companionship and a synchronic and attuned silence while staying connected to any shifts, movement, or stillness in their inner world. Like a kaleidoscope that changes in response to movement, the client's and clinician's inner configurations shift in response to internal and external stimuli.

A 5-year-old attending therapy to address his aggressiveness and oppositional behaviors breaks every boundary established in a therapeutic session. He becomes agitated and throws sand and figures against the wall. After unsuccessfully attempting to engage this child in multiple ways, the clinician notices a sense of hopelessness and sadness emerging in her. She allows herself to connect to these internal states and face them with curiosity, compassion, and acceptance. She realizes, as she continues to mindfully observe and accept the movement of these emotions as they come and move through her, that she is picking up on the client's affective states. She becomes aware of the feelings of powerlessness and hopelessness that are his frequent companions. Compassion fills her mind and heart as she gives herself the space to welcome these states while redirecting the child's play and engaging him in coregulation.

Shifts in this child's behaviors began to occur; the shifts were seldom in the beginning, but eventually the shifts became quite noticeable. This is a child whom adults always tried to change to their liking, and once again, unknowingly, the clinician was following this pattern. The clinician's gift of acceptance and compassion while maintaining clear boundaries within their relationship provided the corrective experiences that created the foundation for healing. The clinician also consistently used passive pathways and signals of safety (Porges & Dana, 2018), mindfully and intentionally using her voice intonation, facial expressions, internal state, and movement to increase or decrease physical closeness as required to meet moment-to-moment the child's demands for safety. As this child's sense of safety and trust grew, he began to bring into the tray the hidden injuries and pain that had surrounded his life. Safety in the relationship and the tray needed to be established before consciousness could reach what was conflicting.

Once the client seems done placing the figures inside the tray, the

Phase 1: Foundational and Advanced Skills   **37**

clinician should ask whether the client feels their creation in the tray is complete (Badenoch, 2008). If it does not feel complete, the clinician invites the client to continue searching for figures that need to come into the tray or to remove those that don't feel right. This process continues until the client reports a felt sense of completion. Here is an example:

> I would like to invite you to look at the tray and what you have created and check inside to see if this feels complete/finalized/done to your liking (choose language appropriate to the client's age). If it does not feel finished or complete, I invite you to consider which figures need to come in, which ones need to step out, and which ones need to move."

Embracing the World: "Being With" and "Sitting With"

The next step is to support the mind in connecting with and witnessing its new creation. "Being with" refers to a state of awareness and mindfulness, a "moment-to-moment awareness" (Germer, 2013) of what is unfolding in the tray. Once the storyteller has a completed world, the clinician encourages them "to be or sit with" what is emerging in the tray. This opens the mind to the data emerging from the symbols as well as to sensorimotor, emotional, and cognitive experiences. This process may begin by asking:

- I would like to invite you to sit for some time with the world you created.
- Let's spend some time (or just be) with what you created in the tray without judgment.

The concept of "sitting with" or "being with" may be foreign, especially to children, so further explanation may be needed. We may clarify that when we hang out with friends or our pets, we are "sitting with them," spending curious time "being with them," and visiting them without judging them as good or bad. In the same way, we can "sit with" or spend time with a feeling, a thought, a body sensation, a world, or a story. Eventually, these two terms and concepts will become familiar to children, as they are used often throughout the eight phases of EMDR-sandtray-based treatment.

According to Siegel (2010), when we explain, we rely heavily on the left hemisphere. When we describe, we draw upon the deeply experiential richness of the right hemisphere, inviting it to collaborate with the left brain. Companions describe what the client is doing or mirroring and use reflective communication, rather than explaining and interpreting. Furthermore, requests should be given as invitations to "sit with," "be with," and "notice" what happens or what unfolds from moment to moment.

38   EMDR-Sandtray-based Therapy

World Exploration

Once the client has had sufficient time to "sit and be with" the world and story created, the clinician may start with general questions and then move to more specific questions (Rae, 2013). The process should be tailored to the client's needs and characteristics. Some clients will respond to multiple questions about the tray, while others may want minimal verbal interactions. We are embracing the richness of the nonverbal, symbol-driven brain and gradually inviting the linear, verbal left brain. According to Badenoch (2008, p. 224), "We don't want to catalyze a leap from right- to left-hemisphere processes, but rather open the highway for the right to offer itself to the left." Starting with general questions may open the door to the linear, verbal brain without quickly flooding the experience with words. For instance:

- What would you like me to know, see, or witness about your world?
- What about this world is ready to be seen and known?

Remind the client that their story and inner world can be expressed in the outer world in whatever way feels most authentic and honoring to them. Offer a gradual and titrated approach, and use coverings to allow the world to reveal itself at a safe and appropriate pace.

- Your world may be ready to reveal itself completely or partially to you and me. The entire world, or just a small part, may be ready to be witnessed. Just notice what you want me to know about it.
- You may share about your world as little or as much as it feels right and safe for you now.
- I wonder if you would like to invite me to visit the world (part of the world) you created.
- Would you be open to giving me a tour of your world (or a part of your world)?

After the questions are asked, the client should be given time for the words to come at a rhythm appropriate to each client. Some sandtray therapists ask clients to give a title to the world. This may be one of many ways of starting to explore the world, but it is not essential.

Focusing on the world and the story created by the storyteller releases them from the pressure of focusing their attention on themselves. According to Homeyer and Sweeney (2017),

> The sandtray and its contents become the focus of the discussion rather than the client. With the focus removed from the client, the client is able to more freely discuss his or her issues. (p. 54)

Phase 1: Foundational and Advanced Skills   **39**

Attempting to link what unfolds in the tray with the client's life accounts is discouraged. Allow the client to stay with the avatars and stories emerging in the tray and only switch when the client organically switches.

Distance is one of the greatest gifts and assets that sandtray therapy offers. To maintain the distance that the mind needs to approach trauma and adversity, we must honor the symbols and metaphors in which the wounded mind has found refuge. In standard EMDR therapy, interpretation is discouraged. According to F. Shapiro (2018), the client's innate information-processing system is assimilating and integrating traumatic material. Integration in EMDR–sandtray is not confined to the cognitive–verbal level of information processing; it encompasses the symbolic–nonverbal and somatic dimensions, resulting in an embodied synthesis of memory. Words are welcome, but not always needed, for information processing and memory integration to occur.

When exploring the tray, use reflective communication and statements that mirror and validate the client's unfolding data, and gently invite new information into the tray. When using questions, be mindful not to overwhelm the client's system. Remember that every question may elicit new information potentially unknown to the client and that can enter the mind too rapidly and intrusively. On the other hand, some clients tolerate questions delivered quickly, so adjust your rhythm based on each client's qualities, characteristics, preferences, and capacities. Several questions will be offered in this chapter; use them intentionally. As Homeyer and Sweeney (2017, p. 66) state, "Be more reflective than interrogative."

Once initial and general information is provided, the companion can gently move into more specific questions.

- What stands out to you as you visit or sit with the world you created?
- What is the easiest/safest part/side/area of this world to visit or sit with?
- What part/area/side of this world do you feel drawn to visit or sit with?

As you move into more specific questions, curiosity and your capacity to mentalize and reflect are your best assets and companions. The following are examples of invitations and questions to help you create your own repertoire (Rae, 2013; Homeyer & Sweeney, 2023; Homeyer & Lyles, 2022).

- Let yourself/allow yourself to be with . . . and let's learn more about . . .
- Let's try to stay a bit longer with [character]'s feelings and see what happens.
- Let's see what happens if we watch and stay with [character].
- Let's notice, watch, or stay with [character] until you know it.
- How is it for [character] to be/feel left out?

40   EMDR-Sandtray-based Therapy

- What does [character] say/feel about being left out by the other [characters]?
- How was it for [character] to push [character]?
- Tell me more about this one.
- Is this a female or a male (or both)?
- What do you know about her/him/them?
- What is it doing?
- What does [character] see in this world?
- What does [character] know of the rest of this world?
- Is this the world [character] wants to be in?
- What does [character] see from where they are?
- I wonder what it is like for [character] to . . .
- Let's learn now about . . .
- Now let's see . . .
- Does [character] know [character]?
- Do they know each other?
- How does [character] know . . .
- Does [character] want to say something to . . . ?
- How does [character] feel about it?
- Let's guess how [character] may feel inside.
- How do you think [character]'s body may feel?
- What is the job of [character]? How does it like or dislike the job?
- What would happen if they stopped doing what they are doing?
- What is [character] afraid of if they . . . ?
- How does [character] know this feeling has arrived?
- Is this a feeling only [character] has? Or is it shared with others?
- How is it for [character] to be the only one having this feeling?

You may also use reflections and statements that mirror while supporting the client in expanding meaning. Reflective statements arise from presence, intention, and mentalization and are offerings from one mind to another to support integration and healing. These offerings may be rejected or embraced, but when rejected, the client often adds information to negate the offering. This is still data that expands the client's field of awareness.

The clinician's mentalizing capacities play a fundamental role in exploring the tray. Fonagy et al.'s (2002) division of low- and high-intensity mentalization interventions has proven helpful in understanding when and how to intervene during tray exploration throughout the phases of EMDR-sandtray-based treatment, especially when processing trauma. Low-intensity interventions are used when the client is overwhelmed and too much information is flooding their mind. In EMDR therapy, we call this over-accessing (F. Shapiro, 2018). Asking more questions or using reflecting

Phase 1: Foundational and Advanced Skills **41**

statements that elicit additional material or expand meaning could further flood the client's mind. Instead, empathic statements of companionship and passive pathways to safety, such as modulating your voice, facial expressions, and closeness (Porges & Dana, 2018), will provide the needed coregulation and corrective experience.

When using low-intensity interventions, the clinician provides support, reassurance, and validation:

> ❝ I see how hard it is for [character] in the story. I am right by your side as we witness [character]'s pain."

The more connected we clinicians are to ourselves, the more we move away from fixing and into being.

High-intensity interventions involve active and expanded reflections and questions that support the client in accessing and developing their understanding, self-knowledge, and awareness. The following are interventions and approaches for using reflective communication and mentalizing strategies while exploring the tray and keeping in mind the client's moment-to-moment shifting capacities and the emerging data (Fonagy et al., 2002; Reynolds, 2020).

1. Slow down before reflecting whenever the client is overwhelmed by the tray's emerging information. Become their external bioemotional regulator.
   a. "Would it be okay if we slow down what is happening in the tray?"
   b. "Would it be okay if we slow down the pace in which information is unfolding in the tray?"
   c. "Let's pick just one area or character that is the easiest to focus on right now."
   d. "How does the speed of what is happening in the tray feel to you? Is it too slow or too fast? If it is too fast, let's slow it down, and let's only watch, observe, or witness what seems more relevant or easy for you now."
2. Demonstrate curiosity and a genuine desire to understand. Clarifications serve as a break to slow down the client and the emerging data and convey to the client that the clinician is engaged and interested. Additionally, they yield new information and organize the existing one.
   a. "I am curious about how [character] went from one house to another without anyone noticing. Can we be curious together about it?"
3. Affect clarification gives the emotion a name, context, and a space to exist in the tray and the client's field of consciousness.
   a. "I am wondering if [character] in the tray is feeling anger (client's

word), pain and sadness (client reports the woman is crying), or all that and more?"

4. Recognize, verbalize, and mirror the emotions without trying to fix them, change them, or rescue the client. Allow yourself to be uncertain while holding the space for your client to safely embrace their inner world.

   a. A client stated that a big fly hurt a kitty, but as the kitty reported, she could not get away or defend herself because she was afraid. The therapist's response may be: "The kitty wishes she could escape or fight back, but the fear is big and taking over and not letting her break free . . . I am just noticing that despite the big fly's hurts, the kitty can still know, see, and share her fear."

5. Notice emotional shifts without trying to interpret or seek a meaningful narrative. Meaning exists in somatic narratives even without a verbal counterpart. We may be biased toward narratives with verbal and linear content while denying the richness of right-brain, body-based storylines. A way to reflect may be by saying: I noticed, I heard, I observed, I sense, or I see . . .

   a. "*I noticed* that you looked down/away as the fly began to hurt the kitty again."

   b. "*I heard* [your voice changing/you become silent/you become louder/your tone of voice was excited and vibrant] when . . ."

6. Label the implicit emotions.

   a. "The little girl feels like screaming, and at the same time, she worries about what the monster could do if she does (client's report). This must be terrifying for the little girl (clinician's addition)."

7. The clinician is a coorganizer of experience that supports the client in putting together the story with increased clarity. In this role, you may summarize essential points and expand the meaning of what has been said and what has unfolded in the tray. Use the client's words when summarizing.

8. Bring resources and adaptive information into the client's field of consciousness.

   a. "I can see how scary being around the big fly that hurt her is for the kitty. The kitty finds it difficult to escape on her own . . . but there are helpers on the other side that the kitty knows (already disclosed by the client) . . . hmmm."

9. Reflect on the polarity or the meaning of the information unfolding in the tray, capturing the client's ambivalence and conflict. Recognize the conflict and contradictions in the tray.

   a. "When the cat is on this side of the tray with his mom, he feels love, but he struggles with the other side where he feels sad because his mother hurts him. It is hard for the cat to put together in his mind

FIGURE 2.4 A child creates a sand world where, on one side, a mother cat hurts her son and keeps him trapped. Eyes represent the mother's power to see and know everything the cat is doing, thinking, and feeling. An alien figure holds a heart in sadness.

FIGURE 2.5 On the other side of the tray, the mother cat is loving toward her son. Trees and a large pink gem represent the cat's love and safety. Each side of the tray represents a polarity in the cat's relationship with his mother.

and understand the feelings that come from being with a mom who loves him and, at the same time, hurts him. Having two feelings at the same time or for the same person may be very challenging and conflicting for the cat. He may be trying to figure out how to handle two very opposite feelings."

10. Draw distinctions while unveiling the polarity.
    a. "On one side, the 'you' in the tray is exhausted from working long hours, and at the same time, she finds it challenging to say no to new opportunities."
11. Reflect on the needs surfacing in the tray and differentiate them from wants.
    a. "The lion is finding out how much rest he needs, but he is still working hard to get more and more money (disclosed by the client). Money seems to satisfy something he wants, and at the same time, his body is showing him what he needs."

12. Amplify and extend the meaning, and expand perspective.
    a. "It seems like both feelings, love and sadness, visit/coexist in the cat's inside world. Both have important reasons for coming and both hold information for the cat."
13. Use metaphors within the metaphor to reflect and paraphrase (Reynolds, 2020).
    a. "It seems like the little girl in the tray is so tired of trying (disclosed by the client) that it feels like pushing a huge rock up the hill."
    b. "I am noticing that the cat feels overwhelmed with his emotions (using the client's words); it feels like he is sinking in big, big feelings."
14. Reframe the occurrence in the tray.
    a. "The cat is overwhelmed with big feelings now. However, he has survived and is still alive and trying."
15. Use zoom-in and zoom-out strategies. Activation may overtake a part of the tray while another side remains unseen, despite holding resources and soothing forces. The clinician may invite the client to zoom out from the activation and zoom in on the resources.
    a. A princess is losing her battle against a small dinosaur, while on the other side of the tray, her powerful friend, Wonder Woman, is ready to help. The adolescent is completely absorbed in the princess's powerlessness despite the power existing in the tray. The clinician invites the client to zoom out and look at the entire tray with curiosity. At this point, she connects to the princess's powerful ally.
16. Validate and acknowledge the issue, situation, or emotion witnessed based on the client's readiness to do so.
    a. "I wonder if the little girl in the tray knows that I am now a witness to her story. I see what the monster is doing, I hear her cry, and I witness her pain."
    b. For clients that are not ready yet for this level of witnessing: "I wonder if the little girl in the tray wants me [or the caregiver, or the child] to witness her story."
17. Pair, reflect, and summarize with questions.
    a. "I wonder how this lands in the little girl's mind, heart, and body."
    b. "How does the little girl in the tray receive this?"
    c. "How does the cat know this feeling arrived in his body?"
18. Show curiosity.
    a. "I wonder how the mother in the tray reached this conclusion."
    b. "I wonder where he/she/they learned that."
    c. "Can we be curious together?"
19. Use active silence and pauses. While physically and emotionally present, silence often yields abundant data as it gives the client permission to be without words. Silence may be uncomfortable for some clinicians,

but as you become more comfortable with being instead of doing, you open yourself to a field of possibilities.

20. Acknowledge your humanity, uncertainty, and the unknown. Sometimes, clients ask for our opinion or we face an issue we do not know how to handle. Acknowledge uncertainties and invite the client to step into the unknown while in the safety offered in the therapeutic relationship.
    a. "I do not know. I am trying to figure it out myself."
    b. "I am sitting in complete uncertainty. I am sitting with the feeling of not knowing and wonder how it would be for you to join me."

21. Acknowledge and recognize ruptures. Moments of asynchrony will happen; they are part of our human existence. Gently bring them to the surface and work toward repairing them.
    a. "I notice that you may have been wanting me to say or do something with what is happening in the tray, and instead, I remained silent. Let me try again and see if I can be there for you in the way you need me to [long for me to be]."

Every single reflective technique can be used as an interweave during processing sessions. Reflection can bring insight and information that support the expansion of consciousness and integration. Anything verbalized may be represented in the tray and physicalized.

- Is what you are telling me ready to show up in the tray?
- How does it want to be or to show up in the tray?
- I wonder how this feeling wants to be [be represented] in the tray?
- Let's have its presence and voice in the tray how it wants.

We provide titration and a space for the stories to show up as they are ready to be witnessed, seen, and known. The clinician should consider a titration continuum and inquire about how the client's inner world longs to be seen and known in the outer world. A figure and its story may want to enter the tray completely buried under the sand or otherwise covered. Offering multiple levels of visibility may be useful. For instance:

"I wonder if the [sad] feeling of the [birdy] is ready to be seen and show up in the tray. If it is, it can show up as it wants: completely [seen/revealed], halfway seen and partly buried in the sand, or completely covered (tray coverings or other objects such boxes may be used)."

Sometimes, a conflict may arise at this point. For instance, one character may want—and even demand—to see the feeling, while another may refuse. In this case, both polarities are invited into the tray.

46   EMDR-Sandtray-based Therapy

The sandtray process also invites somatic consciousness to promote embodied integration and coherence. Clinicians closely observe the interconnectedness of the information unfolding in the tray and the client's physical sensations, breathing patterns, movement dynamics, posture, tightness, tension, tone of voice, areas of the body that seem activated or restricted, and gestures, which are informative and provide insight into the client's inner experience. Clinicians can use reflections, mirroring, and questions about what is developing and what the client's body is expressing. "We might say that the body has its own consciousness, which is not connected with rational thinking, but rather with the imagination." (Turner, 2017, p. 120). Clinicians can invite the client to move their awareness from the objects to the self or body at any given point. For instance, the therapist may describe and reflect on what is occurring in the tray and in the client:

- As you moved the kitty away from the big tiger, I noticed that your body started to shake, and then it became really quiet! I wonder if you are noticing that.
- As you move the kitty to the other corner of the tray, can I invite you to check what is happening in you or your body? What sensations are you noticing in your body? Can you show me with your body how you are feeling right now? Is there a movement or gesture that feels particularly [important/resonant] or connected to what is happening in the tray now? How does your body respond as you watch the [princess] fighting for her life? You may also track changes in the client's embodied patterns: Where is this feeling/sensation moving in your body? Does it feel sharp, dull, heavy, or light? Does it poke, push, or pulsate?

Any of these somatic experiences may be represented in the tray. You might explore the patterns of movement associated with this sensation:

" Does it prompt any urges or impulses? Does your body want to move in a certain way?"

Inviting movement may facilitate embodied integration, the completion of truncated responses, the release of stored tension, and the restoration of mobility in areas where immobilization has governed while prioritizing the client's autonomy and choice. The movements may happen inside and outside the tray, yet the client may remain completely connected to the sand world.

Awareness shifts from object to body or self do not represent a transi-

Phase 1: Foundational and Advanced Skills   **47**

tion out of the story, metaphor, and the implicit channel used to access the client's inner wound. The clinician should honor the mind's refuge and not force awareness or push the client abruptly out of the implicit road. Instead, the movement toward the body should maintain the distance the client needs from the story while actively inquiring about how the sand world contacts the client's body and nervous system. This is an intentional decision based on what is emerging. For instance, when visible sensorimotor data is emerging, the clinician may meet the moment with a question that connects the client to the self and body, especially if this is done during reprocessing phases in the form of an interweave.

Areas of Exploration of the Sand World

The tray provides a space that facilitates dialogue between different aspects of the self while accessing internal conflicts, relational templates, and nervous system patterns. The information unfolding may sometimes emerge in a well-organized fashion, while in other instances, it may emerge in complete chaos, yet we must trust that the client's consciousness has its own organizing principles. How we respond and what we do with what is arising in the tray depends on the present context and the phase of the EMDR treatment. Remember the goals of each phase, as they will be one of the factors that will guide your responses to the client. Phase 1 aims to explore the client's history and develop a treatment plan and clinical landscape. Due to the complexities of working with individuals affected by chronic and complex trauma, clinicians will benefit from having guidelines that can help them organize the flow of information in the tray. The following domains and areas will help systematize the information that is reported, over-reported, or under-reported in the tray.

Cognitive Data. Pay close attention to negative beliefs that point to adverse and traumatic material and to positive metaperceptions that indicate the presence of resources and capacities. Characters who are unable to escape may represent a client's beliefs, such as, "I am powerless" or "I am trapped." The negative belief, "I am bad," may be depicted by avatars that present themselves as bad and unworthy. This metacognitive data does not need to be translated into acknowledged beliefs, as they may continue to exist in the nonverbal and symbolic world. However, the clinician acts as a midwife, supporting the client in birthing and bringing these deep-rooted beliefs into awareness through their presence, questions, and reflective statements.

Emotional Data. The tray reveals a wealth of affective information. Some emotions emerge explicitly, while others remain in the realm of implicit awareness. Emotions may reach consciousness through a character or

48   EMDR-Sandtray-based Therapy

story without the client owning the emotional state. The characters and avatars provide the client with opportunities to expand their affect tolerance and to develop a relationship with their emotions. These emotions may appear orderly, unruly, jumbled, hidden, or overtly expressed. They may have words or exist in silence. Do you observe an abundant display of emotions or a substantial constriction and limited access to emotional states in the client's sand worlds?

Sensorimotor Data. Close observation of bodily states and shifts can yield critical and essential evidence of what the client's mind is discerning. How is the body telling its story? Is the body corroborating or contradicting what the stories in the tray are expressing? Is the material arising coherently or in a disorganized form? The somatic landscape may become frozen or be in a continuous state of change. It may present with constriction or dysregulation. Gestures, subtle movements, changes in breath patterns or skin color, eye and pupil variations, and other physiological expressions constitute the somatic panorama accompanying the EMDR–sandtray work.

Areas of Heat and Activation. Notice areas where activation and mobilization are unfolding. Watch for areas where fear, anger, jealousy, aggressiveness, and fight-or-flight responses are depicted. These are hot and vehement areas of the tray that may signal the arousal of the sympathetic system. Notice how much of the tray is overtaken by this mobilized energy. If you are in the reprocessing phases (4, 5, and 6), you may need to use interweaves to support the completion of these mobilized responses. If you are in Phase 1, data collection will be your primary goal, as well as creating safety, building rapport and connection, and actively accompanying the client as you move into the preparation phase and the building of regulatory capacities.

FIGURE 2.6 **A teenager creates a world where two powerful gangs fight for power and goods. Gang members face each other in the tray, exhibiting anger and overt expressions of aggression.**

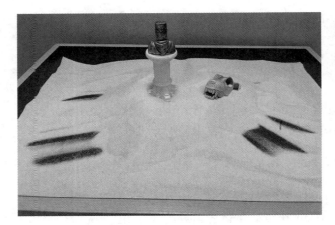

FIGURE 2.7 **A lonely, faceless soldier stands on top of a mountain, and the remains of his dog are his only companion.**

Areas of Collapse, Immobility, and Shutdown. Contrary to a mobilized system, a shutdown and collapsed system can make its way to the tray. These areas are cold and immobilized, where loneliness and silence govern. The client's accounts are usually short and lack detail and richness, as the dorsal vagal system dominates and mediates the sand narratives. Sometimes, only a small portion of the tray carries this collapsed, dissociative energy; other times, it may dominate the entire tray.

Areas of Conflict and Relational Dynamics. Study how the characters in the tray relate to each other. Are they friends or enemies? Do they get along or fight? Is anyone getting injured in the tray? Who holds power, and who are the decision-makers? How are the other characters responding to the injured and injuring avatars? Are there secrets and cover-ups? Do the characters feel safe or in danger? Are the characters in an eternal state of fighting, bickering, and discord? Are they willing to negotiate? Who loses, and who wins? Are there patterns that show polarizations in the relational dynamics? Sometimes, one of the polarities is embraced while the other is denied. For instance, a client may ally with the aggressive forces of the violent character while denying or rejecting the submissive and vulnerable ones. Both need acknowledgment and integration. The clinician observes, uses reflective statements, and invites curiosity, as they both are part of the experience. The most profound realization may be that all these polarized states coexist within a single consciousness—the "Self"—which can observe and own these affective states without becoming them. Deeply polarized states may take multiple reprocessing sessions throughout various developmental stages so the mind at different periods of growth can integrate its multilayered roots and stems. For instance, deeply entrenched perpetrator–victim dynamics that originated in early life will set up profound polarizations and alliances that may extend throughout an individual's lifespan.

FIGURE 2.8 A three-headed, powerful monster keeps a small turtle hostage. The monster can see and control everything the young turtle does and feels. Surrounded by the monster's allies, the turtle is utterly powerless and obedient.

Approach Versus Distancing, Autonomy Versus Dependency, Power, and Powerlessness Tendencies. Do the characters show a sense of agency, autonomy, capacity, and sovereignty? Or do they tell a story of submissiveness, powerlessness, and obedience? Do they seek help, connection, and support? Or do they withdraw, distance, and retreat in the presence of danger and fear and/or when there are opportunities for connection and relationships?

Defenses and Self-Protection. Does the story depict a false presence, hiding the real self and its fears, predicaments, and dilemmas? Avoidance, pleasing, controlling, and dissociation are just a few of the mechanisms of adaptation that may accompany the mind exposed to trauma. Clients may avoid the themes and emotions that are consistently excluded from their sand worlds. They may also evade exploring areas or figures in the tray, devaluing their importance. Some clients may control the world's creation or work excessively to avoid imperfections. The world may be superficial or consistently positive, avoiding uncomfortable emotional or challenging content.

Areas Where Adaptive Information and Resources Exist. Explore the presence of resources and positive and adaptive information emerging in the tray. Notice protectors, helpers, and wise characters that materialize in the tray. These packets of adaptive information and resources will be useful when information processing stalls, especially when preparing to reprocess the world. Support the client in indulging, observing, and taking in such assets while connecting with the figures that hold the space for them.

Regulatory Capacities. The avatars and their inner dynamics often reflect the client's regulatory capacities. Does the character pursue solitude and quietness, or does it seek support from others in the tray? When distressed, do the characters pursue others for help or protection, or do they deal with distress on their own? Do characters direct aggression to themselves or to others?

Actions and Urges. What actions and behaviors surface more often in the story? Covert and overt urges and repetitive movements in the tray hold important stories. Do characters often run or move or usually remain quiet and immobilized? When exploring the tray, what actions and impulses (or, for children, "itchy wishes") do the characters report or wish they could execute? Do they report wanting to move or escape but cannot do so? Are the characters or the client moving the entire time the story unfolds, or is the client quiet and moving very little?

Grief and Loss. The sand world may be overtaken by loss and grief. The deceased individuals or lost relationships may appear as active participants or be utterly ignored and absent from the tray. Scenes depicting moments of loss and experiences surrounding the loss may surface. Clients may depict how they integrate their loss into their ongoing sense of self.

Intersubjective Field. So much can be learned from our own subjective and inner experiences. According to Schore (2019), the intersubjective flow and affective communication of the mind of the client and the therapist as they ride together through various patterns of activation represents a powerful source of transformation and change. Schore (2019) further adds:

> The psychobiologically attuned intuitive clinician tracks the nonverbal moment-to-moment rhythmic structures of the patient's internal states and is flexibly and fluidly modifying his or her own behavior to

FIGURE 2.9 **An adolescent female client creates a sand world depicting the death of a little girl and her dog. Candles, skulls, and death symbols surround this world. Inside the coffin lie the dog and the little girl. The red figure of a lonely teenager next to the skeleton of her dog is crying for him (The client does not recognize herself or her story in this world.)**

synchronize with that structure, thereby co-creating with the client a growth-facilitating context for the organization of the therapeutic alliance. (p. 30)

In the depth of EMDR–sandtray work, internal working models and memory systems reemerge within the footprints of past injuries, present struggles, and rooted defenses. Reenactments occur in the tray and the therapist–client relationship. However, the companionship and synchrony in which the client experiences various states of activation provide the opportunity for correction, coregulation, and the cocreation of new meanings. Clinicians stay connected to what emerges in their own nervous systems and embodied minds, as this data is part of the therapeutic moment that holds information for the clinician and client. Do *you* feel overwhelmed by the content or the amount of energy and movement generated in the tray? Do *you* feel heavy and tired as you connect with the information unfolding? (See Chapter 10 for extensive information on the clinician's mind and the intersubjective field.)

Resources, Capacities, and Realizations

When resources, capacities, new realizations, and acts of triumph arise, they may be explored and installed using slow and short sets of BLS/DAS if the client is acquainted with the procedures of EMDR therapy. You may inquire about how the client experienced moments of triumph and insight:

> " Is there something you take with you from the sand world, the story, or the experiences in your inner world?"

Sometimes, you may bring up moments of victory and awareness that were witnessed in the client or the characters and avatars in the tray:

> " I notice that the kitty pushed the monster away, and you said he felt free and strong. How is it for you to see what the kitty experienced and felt empowered to do?"

If the client resonates with the clinician's statement, the clinician may invite the client to notice their emotions and where they "hang out" in the body as they observe the victorious moments of the characters. The clinician is installing the comfortable, life-affirming emotional state prompted by the character's experience and its act of triumph (Ogden, 2019). This is not about trying to connect the story with the client's life; it is about enhancing their awareness of and connection to the often-unseen capacities, insights, and acts of triumph experienced in the tray.

The integration of resources and insight in the client's mind occurs at a symbolic and implicit level or explicitly as they recognize themself in the tray.

In some cases, the material that emerges from the tray is surrounded by hardship, and the presence of resources is scarce. However, even in these cases, the clinician can mirror the victorious acts and the capacity of the character—or client—to be with such uncomfortable stories and states. The use of BLS/DAS should be a clinical decision based on each client's capacities and the severity of their trauma. Short, slow sets of BLS/DAS could potentially activate memory systems that hold traumagenic material in clients with complex trauma and dissociation. Depending on the client, identifying and installing resources are optional and should not be imposed.

Closure

At the end of every session, the clinician must assist the client in returning to homeostasis and emotional equilibrium. Closure includes containing any disturbing material that was awakened in the tray and guiding the client to regain balance and stability. Closing also involves enhancing new realizations and understandings, as well as fostering homeostatic states. The first step is to announce that the time with the session will come to an end with sufficient time to close the sand world and support the client's homeostasis. Usually, it will be appropriate to invite the client to sit with the world they created to see what needs to happen before they end their time with it. Ask if there are voices from the tray that still want to be heard or witnessed before the end of the session.

> "As we end our time together, I invite you to sit or be with your world or story. . . . Let's check what needs to happen in the tray before we go. Are there figures that need to move, hide, come out, or be seen? Are there voices that need to be heard before we go?"

Once whatever needs to happen in the tray is manifested, invite the client to visit each aspect to ensure that every character and figure is where they need to be.

For instance, a 17-year-old female client must end her session at a critical point in developing her sandtray story. A little girl is taking refuge inside a car after going through a car accident. Despite invitations to find who could rescue this child, no help or support is found. She is invited to sit with the tray and decide how she wants to leave the scene until the next meeting. She says she wants to leave the little girl in a safe place in the tray.

54   EMDR-Sandtray-based Therapy

When clients opt to leave characters in danger, it reveals the client's internal or external state of activation, fear, and hypervigilance. Many clients with complex trauma carry a neuroception of danger, even in the presence of safety. Screening for danger and safety in the client's life is a fundamental step that should be taken into account throughout the eight phases of treatment. A tray with substantial fear, danger, and powerlessness may signal past traumas and current situations of danger that the client feels powerless to address. When the session ends with a character in danger, if the client cannot find refuge and safety for the character, you may offer to keep it safe until the next session. However, if the client declines, grant their wishes.

The literature on sandtray therapy consistently places the responsibility of dismantling the tray in the clinician's hands. This is how to preserve in the client's mind the story and the images that emerged during the session. However, we must wonder if preserving absolutes has the potential to negate individual differences and diversity. The first time a client refused my offer to dismantle the tray, the client stated that leaving the tray open felt unsettling and anxiety-provoking. When given a choice, she invited me to join her in dismantling the tray. She stated that disassembling the tray together gave her a sense of mastery and agency over her pain and trauma. Multiple clients have taught me that the client should decide on this sacred process while we remain faithful companions. When the client chooses to engage in the deconstruction of the created world, they have the opportunity to experience the ephemeral and intangible dimensions of memory. This endeavor imparts a sense of empowerment to the client stemming from the capacity to create, dismantle, obliterate, and once again create a world with newfound awareness and sense of identity. Through this cycle of creation and destruction that occurs in every session, the client closely witnesses the reorganization of sensorimotor, cognitive, and affective structures formed in the service of survival while beholding how the mind redefines its relationship with its life stories. Each session will bring a different choice and a distinct approach to fulfilling the longings of the client's heart. Gratitude may be expressed to the figures that accompanied the client (Homeyer & Lyles, 2022), for the experiences and opportunities these avatars provided, and for the new realizations they brought. Picture-taking usually happens before the tray is dismantled, and the client and the clinician can take pictures of the client's sandtray work.

Once the tray has been dismantled or pushed aside, the container exercise used in standard EMDR therapy or another containment strategy may be used. Once the client is ready, the clinician can extend an invitation to contain what is still disturbing or "yucky." The following is a container exercise that can be used with clients of all ages. This is a modified excerpt from the book *EMDR and Adjunct Approaches with Children: Complex Trauma, Attachment, and Dissociation* (Gómez, 2013):

> We are going to create a cool thing that you can use to help yourself when you have mixed-up (for adults, negative or disturbing) thoughts, feelings, or sensations in your body. Let's start by creating an imaginary container, jar, or box in your mind. This jar or box is very special because you can put anything that bothers you or that is mixed up (disturbing) inside. First, choose the shape of your container, jar, or box. Once you have the shape, choose the material you want it built of. It may be made of metal, wood, glass, or any other material you want. Once you have the shape and material, pick the color. Now, make sure that it has a lid. You can also choose different things to decorate your container with (you can add any features you want to this container to make it yours). Once it is decorated, I want you to decide where you will leave your container. That place could be in my office or any other place you wish. You can also choose the protector of your container, jar, or box. You can have Spider-Man (companions and helpers), an angel, or any important helper or guard to keep your container safe.

Once the client has created the container, ask them to visit the three storytellers: the mind, the heart, and the body.

> " Now, we will visit the mind and find any mixed up or negative thoughts. Next, take a breath, and when you let the air out, put these thoughts into your container (or jar/box for younger children). Next, let's visit the heart; find all the mixed-up feelings (disturbing or uncomfortable emotions), and put them in the jar as you continue to breathe. Now, let's visit your body; find anything or any part that feels yucky or mixed up (like holding disturbance or tension), and put the yucky (disturbing) stuff inside the container while you breathe. How do you feel now?"

If the client reports a comfortable and regulated emotional state, ask where these feelings are located in the body and enhance these positive states using slow and short sets of BLS/DAS.

Coverings may be used if the client wants to fully or partially cover the tray while engaging in coregulation and self-regulation at the end of the session. The fabric might cover only the areas holding activation and disturbance, leaving resources, new understandings, knowledge, or realizations exposed. However, the coverings are placed on the areas the client

56 EMDR-Sandtray-based Therapy

selects. For clients with low positive affect tolerance, the amplification of positive affective states may occur gradually.

Other activities and resources may be incorporated into the closing of the session, depending on the neural profile the client is presenting at the end of the session. Some clients need up-regulation, and some need down-regulation, and strategies and activities to address those needs and physiological states are selected accordingly. For instance, we may ask children to choose to engage in an activity such as playing musical instruments, singing, dancing, and intentional breathing. Adults may choose breathing exercises, humming, mindful practices, and so forth.

Note-Taking

When using EMDR-sandtray-based therapy, it is essential to keep the session to 50 or 75 minutes so you have time to clean up, print pictures, and write your progress notes. When possible, take notes while the client is building and/or describing their world. This may be quite challenging, especially with children, so the ten minutes at the end of the session are crucial for note-taking (see Appendix 4 for a sample of a session summary).

Picture-taking will be part of your EMDR–sandtray practice, so you will need a digital or phone camera. Obtain a stand-alone written authorization or include it in your general treatment authorization to allow the use of EMDR and sandtray therapy. Additionally, ensure that written permission is obtained for taking pictures, specifying where they will be securely stored and how they will be used. Note-keeping can be challenging when using two complex approaches, such as EMDR and sandtray, especially when working with children. Pictures will help you register what unfolds in the tray during the session. You may want to incorporate the following elements in your progress note format beyond the basic domains that are usually included:

1. When you list the various therapeutic modalities, include EMDR therapy and EMDR–sandtray work.
2. Clearly state which phase of EMDR treatment the session was dedicated to.
3. Record who was present during the session (child/parent).
4. Include the title of the world or story and general and specific descriptions of the world/story.
5. Include the main and other accompanying characters.
6. Note the level of titration: implicit or explicit access to resources or elements of autobiographical memory.
7. Note the resources identified and installed.
8. Record negative and positive cognition, as well as the validity of the positive cognition (VoC) scale, emotions, and subjective units of

Phase 1: Foundational and Advanced Skills **57**

disturbance (SUD), when identified during the session. Note inter-weaves used and "stuck points" if the session was dedicated to the processing phases of EMDR therapy.

9. Record body-based data such as muscle tension, breathing patterns, movement rhythms and tendencies.
10. Note which closure activity was utilized.
11. Attach pictures of the sandtray work. You can write information about the characters and the story on the picture.

While clinicians reflect on moment-to-moment occurrences, they should maintain close attention to the clinical landscape that emerges in every session as a microcosm and concurrently remain aware of the broader clinical panorama of the client's life story. Each session delves into different aspects of the client's mind, which are encompassed by the wider vista of the client's trajectories and journey. Connections to both the macro and the micro treatment perspectives are essential, as they offer diverse vantage points of understanding. Clinicians should be guided by the EMDR road map of procedural steps and the eight phases while closely connecting to the client's clinical landscape. Moreover, clinicians should maintain congruency in their treatment planning so that the client's evolving needs, goals, and rhythms align with the therapeutic interventions.

Portals Into the Mind in EMDR–Sandtray Therapy: Implicit and Explicit Entry Roads

The resurfacing of traumatic memories, inner conflicts, and defenses may not occur verbally, especially when working with children. Information may surface through relational and play reenactments (Gil, 2017). Individuals across the lifespan presenting with complex and developmental trauma may find the exploration of trauma and its legacy overwhelming, pushing the client past their emotional threshold and out of their window of affect tolerance rather quickly. The various levels of distance—from implicit to explicit—emerging in the tray offer a titration continuum that the client can navigate through as they embark on a journey of healing thick layers of accumulated trauma. This access to both implicit and explicit routes provides the mind with expanded possibilities to contact the wound at its own pace and rhythm. The mind can find refuge in a distant and third-person story or come face-to-face with the actual traumatic event while owning as much as it is ready to acknowledge.

Implicit Access and First Level of Distance

This access route into the client's embodied and relational mind is especially suited for children, as it capitalizes on their developmental patterns of communicating and interacting with the world. Children usually do not tell their life stories through coherent and cohesive verbal narratives. Instead, they do so through reenactments in the relationships they form and the play themes they create. The mind seeks refuge in the sand story and metaphor, gently sidestepping explicit acknowledgment of the self within the tray. Instead, the characters and avatars tell the client's life accounts while holding the weight of the affect, wounds, and conflicts.

In implicit access and the first level of distance, the client creates a world where the self is often not recognized as an active participant. There is no ownership of the emerging cognitive, emotional, behavioral, and sensorimotor material. The conflicts in the tray are not yet seen as belonging to the mind that created them. This potentially overwhelming material remains in the nonconscious mind not yet entering into the verbal/explicit world. Trauma-related phobias may prevent the client from accessing and exploring memories that are too painful and dysregulating, opting for a protective route of exploring the trauma, free from ownership. Access to implicit awareness through the tray can provide the containment and distance needed to work around and through such phobias and defenses. Undoubtedly, signs and hints of what resides in the depths of the nonconscious mind are revealed in the worlds created by the child despite the child's strong self-protective system. Traces of hardship and suffering can escape the layers of accumulated survival adaptations.

Marie, an 8-year-old experiencing anxiety and depression after suffering from bullying for several years, creates a world where a horse living on a farm is constantly hurt by other horses. Marie reports that no one knows this is happening, and the "horsey" is scared to tell. Marie speaks about how lonely the horsey feels; however, she does not claim the loneliness as her own. Instead, the horse, Marie's avatar, holds the space for the loneliness to emerge, implicitly and below awareness. Marie's teacher describes her as a loner and a sad child. However, during initial sessions, Marie did not provide nor acknowledge any accounts of her struggles and hardships. She reported feeling good and getting along with her classmates. According to her parents, Marie rarely shared her feelings or challenges. She was a self-reliant child with no choice but to shut down her pain in response to growing up in a relationally impoverished and rejecting environment. However, the distance provided by the sandtray work allowed for the traumatic memory's cognitive, emotional, and sensorimotor components to gradually reach consciousness. Still, these elements surfaced while protected and buffered by the distance and symbolic nature offered by the sandtray work.

FIGURE 2.10 **Multiple strong horses often bully a young, lonely horse. Two older horses have their backs turned, focusing elsewhere as the bullying unfolds behind them.**

Implicit access can be used throughout the eight phases of EMDR-sandtray-based treatment and is especially useful with individuals with reduced verbal and regulatory capacities. For clients with dissociative tendencies, the implicit road provides an opening for dissociative parts to gradually enter the client's field of consciousness. Parts in children may not announce or label themselves as such but instead appear in the child's tray work, protected by symbolic play and metaphors.

A 6-year-old boy refuses to talk with the clinician. He remains silent and ignores any attempts for closeness or communication. He witnessed and was the victim of severe violence and in the past reported to his adoptive parents that he was hearing voices that told him to hurt and harm others. Despite his active defenses, he accepts invitations to play in the tray. Although he does not respond verbally, he places figures in the tray and the dollhouse, usually depicting a violent character that hurts and kills other animals and people. When asked about the primary character of his stories, he always points to the "killing hyena," frequently choosing it as his avatar. Although he is verbally inhibited, the chronicle in the tray begins to tell a story and portray a dissociative part that holds loyalty to the perpetrator, his biological father.

Clients do not need to verbally acknowledge these parts, as placing a figure in the tray is, itself, an act of recognition. The tray often contains and reflects the client's trauma-formed polarizations; in this case, the powerful, violent perpetrator and the vulnerable victim. However, as these polarities become visible, they can enter the client's field of awareness with innumerable integrative possibilities.

Explicit Access

Explicit access into the mind usually occurs in clients with greater capacities for affect tolerance, verbalization, and regulation. These clients can connect and report on their inner experiences and the events that injured them. Within the explicit route, there are two different levels of distance: accessing the trigger and the actual memory of trauma. Some clients can recognize themselves in their work in the tray, but only as related to triggers and symptoms—they are not yet able to acknowledge the traumatic event. This may result from active defenses and phobias of the inner experience and, more specifically, fear of the memory of trauma. Even though the entrance into the mind occurs openly and unambiguously, the tray exploration skills, questions, and steps described for the implicit tray also apply to the explicit one.

Explicit Access and the Second Level of Distance. In explicit access and the second level of distance, the client creates a world where the self is identified and attends to the story emerging in the tray. However, the world and stories mostly discuss triggers, current symptoms, and struggles. Emotional states are owned, but traumatic memories remain hidden and unseen. It is a level closer to the core experiences that injured the mind while avoiding the crux of it. How the mind approaches trauma will vary depending on its capacities, internal conflicts, and the presence of adaptations made to support survival. Some will access the residues left by hardship from the peripheral layers, and some will approach the core and center of the

FIGURE 2.11 A mother stands beside a bridge, hoping to connect, while her daughter places a fence around her and between them. The mother freezes and stares at the child. A dragon holding a mirror focuses on itself, avoiding contact with others. The child, standing beside the dragon, turns her back on her mother.

Phase 1: Foundational and Advanced Skills 61

trauma right away. This level of distance may allow the mind to explore and process the periphery before accessing the core.

A 27-year-old female living with PTSD due to childhood abuse came to therapy searching for help with parenting her 8-year-old child. The client reported being triggered by her child's behaviors, which resulted in constant misattunement and ruptures in their relationship. It became clear that her child was activating her experiences of trauma, which moved her into survival and out of coregulation and connection. The worlds she created in the tray depicted her struggles as a mother and the child's behaviors that activated unhealed and unintegrated traumagenic networks. However, there was very little awareness and a great hesitation to explore the trauma that lay at the core of her struggles as a mother. Identifying and reprocessing the triggers supported her in finding greater stability to respond to her child's activating behaviors more effectively. It also gave her a path into the underlying memory systems holding the trauma she endured as a child.

Explicit Access and Third Level of Distance. In the explicit/third level of distance, the core traumatic memories fully enter the client's conscious and embodied mind. This represents a sentient ownership of the injuries unfolding in the tray. The root of the trauma is unveiled and embraced. Clients may start elsewhere, but this is where they eventually land. Implicit and explicit portals are not divided and independent of each other. Instead, they represent the continuum the mind travels through as it approaches deeper layers of healing. The world depicting the actual traumatic event may spontaneously arrive early in treatment or it may arise later, due to the clinician's consistent, curious, and compassionate invitations. The clinician might pursue this level of distance once the client exhibits sufficient affect regulation and readiness to access distressing and disturbing events.

Clients may bring a traumatic event into the tray during the first session or gradually, over multiple sessions. Many therapists wonder if they should immediately jump into reprocessing when these injurious events first appear in the tray or wait until sufficient preparation has been attained. Processing trauma memories should not occur randomly or by chance and opportunity; it should be intentional and well-planned.

When addressing explicit accounts of trauma in the tray, the amount and manner in which the clinician explores it depends on multiple factors including the EMDR phase and the client's readiness and their distress tolerance. Rich and extensive verbal accounts of the world and story that hold the trauma narrative are not necessary because the symbols and the world, themselves, are telling the chronicle. However, having some, even if rudimentary, understanding of what is unfolding in the tray will support the clinician's decision-making and understanding of the client's clinical landscape.

Samantha, a 12-year-old female, comes to therapy because her sister died in a car accident, to which Samantha was a witness. This child is growing up with a loving mother and father. She experienced some adversity early in her life when her grandmother, whom she deeply loved and admired, died from a heart attack. After two preliminary meetings, Samantha creates a tray portraying her sister's accident. Through three sessions dedicated to building safety and regulation, Samantha demonstrates the capacity for shifting emotional states when necessary, tolerating positive and negative affect, and staying present when accessing challenging accounts and emotions. She also accepts invitations from the clinician to coregulate as well as to self-regulate when necessary. Her past experiences of connection, reciprocity, and safety give her access to resources and adaptive memory systems, creating a secure base. At this level, multiple cognitive, emotional, behavioral, and somatic information can freely touch the conscious mind because it can tolerate, realize, and own them. Samantha is equipped to reprocess the death of her grandmother and sister after a short preparation phase. She quickly attains her treatment goals after reprocessing her triggers and doing a short future template.

As previously stated, the levels of distance are flexible, and the client can navigate through them as they please. Sometimes, a client can even move along the continuum of distance, initially accessing the memory implicitly then quickly acknowledging that what is emerging in the tray is actually their memory, all within one session.

Jill, 14, creates a world where a lamb carries a secret about what her dad had done to hurt her. However, within a few minutes, she tells her therapist, "Actually, the lamb; it's me." Jill's clinician shifts her language and approach to acknowledge the new emerging explicit awareness of Jill's experiences with her father.

Clinicians should remain open and flexible with what unfolds in the tray while honoring the distance the client's self requires at any given point in the process. Clients can also return to implicit processing after exploring and retrieving memories explicitly. Remember that each memory and traumatic event may carry its own matrix; each session and therapeutic moment may demand adaptations to the sandtray work's distance.

Level of Directiveness. Various levels of directiveness are used, and clinicians and clients can switch between nondirective to directive approaches. Sometimes, the client may need the clinician's directions and invitations. Other times, the client may need to let their own material, directions, and urges guide the process. EMDR therapy is a directive approach, but there is plenty of room within the eight phases for nondirective work. The initial phases of EMDR-sandtray-based therapy lend themselves to the diverse use of directive and nondirective methods. During reprocessing phases, a diverse approach can be utilized, blending nondirective moments where the clinician follows the client's lead with directive interventions guided by the clinician. Clinicians are encouraged to let what happens happen without disruption or intervention unless information processing stalls. Attunement and synchronicity are guiding principles that accompany the clinician and the client throughout the process.

Additionally, the client's developmental stage will play a fundamental role in which level of directiveness is appropriate. Children communicate through play, so directive and nondirective approaches to play are combined, depending on where they are in the eight phases of treatment and what they are bringing into the therapeutic process at any given moment. During the initial phases of treatment, a nondirective stand allows us to learn about the client, the child–parent dynamic, and their ways of relating The sandtray work may be open to worlds created by the child, the parent, and/or the dyad. Nevertheless, directive approaches and invitations to the client to create worlds with specific themes could provide rich information that would aid the clinician in developing a thorough treatment plan. Some adults may respond well to the nondirective use of the tray, while others may need a directive and straightforward approach from the start.

Directive and Explicit Approaches That Use Sandtray Strategies in Phase 1

As clients feel more comfortable with the sandtray work and the clinical landscape becomes better defined and visible, directive approaches may be interspersed with the nondirective use of the tray. The following are strategies and activities that use directives and themes during the initial phases of EMDR-sandtray-based therapy.

This Is Me

This protocol invites clients to express themselves by creating a world representing their identity. You might say:

> "I would like to invite you to create a world about you. You can pick all the figures that represent something about you in this world—things that people may know or may not know about you; maybe things that you like and dislike."

If the client accepts the invitation, give them a basket for collecting selected figures and the space to connect with themselves and the figures in the tray. Once they have finished, ask if the sand world feels complete:

> ❝ Let's spend some time with what you have created about yourself and see if all you are and all you know about yourself that is ready to be witnessed, is in the tray."

You then have the opportunity to observe and explore the client's capacity to represent and reflect upon themselves, their thoughts, feelings, beliefs, behaviors, preferences, resources, values, and challenges. Start general, and then move into more specific questions, such as:

> ❝ I have learned a great deal about you; thanks for letting me get to know you. Is there anything you want to add to your tray that feels different from what you already have? Are there any voices in the tray that may want to tell different stories about you?"

You may also invite the client to connect to the three storytellers: the mind, the heart, and the body. Then, you may ask them if all they know about themself is represented in the tray.

> ❝ I wonder if we can ask the three storytellers if what they know about you is in the tray. What would you say about the thoughts, memories, and images often coming to your mind? How about your heart? What would your heart say about your past and present feelings? And what stories would your body hold about you?"

Clients do not need to disclose or speak about every figure in the tray. Freedom to disclose or not should govern the session. The client may bring figures that are buried, covered, and not acknowledged. Reassure the client that it is okay to keep information reserved and private. Only when they feel safe and ready should they make a different choice, such as to bring them into the world of words.

My Goals

This activity allows the client to physicalize their goals. What do they want to accomplish? What do they want to be different in their lives, or what do they want to change? What emotions do they want to transform, manage, or cope better with? Are there thoughts or beliefs they are battling that they want to change? Are there relational issues they want to work on? The clinician can support the client with questions followed by invitations to bring in figures that represent their deepest longings and reasons for seeking therapy. Some adolescents say that they do not want to receive psychotherapy and that their parents are forcing them; this can also be represented in the tray. They may want to overcome the conflicts with their parents so they no longer have to attend therapy sessions. What would it take for them to participate? What would they need? Questions such as how motivated they are to come to therapy and participate may be asked and physicalized in the tray. If the motivation is low, clients are invited to represent that and the reasons behind their low enthusiasm and trust in the therapeutic process. Did they have negative experiences with other therapists? What do they expect or wish for in this new experience with a clinician? In general, this work can produce a great deal of information about the client's objectives and aspirations so the clinician and the client can create a thorough treatment plan, tailored to the client's individual needs.

CHAPTER 3

Phase 2: Preparation

When working with complex and developmental trauma, the preparation phase is often multifaceted and is crafted around the client's shifting clinical landscape. The length and organization of Phase 2 will depend on to what extent trauma burdens the individual's capacity to tolerate affect, integrate information, and maintain presence. The unique qualities of each client must be acknowledged and represented in how the preparation phase is structured.

For instance, a child with an emerging personality exhibiting fragmentation will require preparation work that may include active labor with their inner system of parts, while another child may require a much less intensive and extensive preparation. The unique qualities of each client deserve acknowledgment and the chance to be recognized in how the preparation phase is organized.

Preparation Phase: Core Overarching Areas

The following are the main areas that directly impact the organization of the preparation phase for clients with complex trauma and dissociation.

Dissociation

Individuals with a history of developmental trauma and disorganized attachment may present with a wide range of dissociative symptomatology (Liotti, 2004, 2009; Spinazzola et al., 2021). These symptoms exist within a continuum (Putnam, 1997) from mild (inattentiveness, spaciness, trancelike states, etc.) to moderate (depersonalization and derealization) to severe (divisions in the personality). Where the client falls on this continuum will significantly impact how the preparation phase is structured in EMDR–sandtray. If clients present with divisions in their sense of self and identity, the preparation phase may need to incorporate strategies that access, explore, and work with the inner system of parts and their relational dynamics. Inter-

67

nal conflict may be present, and what is soothing and regulating for one part may dysregulate another (Mosquera, 2019). High internal polarizations and conflict may increase symptomatology, creating a neuroception of danger. In addition, it may increase double binds for the clinician, who is often caught in the middle of a highly contentious system. Clinicians working with this population may feel confused when what appeared to be an effective session turns into a self-harming episode (Gonzalez & Mosquera, 2012). When we acknowledge and work with the dissociative system of parts, we can closely monitor and more easily meet the needs and demands of an adversarial and divisive system. The presence of dissociation in any form strongly influences how the preparation phase is organized to accommodate the needs of an often divided and polarized system. Chapter 4 will fully address the preparation work needed with complex trauma clients.

Level of Safety in Five Domains

Depending on the client's level of support, environmental containment, and safety, the preparation phase may need to incorporate significant efforts to restore a state of safety in which the vagal system is most accessible (Porges, 2017). Safety is a visceral and embodied state that emerges from experiences of connectedness and belonging across multiple domains in life. If the client remains in unsafe environments and circumstances, the autonomic nervous system will be recruited for defensive strategies and actions that counteract the therapeutic efforts to support healing. However, safety is convoluted and intricate, since most clients with a history of developmental trauma have challenges in assessing safety and danger. They may neurocept danger in the presence of safety and vice versa as the threat-regulating system governs.

According to van der Kolk (2014), "After trauma the world is experienced with a different nervous system" (p. 53). A neuroception of danger may prevail as the client confuses signs of safety with stimuli rooted in unintegrated traumatic experiences (Cozolino, 2014). Even in the absence of physical danger, individuals with chronic exposure to trauma may not feel safe in their relationships because their nervous system is organized to mistrust others, even when there is connection, safety, and mutuality. Clients may struggle to accurately assess relationships and the possibilities for belonging and connection, often approaching them from insecure networks formed through relational trauma. They carry the fear of abandonment, shame related to a rooted sense of defectiveness, and hypervigilance, because they always expect the worst from life, their relationships, and their surroundings. They learn to fear and avoid their emotions and intensity, fostering defenses and affect phobias that later sustain their internal self-organization. When safety is absent in one or all domains, it can hinder or slow treatment, healing, and recovery. The five safety domains (i.e., external, physical/somatic, emotional, internal, and relational) should be explored and when possible restored to reestablish homeostasis.

If trauma is still happening in the present, memory networks holding maladaptive traumagenic material will continue to be enforced along with entrenched defenses. Each moment carries its own challenges and threats to safety, so the clinician works moment-to-moment to help the client attain greater levels of safety.

Information about the client's sense or level of safety may arise through directive and explicit sand worlds that address the five domains or through nondirective and implicit stories depicting safety, danger, fear, and/or hypervigilance in their characters. The tray becomes a vehicle for assessing and restoring safety and social engagement. The sand world and its characters offer the client's nervous system an opportunity to experience the activation and repair of previously disrupted autonomic states. Trauma leaves biological imprints, as do states of safety, even when they emerge from the avatar.

Sandtray work can offer valuable insights into the client's perceived sense of safety and can provide pathways to restore and enhance a client's sense of security. The lack of safety, fear, and hypervigilance will also emerge in implicit and nondirective worlds. Fear, danger, threats, criticism, humiliation, and relational wounding may overtake the sand worlds. These stories reveal information that is not readily accessible to the conscious mind or that is hidden from awareness.

Neural Tendencies

How does trauma exist in the nervous system, and how has it shaped the brain and ANS? Does this client exhibit a tendency toward emotional dysregulation and a mobilized sympathetic system? Conversely, does this client tend toward hypoarousal and emotional constriction, mediated by the dorsal vagal system? Some clients will benefit greatly from down-regulating protocols and strategies, while others will need an up-regulating approach to stabilization. A client's pace and rhythm may change from session to session, so mentalizing the client's shifting capacities will aid clinicians through the moment-to-moment organization of Phase 2.

The nervous system's rhythms will inform the pace, moment-to-moment adjustments, and specific interventions used throughout the preparation and eight phases of treatment. The sand tray will also serve as a container, sensory modulator, and vessel for burdens left by trauma and its accompanying nervous system activation patterns—whether implicit and unrecognized or explicit and acknowledged.

Phase 2: Preparation **69**

Attachment Patterns, Defenses, and Trauma-Related Phobias

Clients with early wounds and exposure to chronic traumatization often develop ways of surviving and defending against complex and painful emotions and somatic patterns (Hill, 2015). Their internal self-organization represents their best approach to surviving the pain they endured early in their lives (Porges, 2017). Unfortunately, their defenses and phobias may also constrict their capacity to embrace and develop relationships with their inner world, affect, and autobiographical accounts, influencing their work in the sand. These clients fear their internal reality and their emotions, body sensations, and any associations or stimuli reminiscent of their traumas. They build inner landscapes and rigid barriers, crafted to protect, hide, and defend from their life stories.

According to Kalff (1980/2003), sandplay relaxes the control the conscious mind exerts over the unconscious mind, allowing penetration to the material lying beneath the surface. "The dignity of the symbol allows and even stimulates different degrees of comprehension. . . . The symbol embodies the image of a psychic content that transcends consciousness" (p. 3). The symbols and three-dimensional images awaken awareness and the insight that lies beneath the conscious mind, making it easier to circumvent the inner structures created to bolster defenses and increase self-protection. Additionally, symbols connect the implicit and explicit mind, facilitating the exploration of deeper layers of meaning and the navigation through the complexities of one's inner life.

Rose, a 29-year-old seeking therapy to address her extreme anxiety and relationship difficulties, insisted that her childhood was good and that she had a "great" relationship with her parents. She did not understand why she had such intense relational and emotional struggles. She insisted that she had a close relationship with her father, despite him killing her dog in front of her when she was young. She stated that this event was in the past and that she had no emotional connection to it in the present. This is a woman who, to preserve the relationship with an abusive and fear-producing father, had to disconnect and disengage from pain, fear, and shame. Emotional numbness and idealization of the wounding attachment figure allowed her to survive and endure what would have otherwise been unbearable. However, the same defenses that allowed her to survive blocked access to her inner world, her emotions, and the possibility of healing.

In Rose's sand worlds, positive occurrences were often displayed. She sometimes depicted overpowering characters that expected others to satisfy their constantly shifting desires. Slowly, the stories changed to accommodate the pain and discomfort of the people who had to fulfill the king's demands. The world of symbols created channels that began to penetrate Rose's implicit mind, bypassing the barriers forged to safeguard her young mind from a wounding relational milieu.

The EMDR–sandtray clinician remains open to mentalizing the tapestry of the client's mind and how they have come to organize their life accounts. Chronic and developmental trauma often places individuals on a path of self-betrayal and self-abandonment, creating a sense of chronic disconnection, self-hatred, chronic shame, and guilt. When traumatic networks are accessed and activated too quickly, the mind can move into defensive postures that prevent integration. Each individual will have a pace and rhythm at which they enter states of vulnerability associated with trauma and attachment ruptures. Some may initially create worlds colored by positivism that portray happy and exciting narratives, representing the opposite of what they have experienced. Others may create highly disorganized worlds full of polarized and conflicted dynamics, portraying battles, conflicts, and fights or fear, hopelessness, and powerlessness.

The preparation phase in EMDR-sandtray-based therapy may be complex and convoluted as the clinician incorporates the building blocks that honor the client's capacities, inner organization, and bioemotional rhythms from moment to moment.

For three consecutive sessions, Samantha, 12, created fantasy worlds where princesses were having fun. When the trays were explored, the child reported only positive feelings.

Samantha's parents reported that she was often busy playing computer games, reading books, or watching TV. She rarely spoke about her feelings or sought support or help from her parents. The stories she created also showed a fantasy world where the characters were happy and did not face challenges. When asked if the princesses ever felt any other feelings, Samantha responded they were always happy.

Despite Samantha's daily struggles with severe anxiety, depression, and nightmares, she found shelter in mechanisms of adaptation that disengaged her from her emotions, finding refuge in fantasy, avoidance, and detachment. However, the tender and consistent safety offered within the therapeutic milieu alongside the symbolic infrastructure and integrative power of EMDR–sandtray work eventually opened the space for the processing, integration, and restructuring of Samantha's relationship with her life story and herself. Additionally, the clinician supported Samantha in fostering a compassionate relationship with her defenses, which had functioned as vital safeguards during periods of deep vulnerability and trauma. The newfound relationship with her protectors opened novel possibilities and portals into herself.

Phase 2: Preparation 71

For some clients, like Samantha, the preparation phase should incorporate the active exploration, representation, and recognition of the self-protective system before entering the memory networks holding the trauma.

The Multifactor Model of Preparation Phase

The multifactor model serves as a road map and compass supporting clinicians in navigating the intricacies of the mind impacted by complex trauma during the preparation phase. This model is multifaceted and should be customized to each client's unique needs, circumstances, goals, and capacities. This approach underscores the importance of flexibility, as each session and each moment demand strategic alignment with the client's evolving needs. As such, the organization and structure of the preparation phase should be individually crafted. Additionally, the organizing principles (dissociation, safety, neural tendencies, attachment patterns, defenses, and trauma-related phobias) of the preparation phase should be considered, as they each influence the length and moment-to-moment assembly of Phase 2.

Explaining EMDR-Sandtray-based Therapy

How we explain EMDR-sandtray-based therapy to clients depends primarily on the client's developmental level and individual characteristics. Some clients require extensive information, while others need a short explanation. Some children may just need to know that this is a way to help the mind, heart, and body sort out hurtful, bothersome, and difficult stuff so they get to feel better.

For children and young adolescents, you might offer this more detailed explanation:

> We carry many stories within us, and we better understand who we are as we discover and sort them out. We may have stories of hurt and pain, shame, fear, anger, and sadness. When we keep these stories inside, we are not giving them a voice or a space to be seen, heard, and known, especially by ourselves. These stories often cloud our happy feelings and best intentions. When the inner stories are sorted out, something remarkable happens: We get the gift of the story, whether it is the freedom to leave it behind, the ability to get back our sense of strength, the opportunity to recover some truths about ourselves— like that we are good and deserve love—or just that we find out something new about who we are. The sandtray, the figures, and EMDR can help our three storytellers—the mind, the heart, and the body—sort

out hurtful/difficult and painful stuff/experiences so we can let go of what is not letting us enjoy ourselves in the present."

For older adolescents and adults, you might say:

> " A traumatic event can disrupt the brain's natural ability to process and integrate the experience. Later, current triggers can resurface those distressing memories. When this occurs, the thoughts, images, emotions, and physical sensations linked to the past event can overwhelm your mind, influencing your perception of the present. EMDR therapy's procedural steps empower your innate capacity to process and integrate the traumatic event, enabling you to fully engage with the present without the cloud of past trauma. Sandtray therapy—working with the power of symbols—also supports integration. Together, they provide a space for healing and empowerment."

Next, introduce the different forms of BLS/DAS to discover which they would find comfortable.

Introducing EMDR Therapy and the Dual Attention Stimulus (BLS/DAS)

Technology now provides numerous ways of using BLS/DAS, including devices that provide bilateral eye movement, vibration, or sound, thus giving the client freedom to move around, play, and move figures throughout the tray.

The following are forms of BLS/DAS that may be used when delivering EMDR-sandtray-based treatment:

- **Eye movements:** The clinician may move a wand from side to side, lighting up the sand world. This allows the client to engage in eye movement while remaining connected to the sand story.

FIGURE 3.1 **A clinician moves a light-up wand from side to side to induce specific eye movements.**

- **Light bar:** The clinician may place the light bar in front of the sandtray and the client.

FIGURE 3.2 **Using the light bar to stimulate eye movements when reprocessing in the sandtray.**

- **Tactile stimulation:** BLS/DAS may be provided by using brushes to "paint in" resources by brushing on the hands, alternating slowly left and right, and "sort out" memories by brushing as fast as it is tolerable to the client (Gómez, 2013).

FIGURE 3.3 **Reprocessing in the tray using brushes for tactile BLS/DAS.**

- **Self-administered tactile stimulation:** The client uses the butterfly hug (Artigas & Jarero, 2014). The client can also drum back and forth on the corners of the sandtray and may add eye movements by following their hands with their eyes. The client may also tap the chair or table with only one hand, first on the left and then on the right, back and forth, while following their moving hand with their eyes.
- **Movement-based:** Clients may march (e.g., high knee marches) or stomp around the tray while staying connected to the sand story. This may support clients who need to movement to remain present and engaged.

Psychoeducation and the Building of the Corrective Network

The multifactor model allocates space in the preparation phase for clients presenting with missing occurrences, unmet needs, acts of omission, and scarcity of experiences of safety, security, connection, equitable distribution and assignment of responsibility, developmentally suitable experiences that provide an age-appropriate sense of autonomy, power, or control, among others. Clinicians may incorporate preparation-specific work to support the development of new synaptic networks and strengthen existing ones that hold adaptive information. According to F. Shapiro (2018), these networks link to traumagenic systems during processing, allowing "the memory to take its place as a functional part of the client's overall life history" (p. 350). For clients with missing formative milestones and relational insufficiencies, the labor of providing corrective experiences, fulfilling developmental omissions, and building a new adaptive network begins during the preparation phase.

We should also recognize that the boundaries of what constitutes "adaptive" are fluid and at times not well defined, considering that what is adaptive is also subjective and influenced by the conditionings held in the clinician's mind. Discerning what is adaptive or corrective is complex because it is strongly influenced by individual and cultural identities. The clinician should exercise caution when assuming information to be adaptive or corrective and should demonstrate cultural humility, recognizing the diverse backgrounds of each client. Ask, wonder, stay curious, and reflect as you support the client in accessing their inner truths.

Universal human needs have been extensively studied across various disciplines, with Maslow's hierarchy of needs offering a foundational understanding of the essential role that fulfilling these needs plays in human existence. However, in EMDR-sandtray-based therapy the sequence in which these needs are addressed often depends on the unique experiences and priorities of the individual, rather than strictly following proposed orders. Critics, including Liberman (2013), have challenged the structure of Maslow's hierarchy, particularly its positioning of social needs—such as affiliation and social connectedness—toward the lower tiers, arguing that their significance may not always be secondary to physiological or safety needs.

In the therapeutic context, this perspective is particularly relevant during the preparation phase, which is designed to provide corrective experiences, address developmental gaps, and establish a new adaptive framework. While clinicians draw on established knowledge, including insights from models like Maslow's, they must remain closely attuned to the client's unique experiences, longings, and therapeutic directions.

When stories and narratives surface in the tray during the preparation phase, they open a space to provide or elicit existing corrective information through the characters and stories. In addition, the client can be a receiver and an observer of how the character gets its needs met and its feelings validated, represented, and known.

The adaptive information is built in ways that recognize and honor the client's development, especially for children. By attuning our biology to the client's verbal and nonverbal narratives while maintaining an open heart, we create a nurturing space that promotes growth and repair. This attunement fosters the client's healing and integration as they—often for the first time—engage in an affective dialogue with a resonant, synchronously attuned other. In this process, we support the client's system in metabolizing the emotional energy emerging within the tray, which represents their internal states as they are deeply felt and witnessed by another's embodied mind. Clinicians should explore their own life experiences, habituations, intersectionality of identities, conditioning, metaperceptions, and belief systems, because these may permeate and intrude into the therapeutic relationship via the clinician's moment-to-moment decisions and responses to the sandtray work (see Chapter 10).

The stories that emerge in the tray provide clinicians with countless opportunities to provide corrective experiences and completions, to introduce new data, or to elicit and enhance existing adaptive information through the characters. For instance, if a character is struggling in the story yet the client is silent and not expressing what is unfolding for the character, you may invite them to have a "moment of curiosity" and wonder out loud what may be happening to the character and what they may be feeling and experiencing.

If you remain open to the stories emerging in the tray, you can model and invite the child to join you to dance with what is unfolding. If sadness is in the air, share how you are noticing it. If the client resonates with that feeling, invite them to notice how it moves or dances. Even though you are working with the tray, movement may be invited and encouraged. Breathing and letting feelings move through you while sharing your experience with the child will allow them to observe and experience it with you.

Synergetic play therapy (Dion, 2018) invites clinicians to share their authentic selves and to model ways to up- and down-regulate emotions. This is a powerful addition to the work in EMDR-sandtray-based therapy that can allow the client to encounter emotions procedurally and experientially while actively accompanied by the clinician. Information is delivered in a way that reaches the right as much as the left brain and the body as much as the mind.

We also invite the client to join us as we breathe, move, or dance with emotions and stories that awaken fragments of our own tales. We wonder together as we see the character's emotions and struggles come out into the

76 EMDR-Sandtray-based Therapy

world. This is not about jumping into a solution-focused approach and moving the client out of the tray into their own life stories. It is about dancing with what is and what transpires from the tray. These heart-opening experiences will accompany the client throughout the eight phases of EMDR therapy in the sand tray. When the character rides the wave of emotions and embraces the movement occurring in the tray, arriving with it to a comfortable and, at times, joyful feeling, you can bring attention to and enhance these affective states by using BLS/DAS. Invite the client to witness and observe the character experiencing joy or acts of triumph while providing segments of psychoeducation.

Affect Tolerance and Affect Regulation

Increased affect tolerance and the modulation of its intensity are crucial factors in the healing of individuals impacted by complex trauma (Hill, 2021). Affect regulation is a vibrant practice that involves the amplification of both self-regulatory and coregulatory capacities and the expansion of emotional bandwidth to adapt to moment-to-moment changes in environmental demands and the relational milieu.

The sand tray provides the space for affect to emerge completely visible or hidden and protected. The conscious mind may disown the feeling or completely and openly acknowledge it. The tray and its stories provide opportunities for titration, gradual entrance, or full access to a wide range of affective possibilities.

An overfocus on state change strategies may lead to lengthy preparation phases. Certainly, self-soothing and self-regulatory capacities are fundamental to stabilizing clients; however, if the only focus is on distancing, separating, and changing uncomfortable emotional states, the client may not develop the tolerance required to enter the reprocessing phases. It is recommended that clinicians support the client in developing the capacity to move into and away from the activation (state change) considering that both contribute to the client's overall integrative capacity.

The sand world offers fertile ground for clients to practice moving into activating states and contentious and unsettled areas of the tray. The sand story provides opportunities to sit, be with, and embrace the affective states, metaperceptions, sensorimotor material, conflicts, and relational dynamics. The client may experience the character's sadness in the sand world in the company of the clinician and other story characters. You might ask some of the following questions:

- How big is [character]'s sadness?
- How is it for [character] to visit this sadness?
- How much of this sadness does [character] feel safe enough to feel now?

The sand world avatar becomes a bridge for the client as they explore affective states that are unrecognized and intolerable. Titration and a gradual entrance into uncomfortable and disturbing states should be the norm when working with clients with a narrow window of affect tolerance. The clinician might invite the client to start with a kernel of information, and can use measuring spoons, droppers, and spray bottles to titrate the amount of affect the client is accessing at any given point.

For instance, the character in the tray can choose how much of a feeling is appropriate to experience at the moment. You might say:

- How much of the sadness does [character] want to feel now, a medium, small, or a tiny spoon/drop/spritz of that feeling?
- How much of the sadness is safe for [character] to feel now, a medium, small, or a tiny spoon/drop/mist of that feeling?

Nesting dolls, spray bottles, and dropper bottles are an excellent addition to the sandtray collection as they can support the gradual accessing of emotional states that initially may be experienced as too big or too difficult.

Additionally, clients with the tendency to dissociate, disconnect, and detach from their surroundings and themselves often struggle with the feeling that some aspects of themselves are alien, resulting in a "not-me, not-mine, and not-self" state of consciousness (Steele et al., 2017). They may frequently disavow their affective states. Sandtray work accommodates various levels of ownership and realization, inviting gradual awareness, as it becomes tolerable to the client.

Other ways of supporting clients, especially children and young adolescents, in accessing and befriending their inner world include "feeling carnivals" and "feeling parties" or reunions in the tray. These are important opportunities for clients to gently push the edges of their window of affect tolerance to provide greater access to their inner system and emotions. These gatherings begin to soften the boundaries of their window of affect tolerance and decrease trauma-related phobias of affect. When doing feeling parties (for adults, this would be connecting with emotions), invite the client to select their "feeling guests" and represent them in the tray. Then, invite the client to create an entire world representing these guests and how they exist in the client's mental landscape. You may begin providing segmented psychoeducation that invites and supports the development of a relationship with the inner states by providing information on how these guests are messengers that bring important information to keep us safe (Gómez, 2018, 2024b). As a witness and companion, the therapist can stimulate curiosity by inquiring or reflecting on how the client wishes to relate

FIGURE 3.4 An adult client creates a tray to connect with her anxiety. She places a figure of a ghost chasing a character on a bridge, representing the centrality of this emotion in her life. Around the bridge, she places different characters that represent her long relationship with anxiety: a monster depicts terror; a spiked dinosaur represents sharp body sensations; a lion and panther symbolize fierceness and heaviness; the lost man in the middle embodies a sense of powerlessness; and a Saint Bernard illustrates anxiety's protective forces.

to these emotions. The worlds and stories allow emotions to be deeply validated and understood.

The clinician—in their multiple roles as companion, observer, narrator, and, at times, active participant in what is unfolding in the sand—may be invited into the tray to become an avatar in the client's story. Sometimes, we are called to name the client's experience. According to Siegel (2020), when we name the feeling, we tame it. The amygdala calms down when words are added to the experience. I would argue that the act of assigning a symbol and avatar to an affective experience is also an act of recognition, validation, and naming.

If the client invites you to be one of the characters, ask for guidance on what they want to see, hear, and experience from you as this avatar. How does their mind long to interact with and relate to this character? What experience is their mind seeking? It is crucial to execute this role exactly as the client instructs. Sometimes, the client grants the clinician complete freedom to act, despite the clinician's requests for directions. For example, a 9-year-old boy with significant and painful experiences of abuse at the hands of his older brother asked the clinician to be a fly that was being hurt by a big, mean crocodile (the perpetrator, enacted by the child).

When the clinician asked the child for guidance and instructions, the child said, "You do it. I do not want to tell you."

The clinician opened their heart and embodied mind to the story in the tray. The "mean crocodile" (the child) began vigorously hitting the fly (the clinician). As the clinician connected with the moment and the child's life story, they curiously observed the child's nonverbal and subtle cues.

The clinician acting as the fly decided to try to escape, but the crocodile got it again.

THE CHILD SAID, "You cannot escape. I am bigger than you."
THE CLINICIAN (AS THE FLY) RESPONDED, "I am going to ask for help."
THE CHILD REPLIED, "No one can help you because no one can hear you."
THE FLY/CLINICIAN RESPONDED, "I am feeling so scared and lonely."

By becoming the voice of the powerless fly, the clinician gave recognition to the child's profound sense of helplessness and lack of control that accompanied his experiences of abuse and oppression. The child had dissociated during his abuse and when under stress. To mirror his dissociative experiences while protected by the metaphor and the distance offered by the tray, the clinician described how the fly's feelings were getting so big that his mind was going away. The clinician also highlighted how the fly's amazing body and mind were doing their best to protect it, providing a framework for awareness and self-compassion.

FIGURE 3.5 **The tray of a 9-year-old created by a child who holds a crocodile that vigorously hits a fly. The fly is powerless and unable to escape.**

FIGURE 3.6 **The world of the fly and the crocodile changes to depict liberation and companionship. The fly is rescued by other fly friends and surrounded by protective gems and friendly bugs that keep the crocodile away.**

Once the world ended, in the fly finding refuge and help, the clinician added: "Fly, now we know your story. Now we know of your strength and what your mind and body had to do to survive and make it through such a painful and hard experience. Now, you are not alone with your story."

The shades of emotions emerging in the tray opened a field of possibilities for this child and develop a relationship with his story, revealed in the tray, without having to own it, personify it, or realize it. The child's window of tolerance, along with his field of consciousness and awareness to accommodate the lost fragments of his story, was expanding.

Integration does not happen only during the reprocessing phases. Any time we access the inner world and memory systems through implicit or explicit portals, we alter what is encoded in the synaptic networks. These experiences in the sand tray expand and prepare the mind to transition into the reprocessing phases of EMDR–sandtray treatment, where information processing is accelerated.

Coregulation in the Tray

Clients of any age who were exposed to complex and early trauma did not experience the modulating forces of an external coregulator. As a result, their ability to self-regulate and modulate their arousal is diminished, making them prone to intense emotions, dysregulation, and constriction. Systemic and dyadic work that invites the caregiver as an active therapeutic partner should accompany the comprehensive delivery of EMDR–sandtray (see Chapter 5), when working with children and adolescents.

When characters in the sand world are distressed, we may invite them to coregulate through breathing together, interocepting and checking where the feeling is inside, or engaging in movement. Coregulation is not just a cognitive experience but primarily a somatic and affective one. The tray creates entry roads into dysregulated systems and opportunities for clients to join characters and have a direct experience of regulation.

Pendulation and Emotion Tolerance Protocols

Pendulation (a term coined by Levine, 2015) is an effective approach to accessing emotional states in tolerable portions. The client pendulates between two or more emotional states while in the companionship of the therapist to build affective endurance and capacities as they move from comfortable to uncomfortable affective states through titration. One or two trays may be used; when using two trays, one tray holds the space for comfortable and positive feelings, while the other holds challenging emotions that feel yucky, uncomfortable, or intolerable. The client or a character may travel from one side or tray to the other while physically moving their body to engage the vagal system. The clinician can use reflections or ask questions to deepen the experience and support the client in expanding their capacity to be with and form a relationship with their activation. Individuals exposed to chronic trauma carry the voices of hidden, unfelt, and unsorted pain. Using titrated activities that invite emotions gradually and incrementally into the client's field of awareness supports amplified interoception and affective tolerance. Before accessing an affective or somatic state in the tray, clinicians should, invite the client to build a resource tray that serves as an anchor containing companions, special powers, and advisors.

Adjust the pace and rhythm of the process to be appropriate and acceptable for the client. Clients may connect to and represent the texture, length, weather, color, somatic senses, bodily experience, or other characteristics of the feeling. You might say:

> "Let's see what happens when we watch the [weather] inside this feeling. Is it [windy, stormy, snowy, sunny, or rainy]?"

If the client reports the emotion as being windy, invite them to represent the wind in the tray. You might say:

> "How strong is it? Let's be and move with the wind. Show me in the tray the strength of this feeling's wind."

Ask the client permission to interact with this emotion, and then you can validate and mirror the client. You might say:

> "I feel the wind of your feeling. I can feel it in my heart."

If the emotion is comfortable and pleasant, you may enhance it with BLS/DAS. You might say:

> "Let's watch the wind of this feeling, and while we watch, we can [do the butterfly dance/drum back and forth/march]."

If you want to stay close to the symbol-rich right brain, don't ask any questions. Instead, invite the client to be with whatever is emerging as they sit with the feeling and then to physicalize what arises in the moment. Remind them that the figures can accompany them and be the voices of what is unfolding in the present. Once the comfortable and pleasant

82   EMDR-Sandtray-based Therapy

emotion has been visited, invite the client to pendulate to the tray that holds the space for the uncomfortable feeling. Every time the client pendulates into the uncomfortable emotion, invite them to sit with and visit these emotions that live within them. Utilize a titrated and calibrated approach, giving clients control over how information is displayed, witnessed, and represented: buried or completely covered, halfway seen or partially seen, or completely visible. You may offer coverings as well as boxes and containers. You may ask further questions about the feeling's qualities, such as:

- If this feeling were an animal, what animal would it be?
- If this feeling had music within, what music would it be?
- If this feeling were a season, which season would it be?

The world surrounding the emotion will continue to grow and expand while accessing however much of the emotion is ready for witnessing: a spoonful, a drop, or a pinch.

BLS/DAS can be added to deepen the experience and to gently expand the client's capacity to tolerate emotions, especially if the client exhibits a greater capacity to tolerate activation. Four to six sets at a medium speed may be a good starting point, even with uncomfortable emotions. The sets may be increased to 9 or even 12 if the client shows an increased ability to embrace emotions. However, BLS/DAS should not be used if the client shows signs of increased arousal and dysregulation. In addition, the "feeling visits" should be short and gradual and not occupy the entire session because the client may become overwhelmed. As the client develops greater tolerance, more time may be allocated to visiting feelings through the multiple portals described in this chapter.

The following is a summary of the questions that are part of the emotion tolerance protocol with pendulation:

1. "If this feeling were a color, what color would it be? Would you like to pick a figure of this color and bring it into the tray?" Once the color is identified, invite the client to engage in BLS/DAS while noticing the color of the feeling.
2. "If this feeling had weather inside, what weather would it be? Would it be windy? Stormy? Sunny? Rainy? Cloudy? Snowy? Would you like to find a figure that represents the weather of this feeling?" Invite the client to be with the weather that exists in this emotional state. As they embrace the weather, invite them to engage in BLS/DAS. You may invite the client (especially if they are young) to dance and move with the rain or the wind.

Phase 2: Preparation   **83**

3. "If this feeling were a season, which season would it be? Would it be spring? Winter? Summer? Fall? Can you find a figure that represents the season of this feeling?"
4. "Is this feeling rough or soft? Would you like to find a figure that represents how rough or soft it is? Do you want this to be in your world?"
5. "Is this feeling old and familiar or new? Would you like to find a figure that represents this or shows it in your world?"
6. "If this feeling had a scent, what scent would it be? Does it smell like orange blossoms? Roses? Lavender? Would you like to find a figure that represents it? Do you want this to exist in your world?"
7. "If this feeling had a taste, what would it be? Is it sweet, like sugar? Or fruity, like peaches or oranges? Or bitter, like dark chocolate? Would you like to find a figure that represents the taste of this feeling?"
8. "If this feeling were an animal, what animal would it be? Would it be like a lion? Or a little mouse? Maybe an ostrich or a chameleon? Would you like to find a figure that represents it?"
9. Even though the work occurring in the client's embodied mind is reflected in the tray, clinicians can move from object to self to actively involve the body by asking: "As you watch the tray and visit this feeling, can we check in to see how the body wants to move? Does the body want to stay still? Or does the body want to run and dance? I wonder what actions the body would like to embrace."

Inviting the client, especially children, to allow the forces emerging from their body to dance through them can be a powerful intervention that embodies and captures the somatically emerging narratives. Once again, invite the client to use BLS/DAS while inviting movement and engaging the body.

Sandtray Strategies and the Safe Place Protocol

Sandtray work can enhance and expand how we use EMDR protocols to increase state-change capacities, such as the safe place protocol and the resource development and installation protocol (RDI; Korn & Leeds, 2002). Sandtray work engages and embraces the nonlinear brain as we access memory networks that carry adaptive and corrective resources.

The safe place is a core state change protocol for EMDR clinicians. The following are adaptations to the safe place protocol and some special considerations when using it in the sand tray. The language used in each protocol may need to be modified for accessibility based on the client's age. For instance, children may not understand what constitutes safety, so we may need to call it something different. The following words can be used with

84   EMDR-Sandtray-based Therapy

clients of various developmental stages to refer to the safe place: happy, fun, relaxing, calm, safe, protected, good, okay, comfortable, or just "ahhhh."

Image

The image of the safe place is elicited and created in the tray. The clinician begins with an invitation, which may have different shades and formats depending on the client. Individuals affected by trauma have a convoluted relationship with safety. It may be associated with negative affect and danger and may not be tolerable. There are three possible options, depending on the individual's relationship with states associated with safety: a history of adaptive experiences of safety, no history of adaptive experiences of safety, and significant difficulty tolerating safe or calm spaces.

Clients Who Have Had Adaptive Experiences of Safety and Protection. The clinician's main job is to support the client in retrieving a safe place that already exists in their memory networks and autonomic nervous system. You might say:

> ❝ I would like to invite you to [look inside/have an inside visit] to find a place that feels happy, fun, relaxing, calm, safe, protected, good, okay, comfortable, or just 'ahhhh.' A place that you remember and have been to where nothing negative, bad, or yucky has happened. Once you find it, let the figures accompany you in creating it in the tray."

Once the client informs you that the safe place is finished, invite them to see if it feels complete. Clinicians may use the basic exploration sandtray strategies addressed in previous chapters to get a sense of the client's creation. Some clients may be very verbal, and some may not. The clinician adapts to the client's verbal capacities and the defenses that may emerge while creating resources in the tray.

Clients Who Have Not Had Adaptive Experiences of Safety and Protection. These clients may create a safe place that contains scary and disturbing elements. Trauma-related material may infiltrate the state of safety associated with the safe place, bringing anxieties, disturbing images, and unpleasant thoughts, emotions, and somatic responses. In these cases, the clinician will modify the method of eliciting a safe place. You might say:

> ❝ I would like to invite you to be with all these figures and companions and see which ones give you the warm, okay, somewhat-safe, protected, or happy feeling (use whichever term is most appropriate for the client)."

Clients Who Do Not Tolerate Safety or Calm States. These clients do not tolerate states of safety or calmness, and disturbance invades and disrupts the access to positive affective states even after using previous modifications. For example, Gregory, a 5-year-old with severe constipation associated with high anxiety and attachment trauma, believed there was a monster inside him because he felt excruciating pain every time he had a bowel movement. As a result, he would avoid going to the bathroom at all costs, which created a vicious cycle of pain and fear. When attempting to find a safe or happy place, he stated that he did not want to do that because if he relaxed and felt calm, the monster (poop) would come out. Gregory had to stay tense and constricted to keep the "monster" inside. Another client, an adolescent, stated that she did not like to feel calm because negative events would occur if she were not vigilant to ensure no one would hurt her.

In these cases, the protocol is structured to ensure the client has distance from intolerable affective states by inviting them to create a safe (or any other word that suits the client) place for a character, not specifically for themself. This distance prevents fragments of trauma memories from penetrating the experiences of safety. The client can then transition gradually into accepting states of safety and calmness. You might say:

> "I would like to invite you to find your favorite character(s) and invite them into the tray."

Once the client brings in the character, invite them to create a safe (use the term selected by the client) place for them. You might say:

> "I would like to ask [character] to see what makes them feel [term selected by the client]. Once you know, I invite you to have the figures accompany you in creating this place in the tray for them."

World Building and Creation

Once the client brings in the selected figures, invite them to create a safe place in the tray. Let the client know they can build it any way they want while keeping in mind that it is a safe/happy/comfortable/calm place. Many clients, especially children, tend to bring people into their special places. Despite our best efforts to keep wounding figures out of the safe place, they may still sneak into the tray. Clinicians should remain curious and ask about the safety of these characters. If a client tries to bring a wounding relational figure or perpetrator into the safe place, you might say:

“ Sometimes we may like and even love people who hurt us or that have been unsafe around us, and as a result, we invite them into the [safe] place in the tray."

Encourage them to wait until the person shows they are safer before inviting them to the safe place. If this invitation is discarded, it offers important data on the client's relational bond with the perpetrator or wounding figure. You may encourage the client to invite only the part of the perpetrator that feels safe.

Many of the attachment figures of clients with complex trauma may continue to engage in wounding interactions and dynamics with the client, and it may not be possible to have only safe relationships in the client's safe place. However, it is essential to work on preventing perpetrators and wounding figures from entering the space allocated to safety.

When exploring the tray, keep in mind the client's level of distance from it. If facilitating the safe place protocol for a client who does not tolerate safe and calm states—ask questions to the character and have the client speak for the character.

If intrusions and trauma bonds continue to penetrate the client's mind while crafting the safe place, invite the client to be curious together. The information gathered while being curious expands the client's therapeutic landscape to encompass a broader scope of clinical considerations. Additionally, being curious together reveals important data on how the client is internally organized and how their relational environment is structured to support or wound the client. It may also provide data about the forms of self-protection that emerged or are still emerging from trauma, such as alliances, idealization, and loyalty to the perpetrator. Honor each moment without forcing awarenesses that the client cannot tolerate or will refuse, and allow the information to emerge from its hiding place, beneath the symbol in the sand world. The safe place protocol is diagnostic and may signal the need to incorporate sensory modulation strategies to engage the primal forces of the lower brain. Playing with the sand, burying hands in the tray, and touching figures with open and closed eyes are some sandtray-based lower-brain modulation strategies.

Being With and Sitting With. Once the client is finished organizing the figures in the tray, invite them to sit and be with the world and to notice whether it feels complete. Remember, the world holding the safe place may grow and evolve throughout treatment.

Emotions. Invite the client to connect with their heart (for children, to the storyteller that speaks through feelings), and let the figures accompany the heart/storyteller in giving a voice and presence to these feelings. Emotions associated with the safe place may be physicalized in the tray in the way that best represents the client and their emotions.

Location in the Body. Invite the client's somatic consciousness to reveal how emotions are manifesting in their body and creating an inner landscape of sensations. Directing the embodied mind into itself reveals the intricate connection between emotional and somatic states. Depending on the client's age, you might say:

- Where are the feelings hanging out in your/[character]'s body?
- How is your/their body showing you/letting you know this feeling/emotion has arrived? where do you feel this in your body?

Anchoring or Cueing. The safe place may be anchored in multiple ways. The standard protocol involves using a cue word. Another way is by asking the client to pick a figure from the "visiting figures bucket" (the bucket with figures you can take home) to represent the happy place. The figure will be a transitional object to elicit the safe place and its associated emotions and somatic states when needed. Clients can also anchor the safe place to scents by inhaling a scent or the body by holding a finger, hand, or ear lobe while connecting to the safe place and engaging in BLS/DAS.

Minor Disturbance. The client is invited to create a small or minor bugging, negative, or disturbing situation in a separate tray that can serve as a pendulation station from the safe-place tray. The client can represent the minor disturbance in this tray using one or multiple figures. You might say:

“ I am going to invite you to find in you a small or mildly bothering, negative, disturbing, or bugging thing. Once you have it, choose another tray where the small bugging thing can go. How far do you want this tray to be from the one holding the safe place?”

After spending some time with the minor disturbance, invite the client to use the special word, anchor, or transitional object, and orient their attention to the safe place. The client travels back and forth from the minor disturbance to the safe place. When working with young clients, especially dissociative children, we can capitalize on movement to keep the client present and engaged. For instance, we can invite the client to run, impersonate an animal, dance, hop, or pass through a play tunnel (if appropriate and enjoyable) between the trays.

88   EMDR-Sandtray-based Therapy

Enriching the Client's Emotional and Somatic Field of Awareness

Early experiences can mold the client's emotional life and relationship with affective states. Trauma and adversity can narrow the tolerance threshold of emotions and alter the orienting response. Trauma limits access to a flexible range of emotions by intensifying focus on negative emotions, thereby narrowing the spectrum of emotional possibilities, or, conversely, fixating on dysfunctional positive emotions as a way to avoid confronting negative feelings. As a result, the client's mind may hold a narrow field of affective states.

For instance, some individuals may recognize and express only anger, so if they are hurt, sad, in pain, or lonely, the outcome is always the same: anger. Children, adolescents, and adults may become fixated on emotions they desperately want, such as excitement. They settle for thrilling experiences that give them temporary adrenaline spikes and fleeting moments of excitement. For these individuals, allowing the mind to experience emotions that are out of their ordinary range can support the expansion of their affective threshold while allowing the mind to experience thus far disowned and foreign emotional states. Inviting the child, adolescent, or adult to create "a world of feelings" in the tray may be a good starting point. To introduce this concept, you might say:

> " I would like to invite you to create a world about the feelings and body sensations that come to visit you/that you experience most often. Let's invite these feelings into the tray."

When exploring the tray, invite these feelings to speak about their stories. You might ask:

- What is it like to have this feeling as a visitor?
- When does it come?
- What does it feel like?
- What is the message the feeling is giving you?
- What are the infrequent visitors? Which emotions rarely come?
- How are these emotions received in your mind's living room?
- What is it like for you to live without these emotions?

You may invite the client to create a world about the feelings that rarely visit the mind. Once the newcomers enter the tray, ask the client to embody the feeling and bring in figures that represent these emotions' different shades, aromas, sounds, and textures. You might ask:

Phase 2: Preparation   **89**

- What would it feel like to embrace these feelings?
- What situations, people, and experiences would trigger these emotions?
- Is there a reason this visitor is not welcome in your mind and body?
- Is there a reason this feeling rarely visits?

Use reflective statements that expand meaning and support widening of the client's consciousness field. Invite them to embrace new emotions and travel into unfamiliar feelings, granting their body permission to have novel affective states that have been forgotten or rejected (Dispenza, 2007). You might ask:

- What would this emotion feel like? What would bring this feeling into your life? How would your body feel if you allowed this feeling in you or opened the door to it?
- Does it feel safe to invite the three storytellers to open up to this feeling? It may be just a small spoonful, drop, or spritz of the emotion at first.

If the invitation is accepted, gradually expand the felt sense of each emotion. Reflecting moments of comfort, openness, hesitation, and reticence while inviting the companionship of symbols fosters a safe and accepting space where emotions can be discovered, acknowledged, and embodied. When the emotions evoke positive and comfortable somatic states, you may add short and slow sets of BLS/DAS to deepen those experiences.

Future Template

Anticipating the future desired outcome can foster hope and resilience and can open a field of possibilities for some clients affected by complex trauma. New connections can be forged by supporting the client in embracing their future self. The tray can provide a space for the visions of the client's mind to be physicalized. This powerful work can begin by inviting the client to connect to their "future, older self" and all they envision in their future. You might say:

> " Let's connect with the deepest wishes you carry in your heart and let the figures accompany you in expressing them in the tray. Check how you want your future self to feel. What kind of thoughts do you want to have? How would your body feel? What would happen at school, work, home, and with friends and family? Let's teach every cell of your body how it would feel to actually *be* your future self."

Let the client relish the experience. If the client wishes to carry this experience within, you might say:

90   EMDR-Sandtray-based Therapy

"Let's find the place within you where you want to carry these feelings and visions."

Identify the emotions and their location in the body and enhance the experience with BLS/DAS. It is important to consider that some clients may find this experience intolerable because it exceeds their affective threshold. Each individual has a unique capacity for emotional and physiological engagement. For the client with a restricted capacity for positive affect, positive emotional and somatic states should be introduced incrementally as the client's tolerance expands.

Resource Development and Installation

The sand tray and miniature collection will support the access and installation of various resources and the use of the RDI (resource development and installation) protocol (Korn & Leeds, 2002). Every procedural step can be physicalized and externalized in the sand tray. Clients of all ages often report that having all the resources represented in the physical world allows them to access these images more quickly and effectively when in distress and emotionally activated. Parents can print sandtray pictures on T-shirts, pillowcases, and fabric napkins, which can facilitate the access to these resources when the child is triggered.

The RDI protocol is organized around supporting the client in coping with and handling a specific challenging situation. It begins with the clinician asking the client to create a world that depicts an obstacle or challenge, then the two work together to identify the quality necessary to manage the situation. The clinician assists the client, through reflections and questions, to select the resource(s) that could support them in navigating, managing, and handling the challenge. Resources may be relational, symbolic, or spiritual, or they might incorporate mastery experiences.

The clinician enhances the affective states and body-based responses associated with the newly found resources by using BLS/DAS if the client is comfortable and regulated. The resources are embedded into the word depicting the challenge while the client progressively builds a framework in the tray that encompasses their vision for the future, which outlines and represents their aspirations for how they want to communicate, feel, and think and how they envision their bodies responding. If positive/comfortable emotions emerge as the client witnesses their creation and future vision, deliver slow and short sets of BLS/DAS. This future vision will serve as a steadfast companion, continually reminding the client of the vast possibilities for the future and the power of their own resources.

My Team of Companions

Considering the nuanced nature of developmental trauma, which often stems from attachment ruptures and relational wounds (Spinazzola et al., 2021), the preparation phase should include resources that increase the client's access to corrective relational experiences. The team of companions, inspired by Greenwald (1999), is a relational resource designed to provide restorative experiences of affiliation and kinship.

Companions may be anyone or anything, from safe people and family members to animals to religious and spiritual figures to superheroes and symbolic characters to nature characters (trees, flowers, mountains, and rivers). Individuals with histories of developmental trauma hold implicit and embodied internal working models and relational templates that developed from relationships with betraying, misattuned, wounding, unavailable, and inconsistent caregivers. As a result, these individuals' defensive strategies become activated with the prospect of new relationships. Relational templates of mistrust, avoidance, enmeshment, or idealization may emerge while accessing relational resources. Idealization and loyalty to a perpetrator may unfold in the tray as the client creates their team of companions. The relational tray provides an opportunity to explore the client's relational templates and internal working models. Remain open, inviting, and supportive of the client while encouraging curiosity about the relational ecosystem in the tray. Invite the client to spend some time with their team, and notice if all its members promote a sense of safety. You might say:

FIGURE 3.7 **An adult client's team of companions. She includes her animals, guitar, and music, as well as family and friends. The lighthouse represents the universal mind that guides her.**

> " I wonder if we can sit with or visit your team of companions and see if you feel safe enough to have them be part of your team. Sometimes, we may really like someone who hurt us or was unsafe. A part of us may love this person, while another may know of the hurts and fear they created."

Explore what the client wants to see happening in the tray. How do they reconcile the internal conflict wherein one part idealizes the relational figure while another rejects it? The client may physicalize the conflicting emotions while the clinician validates and normalizes the experience with compassion, curiosity, and acceptance. The clinician mediates the communication and offers potential alternatives, such as placing the contended figure in another tray. However, what happens should be the decision of the client's inner system, as they navigate the polarizations around the perpetrator. If the "team of companions" continues to be filled with struggles and divergences, BLS/DAS should not be used. If the wounding figure plays an important role in the client's life (especially a child's), caution must be taken because maintaining the relationship is more important for the child than the conflict (Hughes et al., 2019). In these cases, the clinician must work with the child's relational milieu to address this complex interplay.

The internal conflict should be externalized and worked through before continuing to install the team of companions. Once the team is fully created in the sand tray, encourage the client to notice whether it feels complete. Invite the client to be and sit with the team and to physicalize the emotions and how their body responds to their arrival.

The procedural steps of the team of companions protocol may be brief or extended to incorporate the safe place steps. If extended, resources may be anchored somatically or linked to a word or scent. Pendulation back and forth from a minor disturbance to the team of companions may also be used to strengthen the client's regulatory and state change capacities. In this case, two trays should be used, similar to the safe place protocol where the client can travel from the resource tray to the one holding the minor disturbance. As the end of the session approaches, the clinician should use a container or other state change and regulatory strategy to bring the client back to homeostasis and emotional equilibrium, especially if the client navigated through polarization and conflict.

Meeting Unmet Needs: Tolerance and Amplification of Positive Affective States Protocol (TAPAS)

Clients with complex trauma and dissociation carry significant attachment wounds. Acts of omission and missing experiences from early life often lead to profound grief and deep pain. Frequently, they carry relational insufficiencies tied to early attachment experiences as well the imprints of relationally impoverished environments that surrounded them during critical periods of development. As a result, the synthesis and assimilation of memory may be complex and fraught with obstacles, causing it to stall frequently due to the "absent network." In cases of neglect, the process of building new synaptic systems as well as of fulfilling unmet needs may begin during the initial phases of treatment as a way to more rapidly resource and regulate the client when they do not meet the markers of readiness to move into trauma reprocessing. Beneath dysregulated states lie unmet needs, and fulfilling these needs helps clients restore balance more quickly. The process of fulfilling needs holds the potential of expanding the window of affect tolerance and the intimacy threshold, increasing the client's overall integrative capacities.

The TAPAS protocol focuses specifically on the fulfillment of attachment yearnings with children presenting with deep deficits and unmet needs. The language may be tailored for adolescents and adults.

One of the major challenges in accessing and fulfilling missing experiences is the neglected mind's diminished tolerance threshold to endure having what it needs but has not received. Trauma-related phobias create ambivalence where the client may long for connection, nurturance, and closeness and yet cannot tolerate these experiences, which brings them into a double bind. The client may need validation or reassurance of their worthiness and value yet reject and even feel anger at any offer of appreciation. The work required to rearrange the client's relationship with their needs often requires distance and titration to avoid dysregulation and activation of the self-protective system.

For example, instead of directly meeting the child's needs, the clinician will start with trying to meet the needs of a character in the child's story or a figure representing someone they know. Directly asking the client what they need may be received with opposition, defensiveness, and bewilderment. However, the sand tray and miniature collection provide a space and refuge for the mind to playfully and gradually embrace its needs. Inviting the client to identify the character's longings allows them to learn, practice, and indirectly experience what it feels like to have a need seen, acknowledged, validated, and fulfilled.

The tolerance and amplification of positive affective states (TAPAS) protocol uses Phillip Manfield's (2010) three levels of distance from his dyadic resourcing protocol as a foundation but expands it by four additional levels. These levels of distance give the client a gradual entrance into the intricate inner space left by neglect, invisibility, and acts of omission.

TAPAS Protocol Step 1: Psychoeducation

Using a titration continuum, the clinician finds an entry point for addressing needs while playing in the tray. This may occur when the child plays with a figure in the tray and the clinician invites curiosity about what the character needs. Depending on the child's threshold and tolerance, the clinician may incorporate segmented psychoeducation; where information about needs is delivered in small kernels as opportunities arise in the tray. A psychoeducational sand world may be created about needs by inviting the child to play at fulfilling the needs of the plants, animals, and humans in their tray.

You might say:

> "Let's think about a tree. What does the tree need? Does it need water, food, or light?"

This may be all that is addressed initially. We do not want to overwhelm the child with information and multiple questions at once. Gradually, over multiple sessions, other segments of information may be offered, such as:

> "I wonder if we can go back to talking about needs. Can we be curious about what animals need? I wonder what doggies and kitties need. Do they need food, love, or shelter?"

FIGURE 3.8 **A psychoeducational sand tray focused on the needs—such as water, food, light, companionship, protection, play, access to their feelings, and a home—of plants, animals, and people.**

Phase 2: Preparation 95

Let the child physicalize the animals' needs in the tray. Then, when appropriate, move to human needs. Have a menu of needs handy (see Appendix 2), and invite the child to create a tray about needs. Observe how the child receives this invitation. Do they reject it or readily accept it? Be curious about the tray and the messages the child expresses about needs. Some clients, especially children, get confused and see needs as obligations rather than attachment longings or nourishing experiences. Often, the clinician must make this differentiation. For instance, the child may say that the character "needs" to behave well. The clinician should receive this request with acceptance and curiosity:

> ❝ I can see that [character] wants to behave well. I wonder what he will receive if he behaves well. Will he get approval from people he cares about? Will he get love and acceptance from others? Will he have other [characters] play with him? Can we wonder together what [character] actually needs underneath the good behavior?"

TAPAS Protocol Step 2: Accessing Needs

In this step, the need is accessed using several levels of distance, beginning with the character and navigating all the way to the actual need of the client while in the companionship of the caregiver (if possible). These levels of distance titrate the entrance into positive affective states and the fulfillment of attachment needs while reducing trauma and attachment-related phobias. The avatar and characters become the mind's vehicle for exploring, identifying, expressing, and experiencing the fulfillment of these longings. Pace, rhythm, and tolerance thresholds will vary from client to client and from moment to moment, even for a single client. Dance with each client's pace and avoid pushing the client to accept or receive offerings when their inner space is not ready yet. To avoid overwhelming the client's system, dedicate only a few minutes each session to meeting needs, and expand the time gradually.

If this work is initiated with the character or avatar, two entry options are available:

Option 1. Invite the client to create a world using the sandtray procedures described in earlier chapters. Once the client reports that the world is complete, identify their main or favorite character. Next, carefully question the needs of this character, offering menus of needs as a scaffold. Children who never or rarely had their needs seen, felt, mirrored, validated, recognized, and met have not developed literacy and awareness of their needs and the needs of others, so menus are paramount. You might ask:

96   EMDR-Sandtray-based Therapy

❝ I wonder what [character] needs. Does she need food, someone to take care of her, someone to protect her, someone who can tell her and remind her that she is good? Or does she need someone to play with?"

Option 2. Invite the client to pick a character, any figure the client wishes, in advance. You might say:

❝ I would like to invite you to look at the figures and pick the one that you most want to play with in the tray."

Once the world is created around the character, the clinician utilizes reflections and questions directed at identifying and fulfilling needs. Curiosity is invited as the child and the clinician "sit with" this character and wonder what it needs. To provide menus of needs that assist the child in uncovering what the character requires (see Appendix 2 for a list of needs and menus), you might say:

❝ Let's be curious together about what this character needs."

TAPAS Protocol Step 3: Meeting the Needs

Once the child has identified the need, the next step will be to fulfill it—if the client chooses—based on the level of distance (character or child). Sometimes, children may become angry at the characters and deny them what they want. This offers data about the child's inner organization, especially their relationship with their needs and the needs of others.

At times, we will diverge from this or any other protocol based on the client's needs. Structured interventions are tools and bridges that support integration and a homecoming to self, yet these tools are only part of the multiple, multifaceted, and complex processes that operate within the therapeutic journey. Ultimately, the clinician should follow the therapeutic pathways that best support the client in their journey into themself.

Once the need is identified, who will meet and how this need will be met should be determined. It is up to the character/child to make decisions that honor the longings of their heart. If a caregiver is participating in the session, they may be appointed to provide what the character needs. You might say:

- I wonder if we can let [character] decide who will be giving them what they need or doing what they want.
- How does [character] want to get or receive what it needs?

Phase 2: Preparation   **97**

FIGURE 3.9 **A group of women (princesses and a fairy godmother) fulfill the character's needs for food, play, love, and protection from a witch.**

Allow the character, guided by the client, to select all the options and how the need will be satisfied. You might say:

> Let the [character] show you exactly how they want to be held or how they want to receive love and attention. Let them tell you; let them show you."

You may also ask how the character or the child wants to be loved, fed, held, or protected.

TAPAS Protocol Step 4: Installing Affective States

Once the identified need is met, invite the client to check in on how the character feels about receiving the love, attention, or food and how their body receives it. Next, the comfortable, positive, and regulated affective states can be enhanced using BLS/DAS.

From a distance and under the protection of the metaphor and avatar, the client experiences the fulfillment of important needs, ranging from physiological and physical needs (e.g., food, shelter, air, exercise, and movement) to emotional needs (e.g., love, belonging, friendship, play, emotional support) to attachment-based needs (e.g., acceptance, appreciation, validation, companionship, protection, reciprocity, and mirroring). Additionally, the playfulness and distance of this process offer highly defensive and protected clients access to a portal into a deep sense of fulfillment—without requiring them to own it—by bypassing and down-regulating their defensive strategies.

However, uncomfortable emotions may still surface during this process. For instance, sadness, grief, and jealousy may arise as a client witnesses their character obtaining what they implicitly and nonconsciously want for themselves. Such a response may be an opportunity for them to be and sit with these emotions and to bring them out of anonymity. Once these visitors have been seen or acknowledged, invite the client to explore what the avatar or self needs while these emotions are "visiting." Sometimes, the emotion is fully admitted and recognized; sometimes, it is visible but not acknowledged. The clinician can use reflective communication and invite the emotion into the sand space and may inquire about how others in the tray feel about the character receiving what it needs.

A 10-year-old girl, working in the tray with a rat named Ricky, started to push and hit the rat. The clinician described and reflected on the actions without interpretation. The child remained silent for some time while the clinician continued to accompany her in active and reflective silence. After some time, the clinician wondered aloud if anyone in the tray or outside the tray was having feelings about Ricky getting so much love and attention. This child stated that another rat, named Bobbie, was feeling jealous. The clinician and the client invited Bobbie to tell them what he needed while he was feeling jealous from watching Ricky get attention. Once the need was identified and met, Bobbie continued to feel jealous and, at the same time, happy because he now had attention from others, too. Through the character, the child remained connected and accepted that these two emotional states could coexist simultaneously while holding space for both.

TAPAS Protocol Step 5: Decreasing the Level of Distance

Once the child can tolerate the affect emerging from the fulfillment of previously unmet needs through the avatar, invite movement into a witness perspective. You might say:

> " How is it for you to watch [character] having someone tell them that they are good and loved? What do you feel? Where is this feeling hanging out in your body?"

Enhance the emerging comfortable and positive states using short/slow BLS/DAS while the client can at least partially own them. Once the client feels comfortable in the witness position, invite them to be the direct recipient of protection, love, food, or whatever supports the fulfillment of their longings. Once the client is comfortable at this level, a caregiver may be invited to meet the needs of the character or the child as represented in the tray. The child at this level has an increased capacity to identify their needs and to signal the caregiver regarding how they want the needs fulfilled.

Phase 2: Preparation   **99**

Working With Defenses: A Directive Approach

The mind that is impacted and affected by chronic experiences of trauma and adversity must find shelter from intolerable pain, embarking early on a journey of self-protection. Often, fragments of isolated, implicit trauma-genic memories are subjectively felt as if they belonged to the present even though they are familiar visitors from the past. These slivers of memory do not belong to coherent, cohesive, and integrated verbal narratives. They exist, instead, in somatosensory data that has not been anchored or located in time and space (Cozolino, 2020) and, as such, has not been recognized by the individual's mind as their own. Often, these individuals master the art of self-protection, defending against their own painful stories and often disowning, disengaging, and rejecting any stimulus that may bring these unwanted visitors. The work in the sand tray provides containment, distance, and refuge to the mind seeking integration and the realization of wholeness. It also gives the mind channels of nonverbal expression and communication between the inner and outer worlds that remain intimately connected and radically differentiated, like the ocean and the shore. When defenses are not explored and brought into the client's field of awareness, they have the potential of stalling treatment and causing stagnation.

In some cases, defenses must be explored to initiate the process of recognition, realization, and ownership to facilitate entry into the inner world. The following steps can guide you in the process of working with defenses; however, they are not intended to be rigid procedural steps. Instead, they are meant to support and offer flexible guidance.

Psychoeducation and Physicalization

Working with defenses is a nuanced and multifaceted process. For some clients, especially children and young adolescents, working with defenses may be initiated by creating a psychoeducational tray that invites figures, particularly animals that, by nature, hold multiple defenses. With adults, a conversation may precede the creation of trays focused on their defensive and self-protective systems. The entrenchment and rigidity of a client's defensive system may be more pronounced in some older clients, as they have depended on these protective "soldiers" for much of their lives. Work within the client's tolerable threshold, but persevere and remain consistent.

There are multiple implicit and explicit entry roads into defensive systems that involve nondirective and directive approaches. When using an implicit road, bring awareness and invite curiosity to the client's or character's protective and defensive tendencies. If embracing an explicit portal into these systems, clinicians may implement one or both of two tracks to initiate the exploration of defenses.

FIGURE 3.10 **A psychoeducational tray with representations of defenses, such as aggression (dragon), submission (dog), avoidance (ostrich), control (lion), manipulation (snake and spider), overworking (ant), self-sufficiency and avoidance of interdependence (cat), and hypervigilance (prairie dog).**

Option 1. Invite the client to pick figures of animals that depict defenses. Explore each animal and be curious about how it protects itself, while also validating and normalizing the protective and defensive tendencies humans hold. You may invite a representation of the defenses in the tray if it honors the client and the character.

Option 2. The client and the clinician cocreate a tray: So, you may bring in an ostrich, for instance, to represent avoidance and hiding. Once the defense is represented, inquire about how people do "ostrich stuff" or use similar defenses. Continue with other animals, such as the chameleon, which may represent pleasing others and meeting other's expectations, or the cat, which may represent self-sufficiency.

Some common defenses and mechanisms of adaptation, as described by Gómez (2023c), utilize animal metaphors, including:

> Avoidance—ostrich
> Pleasing—chameleon
> Dissociation—seagull, or birds in general
> Control—lion
> Loyalty and idealization of wounding figures—dogs and puppies
> Manipulation—spiders and snakes
> Self-sufficiency—cats
> Perfectionism—bee

The full list of possible animal–defense associations is much longer. some defenses may be unique to a specific client. Cultivate openness to the tapestry of meaning the client's mind possesses. Additionally, each client will choose the animal that resonates most with them.

FIGURE 3.11 A sand world depicting an adult client's self-protective and defense system: shame/criticism—queen; submissiveness and a desire to please authority and aggressive figures—princess and shy woman; rescuing and overdoing for others even when self-detrimental—nurse; overworking—woman with briefcase; and hypervigilance and catastrophizing—head.

Invitation to Uncover the Self-Protective System

Invite the client to physicalize their protectors while normalizing, validating, and exalting the work these protectors have done to shelter the client from further pain and how the protectors were adaptive strategies to ensure survival. You might say:

> "I would like to invite you to choose figures and animals that represent your own protectors."

If the client cannot find any, invite their inner world processes to unblend in the tray. How does the client relate to the inner protectors? The prospect of their physical existence and visibility may frighten the client and their protectors. The act of realization and acknowledgment is courageous and often painful. Give the inner system time, comfort, and companionship, and wait for the client to find the right moment to face their protectors. Recognition may occur without words while under the safeguard of the symbols. However, when the client exhibits a much greater affect tolerance threshold, you may be more directive and forward in assisting the client and their inner defense system. You may point to or hold an ostrich (or another defense holder animal selected by the client) and wonder if you may have found a protector. You might say:

> "I wonder if an ostrich (a side of you that avoids) is protecting you when you say that you do not know what you are feeling. Can we be curious together and see if there is a protector when this happens?"

Exploration of the System

Once contact has been made with the inner protectors, invite the client to explore these inner defenders and get to know them well. Use reflective statements and, when appropriate, ask questions about the work they do, how they protect the client, how long they have been around, and if these protectors have been in the office/playroom. If they have, inquire about what brings them here and how they are protecting the client now. Support the client in developing a relationship with the defender(s), one founded in self-compassion, kindness, acceptance, and gratitude for the protection they have provided.

Recognition and Gratitude

The sand tray provides a space to celebrate, honor, and express gratitude to these tireless protectors. The self-protective system may be invited to a celebration, an honoring, or a gratitude party in the sand tray, wherein their work and service are recognized and exalted. It is essential to establish the client's readiness to experience gratitude and compassion for their inner protectors. Before reaching this state of gratitude, the client may need to journey through a range of emotions as they realize how these defenders emerged in their lives.

With children, the concept of compassion may be complex, and a separate tray may be turned into a cooking pot. The clinician invites the child to bring ingredients from the miniature collection, such as love, kindness, understanding, and anything else that may be an ingredient of compassion. The clinician invites the child to pretend to taste the "compassion soup" until they agree that it is completely cooked. Sand from the "cooking pot" is brought to the protector's tray and any future trays and stories that need compassion. A spoonful, a pinch, a bucketful, or even greater amounts of compassion are given to the protective system for their service.

Adult clients are invited to find within themselves even a pinch of compassion and gratitude for these inner companions. The state of appreciation promotes healing and empowerment so the client can harness the strength and wisdom of their inner helpers, facilitating further growth and transformation in the sandtray process.

Negotiation

The goal is *not* to overturn or eradicate these protectors but to create a dialogue with them. By doing so, we create the space for these protectors to trust the therapeutic process and to allow themselves to become active parts of the client's healing journey. Through this compassionate approach, the client can see their protectors not as hindrances but as vital allies. This shift in perspective cultivates a sense of inner balance and collaboration, reassuring the client that they are not alone and that they are supported by their protectors in accessing more profound levels of healing and transformation within the sandtray process.

Negotiation with protectors may be necessary before identifying, exploring, and processing trauma. Protectors are actively invited to participate in and/or monitor the session and to give the client permission and space to feel and embrace thoughts, emotions, memories, and bodily sensations. For instance, the protectors and defenders are invited into the resource tray in preparation for accessing memories of trauma. The work may be titrated, and the protector may be asked to let the client hold a feeling for just five seconds so they can connect to their inner experience. This essential work will lay the foundation for building a trusting relationship, especially as they transition into the reprocessing phases.

Closure

At the end of the session, invite the client to communicate with their protectors to find out what they need before leaving the session. Use regulating strategies to bring the client and their inner system back into balance and homeostasis.

Working With Defenses: A Nondirective Approach

After working with EMDR-sandtray-based therapy for a while, you will come to trust that the tray will mirror and reflect the client's mind, including its defenses and protections, in whatever way the client is ready to face. Protective guards may manifest as hidden and unrecognized by the conscious mind, expressed but covered by the avatar's costume. If we remain present and curious, portals to explore defenses will open when they are ready. These protectors represent the client's best response and adaptation to support survival; though they strive to achieve homeostasis, they may paradoxically hinder the client's ability to attain it in the present. Reflective statements that expand meaning are offered to invite and support the client's dialogue with their defense system. Statements that provide small segments of information may be included to support realization. If the client has explicit access, invite curiosity about the characters in the tray that represent the realized self. Invite reflections and pose questions about how the "you" in the tray protects them from pain or other challenging emotions. The clinician can offer invitations to honor and compassionately engage with the defense and self-protective mechanism. You might say:

> "The boy in the tray was overwhelmed by his pain, so he had to hide it and bury it [reported by the client]. Covering up the pain was his best attempt to survive."

The clinician may also use reflective communication that supports the client in building awareness and understanding:

> " In burying the pain, I wonder if the boy also abandoned the possibilities for healing it. Hurts and wounds need to be heard and seen to heal."

Gradually, begin to peel away the layers of protection while expanding the client's awareness.

One 19-year-old woman often engaged in abusive relationships, idealizing her friends and partners and betraying herself. In the tray, she created a world of a child living with an abusive dragon. The child was loyal to the dragon and fulfilled all the dragon's desires and orders while abandoning her own wants and needs. Once the clinician spotted the protective strategy, she reflected and mirrored it while supporting the expansion of meaning and the field of awareness:

> " The child in the sand world idealizes and is loyal to the dragon [adult client's statement]. This is her way to survive while living with a wounding dragon. To survive, she must be loyal to the dragon while betraying herself."

Openings and expansions may occur directly with the fully recognized and acknowledged self or through the character and avatar, which give the self shelter and the possibility of self-discovery.

Identifying and Exploring Targets During the Preparation Phase

The accessing and exploration of memories of trauma and adversity can be challenging for children, adolescents, and adults with developmental and complex trauma. Information may surface through embodied states and reenactments in the therapeutic process and through play, particularly in young clients. Traumagenic material may not emerge verbally but through the stories clients create and the themes that arise in their therapeutic sandtray work. externalizing and physicalizing targets give the mind a sense of mastery while maintaining a safe distance in the tray. In addition, targets may emerge fully acknowledged or hidden, without ownership or recognition by the client's conscious mind. Directive and explicit as well as nondirective and implicit approaches may be used in the tray to explore memories of trauma and adversity. If remnants of trauma-related phobias persist, we would need to work from a titration continuum that actively recognizes the client's fluctuating capacities. The exploration and identification of targets should be structured to promote repair and a restorative experience.

The client must be anchored in the present safety, surrounded by ample companionship and support as they travel into previously intolerable affective states. This begins the journey into self-discovery, with abundant opportunities to restructure the relationship with themselves and their life stories. From this space, clients can move from a state of disempowerment and self-contempt into one of self-acceptance, compassion, and resilience. One of the assets of sandtray work is that it provides the space for targets to surface freely while remaining contained and held by symbols that supply distance. Targets that the client has not realized nor owned can still be processed through sandtray themes and stories. Targets can also be accessed using directive and explicit approaches with clients, especially adults who possess greater language abilities and regulatory capacities. Now, we can openly invite the protector to collaborate and/or step aside for just a short period of time so the client can access their inner world and the memories of trauma and adversity.

Nondirective Access of Targets

Targets may emerge in the tray organically and without much direction. Recognized and owned targets, as well as implicit and unacknowledged targets, may surface. The client holds the control, choice, and rhythm from which the information travels from the nonconscious into conscious awareness. The client's mind directs how inner data wants to emerge in the tray, how it wants to be witnessed, known, and realized, and when it is ready to be reprocessed.

Targets may surface when creating implicit and nondirective worlds. One of the characters may experience a negative or traumatic event. The clinician moves strategically and synchronously between the client's conscious and nonconscious emerging information, cocreating the affective equilibrium the client's mind needs to find itself from moment-to-moment.

Directive Access

Resource Trays. Due to the often-narrow threshold of affect tolerance of clients affected by complex trauma, resource trays frequently accompany the explicit exploration of traumagenic networks to increase the accessibility of the client's resources. The trays that hold the client's resources or their memories of trauma can be moved closer or further away as needed at any given moment. When two trays are used, the clinician can capitalize on the opportunity two locations offer for movement and social engagement, especially with children. We invite the child to run, walk, dance, or creatively move from one tray to the other while impersonating animals.

Pendulating supports the gradual and tolerable access to disturbing material. From the resource tray back to identifying trauma memories and back to the resource tray. Individual trays can be partitioned to hold space for both adaptive, corrective elements and maladaptive, traumatic content. The resource tray may have multiple assets that are relational, spiritual, or that represent mastery experiences and capacities. The team of companions, the client's strengths and special powers, or the safe place may also be symbolized in the tray. The defense system that has already agreed to let the client access their inner experience and autobiographical memory should also be invited to the resource tray as a faithful companion. Clinicians should pursue and request permission from the client's protectors in advance.

The Worry World. This directive protocol begins by creating a resource tray. Once completed, the client's awareness is directed to choose figures that represent their experiences of adversity, pain/hurt, or trauma. The client connects to their inner world to find and unblend yucky, bothersome, worrisome, hurtful, disturbing, upsetting, traumatic, or "bad" (use the term most appropriate for the client) experiences from their life stories. You might say:

> ❝ I invite you now to pick the figures that will accompany you in representing challenging experiences or stories you carry within. You may bring as many figures as you feel ready to witness and represent in the tray. Words may or may not accompany the representations in the tray. The figures themselves give your stories a voice, a presence, recognition, and wings."

While the sand tray and the miniature collection offer the client's mind a safe and sacred space, the clinician provides a compassionate and nonjudgmental presence that serves as an important anchor into the present while fostering trust and a sense of belonging. The therapeutic companionship is very impactful, so verbalize, announce, and make your presence known to the client:

> ❝ Remember that you are not alone. I am with you right here, right now, and all the way through our journey today."

Support the client in staying rooted and grounded in the here and now. You might say:

Phase 2: Preparation **107**

"Remember that this is not happening now. None of these things or stories are happening in this moment."

The trauma/worry tray may be built gradually, one experience at a time. Once the sand world containing the memories/experiences or events associated with trauma/pain/hurts or dysregulated affect is complete, invite the client to be with the space as long as it is tolerable. The exploration of the tray should be gradual and titrated and does not require words or deep explorations of what each figure represents. At this point in EMDR–sandtray, we should not get too many details or make long inquiries about each figure that can unnecessarily activate and potentially dysregulate the client.

If defenses show up—for instance, if the client becomes very quiet or often says, "I do not know" or "I cannot find anything"—explore the client's current experience and invite curiosity. You may direct the client to the resource tray to connect with their protectors/defenders and inquire if they have concerns about what unfolded in the sand world. Search, through reflections or questions, for what the client and their "soldier" need to continue, such as a greater connection to safety, companionship, or a slower pace. The client may need space to regulate or coregulate with the therapist before continuing the exploration of targets. Once the client is back to a regulated state, explore if the protective system is willing to continue now or if stopping seems more viable.

This work can last a few minutes or the full session. It is up to the client. When the end of the session arrives, the client is free to dissemble the tray, have the therapist dismantle the tray, or work with the clinician to put the figures back on the shelves. The clinician mirrors the client's strength and courage so they can savor this important act of triumph. You might say:

FIGURE 3.12 **A 10-year-old creates a worry world, depicting her numerous surgeries on one side of the tray. Freddy Krueger, with his knife-like fingers, stands next to her and represents the multiple doctors who have cut into her body over the years. She represents herself with a beheaded girl figure surrounded by medical personnel and her father.**

"Visiting yucky, bothersome, hurtful, disturbing, and bad stuff (adapt the words to the client's developmental stage) is a courageous thing, and you did it today. I wonder if we can spend some time just noticing and sitting with what just happened and what you managed to do."

This act of triumph may be physicalized in the tray on the resource side and, if possible, installed using slow and short sets of BLS/DAS. Additional regulatory strategies, including physical activity, may be used to either up- or down-regulate the client's system before ending the session.

Timelines. This entry road into memory systems is straightforward and effective with children, adolescents, and adults in identifying targets for reprocessing. When working with children, the caregiver can provide companionship and add valuable information to the timeline and the child's life story. The child should be an active participant in deciding whether to invite the caregiver. If the parent will be part of the session, a preparation session should be scheduled with the caregiver to make the treatment session and process predictable and safe. Please see Chapter 5 for information on dyadic EMDR–sandtray procedures. We certainly want to prevent the parent from disclosing information that the child has not been explicitly exposed to, which could potentially retraumatize the client. For instance, disclosing sexual abuse that occurred in the client's first years of life could be shocking and dysregulating to the child. Even if there is an agreement on the need to disclose a traumatic event unknown to the child's conscious mind, how it will be disclosed should be discussed thoroughly with the

FIGURE 3.13 An adult client's timeline. It begins with experiences in her childhood, represented by a raging father (Hulk), a narcissistic mother (dragon with a mirror), and two older brothers who physically abused her (two boy characters with the client, who is under a rock). Her best friend died at the age of 12 (hippopotamus represents the best friend). Her dog was also killed when she was 13. At 23, she married a narcissistic and abusive man (bride and man with a straitjacket). Shortly thereafter, she developed an autoimmune disease (woman next to the eye). In the front of the tray, a figured labeled as happy is buried, a sad alien holds its heart, and the client is depicted as a bound and gagged character, representing her current symptoms.

Phase 2: Preparation 109

caregiver. In children, the injury will often surface through implicit and nondirective worlds without having to explicitly disclose traumagenic experiences/memories.

Timelines in the tray do not need to be linear and may be organized in multiple ways. A resource tray should be set up before initiating the timeline tray to bolster the client's accessibility to resources.

Once resources have been set up, invite the client to visit or "make contact" with life events, in chronological order, that are yucky, difficult, bothersome, disturbing, or distressing as well as events that are joyful, happy, courageous, or that represent mastery experiences. The client then chooses figures that accompany them in telling their chronological stories, beginning with their life inside their mom's belly/mother's womb (life in utero). At this point, one might say:

> ❝ I am wondering if we can start with the time when you were in your mom's belly (your mother's womb, or, if adopted, your belly-mom's belly or biological mother's womb). Let's find figures that represent that time in your life."

Once the client picks the figure(s), invite them to place them in the tray however they please. When working with children, the parent is invited to join the child in selecting figures. If there is something that the child does not know and the parent and clinician have previously agreed to share, then the parent should be invited to pick figures to represent the story that they hold and place them in the tray. The verbal brain may be called in to speak about the selected figure(s). Details about the traumatic event are not summoned, only short descriptions of how this figure tells a story about a specific time in the child's life. The child is reassured that sufficient time will be allocated to each memory or experience so they are fully honored and the voices that speak about the child's stories will be heard. However, if the child wants to volunteer more information, space should be provided for them to do so, as long as it is understood that this is not expected of the child.

Creating a timeline in the sand tray may take multiple sessions, as the pace and rhythm of each client are met with synchrony and resonance. Once a developmental stage has been explored, move to the next one and repeat the process. Make sure that you check in to determine whether a specific time in the client's life has been fully addressed and is complete. Timelines can offer rich information, especially for children accompanied by parents who can supplement with additional information to deepen the process. When a parent reports on something the child did not know, make sure the delivery is developmentally appropriate. For instance, if the mother experienced anxiety during pregnancy that could have affected the child's nervous system, the mother may say:

> " When you were in my belly, I had big feelings, not because of you but because Mommy was dealing with things in her life that gave her these big feelings. Because you were in my belly, your little self may have felt the winds of these big feelings. Although I am fine now and can handle big feelings, your mind, heart, and body may still remember."

Remain aware of the client's pace, and slow down or stop if you suspect the client is overwhelmed, even if the client does not verbally express it. For some clients, the timeline may be titrated through multiple sessions, dedicating only a portion of each session to it. Remember to allocate time at the end of each session for containment and regulation.

When using timelines with adults and older adolescents, guide them chronologically through each developmental stage. Identify significant generational events from their lifetime and their parents' lifetimes that may have been passed down to them.

Tracing Back and Affect Scan. Sandtray explicit work kindles adaptive and trauma-formed networks, which can serve as springboards to trace back or affect scan into other events. While some clients may be ready and have the capacity to enter trauma-related associative channels, others may not tolerate this rapid access. When doing a traceback (Young et al., 2002; F. Shapiro, 2018; Gómez, 2023a), the client identifies the negative cognition specific to an experience emerging in the tray followed by exploring other associative networks that contain similar metaperceptions and cognitive tendencies. Clinicians can also use emotions and body sensations to further explore adverse and traumatic experiences through an affect scan. Any new emerging data is represented in the tray in whatever way best honors the client's embodied mind. The client should always have a stop or a slowdown signal they can use to control the rhythm in which trauma-related information emerges in the mind and the tray to prevent emotional flooding. Closure will support the client in containing and regulating before exiting the session.

CHAPTER 4

Phase 2: Advanced Capacity Building and Strategies to Work With Complex Trauma and Dissociation

EMDR–sandtray work promotes presence and groundedness, which both support clients who tend to disengage, detach, and dissociate. A thorough assessment of the level of dissociation in clients with complex trauma will support treatment organization and moment-to-moment therapeutic decision-making. It is essential to learn where the client is on the dynamic integration–fragmentation and association–dissociation continuum, which impacts treatment configuration (Putnam, 1997).

Sandtray work can keep clients grounded, engaged, and present—especially children who present with mild dissociation and seem spacy and inattentive. It also provides multisensory opportunities for tactile and visual stimulation. The movement of picking up figures and placing them in the tray imparts sensorimotor, kinesthetic, and proprioceptive stimulation. Exposure to chronic trauma can make an individual's nervous systems vulnerable to faulty neuroception that causes them to detect threats in the presence of safety or safety in the presence of danger (Porges, 2017). Working through emotional and body-based states in the sand characters or themself supports the client's interoceptive intelligence and the resetting of faulty neuroception. Additionally, play—a neuroexercise and nervous system regulator (Porges, 2017) that is essential for neurodevelopment (Kestly, 2014)—provides containment and a developmentally sound road toward healing.

Depersonalization (separation between the observing and experiencing self) and derealization (disruption in the perception of reality) manifesting in the tray are often recounts of the dissociative experiences that occurred during the traumatic event. Moderate dissociation may manifest in the tray as "observant characters" that look over the occurrences in the tray. An adolescent who depersonalized whenever her father, who often fell ill and

112

lost consciousness, placed an observing owl in her tray. When invited to share about the sand world, she stated that she was the owl watching how a dad was dying in the tray, and at the same time, she was the little girl experiencing the fear and despair of trying to bring the dad back to life. Clients may also create sand worlds that represent feelings of detachment, disconnection, emptiness, isolation, chaos, and lack of emotional connection. Tray stories may exhibit lack of coherence and disorganization that reflect the client's altered awareness of reality. Peritraumatic dissociation may emerge as part of the sand story, or it may happen in the session, while the client is in contact with an activating and traumatic story.

If severe and structural dissociation is present, and with it a dissociative structure of parts, EMDR–sandtray work can support exploring the inner system and unblending dissociative parts into characters and avatars that give the dissociative system an outlet of expression. In the tray, dissociative parts can have a voice, reconcile inner conflict, and increase coconsciousness. The figures can accompany the client as they dive into deeper layers of their often convoluted and intricate inner matrix. Internal conflicts may arise when a client's dissociative part creates a sand world and another comes to destroy it. Clients may have difficulty recalling what and why they created the scene or the reason they selected a specific figure. Figures may be scattered across the tray, cut off and disconnected. Polarizations, conflicts, and abrupt changes in the story line emerging in the tray may signal a highly conflicted dissociative self-system. The tray is also a fertile ground for dissociative parts to emerge. Sometimes, the parts surface after being hidden under the costumes of characters and stories without ownership or acknowledgment. Other times, they are fully disclosed and visible. Parts may emerge all at once or gradually. In general, dissociation across its continuum manifests in sandtray creations through expressions nuanced by symbolic gaps, reenactments of trauma, and disjointed and confusing worlds.

The Assessment of Dissociation

Onno van der Hart et al. (2006) wisely stated that the heart of trauma is dissociation. Therefore, if we are working with traumatized clients, we are working with some level of dissociation. The assessment of dissociation must be initiated early and continued throughout the eight phases of treatment. When assessing dissociation, the client's history will provide initial cues. Disorganized attachment appears to set the foundation for developing dissociative processes (Farina et al., 2019), as does early disruption in the child–parent affective dialogue (Lyons-Ruth et al., 2006). The combination of traumatic experiences, disorganized attachment, and unavailable primary caregivers—especially in the early years of life—creates a framework that significantly increases the likelihood of dissociation becoming a primary defense and an organizing factor in the client's inner configuration. A child without a relational environment that provides what they need to attain an integrated sense of self and identity may instead follow a path to fragmentation. Exposure to multiple and incongruent models of the self (Liotti, 2009) may provide the fertile ground for dissociative processes to settle in.

The assessment of dissociation is multidimensional and should begin in the initial sessions. Various methods aim to evaluate dissociative experiences, such as self-reports, standardized instruments, structured and semi-structured clinical interviews (with the child, caregivers, and teachers), and observation (Silberg, 2022; Waters, 2013, 2016). Using a combination of methods will provide comprehensive data about the nature, severity, and frequency of the client's dissociative symptomatology.

Dissociation and EMDR-Sandtray-based Therapy

According to F. Shapiro (2001, 2018), dual attention (grounded in present safety while accessing traumatic material) is fundamental during trauma processing because EMDR therapy does not encourage the client to relive the event. Instead, EMDR therapy aims to keep the client grounded in the present safety while accessing the biological imprints left by trauma. When dissociative processes govern the mind and its configuration, the traumatized client can move quickly through time and space and begin to experience the event as if it were happening in the present, stripping away the protective layers of the present safety and the connection to the social engagement system. This results in the activation of overwhelming affect that will set dissociative processes in motion in clients who are vulnerable to dissociation. Mild, moderate, and severe dissociative processes may be observed, especially during EMDR–sandtray reprocessing sessions, which results in the loss of dual attention.

As stated in Chapter 1, EMDR-sandtray-based therapy takes a depathologizing approach to dissociation, recognizing that fragmentation was the only road possible for the client to coexist with the unbearable psychobiological imprints left by trauma.

The initial phase of EMDR treatment should yield sufficient information about the extent to which the client dissociates and how/when their dissociative processes manifest. The preparation phase should be organized in a way that attends to the dissociative defenses and the client's dissociative self-organization before attempting to access traumagenic data using implicit or explicit portals. Dissociative symptoms present in clients across the lifespan are complex and intricate and thus require further exploration that is beyond the scope of this book.

Utilizing the Tray in the Assessment and Exploration of Dissociation

Sandtray work can aid and mediate the process of exploring dissociative processes with clients. It opens the door to a nonpathological and nonshaming approach to assessing dissociation. The tray, the sand, and the miniature collection bring multiple options to investigate and study dissociative experiences using an approach that goes from nondirective to directive. When the client reports or identifies a dissociative experience, invite them to represent it in the tray using the miniature collection or to create a world about their dissociative symptoms and experiences. The client can sit with their creation and honor their inner milieu and the dissociative strategies that emerged for self-protection and survival. The sandtray process also allows the clinician to validate and provide the client with psychoeducation (if needed) on dissociation. The sandtray work mirrors the client's embodied mind, reflecting inner realities, tendencies, and dynamics while in the refuge of symbols and metaphors. For some clients, it may take the creation of multiple sand worlds for the full spectrum of dissociative experiences to arrive in the sand. Initially, the dissociative system may provide only a partial view of itself in the tray. However, as safety in the therapeutic relationship increases, so does the client's openness to showing in the tray how they are internally organized. Due to the symbolic nature of the work in the tray, clients may find the freedom and safety they need to explore and represent dissociative dynamics and experiences without verbally naming them. This data may remain in the refuge of the metaphor and the symbol, keeping it verbally invisible.

FIGURE 4.1 **In the middle of this tray, created by a 10-year-old client, a bridge depicts the client's frequent crossings into a safe, imaginary world. To endure the pain of her frequent surgeries, she often crosses this bridge represented in the tray from reality into a painless fantasy world where nature and loving fairies surround her. In her daily life, she frequently retreats into a disconnected world of fantasy when facing distress.**

You may set up trays for the client to create worlds that represent what they realized after responding to one of the standardized instruments assessing dissociation and what they learned about themselves. You may invite them to create multiple sand scenes depicting their dissociative tendencies and how they relate to their inner world. Clients can name such experiences as they please (dissociation, going away, splitting, etc.). The following questions are intended to provide opportunities for expanding awareness, but they should be delivered gradually, interspersed with reflective statements and moments of silence.

- When and how did you discover them?
- What triggers such experiences, and what attenuates them?
- Are there periods when you do not have them?
- Are there times in your life when you had them most?
- Do certain people, circumstances, or environments make them better or worse?
- What happens before, during, and after you have them?
- How do they help?
- Are there parts, voices, and so forth? And are they willing to make themselves visible in the tray?
- How do you relate/feel about your inside world and inner voices, and how do you feel about these inner experiences and dynamics?

The information emerging in the tray related to dissociative experiences will further expand on the presence of defensive dissociative processes or characterological dissociation nuanced by divisions and compartmentalization. In the client–therapist relationship, both nervous systems make contact through both verbal and nonverbal cues such as tone, facial expressions, and body language. This allows their nervous systems to tune in to each other, often creating a sense of safety, connection, or presence. The clinician often makes psychobiological adjustments to support the client in up- or down-regulating their internal states. The clinician offers options from a titration continuum so the client can choose how they want to be witnessed in the tray and how they want to connect with themselves in each moment. For instance, a figure may appear in the tray hidden and buried under the sand. Clinicians may also offer coverings, giving the client possibilities for how they want to be seen and how their inner world makes contact with the outer world.

Clinicians also remain curious and observant of any shifts in attention, present awareness, energy level, muscle tension, facial expressions, or anything that could indicate that the client is beyond their tolerable threshold and moving out of presence and social engagement and into dissociative states. Inner or outer world occurrences, including happenings within the tray, may activate these changes and alterations in consciousness. Sometimes, material emerging in the tray may be overstimulating to the client's mind, while other times it may be regulating, soothing, and containing. The clinician must make moment-to-moment adjustments to meet the client's demands for safety and regulation.

Working With Mild to Moderate Dissociation

Dissociative children, adolescents, and adults may overfocus or have difficulty directing their attention. They may space out, exhibit trance-like states, or present with a divided sense of identity. Any dissociative manifestations will significantly influence the organization of the eight phases of EMDR–sandtray treatment. If the client presents with mild dissociation, the focus in the preparation phase will be on supporting them in attaining a heightened state of awareness, presence, and connection to the present safety, increasing their integrative capacities, and cultivating their interoceptive and exteroceptive intelligence even while they present with some level of disengagement and dissociation. "Safety checks," which invite the client to look around and orient in time and space, can support the client's regulation, orientation to present safety, and resetting of faulty neuroception. Once the client is sufficiently grounded in the present safety, invite them to select a figure that represents the experience and associated affect. Let the client savor and connect to the affective and physiological state resulting from the experience of safety in the present before inviting the client to engage in BLS/DAS.

A developmentally sound way to assess here-and-now consciousness will support interoceptive awareness and give the client a pathway to gauge and communicate their connection to the safety of the present moment. The back of the head scale (Knipe, 2019), created for adults, provides a tangible way for clients to do presence checks. Children may use the "fanometer," which is a fan that when entirely open represents an extensive connection to the present. If it remains completely closed, it indicates narrow interoceptive and exteroceptive awareness (Gómez, 2013). Measuring spoons may also give children a means of expressing their high or low connection to the present. A small spoon would indicate narrow access to present awareness, and a large one would represent abundant connection to safety in the here and now. The client may also opt to select figures to represent their entire safety spectrum. For instance, an elephant may depict the experience of complete safety, while a snake may embody the sense of threat and danger and the disengagement from the present. Other figures may be used to represent an assortment of intermediate states. The clinician can, for a safety check, invite the client to select the figure that represents their current state.

Reflective communication and mirroring allow the client to expand their awareness of how they distance, disengage, and return to presence. The clinician and the tray are echoes that emulate the client's mind so clients can find themselves in the clinician's reflections and the emerging themes, creations, and motifs of the tray. The following template may be employed as a bridge into presence:

> " Let's take some time to do an 'inside visit' (or for an adult, 'let's direct your awareness within') and see how present you feel. Do you hear my voice well? Do things around you feel real and close enough to know where you are? Do you feel alert and awake or sleepy and far away?"

Invite the client to pick figures that represent how present they feel. For instance, if the client selects a sleepy tiger to represent how they feel when tired, disengaged, and away, this figure can continuously accompany them. If the client feels they are starting to drift away, they can bring out or point to the sleepy tiger figure; thus, they need not rely solely on their verbal capacities. The clinician, in response, can implement strategies such as inviting the client to connect with and touch the sand, to stand up and walk around until presence is restored, or do a safety check to reorient to here and now.

Once the client reports feeling grounded in the present, they may choose another figure to represent their "present" or their "I am safe right here, right now" state which they may continue to use to indicate their presence. The client also borrows from the clinician's ventral vagal energy and presence through coregulatory processes (Dana, 2023). The clinician becomes an anchor that connects the client to the safety of the here and now.

Severe Dissociation and Fragmentation: The Absence of a Unified Sense of Self

The most traumatized children, adolescents, and adults often did not receive what they needed to develop an integrated sense of self and identity. When the client shows fragmentation in their (emerging) personality, the organization of the preparation phase is tailored to work with a system that shows divisions, polarizations, and conflicts. Therapeutic work with dissociation should involve exploring internal conflicts and encouraging inner dialogue, aiming for consensus when achievable. Parts may coexist within an unintegrated constellation of meaning. While honoring the nuanced discrepancies and distinctions that cohabit within the inner milieu, we should relate to parts as manifestations of one's psyche (Steele et al., 2017). We want to honor the system while gradually conveying that there is only one individual in existence.

One way to address the inner system of parts, especially with children, is by using the language of stories and storytellers. Children learn that "parts" are "storytellers" and "story holders" that carry essential information about their lives. These story holders carry fragments of experiences, memory traces, emotional imprints, relational patterns, and body-based encryptions left by trauma. A story holder may carry disowned emotions and experiences where anger, resentment, and hatred govern. At the client's pace, the clinician supports the uncovering of a polarized system of parts that carry the client's disclaimed, repudiated, and fragmented life story that has not yet entered their field of consciousness. Titration and gradual entrance into the constellation of meaning and embodied states left by trauma can better support the reparative work that moves the client into states of integration and to realizing wholeness.

Through sandtray work incorporated into EMDR treatment, the client can begin the process of uncovering, realizing, owning, assimilating, and integrating the information that trauma left fragmented and compartmentalized. Sandtray work grants a pathway to access and to work with the inner system. Figures can represent dissociative parts, the information and stories they carry, the job they execute, their concerns and assets, their needs and developmental gaps, and their fears and lived experiences. Clients can also represent relational choreographies in the tray that mirror the inner system's interactions and affiliations. Which parts are polarized and in constant conflict? Which ones have created alliances and bonds?

In the tray, the system sometimes emerges without words, revealing and physicalizing defenses and entrenched forms of self-protection. Dissociative parts may emerge implicitly, while hiding underneath a character's costume, or explicitly and openly. The dissociative system may surface slowly, with a few parts making themselves known, or rapidly, with the entire system entering the tray at once. Either way, the clinician remains consistent, attuned, present, curious, always observant and synchronized enough to notice when containment or a slower pace is needed. Parts work in the tray is often a potent route into the client's embodied mind and inner structure. However, the work with dissociative clients expands beyond the process with parts, as it is often comprehensive, encompassing multiple layers of work and complexity.

Accessing the Inner System

An Implicit Portal

Self-states may show up in the client's worlds quietly and without ownership, beneath the protection of metaphors and avatars. This is an access route often used by children, though it may also be a portal into the systems of adolescents and adults. Nondirective and implicit portals and approaches can lead the way into the client's mind and inner system. Characters may represent parts of the self and internal battles and struggles within the perpetrator, rescuer, and victim trauma triangle (Danylchuk & Connors, 2024). Conflicts among characters that portray polarized self-states are visible in the battles between good and bad, victim and perpetrator, powerful and powerless. The tray often reflects how the mind has organized itself to respond to and adapt to trauma.

A 12-year-old girl created a world in which a dragon attacked a little zebra and would lay on top of her. The zebra's mother would turn her back and remain peripheral and unmoved by the little zebra's pain. The girl said the dragon was powerful and was the story's main character. The other animals worshipped him and did what he wanted. At the same time, an elephant hated and was angry at the dragon. In a single world, inner dynamics and self-states portraying introjects and internalizations of wounding figures emerged, as well as a constellation of conflicts and alliances with perpetrators and injurious figures. One part is victimized, fearful, and powerless, while another is angry as it witnesses the wounding acts. This child presented nuanced metaperceptions, depicting the perpetrator as omnipotent and almighty while portraying the mother (caregiving system) as absent

FIGURE 4.2 In the tray, a giant dragon traps and attacks a little zebra, while three other zebras, representing her family, have turned their backs on the attack. A giant elephant watches angrily, and other wild animals watch in turmoil but cannot do anything for the zebra.

and neglectful. Although the child is not labeling or owning these parts, they are making themselves visible in the tray, seeking recognition from the child's conscious mind.

Communication among parts can also occur with distance and without acknowledgment and ownership from the client's mind. Robert, a 16-year-old with an extensive history of trauma, created a world where a malevolent king terrorized vulnerable children, especially a small boy. A wrestler witnessed the abuse in rage, unable to face or challenge the king. The king had a wife, who was also victimized and unable to defend herself. Relational patterns between the victim, perpetrator, and witness mirrored the adolescent's life story. Parts that imitated the perpetrator, the vulnerable and victimized child, and the angry bystander all existed in his dissociative system and the tray. Although they were only acknowledged as parts after several sessions, all the parts and their relational dynamics were implicitly present in Robert's initial world.

Implicit access is initiated through a nondirective and open invitation to create a world in any way the client wishes. This open permission to create while in the refuge of the metaphor allows the client to visit the frontiers of their inner landscape. Just like the ocean touches the shore and recedes, the mind contacts the inner world and then distances. Through this rhythmic movement of approach and distance, the mind pendulates from the known into the unknown, the tolerable into the intolerable, and the comfortable into the uncomfortable. Implicit access is one of sandtray therapy's greatest offerings to EMDR. Through the characters and avatars, the client gets to experience corrections, completions, and a channel that bridges the gap between the inner and the outer world. As the client implicitly makes contact with and touches their inner world, the barriers created for survival begin to erode, permitting the system of parts to gradually become more perceptible. Clients may spontaneously report that a previously unnamed part represents an acknowledged one. The movement from implicit to explicit parts recognition should happen at a rhythm uniquely established by each client. The symbolic nature of sandtray work provides a refuge for parts to remain unacknowledged and disowned in the tray for as long as the client's mind needs them to be.

An Explicit Portal

Dissociative parts or ego states may appear spontaneously and uninvited while recognized and acknowledged as existing within the client's inner milieu. Other times, the clinician may directly invite the client to unblend in the tray.

A 17-year-old started to bury multiple figures in the tray. After a few minutes, the teen stated, "They are all inside me." The teen unburied one of the figures and said, "This is the 'ringmaster' inside me, and he is angry because he does not want to be here."

The clinician used reflective communication to let the teen and his parts know that she had heard his message and discomfort. She invited curiosity and wondered if there was anything else the ringmaster part of him wanted them to know. The adolescent stated that this part of him did not want to disclose any further information and wanted to hold on to what he or every other part knew.

The clinician, in presence and synchrony, responded using reflective communication, "It seems like the ringmaster not only has information but knows how to carry it and protect it well. He seems to be a very important story keeper and a powerful part of you." The clinician also wondered out loud, "I wonder how it is for this part to hold such power." The clinician also inquired about the inner system and how other parts felt or responded to the ringmaster, "I wonder, how is it for the rest of the parts inside you to hear what the ringmaster part of you is saying?"

In this case, an angry and oppositional part appeared, while four other parts remained buried in the sand. This part strongly allied with the ringmaster, and the rest of the system remained silent and fearful. As a bioemotional regulator for the client, the clinician maintained curiosity, acceptance, and compassion for the adolescent and his inner storytellers, supporting the communication among parts to increase coconsciousness, realization, and homeostasis.

Sometimes, the dissociative system does not surface spontaneously, and rigid defenses may block the access and exploration of dissociative parts. In these cases, the clinician may start by using reflective communication that incorporates parts language when the client brings figures representing emotions, thoughts, movements, or memories into the tray:

> "It seems like a part of you feels really big feelings. I wonder if you can connect to this part of you. Where in your body do you feel its presence [or where is it present or hanging out in your body]? Can you pick the figure(s) that represent(s) it? Can you place it/them in the tray in where it feels right or safe for this part of you?"

You may continue to investigate the system by asking if other parts of the self may have the same or different feelings:

> "Is this how all the different parts of you feel? Can we be curious together and see if other parts feel the same or different?"

Curiosity and presence will help clinicians understand how the client is shaped and structured internally.

122   EMDR-Sandtray-based Therapy

Polarizations and the Inner Conflict

Inner-systemic work is pivotal during the preparation phase. Inner polarizations and conflicts lie at the core of many of the client's struggles and challenges. Reducing them will result in more rapid stabilization during this phase.

You may explicitly invite the issue, conflict, internal tensions, or conflicting inner dialogues to come into the safe and supportive space offered by the sand tray. Other times, conflict arises spontaneously and implicitly in the tray. Either way, summon the conflict into the tray to enter the field of possibilities that exist in awareness as it becomes tangible to the client's mind. This level of work will support a shared consciousness, interoceptive intelligence, and increased internal dialogues.

Depending on the client's capacities, they may observe from a compassionate and curious standpoint, wondering about what is happening as they observe this tension.

> " Is there something these parts of you can learn from each other? Are there other parts involved in this conflict? Are they willing and open to share ideas and possibly reach 'inside compromises,' even if they are very small?"

The initial work is not about the therapist resolving the internal struggles and clashes; it is about facilitating communication and compromises among polarized parts. Questions from ego states therapy (Watkins & Watkins, 1997) and internal family systems (R. Schwartz, 1995) can support self-discovery and connection to the inner milieu that is in distress. Parts hold trauma-bound compartmentalized life experiences with their accompanying cognitive, emotional, behavioral, and somatic schemas as well as entrenched forms of self-protection and relational dynamics. It is pivotal that the clinician honor the client's story without getting lost in a convoluted and intricate inner system.

Exploring the client's internal structure and interplays may begin superficially and then move toward revealing and uncovering deeper systemic layers. Be curious about each part, how each functions in the system, and how they manifest in the tray. Where are they placed inside the tray? Is there distance, closeness, or battles between one part and others? How does each part relate to other parts and to the client's self? How long has the part been with the system, and what is its main job? Who gave them this job, and how has the job changed or stayed the same throughout the client's life? Each part's qualities, struggles, stories, duties, or missions can exist within the client's sense of self and be represented in the tray. Initially, each part and its relational nuances may not exist in the language realm, existing only in the richness of the image and symbol domain.

The concept of polarities from gestalt therapy (Mann, 2021; Perls et al. 1951) is also useful in helping us understand how the traumatized mind constantly moves along continua of opposites: joy and despair, love and hatred, connection and separation, idealization and devaluation, submissiveness and aggression, powerlessness and overpowering. This results in constant movement toward internal conflicts. Once the conflict arrives and is encrypted in the sand (the physical world), the client is invited to be with the conflict and polarization of their internal reality, allowing this information to enter awareness and promoting recognition, ownership, assimilation, and integration. When the mind enters this neutral and mindful observation of the polarization intrinsic to the inner conflict (in gestalt therapy, "the fertile void"), the client can access "what exists before experience, which is an undifferentiated landscape of possibilities that precedes every human encounter" (Mann, 2021, p. 81).

Sometimes, the client may interact with the figures by holding the ones that represent the opposites while moving around the tray, acknowledging the existence of the conflict, and at the same time accepting and dancing with uncertainty and the unknown. According to Mann (2021), it takes courage on the client's and the clinician's part to enter this void, as it represents the risk of being rather than doing. Other times, joint curiosity is invited to support communication among polarized parts. As this process unfolds, so does the practice of self-recognition and self-knowing. The mind begins the process of dialoguing with itself while attaining greater levels of self-awareness and realization.

The clinician makes microadjustments to their approach/strategies/ communication/tone of voice/closeness to accommodate the client's ever-changing states and readiness to access their inner world. Slowing down and speeding up when the moment calls for it is a therapeutic dance. Accessing the inner family all at once, with its relational dynamics in the tray, is attainable with some clients. However, every session and every inner turmoil will have its own rhythm and therapeutic needs. The clinician accompanies the client's mind to discover and mirror itself at a tolerable pace. Clients are not necessarily encouraged to name parts or conflicts unless they choose to do so. Instead, the tray physicalizations are left to exist freely, without labels. Remember that the image emerging from the sand world already acknowledged and validated the existence of the inner system or the part and its struggles.

Once the inner battles are represented in the tray, invite if the client wishes or is ready to deepen the exploration: When did this start? What

124 EMDR-Sandtray-based Therapy

parts are involved? What exacerbates the conflict, and what helps to resolve it? What do parts need to be able to resolve the conflict? If trauma memories come up, invite the client to place them in the container (which should have been created before engaging in this level of work). You may ask questions about what is needed for two parts to reach even a tiny compromise or to enjoy the benefits of working together.

Polarized parts also can take steps away from and toward each other and practice and experiments together to see how they can work collectively and cooperatively. The purpose in the preparation phase of EMDR–sandtray is to reduce divergences and to support conflict resolution and communication among conflicted parts in the tray, laying the groundwork for trauma reprocessing. Be observant and attuned to any shifts in the client's emotional and physiological states that may signal an increase in activation or a movement into social disengagement and dissociation. Even if the intensity of the conflict is reduced slightly, this will still lessen the internal tension.

Ruby, 11, came to therapy because of multiple somatic complaints. Ruby always worked hard to be the best and to be perfect. In the tray, she created a world where numerous princesses lived. One side of the tray held the space for the princesses who obeyed their critical queen and were always on their best behavior, even though they were deeply unhappy. Three other princesses challenged the queen's rules, removed their clothes, created a pool, and played as they pleased on the other side of the tray. Ruby said these princesses were tired of following the rules and being perfect. She also stated that they felt happy and free. The obedient princesses on the other side became enraged because of the three princesses' behaviors. Instead of taking sides, the clinician named the polarized self-states, "I see . . . On one side, the princesses work hard to follow the rules and be perfect despite

FIGURE 4.3 Ruby's sand world, depicting obedience on one side and defiance of the queen's rules on the other side.

feeling unhappy. However, on the other side, the princesses do what makes them happy, even if that challenges the queen. Both sides have different feelings and perspectives, yet they exist within and are part of the same story."

In some cases, clinicians may use BLS/DAS to reduce and desensitize internal conflict and trauma-related phobias more rapidly for clients with increased affect tolerance (Knipe, 2015, 2019; Gonzalez & Mosquera, 2012; Gómez, 2013, 2019). The BLS/DAS should start short and at a medium speed, which may be increased depending on the client and how they respond to the process. In this case, the client is not focusing on a memory or resource while engaging in BLS/DAS. Instead, their attention is directed to internal conflicts.

The Sandtray-Inner Family

Even though Fraser's table (2003) was born as a hypnotic technique, it has been used and modified to fit multiple approaches. For instance, Martin (2012) adapted the dissociative table technique for EMDR therapy. The sandtray-inner family is a protocol informed and influenced by Fraser's table technique; however, it has its own character and definition that differentiate it. Before using any directive approach or protocol, it is essential that a therapeutic relational environment of safety and trust be established to ensure the client feels supported as they enter the intricate labyrinths of their inner experience.

As stated previously, sandtray work within the framework of EMDR therapy becomes the vehicle for exploring, physicalizing, and unblending dissociative parts, ego states, polarizations, and so forth.

1. Segmented Psychoeducation

Educating the client about dissociation and compartmentalization is an essential component of treatment. Analogies and metaphors will help the client, especially young clients, understand multiplicity and compartmentalization. Clinicians may use an embodied and segmented approach to psychoeducation, in which the information is delivered in small portions throughout several sessions, before mapping the system. Especially with children, therapeutic embodiments are invited as the child dances or moves with a figure(s) in whatever way an emotion, a somatic reaction, or a part longs to move and dance in the sand tray. We may invite the child to connect to the different colors they have on the inside (Gómez, 2013; Gómez & Paulsen, 2016).

> We are like a rainbow with many colors, yet it is still only one rainbow. Or like a flower with many petals that is still one flower. Or a tree

with multiple branches that is still one tree. Or a hand with several fingers that is still one hand. Or a cell phone with many apps that is still one phone."

This conversation may be repeated throughout multiple sessions in small segments so the child becomes familiar with these concepts. The same analogy may be used with adults and adolescents, using developmentally appropriate language.

As you continue with psychoeducation, you might say:

" We have already talked about all the different colors, parts, and sides that are *all* you [use the language that best suits your client]. I am wondering if we can peek in and get to know your inside colors/parts. The figures and the tray will accompany you as they give your inside family a voice and a space so it can express itself. We can do this at a pace that feels right and safe for all the different parts of you. We can go slow or fast; it is all up to you and all the different parts of you. They are free to show up in the tray how they want to be seen, known, and witnessed: open and seen, hidden and covered, or just a part of them showing up."

When using the tray, the client does not need visualization capacities, since everything and every part will exist in the external and physical world while protected under the metaphorical and symbolic nature of sandtray work.

2. Resource Tray

A resource tray can support the client before accessing the system if dysregulation occurs and stabilization is needed. Additionally, an open container may remain near the client throughout the session for any emerging material that needs containment. Using protocols such as the calm/safe (happy) place may require special attention because what appears calming and safe for one part may be dysregulating and terrifying for another part. Some clients may benefit from creating a safe place before accessing the inner system. In contrast, others will first need to access the internal system of parts to facilitate the use of resource EMDR-based protocols that invite inner communications and settlements. Another option may be to start with simple resources the client can use while accessing the internal system. For instance, the client may begin by picking a figure that connects them to a resource or the present safety in the clinician's office. The client may also choose animals, pets, superheroes, and, in general, characters that represent or provide a sense of safety, strength, and empowerment. When selecting figures and characters, invite the client to pause, reflect inwardly, and do "inside check-ins" to foster a deeper connection with their inner world and to bring potential internal divisions into awareness. The clinician supports the client in creating enough consensus from the self-system to facilitate resource creation. If the system lacks capacities and is in a constant state of crisis, exploring the entire system at once may be overwhelming. Keep in mind that, in general, acknowledging that there is an inner system of dissociative parts may be very challenging for some clients who feel abnormal in the process of recognition. The readiness for this level of exploration needs to be established before engaging the self-system.

Allocate a tray for the client to place all the resources that will accompany them. When the resource tray is complete, invite the client to connect with it, and pause to direct their attention and awareness toward their inner world to ensure that all the different parts share a state of resonance in connection to the resources that are symbolized in the tray.

If it becomes clear that the client may be drawn into traumagenic memories encourage them instead to take breaths and ground themselves in the present sense of safety, containment, or emotional regulation. This approach helps to minimize the risk of retraumatization. Make sure the client is grounded and that the "I am safe here and now" figure, the "safety reminder" rock, the "I am okay now" figure, or whatever item and label resonates with the client is placed in the tray to keep the client and their parts grounded in the present safety.

3. Preparing the Tray for the "Get-Together"

The next step is to ask the client to look at the tray, where all their different parts will be invited to a "get-together," and see if they need to add anything before proceeding.

> *Is there anything you or any of the different sides of you need to place in the tray before we start?"

Sometimes, clients may want to represent a house, where each part has its own room (Forgash & Copeley, 2008). Sometimes, clients may want to put up fences or doors and create a safe space in the tray for all the parts to feel comfortable and safe. Some clients like to create the world and prepare it before the parts arrive, and others like to have the parts unblended first into sand figures, and then create the safe atmosphere and environment for each. Allow the client enough time to create the world and landscape in which the parts will come into awareness. It may take an entire session to construct this world.

128   EMDR-Sandtray-based Therapy

4. Inviting the Guiding and Wiser Self

In internal family systems (R. Schwartz, 1995, 2021), the clinician supports the individual in developing a part–self relationship. The self is seen as a spiritual entity from which parts can be observed from a place of compassion and acceptance. Others use the concept of the wise self (Fisher, 2017), the adult self, the guiding self, or the most competent self. According to Steele (2021), the adult in therapy is grounded in the self that holds the greatest capacities. Whether working with the self, the wise self, or the most competent guiding self, we prepare the client's field of consciousness to enter their internal landscape. When working with children, we present the concept of the "bigger and wiser self" or the "older self," which is the one that does the "inside visits" and "inner checks." This self is grounded in the present but also knows about the past. The bigger and wiser self, or the "owl self," will often be invited to the tray. Some children may want to have the "bigger self" represented outside the tray; for instance, the child can wear different hats when observing and interacting with each part in the tray. At times, the invitation will be about being with or sitting with "this side of you" or "these sides of you."

Occasionally, an entire session is dedicated to connecting with the bigger and wiser self. The child may be invited to create a tray about the self that knows they are safe now (if true), that knows they are bigger and that they have family, friends, pets, and strengths now. In addition, the bigger self has the greatest proficiency at changing states, tolerating affect, and more. This concept may be too complex for young children; this approach is recommended for children over seven.

Before initiating this protocol, the client may be invited to create a sand world that symbolizes their expansive, guiding, and deeply wise self, embodying the essence of their internal wisdom and resilience. This experience allows them to tangibly represent and connect with this part of themselves, offering a grounding presence throughout the therapeutic process. Additionally, we support the client in forging a profound connection to this wiser self, reinforcing their capacity for insight, self-compassion, and inner guidance as we move through the work together. What happens when it is at the forefront? How does the client know of its presence? Once this connection is established, invite the client to create the tray for this wiser or guiding self. Playfully, begin to bring into awareness the relationship with the wiser self and guiding self; this will facilitate further work with the inner system.

5. Inviting Other Parts of the System to Join

Now, invite all the other "sides" or "parts" of the client to join their wiser and guiding self. The client can perform a check-in to decide which parts will come into the physical realm, then select the first symbols. Once the parts are physicalized, the client chooses where to place them in the tray.

Sometimes, parts may be locked up and thus cannot come into the tray, or maybe they cannot come into the tray because others may feel unsafe in their presence. It is not a good idea to free a part that was previously locked up by the system. Usually, parts remain locked up because they cause harm to the body, triggering suicide attempts or creating other crises. Imprisoned parts may delegate a speaker or another part that can represent them or provide information about them (Forgash & Copeley, 2008). Before using this protocol, a safety agreement may need to be created to ensure that all the parts feel secure. Some clients may build barriers, fences, and barricades in the tray to house parts and create boundaries. If the system has perpetrators locked up or if multiple parts do not feel safe with unblending the system all at once, use a more gradual approach.

Multiple figures may represent one part, as more than one may be needed to speak about different nuances of this part, ranging from its main job to its needs, desires, and relational map.

6. Getting to Know the System

This is an opportunity to get to know the client's inner structure and self-organization. To this end, the clinician may invite the client to spend time being with the reflection of their inner world without judgment, in the neutral space of being. Next, the clinician would summon the client to be curious and get to know their different sides in whatever order they wish. Here are some sample questions for exploration:

- What has this part of you been doing for you?
- Who gave this part their job?
- What keeps this part performing this job in the way it does now?
- How long has this part been with you?
- How long have you been aware of its existence or presence?
- How does this part get along with the others?
- What does this part need, and what are its missing experiences?
- What are its concerns, conflicts, worries (and so forth)?

Questions should be delivered gradually, one at a time, giving the client plenty of space to reflect on each one; and their delivery should be infused with reflective pauses, silent observation, and in a contemplative atmosphere that fosters the expansion of consciousness. As the history of each part unfolds, the clinician invites the client to physicalize their responses in the tray. This means the client is invited to choose a figure to represent the role a newly explored part has been fulfilling within the system, along with this part's specific needs, concerns, and internal conflicts. This figure can also reflect the relational dynamics between this part and the broader dissociative system. Parts may choose to be near each other in the tray, which may represent a deep bond or a symbiotic relationship between them, or far away and separated by rocks and fences, which may represent their dislike for each other and, potentially, conflict and polarization. Distance and closeness have constellations of meanings assigned solely by each individual's mind. Cultivate an attuned presence and resonance with the client's rhythms to ensure intersubjective congruency with what is unfolding for the client and in the tray. Asking whether it is okay to continue and reaffirming that the client may stop, slow down, or take a break when they feel they have had enough—before the work becomes too uncomfortable and overwhelming—is a good way to maintain checks and balances. Maintaining a dedicated "rest area" space in the office where clients' nervous systems can reset and regulate, will aid, especially for young clients, coregulatory processes and provide reparative experiences to previously disrupted autonomic states.

The clinician reassures parts that they have the right to abstain from participating if they do not want to partake or be represented. However, parts are asked not to sabotage other parts' work. Separate trays may be created to hold just these parts if they want to externalize their concerns

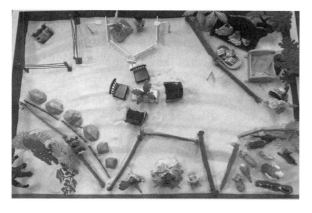

FIGURE 4.4 This is the sand world of a woman, representing her inner system of parts. Each part has its own space and boundaries, represented by fences. Three fairies represent the wiser self, and to the right is a mute, dissociative part that uses nonverbal language. This part loves and connects well with animals. To the left of the wiser self is a perpetrator-imitating part, isolated and under constant surveillance by another part. A dormant part that carries trauma memories is in the upper left corner. In front of the wiser self (top center) is a part that is highly dedicated to studying and reading and highly invested in perfection. This part falls apart in the face of shame. Two young parts and their caregiver are in the upper right corner. In the middle, the inner system has created a meeting place to communicate and resolve conflicts.

FIGURE 4.5 The communication between dissociative parts is represented and physicalized in the tray. An adult transgender client represents their dissociative parts that live in conflict. The client often hears the voices of a priest and a nun, shaming them for who they have become. Three teenagers rebel, become aggressive, and frequently encourage the client to oppose and become belligerent. A vampire represents a perpetrator-imitating part that abuses the little girl and the alien next to him. This usually results in self-harming incidents. For a while, only a few parts met, but after multiple sessions, the client wanted to have them all communicate in their gathering place.

about therapy and what they need to move forward and feel safe with the process. The clinician also reminds the parts of the titration continuum, in which they can appear hiding under the sand or other coverings. It is up to them to decide how they want to be witnessed.

7. Closure

Bringing the session to a closure that restores homeostasis, balance, and stability is essential. Opening up the system may be stressful for the inner milieu and the client. We want to ensure the parts return to balance and are "tucked in" (Paulsen, 2009) in the tray and in the client's embodied mind. Additionally, if enough connection to the wiser self exists, the wiser self is invited to lead the system as the client prepares to exit the session. What do the client and their inner system need before departing? How can these immediate needs be nurtured and fulfilled? Sometimes, expressing gratitude for the work, courage, and willingness to bring the self-system into the openness of the tray is part of the closure process. Movement may be invited, especially for children. The stories and energy emerging in the tray extend beyond its frontiers and may mobilize the client's body. A child may want to dance, move, or use rhythm during closure. Resources that emerge during the session can be enhanced with BLS/DAS while adding movement.

Skylar, 10, ended her session in complete excitement and bliss as she realized that her inner family could have arguments, negotiate, and reach agreements. Skylar was invited to represent the excitement shared by the system. She began dancing as she chose the figures depicting her emotional state. Her therapist joined her and invited her to savor the moment and embody it through movement. She held some figures and moved around the office while the clinician invited her to notice her feelings and where they lived in her body and to jump back and forth while dancing, providing BLS/DAS to enhance these moments of repair and homeostasis.

Resourcing Parts

Implicit and spontaneously emerging resources may surface in the tray from the very first session. The tray offers the client a field of potential and a platform for treasures, riches, and assets to be discovered and embraced by a system that may be unaware to its own hidden powers, potentials, and strengths. Empowering endowments, inner connections, and life-affirming intrapersonal interactions may enter hidden in implicit worlds and stories.

Once the client is familiar with EMDR-sandtray-based procedural steps and various forms of BLS/DAS, clinicians can enhance these resources using BLS/DAS.

When using directive and explicit resources, such as the safe place protocol or RDI, the system must be consulted. For example, when building the safe place in the tray, invite the client to journey inward or do "inside check-ins" or have "inside visits" to consult with the dissociative system and ensure the safe place selected does not negatively affect or activate another part. Inquire about different needs and perspectives around safety and invite parts to provide input about what needs to change or be different in the tray to foster security in the self-system. Encourage the client to make adjustments, additions, and removals and to reconfigure the tray based on the inner agreements and compromises as the safe place is refined in the sand. Once there is a systemic agreement about the positive associations and elicited feelings, install the resource with BLS/DAS. Resources may be collective or individualized to each part. Each part may identify and create a calming place or resource in the tray. It may be necessary to use multiple sand trays or bring dividers to separate resources for each part when consensus is not possible.

Anchors and Anchoring

When trauma has burdened human biology and integrative capacities have been exhausted, assimilation of the traumatic event is thwarted. As a result, the embodied mind, like a wheel spinning without advancing, continues to respond to the internalized past. The individual continues to live psychobiologically in the time when the trauma occurred (Steele et al., 2017). Anchoring work provides a touchstone for stability, empowerment, and regulation that supports the client in maintaining a connection to the safety in the present. The sand tray and the miniatures collection are powerful anchors for the distressed mind. Clinicians may add a multitude of sensory-based anchors to accompany the sandtray work and strengthen a client's orientation to the safety of the present.

Smell

Lotions, scented sprays, or essential oils can provide a bridge to the client's sense of safety. Clients select scents that they associate with their embodied connection to the safety in the here and now. Trauma can significantly impact one's perception of safety and danger, so clinicians often need to support the client in expanding their awareness and discernment around cues of safety and danger. BLS/DAS can be used to enhance the connection between feeling safe and the chosen scent. Once the scent associated with present safety is identified, it is used before initiating the work in the tray or in moments of rupture when the security of the present needs to be reaffirmed.

Sound

The physical space where therapy is delivered should be vetted for sounds that could activate defensive states via neuroception (Porges, 2017). According to Porges (2017), feeling safe is a precursor of treatment. Clinicians could use sound therapeutically by inviting the client to select sounds they associate with groundedness and connection to present safety. Clients may choose the sound of water in a stream, bird songs, rain, and so forth. When using sound, it should be audible but quiet enough not to interfere with the work and connection with the tray.

Touch

The tray, sand, and miniatures can serve as potent anchors. Before further engaging in the world creation, the client may use the sensory engagement with to the sand and water to access the safety emerging from the connection to the present. Each session may begin with a grounding ritual, inviting the client to make contact with the sand, water, or miniature collection to establish a sense of present safety. When working with children and the caregiver is a source of safety, the caregiver may be present and provide touch to support grounding, companionship, and containment. Hand holding, crossing/interlocking feet, shoulder or arm touch, and hugs can be powerful anchors to safety and trust, especially during challenging therapeutic moments. It is essential to approach touch with clear boundaries, respect, and consideration for the client's safety, autonomy, and cultural identity. In each moment, the child decides what level of physical proxim-

134 EMDR-Sandtray-based Therapy

ity and touch is appropriate. Clinicians should invite inside visits to consult with the inner system when working with dissociative children.

Elements

Element-based rituals performed before initiating or before ending an EMDR–sandtray session can offer a rich, multidimensional experience involving the five senses. Sandtray work provides the vessel and the space for the four elements to come into the client's awareness. The client is invited to touch the sand (earth), water, fire (represented by miniatures), and air (whether physically represented or embodied by the client through breathing) and become aware of their presence and how it connects to their autonomic states when a sense of safety is present. When the client is grounded in safety and regulation, the clinician can deliver BLS/DAS to enhance the experience. Be aware that some of the elements may be triggering for one part or for the entire system.

Temporal and Spatial Orientation in the Sand Tray

Dissociative parts often live in the past, holding on to memories, metaperceptions, somatic responses, and defenses needed for survival. They continue to react and respond to the present as if the past were still occurring (F. Shapiro, 2018). Parts may be convinced they are younger or older than the body, remaining stuck in different developmental periods. This may happen for a multitude of reasons but often is due to trauma and acts of omission or commission that took place during a specific period of development, or stalling at a certain age, which enabled them to maintain a connection with an important attachment figure (Paulsen, 2009; Mosquera, 2019; Steele et al., 2017).

A 27-year-old female client holding a 2-year-old part spent the first 12 years of her life with an abusive mother, who would shame her for being "too big and too sexy" and for calling the attention of men. The client's mother had been more accepting and less critical of her when she was much younger. Due to the mother's unresolved trauma, as her child was growing up, the mother would accuse her of trying to seduce men sexually. This client had a very young part in her system that refused to grow up because that would threaten her connection with her mother and expose her to verbal, sexual, and emotional abuse. Living in an older body became dangerous to this woman, so a part developed that refused to grow up so it could stay safe and in relationship with her mother. Each part has a story and a reason for remaining at the age and in the body they are convinced to inhabit.

The tray can hold these early adaptations developed to support survival, while also fostering exploration, curiosity, and an expansion of awareness.

When clients create worlds depicting their inner system of parts, you may invite curiosity and use reflective statements about different parts' temporal existence and identity.

> "I am curious about the part of you that has the body of a baby and feels like a baby (client's report), yet lives inside you."

If the client is open to the concept of "parts as storytellers," invite curiosity about how this baby may carry "baby stories." Invite representations in the tray of the baby part and the client's present body. Allow information to enter consciousness:

> "Let's just sit with this in the tray and see what happens."

Any new awarenesses and realizations may be represented in the tray if the information revealed is ready to be witnessed:

> "How about if we find a figure or figures that represent or show this new information that you just discovered/realized?"

These explorations in the tray should honor the client's rhythm and may be spread over multiple sessions to avoid overwhelming the client and their internal family.

Orientation to the Body

Individuals with a fragmented sense of self hold parts that maintain schemas about separateness. Their lack of realization and level of compartmentalization makes them believe that they have a separate body or that their body has a nonhuman shape or is from a race and gender that is different from the client's body. The work to support the realization and access to adaptive information is initiated during the preparation phase with this population. The miniature collection opens possibilities for individuals affected by trauma to reorganize such rooted metaperceptions. For instance, if a part of a child strongly believes it is an animal, invite them to find an animal in the miniatures collection to physicalize it in the tray. Once it is externalized, invite them to compare their body with the one in the tray. Invite them to bring human hands and compare them with the animal part.

- Can we just observe and see what happens?
- I wonder how they are similar or different?

136 EMDR-Sandtray-based Therapy

- I wonder how having a [lobster]'s body helps this side of you.
- Sometimes, this may be like a costume that parts of us wear even though we are still under the costume. May I invite you to pick the figure that represents how this animal costume helps, protects, or serves this part of you?
- Can we be curious to discover how being this animal helps you?
- How did this part of you choose a [wolf] to represent it?

The information provided by the child is physicalized in the tray, and invitations are made to be with this new information and explore it in a nonjudgmental and compassionate atmosphere:

- Can we sit with this new stuff we are learning about this part of you?
- Let's look at the figures that speak about this new information.

A 7-year-old had a lobster part in her internal system. This part pinched children at school, and as a result, she would be sent to the principal's office quite often. This part held a fight response that was activated when her biological father physically, emotionally, and verbally abused her. This fight response needed a space to be held even though it was not yet realized. The therapist invited the child to create a sand world about her lobster part and their relationship. Aloud wonderings invited reflections about the important job this part was doing for her. This child never felt safe and had difficulty discriminating between friend and foe. She felt like other children could hurt her, so this part was always on the defense and attacked other children by pinching them. The clinician brought people to the tray, and even a picture of the child into the tray, to help the young client compare the lobster body to her body. When the child was ready, she was supported to bring gratitude to the lobster part for its incredible work and dedication to keeping her safe. The lobster part was validated and recognized for keeping the child safe, and it was awarded a medal and trophy. As the child and her lobster part became more open to exploration and change, the clinician asked the child if this part was ready to change its name and costume or if it felt that they were still needed. The child was reassured that making these changes did not mean the lobster part would disappear or be unnecessary. Sometimes, parts want to preserve their costumes. In this case, invite the client to create a world that represents the part's story and why it still needs the costume.

Parts may be challenged if enough tolerance and trust have been built through the therapeutic relationship. Ask questions about how this part could continue to protect the client and keep them safe while modifying how they do their work. Some parts may initially be reactive and become defensive when their deep-rooted schemas are challenged (Paulsen, 2009; Mosquera, 2019). Remain compassionate and slow this work to accommodate the client's rhythm. However, do not be discouraged by highly defensive parts. It important to remain consistent and continue to gently engage with the part and the inner system while staying curious and playful. You might say:

- I notice that this part of you gets some big feelings and reactions when discussing the body and its costumes. Can we invite this side of you to bring these feelings into the sand tray in a way that feels safe or appropriate for this part?
- It can be very challenging when you are invited to see things differently.
- I am glad this part is letting us know this is challenging.
- Let's be curious about how staying at this age helps you and this part, or how it may challenge you.
- The big feelings may be speaking about how important it is for this part to hold on to a separate body.
- May we ask what this part of you is getting by having a separate body?
- Is there something this part is afraid of or concerned about?

Do not overwhelm the client with questions; intersperse them with silence and verbal and nonverbal reflection. This work may take time, patience, acceptance, and compassion as you honor the client's inner rhythms.

One thing to remember is that there is meaning behind every piece of information and choice made by the client and their parts. If a lobster was selected and the lobster part executes certain actions, there is an important reason and meaning behind it.

Mark, a 15-year-old boy, reported having a 35-year-old part. When this part was present, it would care for his mother. However, it would become sexual with her and, at times, try to touch her breasts and kiss her in inappropriate ways. The mother tried, unsuccessfully, to set boundaries.

When Mark was two years old, his father died; and after his death, his mother became depressed, and her sex addiction became more visible as she brought men to the house. Some of the men would physically and sexually abuse Mark. Mark's adult part was not just attentive to his mother's needs; at times, it would become verbally and physically abusive toward her. It expressed a lot of the same traits his father and his mother's sexual partners did.

Mark would exude power and control when this 35-year-old part was active and at the forefront. No other parts were allowed when this part was present, so Mark and his adult part were invited to create a sand world. The

138   EMDR-Sandtray-based Therapy

clinician validated and acknowledged the part's power. As they explored the tray with curiosity, the clinician wondered aloud about this adult part's job, function, and age, as well as the age of Mark's body. Initially, these questions were received with resistance and opposition. However, consistency and persistence crafted a space for awareness and realization. Over time, Mark started to bring into the tray figures that represented some of the traits and responsibilities of the adult part while also selecting figures that depicted the stories this powerful and important part of him was carrying.

Binding and Differentiating

Integration and synthesis involve the linking and differentiating of information (van der Hart et al., 2006). "Integration involves maintaining differentiation while also achieving linkage, creating a synergy that enables the whole to be greater than the sum of its parts" (Siegel, 2020, p. 15). For instance, parts may share interconnected and differentiated emotions that the individual begins to bind and own. When reprocessing memories of trauma, the client may start to differentiate past from present and locate the memory in time and space while reclaiming dissociated networks. Binding and differentiating occur often with perpetrator-imitating parts. Dissociative individuals often believe that these parts are the actual perpetrators. When they surface in the sand, the clinician supports the client in linking and associating the emotions, thoughts, memories, and actions emerging from the perpetrator-imitating part while promoting differentiation from the actual perpetrator. Exploring, establishing, and maintaining personal boundaries that define the limits of the client's identity, personal space, and autonomy within the inner system of parts and the relationship with others are fundamental pathways of differentiation. Clients may differentiate between the inner and the outer world, or reality and fantasy. All experiences can converge into a single moment in the sand, encompassing actions, emotions, bodily states, and cognitions. Emotions from the wounding caregiver or perpetrator are differentiated from the client's own, allowing a sense of self in relation to others to begin to emerge. The clinician may use dividers in the sand or two trays to represent the self and the other. Figures may physicalize linkages and connections and reflective communication that can support the client in feeling internally and externally connected while simultaneously differentiated.

- Is this the [monster]'s or the child's behavior?
- Whose feelings are these?
- Does the [anger] belong to the [ogre] or the [zebra]?

- Who knows about this emotion/behavior/action in the tray beside the [mother bear]?
- What is keeping others/you from feeling/seeing this emotion/action?
- Is this part helping you understand and deal with what the [lion] did to you by carrying the [lion]'s story?
- Let's bring this new knowledge and understanding to the tray. How would you like to see this represented in the tray?

Invite linkages and moments of differentiation to come into the tray through symbolic representations. To enhance and expand moments of knowing and expansion in the tray, invite slow and short sets of BLS/DAS.

Target Identification and Exploration of Trauma

The view of parts as story keepers is a depathologizing and deshaming way to address the dissociative system of clients of all ages. There is a story holder for every memory, truncated defense, emotion, belief, and somatic reaction. The healing process and the exploration and processing of traumatic events become part of the client's journey to reclaim their stories. These stories speak of the events the client had to endure and how they accommodated the demands of living in traumatizing and relationally impoverished environments.

Accessing and exploring memories of trauma should happen only once enough capacities have been built within the client's system. Accessing trauma within a highly contended and polarized system will only add to the current chaos and dysregulation. The clinician may feel they are in a double bind between a divergent system and the need to work through the traumatic experiences that are at the root of these trauma-formed internal relational dynamics. For instance, reprocessing traumatic events related to a highly abusive attachment figure may activate one part that holds a solid alliance with the perpetrator and another part that holds rage toward the perpetrator. These dynamics can spiral downward in the client's system into a rabbit hole of dysregulation or collapse. Waiting to begin memory reprocessing until all the internal conflicts are completely resolved is not expected. However, preliminary work addressing entrenched conflicts should be initiated during the preparation phase. Once enough capacities exist, either the trauma will begin to surface implicitly more abundantly, or the client will accept invitations to represent trauma and adversity in the tray. The inner system, with its expanded capacities for communication and collaboration, will be involved in deciding when and how to invite the trauma into the tray. In this process with highly traumatized clients, the

140   EMDR-Sandtray-based Therapy

steps should be titrated and gradual (Gonzalez & Mosquera, 2012; Knipe, 2015; Gómez, 2013). You may commence by addressing peripheral targets associated with current triggers and struggles. Alternatively, in some cases you may break down the memory into smaller kernels of information. This clinical decision should be made with care and in collaboration with the inner system.

As the client's external bioemotional regulator, you must check with the inner family to see if the story is ready to be fully or partially disclosed and witnessed. If the system is not yet ready, it should be guided to support, validate, and resource the part holding the memory or story in the sand tray. Dialogues, conflicts, and resolutions are physicalized in the sand. The memory can be placed in a container for later, and the client should be reassured that the right time will be found for the inner family to embrace it.

When these life experiences exist in the world of symbols, they remain contained and validated by their existence in the physical and symbolic world. We offer the client a titration continuum and gradual entrance through the portals that lead to traumatic events. Information may emerge in the tray without words, hidden under the sand or coverings, partially or fully seen, or accompanied by verbal narratives.

If the client and their system have not developed enough integrative capacities for memory processing, preparation-based strategies described in Chapter 3 may be used, with modifications to accommodate the internal system of parts. For individuals impacted by chronic trauma, a resource tray and an open container are often set up and kept accessible for regulating overwhelming affects when they arise. This is especially important when accessing trauma explicitly and directly. The resource tray is created before the clinician invites any trauma exploration, identification, or processing. Integrating verbal and symbol-based narratives offers a comprehensive approach to healing within EMDR–sandtray work. Some elements of the trauma emerge more easily through metaphors and symbols, while others long to be verbally acknowledged and explicitly known.

For clients with divisions in their sense of identity, start with the least disturbing experiences. Green, yellow, and red trays provide a titrated and gradual approach to explicitly accessing traumatic memories (clients may also choose their color scheme to symbolize the spectrum of activation, ranging from mild to highly disturbing). Green sand carpets a protected area for low-activation memories, yellow sand furnishes a zone for more disturbing experiences, and red sand provides a refuge for the most disturbing events. However, chosen colors may change as the client's mind assigns the appropriate valences of intensity and activation to each color selected.

Phase 2: Advanced Capacity Building and Strategies   **141**

Begin with the green tray, inviting the client and their different parts to pick figures that represent memories of difficult, painful, hurtful, or traumatic experiences *that are the easiest to remember and bring into awareness* (use the language most appropriate to the client's development and verbal capacities). Encourage the client to conduct safety checks and temporal orientations, and to represent safety in the sand tray as often as needed. When and how to travel into the trays that will hold greater intensity in association with trauma will depend on the client's tolerance and capacity to stay aware and grounded in the present.

After working with the "green memories," invite the client to go into "yellow memories," and so on. Sometimes, the clinician may stay with the green tray for some time and initiate reprocessing with green memories before identifying those associated with yellow and red. Use the emerging data on the client's presence, stability, and homeostatic repertoires to guide moment-to-moment decisions. Reprocessing phases will be addressed in greater depth in Chapters 7 and 8.

The exploration of trauma memories in individuals with early and chronic trauma often requires titration and segmentation of the process. In-and-out strategies (Gómez, 2013, 2021a) and pendulation, which quickly move the mind from the trauma back into present safety and homeostasis, may be necessary for treating trauma that exists within a narrow window of affect tolerance. For many, the first entrance into memories of trauma may bring turbulence that can be attenuated by the resources already prepared and installed and the coregulating forces offered in the therapeutic relationship.

CHAPTER 5

Systemic Work
With Parents and Children

Children often present in therapy with issues manifesting from trauma that spans generations. Inner representations shaped by lived experiences, relationships, and the intersectionality of cultural identities create complex memory networks in the parents' minds that influence how they navigate through parenthood. I propose the concept of a shared memory network that extends beyond individual synaptic systems into a shared biological space in which two or more minds are mutually altering and activating their life stories. This includes a shared AIP system in which information processing operates individually and systemically in the caregiver–child space. The biological imprints of trauma mold parenting styles, relational patterns, defensive and self-protective strategies, autonomic tendencies, and resilience. Exploring how the parent's mind is shaped and organized will provide insight into their motivations, emotions, cognitions, and impulses, shedding light on how embodied experiences contribute to their overall parenting behavior. Clinicians explore somatic markers, such as muscle tension, respiratory changes, and arousal, that influence the parent's moment-to-moment decisions, meaning making and responses to their child. Additionally, through sandtray-based strategies, clinicians support parents in developing the capacity to regulate affect and in deepening their embodied knowledge and understanding of bodily cues and inner representations, which guide parenting. In EMDR-sandtray-based therapy, clinicians work with the interaction between the body and the mind to transform and heal the parent–child bond.

Supporting the healing of a child becomes particularly challenging when they continue to experience harm from pervasive toxic and impoverished relational patterns. As such, working closely with the relational ecosystem and engaging in systemic work is crucial. Accessing the deep injuries of the parent and child is not a linear process; it is convoluted and intricate. Caregivers rarely provide well-organized verbal narratives about these rooted

143

relational patterns and generational wounds. Instead, the parent and child disclose these life stories nonverbally, often through relational reenactments. This material usually does not reach the clients' conscious minds. Therapists must, therefore, remain observant, curious, attuned, and in sync to notice subtle shifts, ruptures, and disconnections between the caregiver and child as well as moments of joining in, reciprocity, resonance, coregulation, and connection. When words fail and implicit knowing governs, sandtray work creates an opening for the nonconscious/implicit mind to express itself. Observant, curious, and attuned "companions" can gather data that will aid them in formulating a treatment plan and a comprehensive view of what exists intrapersonally and interpersonally as the child and parent join into a shared memory system and a "we territory."

Systemic work is often necessary when the child's symptoms result from intergenerational wounds. Caregiver–child intervention is among the most effective mental health interventions (van der Kolk, 2021). If the caregiving system is not functioning optimally, it will be reflected in the development and organization of the child's inner world, their relationship with the self, their homeostatic capacities, and their overall ability to navigate relationships and challenges. Intrapersonal capacities (one's relationship to the self), interpersonal competencies (to engage and relate to others), regulatory capacities (to modulate arousal and affect), and neurocognitive capacities are all impacted by exposure to complex and relational trauma (Vliegen et al., 2023).

Sandtray work provides an open space and built-in containment to explore parent–child dynamics, to scaffold dyadic resources, to increase integrative capacities, and to process traumatic memories. In EMDR–sandtray, parents become active companions and partners in their child's healing journey and developmental recovery. The sand world becomes a portal into the child's and the caregiver's internal representations and working models. Shared patterns of autonomic activation also emerge in the tray and the parent–child relational choreographies.

A Shared Memory Network

The AIP model posits that the human apparatus has an innate capacity for information processing (F. Shapiro, 2018; Hensley, 2021) and integration (Siegel, 2020). However, the mind coexists within relational milieus and a shared neurobiological circuitry that holds life stories and affect regulation tendencies. As a result, information processing is a shared and interconnected phenomenon that is stimulated or hindered by collective companions. The child's and the parent's memory systems and biologies continually interact moment-to-moment, leading to connection, regulation, and homeostasis or affective imbalances and profound disruptions in the child's homeostasis and sense of self. In the sand tray, the shared neurobiological and relational circuits become visible, especially to the client's consciousness. The clinician delivers active invitations to unblend the implicit and explicit relational models internalized by the caregiver and the child. The child's strategies to elicit care and the parent's caregiving tendencies and capacities arise as they coconstruct sand worlds, giving the clinician a view of the child–caregiver relational landscape and repertoire.

The Attachment System

The child's attachment system is also a biological, interpersonal, and prosocial system that is fundamentally involved in promoting protection and regulation through seeking proximity to the caregiver (Bowlby, 1988; Liotti, 2017). Experiences during critical developmental periods shape the child's neurobiology, affect regulating systems, and identity formation (Schore, 2019). Children raised by parents who were consistently nonreciprocal and neglectful, emotionally blind, and inexpressive become self-reliant. These children have no other option than to shut down their need and desire for closeness. These recurrent experiences during crucial periods of growth and development, significantly shape the child's brain and nervous system.

According to Siegel (2010), individuals raised in cold, distant, and rejecting relationships develop understimulated right brains, leading to an excessively dominant left brain as a survival mechanism in response to distant, rejecting, and neglectful caregiving. The clients' minds find refuge in the linear, logical, and emotionally distant left brain. These clients may construct worlds and stories that reveal a bias toward the hemisphere that gave them refuge (Badenoch, 2008).

Anxious children of preoccupied parents receive unpredictable, undependable, and intrusive care that prevents and hinders differentiation. These children and their parents may be more influenced by the emotional right brain (Siegel, 2020). These early and repetitive experiences shape the children's biology and relational tendencies. They may construct sand stories that reveal their preoccupation, anxieties, and enmeshment.

Children and adults who have been exposed to chronic traumatization and who carry attachment wounds often develop defenses and trauma-related phobias, which become evident in the tray as the defenses and phobias block access to and expression of inner wounds and conflicts. Dissociation, avoidance, idealization, placation, perfectionism, control, and so forth are often shared generationally. To coexist with the caregiver's insufficiencies, these children had to internalize the parent's defenses and self-protection strategies.

Constriction and dysregulation may be evident in the tray as well. Worlds that lack coherence and that show significant disorganization may tell the story of a child who was/is forced to be in a relationship with caregivers that activated two systems: defense and attachment. These children were exposed to multiple and incongruent models of the self and others (Liotti, 1992) and had to disengage and dissociate to cope (Farina et al., 2019). Preoccupation and anxiety may surface in the tray as may truncated defense responses that could not be completed while the traumatic event was occurring. Fight, flight, and cry for help may appear through characters and symbols. These caregiver–child dyads may surface through worlds where characters engage in constant battles that never resolve.

Clinicians who remain observant of their clients' emerging bodily states can invite them to shift from character to self and character to body to deepen the exploration, especially during reprocessing phases. Clients who use placation and denial as their primary adaptation mechanisms may create superficially positive worlds that depict wishful thinking rather than real issues. It is crucial that highly defended clients not have their defenses stripped away. Remember that these arsenal helped them survive painful experiences.

Further chapters will explore the intricate and delicate work required to navigate around and through defenses while acknowledging their vital role in the clients' survival and coping strategies.

The Caregiving System

According to Panksepp and Biven (2012), the caregiving system is an inborn motivational and social engagement system with abundant neurochemicals that ensure maternal care will provide joy. The authors further emphasize that the child–caregiver relationship is fundamental to the development of the child's homeostatic repertoire and capacity to respond to stress.

However, trauma, primarily relational trauma, within the caregiver–child relationship ruptures the coordination and synergy of attachment and caregiving behavior, resulting in the absence of a coherent attachment and caregiving strategy (Solomon & George, 2011). The child, in an effort to survive, develops a strategy to awaken an abdicated, collapsed, or sympathetically mobilized caregiving system. The child and caregiver as a result of the activation of traumagenic networks can move out of connection, coregulation, reciprocity, and social engagement into defense, self-preservation, and disconnection (Porges, 2017).

The caregiver embodies a complex duality, offering solace and injury. They may alternately be a source of homeostasis, connection, and balance and a force of wounding and trauma. When the caregiver holds unresolved trauma, they feel, experience, see, and give meaning to the child's attempts to elicit care through their lenses of traumagenic memory systems. The parent's mentalization and mutual regulation capacities become compromised, resulting in parenting behaviors that lack consistency, reciprocity, and coherence. The parent's asynchronous responses are manifestations of the activation of memory systems and defensive reactions mediated by disrupted autonomic states that perpetuate trauma into the next generation. This underscores the importance of involving the parent as an active therapeutic partner to break the cycle of intergenerational trauma.

The movie *The Story of the Weeping Camel* profoundly illustrates the healing power of relational bonding. The mother camel, traumatized by a painful birth, rejects her calf, severing the natural bond between them. The camels are gently invited to rediscover and connect with one another through music, songs, caresses, a nurturing environment, and companionship. The nomads create a harmonious, safe, and regulated environment and perform a powerful bonding ceremony through which the mother and her calf can heal and bond.

Similarly, the EMDR–sandtray clinician provides the relational safety, companionship, coregulation, and the transformative power of EMDR-sandtray-based therapy to the caregiver and child. Like the music in the camel story, EMDR-sandtray-based therapy supports the restoration of connection, belonging, and homeostasis in the caregiver–child relationship.

Developmental and complex trauma is relational, interpersonal, and marked by attachment ruptures (Spinazzola et al., 2021). Therefore, the healing process must involve corrective and reparative relational and interpersonal experiences. A caregiver who mentalizes and engages in coregulation and co-homeostasis becomes a powerful bioemotional regulator and healing agent.

Phase 1: Gathering History and Exploring the Parent–Child Relationship Through Sandtray Strategies

The sandtray work provides a profound gateway and avenue to explore the parent–child dynamic and relationship. A myriad of dyadic, nondirective approaches and playful strategies can open a window into this sacred relational territory. The clinician compassionately and respectfully enters the interpersonal realm where caregiving and care-seeking forces join in a relational dance that may occur either synchronistically or in complete misattunement and disorganization.

These asynchronous or wounding parent–child dynamics are often not reported verbally, as they remain outside a client's awareness. Instead, they manifest through reenactments and implicit portals, such as play themes and relational dynamics unfolding in the therapy room or playroom. If these harmful dynamics become habitual shaping forces, they can hinder or slow the efficacy and outcome of EMDR-sandtray-based therapy.

Nondirective Sandtray Strategies

Before inviting a parent to join the child's session, the clinician needs to obtain the child's permission and acceptance. When in the exploratory phase, the clinician should aim to observe how the dyad interacts, makes decisions, and resolves conflicts. However, it is essential to establish boundaries to preserve the safety of each participant.

If both parents or primary caregivers are available, you may conduct sessions with each individual and/or both together. This can provide valuable insights into each parent's relational tendencies and caregiving strategies and to the overall family dynamic.

Once the parent and child are present, invite them to play in the sand tray. You may invite them to play in the sand or you may directly prompt them to create a world. You might say:

> **"** I would like to invite you to create a world together. The first step is to select the figures you are drawn to. Don't think about what you will do with them; just pick the ones that attract your attention."

Once the child and the caregiver return with their chosen figures, invite them to create a world however they want. Remind them that there is no right or wrong way to play or work in the tray and that anything they want can happen in the sand world.

Once the world is crafted and both parties agree it is complete, the decision power, regarding who responds and how they invite words to their creation, is shared. Remain curious (not judgmental) and observant of what unfolds in the tray and what emerges in the intersubjective field between the *storytellers* and the *companion (the caregiver and the therapist)*. Observe and pay close attention to the following:

1. **Organization of the World**
   a. How do they manage the organization of the world?
   b. Identify the roles: Who directs the process, and who follows?
   c. Are they able to cooperate, or do they exhibit dynamics of control, dominance, and submission?
2. **Decision-Making and Conflict Resolution**
   a. Explore their approach to decision-making and conflict resolution.
   b. Identify the leadership and communication style of the client and

caregiver: Is it authoritarian, controlling, critical, collaborative, or punitive?

   c. Recognize areas that generate conflict and those that are manageable and enjoyable.

   d. Does the caregiver deliver invitations to coregulate when there is conflict, and does the child accept their efforts?

   e. Do they engage in power struggles in which coregulatory capacities and reciprocity are largely absent?

3. **Creation of Worlds**

   a. Determine whether they created two separate worlds or successfully cocreated one world.

   b. Note patterns of autonomic activation that emerge during the process.

4. **Parent–Child Interaction**

   a. Examine how the child attempts to elicit care and how the parent provides care.

   b. Observe the relational tendency: Is it disengaged, detached, avoidant, conflict-prone, anxious, or preoccupied?

5. **Coherence of the Tray World**

   a. Evaluate the world's coherence: Does it present as a cohesive narrative, or does it feature disjointed elements?

   b. Assess agreement on the world's content and acceptance of differing perspectives.

   c. Identify conflicting elements: Are narratives dominated by conflict or loneliness and despair?

6. **Attachment Dynamics**

   a. Explore how the attachment system is represented in the tray.

   b. Are there active caregivers in the story? How do they care? Are they absent or immobilized? Are they angry, critical, and authoritarian?

   c. Assess the presence and nature of caregivers: Are they active, absent, immobilized, caring, angry, or critical?

7. **Body-Based Data and Nervous System Patterns**

   a. Observe body signals and rhythms: Pay attention to patterns of muscle tension, respiratory rate, eye contact, and facial expressions.

   b. Note patterns of tension in the upper and lower extremities indicating fight-or-flight responses.

   c. Identify tendencies and impulses present in the parent–child interactions.

   d. Observe whether the child moves away from or toward the parent.

   e. Do they present a highly mobilized story, dominated by wars and grievances, or a lonely and depressed world?

E. Interaction With the Clinician
   a. Assess whether the child and caregiver seek to please or to antagonize the clinician during the session.

Gently explore the world while giving the caregiver and child space to decide who will respond and how they will respond. Through the stories and relational dynamics unfolding in the tray, the caregiver and child can explore and practice new ways of interacting, coregulating, and connecting. For instance, one mother and her child created a story about a small raccoon stuck in a big storm who did not receive help or support from his family or friends. The clinician invited the dyad to be curious about the raccoon's feelings and what he needed. The child stated that the raccoon needed to be rescued, and the mother said he also needed to feel safe. The clinician invited curiosity again and provided small kernels of psychoeducation regarding the need we all have for safety and connection. In the tray, the raccoon was reunited with his mother, and the child and caregiver played the roles of the raccoon and the mother. The mother helped the raccoon return to safety while the clinician continued to wonder how the mother raccoon could support a sense of relational safety, regulation, connection, and homeostasis. Although these practices were challenging in real life, this dyad found joy in role-playing their stories in the tray, which gradually began to transform their relational dynamics. The clinician often invited the dyad to bring their awareness to how the raccoon expressed his emotions and needs and to what he needed from his mother. The caregiver and the child connected through moments of safety, coherence, reciprocity, and regulation within the interpersonal relationships of the characters while observing and guessing the avatar's emotional and body-based experiences. These connections and affective states were enhanced by BLS/DAS. Sometimes, the clinician invited the parent or the child to shift their awareness from a character to their self and wondered how it was for the child and the parent to witness such moments of connectedness and safety while offering BLS/DAS.

When approaching the end of a session, invite the caregiver and child to jointly decide how they want to close the session and to rearrange the world to close the sand story. Additionally, you may inquire about how they want to dismantle the tray. If they want to participate, observe how they manage a task that the child or parent may not enjoy and thus slightly activates the attachment and caregiving system. Observe their individual and collective conflict resolution and coregulating capacities if there is conflict. If escalation occurs, you may intervene to help them manage the divergences and arrive at a place of compromise. Notice whether the invitation to mutually regulate is accepted or rejected. If mediation is not possible, this provides important insights into the vulnerabilities, the effectiveness of caregiving strategies and the child's care-seeking tactics. If a conflict arose around the end of the first session and the dismantling of the tray, allocate more time for closing future sessions while using these experiences of conflict as opportunities to engage the dyad in mutual regulation.

If you receive prior written consent from the caregiver and child, you may use videos therapeutically with the caregiver. Video microanalysis—a method used in multiple approaches, protocols, and coding systems—involves recording and analyzing moment-by-moment caregiver–child interactions. The goal is to enhance parental sensitivity and attachment security while reducing attachment disorganization (Cyr et al., 2022; Moss et al., 2018). This methodology can be used to augment parental capacities for synchrony, regulation, and reciprocity, complementing a systemic approach to EMDR-sandtray-based therapy. I have created a video microanalysis protocol to complement EMDR therapy and EMDR-sandtray-based therapy (Gómez, 2023b), wherein dyadic EMDR-sandtray-based sessions are videotaped. These videos become a valuable resource for supporting the parent in learning, practicing, and experiencing the heart of coregulation and coorganization of experience.

During video microanalysis, the clinician invites the parent to observe the child's emotions, body-based cues, behaviors, and needs as well as their emerging internal representations, emotions, cognitions, behaviors, and somatic data. The videos are also tools for exploring moments of rupture that result from the activation of the child's and the parent's trauma networks. The clinician draws awareness to how and when these ruptures occurred and how they can be repaired.

The caregiver's clinician can also investigate, through the videos, the traumagenic systems and ruptured autonomic states that were awakened by the child. The parent may further explore their past experiences of traumas that have not been integrated and that the child continues to activate. Additionally, the videos allow for the identification of resources and moments when the parent exhibited parental capacities for connectedness, reciprocity, and regulation. These instances can be enhanced with BLS/DAS to promote realization and awareness in the parent–child relationship.

The sandtray themes that the child and parent create can support or challenge the information gathered from intake. In one case, a mother reported that her child, who was coming to therapy due to reports of severe depression and aggression, had a great life and was part of a nurturing family. She struggled to make sense of her child's extreme emotions and behaviors. Despite the perfect picture the parent presented about their lives, they both created worlds characterized by themes of loneliness, fear, and abandonment.

The discrepancy between the verbal narrative and symbolic representation in the tray suggested a deeper conflict within the family dynamic. The meaning attached to the story created by the parent and the child in the tray was dissonant, ambivalent, and conflicted. The child often refuted and opposed the mother's narratives. In response, the mother would become quiet, distant, and disengaged. Her gaze and body were directed away from the child and the tray, and she did not make any attempts to coregulate with the child, who remained emotionally abandoned.

These relational dynamics deeply challenged their verbal narratives about a nurturing and connected family. The findings showed an emotionally distant and relationally deficient environment where the child's needs for connectedness were unfulfilled. Nevertheless, the mother had organized her autobiographical accounts around defenses and a narrative that protected her from pain or responsibility. Despite her best intentions, her own early relational trauma interfered with her desire to support and connect with her child.

Directive Sandtray Strategies

A directive approach can also yield valuable information. For instance, the clinician may invite the dyad to create a sand world about their relationship: what works well, and what is an area of conflict. Using two trays, or dividing one tray into two sections, can help the dyad depict these two facets of their relational tapestry. You can invite the parent and child to create a world with the theme "a story about us" or ask them to create a representation of their relationship. You might use the following prompt:

> " I invite you to take the basket and select figures that represent things about you and your relationship or how you get along. Remember, the tray is a space where anything can happen and what you want to say/show can be expressed. Take a moment to think about you two, how you get along, what you like or may not like, and what feels safe or unsafe about your relationship. When you're ready, choose your figures."

Follow the tray exploration stages with both the parent and the child. You may notice differences between the sand worlds the child creates with each caregiver or within the one created by the collective family unit. The questions and observations recommended when using nondirective work also apply to directive work. Please use the world exploration strategies discussed previously.

Closure is an essential part of every session. Explore how the parent and child want the story in the tray to end. Address whether any figures need to be relocated. Furthermore, the clinician should ensure that both the parent and the child regain (if compromised) emotional balance and return to homeostasis and regulation. Sufficient time should be allocated for regulating the parent's and the child's nervous systems. The clinician may invite them to engage in embodied experiences of play, singing, breathing, humming, or dancing. These activities can help restore the dyad or family to a state of homeostasis, connection, and emotional balance.

Working Individually With the Caregiver

If the parent is willing to undergo individual therapy, the clinician may begin by inviting them to create a world that represents themself as a parent. What is it like to be a parent, what gifts and challenges are present, and what resources have supported them through the journey of parenthood? The parent can begin either with a nondirective/open tray or with one that directs their conscious mind to focus on parenting, such as a tray based on "my life with [child's name]" or "parenting [child's name]."

These trays serve as a portal into the parent's inner world and are a window into their representational system. The tray provides a unique opportunity for the parent to explore what activates them and how they interpret the child's behaviors, emotions, and needs and how they respond.

The exploration of the tray, accompanied by the curious and intentional mind of the clinician, becomes a path toward increasing the caregiver's mentalization capacities. The clinician actively uses reflective listening and communication, mirroring, curiosity, validation, and compassion, which collectively contribute to a corrective experience that becomes part of the tapestry the caregiver and the clinician coconstruct.

For instance, one parent created a tray about her experience with a child who had long and intense temper tantrums. In the tray, she physicalized her child, along with her fear and anxiety surrounding parenthood as tired figures. When the clinician invited her to explore the symbols in the tray, the mother reported that she perceived her adopted child as a burden and believed that the child only wanted to overpower her. The meaning attached to the child's emotional dysregulation, fearfulness, and desperation was misconstrued and negatively skewed.

As the mother and clinician observed the tray and sat with the emerging somatic, emotional, and cognitive data, the clinician validated, witnessed, and accompanied the mother. The clinician facilitated a transition from the objects (miniatures/characters) to the mother's self-awareness and invited the mother to notice how her pain felt in her body while representing it in the tray. Using heavy figures and slow physical movements in the tray, the mother showed how her pain was burdensome and deep. The clinician validated the heaviness and long-standing pain while providing a safe space for dialogue with the emerging information in from the tray.

Systemic Work With Parents and Children   **153**

As the exploration continued, the clinician invited the mother to be curious, without judgment, about what may lie at the core of her child's behaviors. Initially, the mother could only perceive that the child was trying to overpower her. However, the clinician's invitations opened a much greater field of possibilities, which began to emerge within the sand tray and in the mother's field of awareness.

The clinician used a segmented and titrated approach to psychoeducation, giving the mother tiny drops of information at a time that could gradually challenge insecure and trauma-formed internal working models without overwhelming her system. Segmented psychoeducation might sound like this:

- Children with deep injuries may show their pain in challenging ways.
- Children need someone that can help them feel safe.
- Sometimes, children show they need safety and protection in hurtful ways.

Preparation Phase

Working With the Caregiver's Inner Representations

With the information collected in the initial phases, a clinical and relational tapestry emerges that guides the clinician's treatment organization. The clinician creates a plan and road map that highlights the parent's strengths and the areas that need development.

In the tray, we can gradually introduce new relational possibilities, parental responses, collaborative decision-making, and problem-solving. Culturally affirming resources and psychoeducation that honor the parent's unique qualities and challenges are also offered in the therapeutic process. The sand tray is a space where the parent can explore the intersectionality of identities and how these identities intermingle with their parenting. Caregivers may develop complex adaptations in response to long histories of exposure to power imbalances, oppressive practices, and marginalization that have the potential to affect their parenting capacities.

The clinician devotes therapeutic time to promoting the parent's ability to understand and give meaning to their inner reality (thoughts, emotions, behaviors, and sensorimotor responses) and to their child's. By actively addressing the parent's internal working models and inner representations, clinicians can provide a more comprehensive approach that scaffolds the parent's skills and capacities and empowers them to be an active partner in their child's healing and growth.

The child's clinician will initiate some work with the parent and, if appropriate, refer out to determine the most suitable therapeutic approach.

154 EMDR-Sandtray-based Therapy

This process may involve deciding between standard EMDR therapy and EMDR-sandtray-based therapy. Individual treatment for the parent may also be essential, particularly when navigating complex issues such as generational trauma, attachment injuries, or deeply ingrained patterns of emotional and behavioral responses. The child's clinician should maintain clear boundaries regarding how much of the parent's autobiographical memory would be explored in the sand tray. The parents should understand clearly that they are assisting as collaterals, not as clients. Sandtray work with parents should focus on exploring the child's life, symptoms, relational patterns, and so forth. Generally, the child's clinician should avoid inviting the parent to create worlds that depict their histories and personal issues unless the clinician is working individually with the caregiver. Sandtray work has the potential to open up the mind in ways that cannot be predicted. Even regular talk therapy can expose and activate a parent's history of trauma, so sometimes intruding into the deeper layers of the parent's mind is unavoidable. Understanding the parent and the functioning of the caregiving system can significantly support the provision of coherent and solid treatment. This treatment should address the systemic issues and generational wounds often present in children with complex trauma and dissociation.

The following is an integrative, transtheoretical, and attachment-based systemic model that works with children and their caregivers within an EMDR framework (Gómez, 2013, 2021a). Multiple degrees and domains of parental involvement and interventions may be used in EMDR–sandtray therapy.

1. Safety
2. Psychoeducation
3. Emotion regulation (coregulation and self-regulation), affect tolerance, and mentalization
4. Memory processing and integration
5. Dyadic work and repair

The tray is the vehicle of communication, expression, and exploration in each tier and domain. The extent and depth in which the parent participates will depend on the child's and the parent's goals, vision, and readiness. Clinicians should tailor EMDR–sandtray to meet each child's and parent's particular needs and capacities.

Safety

Cues of safety, relational reciprocity, and belonging provide the foundation for repairing and reestablishing social engagement after trauma (van der Kolk, 2021). These safety cues within the therapeutic process in EMDR-sandtray-based therapy promote connectedness, predictability, consistency, reciprocity, and congruency, resulting in a radically visceral and embodied experience. The metaphorical and symbolic nature of sandtray therapy, united with EMDR, provides the space for the child and parent to explore and navigate the intricacies of relational safety while fostering mutual discovery. The sand characters may awaken physiological and visceral states, signaling safety and danger cues and giving the caregiver and child space for moments of shared consciousness.

Trauma, especially relational, represents an assault on the child's sense of safety that permeates their sense of self and identity. As a result, children are unable to accurately assess cues of danger and safety, becoming mobilized/immobilized in the presence of safe relationships or misreading actual cues of relational danger. The sand tray becomes the theater that offers the child many possibilities to experience themselves and the world in different ways while in the safety, companionship, and containment offered by the clinician and the caregiver.

Through individual sessions, the clinician actively invites the parent to engage in sand world explorations to discern multiple domains of safety that can be transferred later to the we-space between the child and the caregiver. These repetitive experiences support the creation of a new synaptic architecture and adaptive network and the repatterning of previously disrupted autonomic states in the caregiver. The clinician cocreates safety moment-by-moment with the child and the caregiver. The clinician may use microadaptations such as intentionally changing intonation, using silence, becoming more verbal, or moving closer or creating distance to allow the child and the parent to pause and down- or up-regulate their emotional states. These adaptations promote safety, coregulation, and co-homeostasis and offer opportunities for new meaning-making that is radically grounded in the visceral felt sense of safety.

Active pathways recruit social engagement by challenging feelings of safety through neural exercises that intentionally move the child and parent in and out of a ventral vagal state (Porges, 2021). In the sand worlds, the child and caregiver experience various physiological rhythms through the avatars that challenge their sense of safety and open up a space to repair previously ruptured autonomic states of safety. The presence of the parent and the clinician broadcasts safety cues while embracing traumatic stories that challenge safety, simultaneously offering the autonomic nervous system a possibility for repair. For example, when an angry lion chases a baby giraffe in the tray, the parent, under the guidance of the clinician, can protect the giraffe and contain the lion. This allows the sympathetically mobilized child to return to homeostasis, safety, and social engagement.

156 EMDR-Sandtray-based Therapy

Psychoeducation

The sand tray provides a powerful and sacred space for symbolic representations of parent–child dynamics and the expansion of awareness and consciousness. The tray acts as a passive and active portal through which the parent can deliver safety cues to their child. When the character in the tray fulfills longings, receives previously unavailable information, attains completions, and returns to homeostasis after facing danger, fear, and instability, the child's nervous system receives these restorative offerings.

The tray serves as a reliable and safe vessel for integrating and advancing psychoeducation in both dyadic and individual sessions with the parent. It facilitates the blending of the two hemispheres of the brain—the symbolic wisdom of the right brain with the verbal processing of the left—enhancing understanding and connection. As caregivers gain insights and realizations, the clinician invites them to represent these in the tray. Through this process, the parent is assisted in individual sessions to explore and learn about coregulation, attachment needs, connection, resonance, attunement, and contingency.

Guiding the parent's mind to attune to the child's mind through reflective communication, thoughtful questioning, and symbolic representations in the tray fosters the reorganization of working models and relational templates rooted in insecurity and distrust.

In the tray, clinicians can weave in reparative information and segmented psychoeducation in small, digestible kernels. This segmented psychoeducation allows the parent to integrate these pieces of adaptive information while physicalizing them in the tray. For instance, you might incorporate analogies and metaphors from the parenting wheel (Gómez, 2021b) into the tray (see Chapter 11). These include a thermostat (the role of an external bioemotional regulator), a dresser (the role of a coorganizer of experience), and an accordion (emotional bandwidth and affect tolerance that allows the parent to accompany the child in accessing a wider range of emotions), among others.

When exploring a tray focused on issues related to the child's perceived problematic behaviors, emotions, and needs, challenges may arise if the parent struggles to recognize possibilities for understanding the origins of the child's behavior. In these cases, offer information about how the parent can use their thermostat or dresser in the tray. Symbols and metaphors, easily bypassing the parent's defense system, assist the caregiver in integrating the essence of coregulation, coorganization of experience, and the cocreation of new meanings around parent–child dynamics. When the parent is "educated" on "good parenting practices," they often hear that they are not good enough, triggering shame that often disrupts the therapeutic relationship and, ultimately, the treatment outcome.

You might invite the parent to represent in the tray one of the incidents with their child that challenged their regulatory capacities by asking questions like:

> ❝ As you look at the figures representing your child in the tray, what emotions do you notice they may be experiencing? Could they be lonely, sad, or hurt?❞

If the parent is unable to see beyond their own restricted and trauma-influenced representations, segmented psychoeducation can help guide them toward new possibilities and insights. Here is an alternative approach:

> ❝ Let's be curious and wonder if there are other possibilities. Perhaps they long for connection but do not know how to ask for it. It's possible they haven't learned how to ask for connection and may not even realize that's what they want and need. I wonder what would happen if you used your thermostat and dresser to modulate their emotional temperature. Let's see how this would happen in the tray.❞

If the parent resonates with these new potentialities, invite them to bring figures into the tray that represent them. Sandtray work allows parents to embrace new capacities procedurally as they mobilize figures in the tray, enabling them to practice coregulation and signal safety. The parent's therapist may enhance these new understandings and realizations with BLS/DAS.

For instance, when the parent reaches an aha moment, the clinician might direct them to notice how this new awareness feels in their body. While delivering short and slow sets of BLS/DAS, the clinician might say:

> ❝ As you look at the tray and the new realizations, and your awareness about your child and the possibilities for connection, let's notice what happens in you. Notice the emotions arising and the area of your body that holds this new experience and awareness. As you focus on this, let's tap back and forth to enhance this knowing and the accompanying emotions within you.❞

Using BLS/DAS to enhance the caregiver's progress, should occur in the caregiver's individual sessions—not the sessions in which the caregiver accompanies the child in their therapeutic sessions. When awarenesses arise in a psychoeducation session during the child's treatment, the clinician should invite the caregiver to breathe, to take in and reaffirm their new insights and realizations.

158   EMDR-Sandtray-based Therapy

Emotion Regulation, Affect Tolerance, and Mentalization

Inner implicit maps contain cognitive, emotional, somatic, and behavioral schemas that influence meaning-making and that guide caregiving behaviors. Caregiver responses may be rooted in trauma-formed procedural patterns that continue to cause ruptures in parent–child affective exchanges. Sandtray therapy allows the parent to physicalize these internal working models and to explore their parenting tendencies and impulses. As parents learn to use passive and active pathways to promote safety and regulation, they also capitalize on more complex ways to coregulate through reflective function and mirroring.

However, a parent carrying unresolved trauma will see their child through the lens of their pain, assigning, at times, distorted meanings to the child's attempts to elicit care and regulation from them. Hence, the mirroring these children receive is entangled with their parent's misinterpretations that emerged from the parent's past trauma. Consequently, memory systems that harbor a distorted perception of the child, which in turn shape parental behavior, are developed and strengthened.

Mapping and sequencing activating and injurious interactions in the tray can bring these wounding dynamics to the forefront. This process enables transformation, paving the way for restoration of natural rhythms of connection and love. The sand world allows the parent to explore and represent their internal configuration, inner dialogues, and decision-making sequences around parenting. This approach can work more easily around shameful states that would otherwise impede the parent's active participation in the child's therapeutic process.

For instance, when the caregiver comes to an individual session complaining about the child's behaviors, invite them to create a representative moment-to-moment sequence of the behavior in the tray. Felicia, 36-year-old mother of Naomi, a highly oppositional and aggressive 10-year-old girl, would often express disappointment and exhaustion with Naomi's behaviors. The clinician invited Felicia to represent the challenging interactions in the tray, moment-by-moment.

> "Let's start right before the chain of events began. I invite you to pick the figures you need to create this event in the tray."

Once Felicia placed figures representing herself and Naomi engaging in a power struggle, the clinician invited the mother to slow down to notice the emotions emerging for her and her child, her body sensations, and her emerging thoughts and beliefs. The mother was invited to physicalize the child's signals, strategies to elicit care, and her unspoken needs. The clinician delivered small segments of psychoeducation and actively invited the mother to search for possibilities that could allow her and Naomi to connect and coregulate. Frequently sequencing moment-to-moment decision-making in the tray supported the mother's realizations and increased her mentalizing capacities.

EMDR–Sandtray Parenting Protocol: Accessing the Caregiver's Inner Representational World

The following is an EMDR-sandtray-based parenting protocol that integrates parts work and the "wiser and guiding self" to enhance mentalizing and coregulatory capacities. It aims to expand the parent's field of awareness, restructure their internal framework around parenting, and restore their coregulatory synergy and shared coherence. This protocol emphasizes the parent's role as the wiser-older-guiding force and external bio-emotional regulator in the child's life.

Step 1: Create Space in the Tray. To begin the therapeutic process, we invite the parent to engage with the sand tray while exploring the space within that influences their parenting behaviors. Focusing on moments of activation with their child can bring about valuable insights into the cognitive, emotional, somatic, and behavioral schemas activated during parent–child interactions. Here is how you might introduce the concept:

> " The tray is a unique space where we can explore and sequence what happens when you interact with and parent your child, especially during the most challenging moments. In the tray, we can externalize and examine anything that may create conflict or challenge you in your relationship with your child."

We invite the parent to engage with the sand tray and miniature collection while providing safety, acceptance, and companionship cues. This supportive environment encourages the parent to explore their inner landscape and gain deeper insights into their parenting dynamics, fostering a greater understanding of themselves and their relationship with their child.

Step 2: Physicalize the Internal Representation of the Self and of the Child. Once a safe space is established within the tray, invite the parent to connect with their inner representations of themselves and of their child, focusing on the presenting issues and perceived challenges with the child.

Here is how you might facilitate this process:

1. "Can you direct your attention inward while exploring the miniature collection? Hold your child's mind in mind as you pick a figure or fig-

ures that represent your child during one of the most challenging moments for both of you. Allow the figures to guide you without judgment. If judgment arises, pick a figure that represents the part of you that is judging you or the process."
2. Invite the parent to place the selected figures in the tray without interference.
3. "Let's take a moment to sit with this representation. Allow this image (or these images) of your child to enter your awareness and the space of knowing within you at a pace that feels right for you. Does it feel complete, or do you sense that other figures must join for the tray to feel finalized and whole?"
4. Give the parent time to reflect on their tray and add figures if needed.
5. Once the parent indicates that the tray feels complete, encourage them to focus inward: "Let's gently shift your awareness to how you see yourself in relation to your child during this most demanding time. As you do this, let the figures accompany you in characterizing and embodying yourself as a parent."
6. Allow the parent to bring as many figures as needed to externalize their inner configuration during conflicting times.
7. Invite the parent to verbally explore and share the symbols representing the child and themselves.

Sophia, the parent of an adopted child who faced significant behavioral and emotional challenges, chose a big monster with three heads to represent her child. She stated that she always felt she had to walk on eggshells around her child, fearing sudden outbursts and aggression. She then chose two figures with stiff and unyielding postures that radiated a sense of impenetrability, one with arms firmly folded across their chest. To deepen the experience, the clinician invited Sophia to delve deeper into her feelings and experiences by connecting with the symbolism in the tray. This process aimed to help her explore any additional emerging

FIGURE 5.1 A caregiver's representations of their child (monster) and themself during a conflicting moment.

emotions or thoughts, allowing her to gain insight and understanding into her situation.

Step 3: Explore Cognitive, Emotional, Behavioral, and Somatic Schemas and Temporal Orientation. Once the internal representations are physicalized in the tray, explore cognitive, emotional, behavioral, and somatic patterns using the following prompt:

> " Take a moment to notice what thoughts accompany this moment and representation of yourself and your child. What beliefs exist underneath these inner maps? Once you have connected with them, look at the figures and select the ones that will embody them. Now, let's check the emotions that accompany such an activating and triggering moment with your child. I invite you to drop into this place of knowing and notice the emotions that emerge as you interact with your child. Once again, choose the figures that represent these feelings."

Follow the parent's pace and rhythm. Slow down when necessary to deepen the experience, or speed up if the parent's natural rhythm demands it.

You may offer bits of information about how embodiment and somatic intelligence refer to the experience of exploring how we exist in a body and how the body influences cognitions, emotions, behaviors, and relationships. Emphasize the interconnectedness of the mind and body and how entering this dimension opens a pathway into a deeper connection with the self and with important relationships with others, especially our children. Invite the parent to connect to their body and notice how and what their body communicates in response to their interactions and dynamics with their child. Then, direct the parent to pick figures that represent the embodied aspect of their experiences and place them in the tray. Encourage the parent to remain present with the unfolding and emerging experiences, exploring the origins of their affective, somatic, behavioral, and cognitive schemas. This exploration allows the parent to gain insight into how their body carries and expresses memories.

> " As you hold the sense of inadequacy, let's connect to when it first came into your life. What stories surround this experience? When did inadequacy become a part of you? Who holds these stories within you? There is a story keeper and a story holder that has been carrying this for you since the moment the world gave this to you."

Temporal orientation is an integral part of our work, considering that many individuals affected by trauma live in trauma-time, responding to the present as if the past was still governing their lives (F. Shapiro, 2018; Steele et al., 2017).

> ❝ I invite you to discover how long these beliefs, emotions, and body sensations have accompanied you. Are they old and familiar or brand new? Let's find a figure, or figures, that represent where they exist in time and space."

In Sophia's case, after she represented herself and her child, she physicalized her belief of not being a good enough mother as well as her shame, powerlessness, distance, and anxiety. She then connected to her body and represented her shame's slow and heavy rhythms. She identified a little girl in the tray as her shame holder, a girl who had to endure endless criticism from her father.

You may invite the caregiver to trace back (Young, 2002; F. Shapiro, 2001, 2018) or perform an affect scan from the moment of activation elicited by the interpersonal transactions with the child. When tracing back, invite the caregiver to find memory systems that hold traumagenic material that becomes activated by the interactions with the child.

Once again, we invite the parent to deepen the experience and sit with what is developing in the tray. Inviting awareness while weaving in adaptive information will support the development of mentalization and mindful awareness in the parent. You might say:

> ❝ I wonder what comes up for you as you recognize these old stories that your much younger self has been carrying—stories that continue to shape how you see, feel, and perceive your child."

Invite the caregiver to physicalize any material emerging in the tray while considering their needs and window of tolerance. It is crucial for the clinician to continually cocreate a sense of safety as they accompany and support the parent in their explorations.

Step 4: Access and Physicalize the "Wiser, Older, and Bigger Self." Connecting with the wiser and most capable self within the context of caregiving taps into the parent's inner strengths, resources, resilience, and wisdom. This work helps parents navigate parenting challenges while staying connected to themselves. Guide the caregiver to go within and connect with their bigger/older/guiding/wiser self. This self may or may not have a name. Let the parent decide what to call it. You might say:

> ❝ I invite you now to go within, to that inner space of knowing (and wholeness), and connect with your bigger, older, guiding, or wiser

self. You are most connected to this guiding self when you feel capable, compassionate, confident, centered, and balanced. It guides you during emotionally charged moments, offering a sense of direction. As you connect with even a sliver of its energy, pick a figure to represent it, and place it in the tray where it can be witnessed. Notice what it feels like to unite with the natural rhythms of being and the embodiment of your guiding/wiser self."

Once the tray represents and reflects the parent's inner experience, identify their body's response to new insights and realizations and their accompanying affects. Enhance this embodied experience with slow and short sets of BLS/DAS.

" Now, through the eyes of this wiser self, anchored and grounded in compassion and a deeper understanding of your child's essence, take another look at your child. What do you see? Choose figures that represent this new knowing."

Guide the parent to practice observing through the eyes of their wiser self without judgment, fostering a deeper understanding of the child's embodied mind. Slow down to allow the parent to connect with insights and expansions of awareness occurring in their minds and in the sand tray.

You may provide small segments of psychoeducation and adaptive information on how the child's behaviors and actions are their child's best attempt to communicate their longings and deeply held attachment needs, as well as expressions of their unhealed wounds and trauma. As the parent expands their field of awareness, they also realize new potentials and opportunities to see their child's uniqueness and inherent qualities and capacities.

The parent's wiser self can now see the child's pain and challenging behaviors through a lens of compassion, acknowledging the child's life story and their journey toward healing and wholeness. At the same time, the caregiver can see themselves through the eyes of the compassionate, wiser self while understanding the challenges of parenthood. As a representational tool, the tray provides a safe space for the parent to physicalize new visions, understandings, and realizations, depicting these new expansions of consciousness.

If the parent's connection and exploration of their wiser self needs further encouragement, consider using these prompts:

- Think of a time when you felt strong and capable, especially in your interactions with your child. Reflect on moments when you sensed wisdom guiding your decisions and actions during challenging times.

164   EMDR-Sandtray-based Therapy

What capacities and strengths supported you through adversity? Can you recall moments of intuitive guidance that helped you find your way through challenging situations? How does your body communicate messages and signals that guide your actions and parenting behaviors that support your child? Let's explore these moments, as they often indicate the presence of your wiser self.

- Take some time to sit with this information and notice the feelings that arise as you connect with your wiser self. How do you feel now as you reflect on these moments? Let's find figures to represent the different aspects of your experience.
- How do you experience the presence of your wiser/guiding self in your body? How does your body signal your connection to your inner wisdom?
- When you think about your child's challenging behaviors, can you look inside and reach into your inner wisdom? Can you connect with this place in you that can best understand your child's requests for care? The part of you that can see beyond challenging behaviors into your child's deepest longings/needs? This is the wiser self within you.
- Once you find the connection with the wiser/guiding self, let's find a figure or figures that represent it.

Once the parent has established a relationship with the wiser/guiding self, invite them to connect with its felt sense. Help them identify the present emotions and body sensations, and use BLS/DAS to enhance and strengthen their newfound relationship with the self.

As the work continued with Sophia, she was prompted to view her child through the eyes of her wiser self. Reflecting on this perspective, she expressed that she saw a hurt and wounded child who sought the connection he needed in challenging ways. She acknowledged her child's pain, and so she physicalized this new understanding by choosing a figure to represent her child's need for love underneath his violent behaviors and another to represent herself as a supportive mother. Slow/short BLS/DAS was used to enhance this new knowing and realization.

Step 5: Access Additional Resources. Other resources can support the parent in their often-challenging task of parenting children with deep wounds and trauma. Consider the following prompt:

    ❝ Who can accompany you through this journey of parenthood? Think of people, animals, religious figures, nature companions, friends and family, superheroes, or any others who provide you with the qualities and support you need to meet the demands of parenting.❞

Systemic Work With Parents and Children   **165**

FIGURE 5.2 The caregiver's second representational tray. The younger self carries negative metaperceptions (dragon), emotions (ram), and somatic experiences of heaviness associated with parenting (rocks). The other figures represent the caregiver's wiser/guiding self as well as the relational and ancestral resources and assets.

FIGURE 5.3 The caregiver's third representational tray. From their wiser, guiding self, the caregiver now perceives the child's challenging behavior as a manifestation of their pain and deep need for connection.

Externalize any companions in the physical world by placing them in the tray. Once they exist in the tray, they can be installed using standard procedural steps. With guidance from the wiser self and supportive companions, invite the parent to continue mentalizing the child.

Questions about the child's feelings and needs challenge and change maladaptive and distorted internal working models and inner representations of the child and the self. Here is how you might facilitate this process:

1. "As you connect with your wiser self, consider what your child may feel and the thoughts, needs, or impulses they may hold." Invite shared curiosity and the representation of these experiences into the physical world.
2. Allow the parent to be and sit with the sand world, observing the emerging data: "How does this want to be witnessed?"
3. Invite the parent to enter the realm of possibilities: "Is it possible that your child is confused about what is happening? Do they need your acceptance, appreciation, or companionship, but don't know how to ask? Your child has experienced losses and pain within a short life and may be afraid of abandonment."
4. Allow responses or reflections to arise through the expressive channel

of EMDR–sandtray work. If words do not arise, allow the caregiver to resonate with the nonverbal and felt sense of their experience.

5. While embodying compassion, invite the client's wiser self to connect to their younger parts that carry past burdens. Gratitude and compassion may emerge, presenting the clinician with an opportunity to enhance these moments of awareness, gratitude, and compassion using BLS/DAS.

6. Sometimes, these "moments of knowing" may carry feelings of grief or sadness connected to the child or their relationship with the child. "How does it feel to acknowledge and connect with this pain? Let's see if a figure or simply a space in the tray can represent this experience."

7. How any emerging information wants to exist in the physical realm is up to the longings of the caregiver's mind. Sometimes, their mind will be ready to be openly witnessed, known, and realized in the tray; while other times, it may want to remain hidden. Use a continuum of titration that respects the parent's mind's yearnings. "Can we spend some time being with this deeper knowing of what is unfolding in this moment of grief or sadness? Is it ready to show up, open and complete in the tray, or does it want to hide? Let it come out in whatever way it wants to be witnessed. Let's explore how your body communicates this to you, and let's sit with this as you form a connection that flows in synchrony with you now."

8. The clinician now has the opportunity to weave in adaptive information. "As you notice the hurt in your child's heart, let's explore what they might need. Does your child need you to stay connected? Does your child need your internal thermostat to help regulate their inner state? Let's take that in and see what emerges in you. Whatever unfolds, let's represent it in the tray."

Sophia, for instance, placed bridges in the tray to represent her desire to get to know and understand her child. Afterward, she stated that her child needed love, so she placed figures in the tray to represent her son's needs and her newfound awareness.

This protocol is designed to support the parent in increasing their awareness and mentalization capacities when conflicts arise between the child and the parent. Mentalization is state-dependent (Fonagy et al., 2002), so when the parent feels safe and grounded in their wiser and guiding self, they are able to access their mentalization capacities and genuinely understand the deeper causes behind their child's baffling behaviors. However, when the parent's own memory systems that hold traumagenic material and previously disrupted autonomic states become activated, mentalization is no longer accessible. This affects their capacity to accurately assess the child's requests for care. This work aims to transition the parent

Systemic Work With Parents and Children   **167**

from biased, survival-based views and perceptions of their children to an expanded capacity for mentalization, connectedness, reciprocity, and synergy with their child.

Step 6: Closure. Ensuring the stability and emotional balance of the caregiver while moving into deeper explorations of their inner system is paramount. Coregulating while using breathing, state change strategies, or mirroring supports the caregiver in learning and incorporating these capacities procedurally instead of just cognitively. Use closure procedures to ensure the parent's homeostatic state before ending the session.

Dyadic Resources: Working With the Child and the Parent in the Preparation Phase

Invite the child to notice the sand images and emotions and how they are embodied when dyadic resources, strengths, happy memories, and relational assets are spotted in the joint tray. Follow this with slow and short sets of BLS/DAS.

Sand worlds containing shared hopes and visions for their future are essential resources, fostering play, connection, and relational safety. The tray allows the parent and child to witness each other's embodied minds, increasing reflective practices and emotionally attuned connections. They can dive into collaborative explorations of disagreements, tensions, and conflicts. Sequences in the tray are powerful representations of the interactions between the parent and child. They encapsulate and acknowledge both the tangible, concrete dynamics and the subtle, implicit, affective, nonverbal, and embodied undercurrents in their relationship. By exploring these sequences, they can delve into the complexities of their conflicted moments and gain a deeper appreciation and understanding of the subtleties and nuances that contribute to their dynamic.

The sandtray work offers a sacred space for the often invisible, intangible, unspoken affective, and embodied experiences that significantly shape the parent–child dynamics to manifest through avatars in the tray. The characters play out, implicitly and/or explicitly, the child's and parent's struggles and conflicts as well as their assets, fostering empathy, relational coherence, and compassion.

As an external bioemotional regulator, witness, and companion, the clinician guides the parent and child to delve into the interpersonal realm and intrapersonal dynamics that shape the overall relational landscape. When dyadic understandings occur, the clinician may invite short and slow sets of BLS/DAS to further deepen the therapeutic process and understanding. This approach helps facilitate growth and healing within the parent–child relationship.

168   EMDR-Sandtray-based Therapy

In the case of Joseph, 6, and his father, frequent arguments and conflicts arose related to Joseph's defiant and aggressive behaviors. Power struggles and verbal arguments were common, likely exacerbated by the absence of Joseph's mother, who died when he was 3 years old. Since then, Joseph's father has introduced multiple potential mothers into the family dynamic, often blending and rupturing different family structures. Ultimately, all of these relationships were unsuccessful. During the preparation phase of EMDR-sandtray-based therapy, the clinician focused on increasing coregulation, relational safety, and reestablishing trust within their relationship.

The father was invited to multiple sessions with Joseph's consent. During one session, Joseph and his father created separate sand worlds to represent their most recent conflict. Joseph had broken his younger sister's toys. When confronted by his father, Joseph ran out the door, and his father had to chase him. They chose to use separate trays to physicalize their subjective experiences. Afterward, they exchanged trays and shared their perspectives, both tangible and verbal, as well as the aspects of the trays that remained unseen or unnoticed, which the clinician helped them explore together. They agreed to listen to each other's stories. The clinician facilitated mentalization with questions, such as:

> " I wonder how you felt in that moment and how you feel now. Can we ask the boy in the tray what he needs now?"

In cases of complex trauma, the clinician often needs to offer menus and possibilities, especially if the parent or child experienced deprivation and insufficient caregiving early in life. The following questions can help address the deep-seated emotional needs arising from trauma:

- Do you need someone to tell you that things will be okay? That you are not alone? Or that you are still loved even after breaking the toys?
- What do you want your parent/child to see and know about your sand world?

Menus become important when either the child or parent is stuck in polarizations within a restricted field of awareness, constrained by unintegrated trauma. Through thoughtful exploration and reflection, the clinician guides the family toward healing and understanding, fostering a supportive environment for growth and development. You may use BLS/DAS with the child during moments of resonance, understanding, and connection.

Guessing and Meeting Unmet Needs. Experiences of neglect, deprivation, and inadequate caregiving profoundly impact a child's neurodevelopment, often leaving them with unmet longings and attachment needs. The parent serves as a secure base, fostering a sense of safety and belonging, and acts as a bioemotional regulator for the child's stress system. Restoring synergy, coherence, and reciprocity in the parent–child relational dynamic is crucial for the child's emotional security, regulatory capacities, age-appropriate exploration, and identity formation. For the child's needs to be met, the child is encouraged to express their physical and emotional yearnings through signals and actions. In response, the caregiver works to understand and recognize these cues, responding contingently to address and fulfill the child's needs. Additionally, the caregiver needs to accurately represent the child's mental landscape and reflect it. Trauma ruptures the synergy that is required to fulfill the child's deepest longing, and the therapeutic process works on repairing these ruptures.

The sand tray provides a versatile and valuable space for the child to communicate their needs nonverbally, enabling the clinician to support the parent in understanding, accurately representing and reflecting, and fulfilling the need. The protection and containment offered by the sandtray symbols allow the parent–child exchanges to take place while maintaining the distance that a child with complex trauma and a narrow intimacy threshold may need. Trauma-related phobias may interfere with the fulfillment of the child's profound yearnings. In the sand tray, the child can receive the offerings and the fulfillment of having their needs validated, seen, and met without consciously owning the experience. The caregiver is also invited to mentalize and, while holding the child's mind in mind, identify and fulfill the need.

Psychoeducation around needs is often necessary; the child and parent may be invited to bring figures into the tray to represent plant, animal, and human needs. Depending on the child's comfort levels, they may prefer to work through avatars instead of representing themself. The child can create an implicit and nondirective world and select characters to identify and fulfill their needs, like in the TAPAS protocol. The child may give cues to the caregiver, who is invited and guided to guess, represent, and reflect the character's needs and take action to fulfill them.

For instance, a child named Lori created a world where a small, hungry snake walked through the desert. To signal the snake's needs, Lori brought figures, such as a container with food, a small pond, and a house, into the tray and buried the snake to represent her stress. In response, Lori's father was invited to hold in mind and reflect the needs of the snake. Under the guidance of the clinician, the father told Lori the snake needed love, companionship, and water, while describing and reflecting the ways in which the snake showed him her needs and distress. Once identified, the charac-

FIGURE 5.4 **A sand world of a child (Lori), symbolically representing the needs of the snake for water, food, shelter, and love. Her father was asked to guess and fulfill the snake's needs.**

ter and the child determine how, who, and what is introduced into the tray to address the character's needs.

When working implicitly with a character, direct the questions and reflections to the character:

- How does it feel for [character] to have their needs seen and known?
- How does [character] feel?
- How does [character]'s mom/dad guess and understand what they need?
- How does [character] want to be loved?

Sometimes, menus or options are helpful to support the identification of embodied needs. If the parent is invited to fulfill a need, you might ask:

"Does [character] want mom/dad to come close, hug, kiss, or just let them know they're not alone?"

Once needs are acknowledged, reflected, and fulfilled, identify the emotions and embodied sensations and use short and slow sets of BLS/DAS if the response shows comfortable and regulated emotions. The duration of this attachment-focused play can vary based on the child's window of tolerance for positive and negative affect and their intimacy threshold.

Similar to the TAPAS protocol addressed in Chapter 3, the child may be a witness or a direct participant in the tray, as a figure may explicitly represent the child and their needs. Additionally, the clinician mirrors and reflects moments when the parent and child nonverbally and verbally join in shared experiences of joy and connection (if in synchrony with the moment) slightly amplifying their intimacy threshold and window of positive affect tolerance. Inviting physicalizations in the tray and using BLS/DAS to "paint in" or "march in" the experience and its accompanying affect builds and expands the caregiver's and the child's homeostatic and relational repertoire. The clinician supports the parent and the child in finding moments of delight and closeness as they work together in the sand tray. The clinician takes the opportunity to join and use BLS/DAS.

The Defense and Self-Protective System of Parents and Children. Another issue that can be explored in the sand tray is the child's symptomatology's role in the family dynamics. Consider asking:

> "How does the child's symptom serve the system, and what is its function?"

Parents may find that focusing excessively on their child's issues diverts attention from their own unresolved trauma and conflicts. This fixation can inadvertently amplify the issues they want to decrease. Invite the parent to represent the function of the child's problems in their lives and within the family in the tray.

For example, Liz and Joe brought their hyperactive and "clingy" son to therapy. They reported that he was like a "fly," constantly buzzing and "bothering" the family. However, Liz and Joe also shared a distant relationship and never addressed their relational issues. Instead, they focused on their child's perceived problematic behavior. Joe was an attorney, and Liz was a stay-at-home mother.

As they explored their concerns using the sand tray and miniature collection, Liz placed figures that represented her sense of inadequacy compared to her successful husband. Her child's issues, while bothersome, kept her occupied and relevant because she brought her son to multiple professionals and she devoted significant time and effort to his care.

The family lived in a relationally impoverished environment where coregulation and connection were utterly absent. Physical touch and connection were experienced mainly through the family dog.

When Liz and Joe represented these issues in the tray, they began to better understand their child's behaviors and their roles as their child's bioemotional regulators. This process allowed them to acknowledge and address underlying family and marriage issues that contributed to their child's behaviors.

Target Identification and Reprocessing Phases With Caregivers

When working with parents grappling with unhealed trauma and adversity that interfere with their capacity to parent the child and promote safety, regulation, connection, and reciprocity, it is essential to prioritize the processing of the parents' unresolved issues and parenting-related triggers. Sandtray strategies offer a valuable tool to enrich individual work with the parent, allowing the exploration of multiple targets for reprocessing that may emerge during the preparation phase. While the parent physicalizes their cognitive, emotional, behavioral, and somatic responses to their child within the sand tray, the clinician can help trace these responses back to earlier experiences of trauma and adversity. This process provides insight into how past experiences shape present reactions, enabling the parent to understand the origins of their triggers and parenting responses.

Clinicians may also invite the parent to create a tray containing representations of triggers that emerge directly or indirectly from interactions with the child.

The following steps are used in the sandtray to identify triggers and targets with parents:

1. Connect to the Moment of Activation. Before delving into difficult material, assess the parent's regulatory capacities. If needed, allow them to bring companions or resources into the tray that can support them through the exploration of activating stimuli and trauma memories.

When working with a parent who experiences dissociation, assess the severity of their dissociative tendencies and their ability to cope with potential emotional distress. Ensure that sufficient preparation and stabilization occur before delving into any traumagenic material with these clients. Additionally, create a resource tray to anchor the caregiver in the present safety and provide greater accessibility to resources when they are needed.

To begin the session, invite the parent to slow down and connect with themselves, focusing on moments with their child that challenge or trigger strong reactions. You might say:

> ❝ I invite you to take a moment to slow down and connect with yourself, reflecting on those challenging moments with your child that elicit strong reactions. Once you connect to these experiences, take a look at the miniature collection and choose the figures that can support you in telling this story."

Invite the parent to use the miniature collection to represent the challenging moments they experience with their child in the tray. After the parent has finished arranging the tray, invite them to reflect on whether the tray is complete and accurately captures the moments of activation elicited by the child:

> ❝ Does this feel complete and congruent as you compare your inner reality to what is visible in the tray?"

Systemic Work With Parents and Children **173**

Once the tray is complete, invite the parent to share their world. Safety, companionship, and presence are crucial as the parent embraces deeper embodied states left by trauma:

- I am right here with you as you explore these triggering experiences.
- I am holding you right here, right now. Let me know if the explorations feel too overwhelming. Remember that your companions and resources are here with you.

2. Trace Back to the Origin of the Story. Tracing back from parent–child triggering situations may be incredibly powerful in helping the parent understand how the child's behavior, needs, actions, or emotions evoke memories of trauma and adversity. Often, it creates a moment when the parent recognizes that their responses to the child, their perceptions and interpretations, and the meanings they attribute to the child's requests for care are influenced by their own experiences of attachment, adversity, and trauma.

Once the parent has represented the trigger, invite them to notice the thoughts, emotions, and body sensations that arise, and encourage them to select figures to represent the cognitive, emotional, behavioral, and somatic schemas. If multiple triggers are present in the tray, help the parent identify the most meaningful one and use it as a focal point for exploration. Encourage the parent to sit with and fully engage with the moment and the representations of their embodied experience. You might say:

> " As you connect with this moment that emerged in the tray, let's notice the thoughts, emotions, and sensations in your body. Let's trace back to find other times in your life that you have had these thoughts, emotions, and sensations in your body to discover its origins. When did these thoughts, emotions, and sensations, which your child continues to reactivate in the present, first enter your life? When and where did the world give this to you?"

You may guide the parent through an affect scan to help them gain a greater sense of their emotions and sensorimotor reactions. Allow the parent sufficient time to be with this information, and once the memories emerge, invite the parent to physicalize them in the tray.

3. Reflective Communication for Consolidation. Once the tray represents the targets and experiences at the core of the parent's self-organization in moments of activation, invite the parent to spend some time with them if enough affect tolerance exists. As a supportive companion, the EMDR-sandtray clinician can use reflective communication:

174   EMDR-Sandtray-based Therapy

❝ Let's take some time to explore what unfolded in the tray. What words come to mind about the larger picture of what happens when your child or other life circumstances trigger these inner experiences?"

Allow the parent to invite the voice of their left brain to construct the verbal story. You may also ask permission from the caregiver to verbally acknowledge the story and reflect it back:

❝ As your companion, may I reflect on what I see emerging in the tray and connect it with what you have shared verbally? When your child [repeat the physicalized description of the child], this experience may evoke thoughts like [name the figure representing the cognitive, emotional, and somatic schemas, such as, the polar bear symbolizes 'I am not good enough,' and the tiger represents angry feelings]. These experiences connect to memories that left an imprint behind, such as [briefly name the identified memories using the sandtray figures]. Sometimes, unknowingly, you perceive and understand your child through these lenses. These memories, thoughts, and bodily experiences become the glasses through which you perceive and interpret the present moment with your child. How does this reflection land/ arrive in your mind, heart, and body?"

After completing a trace-back or an affect scan, parents begin to recognize how their past experiences influence their perceptions and interactions with their child in the present.

When the parent has new realizations and understandings, invite them to represent them in the tray. You may also invite their wiser self into the tray to explore the contrasting perspectives and their different states of being with their child. While the wiser self holds a compassionate approach that emphasizes connectedness, belonging, and reciprocity, a parent's unresolved trauma, fear, and mistrust result in distorted views of the child, which may perpetuate generational wounds.

As you support the parent, help them recognize the polarity within themselves and in the tray: the vulnerabilities and pain on one end and the wisdom, presence, and compassion of the wiser self on the other. They coexist not as separate entities but as ways of being that seek integration and balance. Encourage the parent by saying:

❝ Let's hold both the wiser, guiding self and the part that holds the pain. They each hold different stories, experiences, and ways of seeing, feeling, and understanding the world, especially regarding your child. Take some time to be with what is unfolding in the tray."

Systemic Work With Parents and Children **175**

This level of work deshames and depathologizes the parent, shifting the perspective from a focus on deficits, pathology, and judgment to recognizing the joys and profound challenges of parenthood. This challenges socially held perspectives of "good parent" and "bad parent" and supports the transition toward a compassionate and growth-oriented approach. This perspective acknowledges the impact of trauma on individuals, how it shapes their thoughts, emotions, behaviors, and somatic reactions, which in turn influence their parenting. Simultaneously, it emphasizes the parent's capacity to find healing, growth, and integration. BLS/DAS is used throughout the process to enhance moments of realization and insight when the client is connected to comfortable and positive affective states.

Investigate Resourcing and Process Triggers

This therapeutic work can empower the parent to recognize that they deserve healing, especially with the understanding that their therapeutic work will positively impact their parenting. The reprocessing may be done in the tray or using standard EMDR procedures, depending on the parent's preference.

Encourage the parent to evaluate whether additional resources are needed. Extend the preparation phase to the point where they feel well-equipped to visit their memories of trauma. For parents who are not ready to process the imprints left by trauma, especially attachment trauma, reprocessing the parenting-related triggers can increase mentalization and reflective function.

Through reprocessing triggers, the intensity of the distress linked to the activating parent–child interactions may decrease, while understanding and insight may increase. This can restore the synchrony, connection, and reciprocity in parent–child relational dynamics.

Reprocessing Sessions (Phases 4, 5, and 6)

Clinicians should be fully prepared to accompany caregivers with interweaves (for a detailed description of interweaves, see Chapter 7) during processing sessions because they offer profound opportunities for integration and transformation that will impact the caregiver's relational capacities. Interweaves are used when information stalls and the caregiver is looping around the same issues. Often, caregivers who engage in wounding dynamics have experienced attachment ruptures and relational wounds that continue to impact the function of their caregiving and attachment systems. During reprocessing, these ruptures and imbalances need to be repaired.

176   EMDR-Sandtray-based Therapy

Reparative and Restorative Interweaves. When reprocessing early memories of attachment trauma with caregivers, the clinician may use interweaves that investigate the unmet needs of the caregiver's wounded younger self. If the caregiver's needs were never seen, acknowledged, and fulfilled, this can profoundly affect their capacity to respond in synchrony to meet their child's longings. When the caregiver can connect to their own missing developmental and attachment experiences and fulfill them, the process often creates an opening for a different legacy to be transmitted to their child and for the reshaping of the parent–child affective transactions. The following are potential interweaves for caregivers:

- "As you notice what is unfolding, I invite you to connect to your younger self. Let them show you or tell you what they long for. Notice their missing experiences and what they needed but did not get." Follow with long and fast sets of BLS/DAS. Once the need is identified, inquire about who will meet this need and how. The who may be the adult or the wiser self or a spouse, close friend, character, or their parent—either at the age they were during the past event or at a more experienced developmental stage (e.g., the much older parent is now capable, whereas the younger version of the parent was not).
- Invite visits to their inner child or the part carrying this hurt/wound/belief.
- Invite the caregiver to mindfully notice initial impulses from their younger self and their adult self and to represent them in the tray.
- Encourage a relationship between their wiser self and their hurt inner child and ask them to physicalize their dialogues in the tray.
- When reprocessing memories related to their actual child, the clinician may use interweaves that inquire about what the caregiver needs to enter the "we terrain," where connectedness and the fulfillment of the child's needs become possible. "What do you need to heal, know, or complete before you can enter the relational space your actual child needs?" Invite the caregiver to remain connected to the tray and to represent their findings, newly exposed wounds, and the pathway into the self that is required for generational repair.
- Invite the caregiver to notice and represent in the tray what was passed on to them by prior generations that they may be passing on to their child. The caregiver undertakes a profound journey of generational healing as they disentangle emotional inheritances and burdens as well as assets and resources while accompanied by the symbols offered by the miniatures. Invite the caregiver to select figures to represent the intergenerational strengths, knowledge, cultural wisdom, and resilience they received. The clinician supports the care-

Systemic Work With Parents and Children   **177**

giver in processing, integrating, and embracing the full spectrum of their ancestral legacy.

- As generational wounds enter the caregiver's field of awareness, the clinician may invite the caregiver to notice the impulses arising: "What is your first impulse? Is it to distance from it, give it back to prior generations, or hold on to it? What keeps you holding on to it?" Invite them to physicalize the impulses in the tray. If they choose to give it back, you may inquire about how they want to return it to past generation(s). If they choose to hold on to it, invite them to notice this impulse and to observe with awareness and without judgment which part of them is still holding on to it. You might ask, "Is there a message you need to get or any information you need to know before you let it go and give it back? How and to whom do you want to give it back?" Invite the caregiver to represent their realizations in the sand. This information may remain guarded by the symbols or emerge verbally. It is up to the caregiver's mind to decide.
- Sometimes, caregivers may have healing ceremonies in the tray, in which they symbolically release the burdens of trauma, emotional pain, learned behaviors, and metaperceptions. The pace and rhythm at which the generational wounds are accessed and integrated depends on the caregiver.
- Caregivers may realize generational and ancestral gifts that can now support their parenting. When the caregiver finds inherited capacities, the clinician invites awareness and observation of the tray and its symbols. How can this ancestral wisdom and capacity support the caregiver now?

Dyadic Work During Reprocessing Phases. The caregiver is invited to actively accompany the child while reprocessing memories of trauma and adversity once the caregiver has been adequately prepared to accompany the child. This makes the process predictable and establishes the readiness for the parent to tolerate the witnessing of the child's pain and trauma. The caregiver may deliver interweaves, under the clinician's assistance, that repair and fulfill unmet needs, support the completion of truncated responses, and accompany, validate, and mirror the child (Gomez, 2013). When the child gives permission, the caregiver is invited to provide support and nurturance, to fulfill attachment needs, and/or to rescue and defend. A wide range of possibilities exists for involving the caregiver in the tray when information processing stalls, helping to facilitate movement and create change. Consider the following example:

173   EMDR-Sandtray-based Therapy

❝[Mom/Dad], we want to invite you to come to the tray in the way [name of the child or the character] wishes. The [child in the tray or character] is alone and scared and needs help and companionship. [Child or character's name], what do you need in the sand world? How do you want to receive [love, companionship, support, etc.]? How do you wish to have [Mom/Dad] help [you/character] in this moment?❞

Let the child guide the process, step-by-step, and as the need is fulfilled or the support is provided, follow with fast/long BLS/DAS.

The caregiver may speak, sing, or provide verbal reassurance and information (e.g., "Little giraffe, I know you are lonely and scared, and I am right here and with you and your lonely feelings right now. I am sorry that the belly-mom giraffe left you. Sometimes moms and dads make choices that hurt others because of the pain they have inside"). Caregivers may repair ruptures they or other parents caused (adoptive parents may repair ruptures with biological parents). Caregivers may be invited to look into the eyes of the character or the child in the tray (or the actual child if this is what the child chooses) to let them know they are lovable and to join them in delight or sorrow if the child/character is longing for presence and companionship during moments of pain. Caregivers can use musical instruments to sing lullabies, celebrate a character, or soothe the child. The child is invited to represent what continues to emerge in their inner world as synthesis and integration occur with the fulfillment of unmet needs.

When completing defensive truncated responses, the caregiver and clinician can support the child by running, pushing, or accompanying them in executing movements, expressing unspoken words, or making other sounds. Vocalizations, grunts, and humming sounds may serve as a bridge to complete actions and access deep-seated emotions and sensorimotor material. The sound may emerge from the character, the child, the caregiver, and even the clinician. Through the avatar, the child may use a guttural sound to express anger or deep humming to convey a sense of sadness. It is often embarrassing for clients to express the sounds of the body. However, if the caregiver accompanies them, the child may find the freedom to embrace these inner sounds. After or while the sound is emerging, the clinician invites or delivers BLS/DAS.

CHAPTER 6

Phase 3: Assessment

During the assessment phase of EMDR treatment, the client's mind confronts remnants of disowned and phantom echoes of the past and faces its traumas and accompanying cognitive, emotional, and sensorimotor schemas. In this phase, the memory system is activated so it can be rewired, consolidated, and moved to integration and adaptive resolution. There are critical junctures and decision points, which require careful consideration as we explore each client's readiness, in the transition from the preparation phase into the assessment and reprocessing phases. However, this is a highly nuanced decision. As we transition from preparation into reprocessing phases, the question is not just whether the client is ready to enter traumagenic networks but how and which portals will be used. As an analogy, imagine the memory system harboring the traumatic event as a house. The house has multiple pathways for entry, including the front door, the garage door, a window, and the back door; though sometimes all these openings are locked, and access is available only through a hole in the wall. Each access route represents either an unbounded, open entrance or a highly constrained, incremental, or titrated entrance into the memory network. This analogy accommodates a rich tapestry of possibilities that capture the nuances of accessing memories of trauma when clients present with a wide range of capacities and challenges. The access route is selected according to the client's integrative capacities and their window of tolerance.

Assessment phase questions support the client's full entrance into the traumagenic memory network by creating a baseline and system activation. This chapter offers scripts, step-by-step procedures, and protocols that provide flexible guidance and options so the clinician can choose the appropriate pathway for each client. The clinician may decide to address each question and procedural step in this phase or deliver a shorter version. These decisions are multifaceted and should come from mastery of the EMDR model, methodology, and procedural steps. How to deliver the assessment phase depends on what is emerging at the moment and the client's overall therapeutic context and integrative capacities.

For instance, after a young client's story has been explored, the clinician may observe that there is already an area/part of the sand world that stands out for the client, along with negative metaperceptions and emotions. This child may not tolerate many questions, and moving forward with assessment queries may disrupt their process. In this case, the image, cognitions, and emotions are already activated and symbolically identified, so all that remains to be assessed in Phase 3 (Assessment) is their level of disturbance and the somatic correlates. The clinician's approach to the assessment phase is informed and guided by their understanding of its goals and procedures; the client's history and developmental and individual capacities and characteristics; the information emerging in the tray; the client's verbal and nonverbal data; and the clinician's felt sense of what is emerging at the moment. A clinician may follow the standard set of questions with an adult or adolescent client who demonstrates greater capacity and tolerance for verbal questioning while simplifying or shortening the procedural steps for a younger child.

The human mind is incredibly complex, and a fluid, responsive, and client-focused therapeutic environment that moves beyond a binary and rigid approach is encouraged. Conversely, the mastery and knowledge of EMDR phases and procedural steps will support decision-making and adherence to EMDR principles.

Decision-Making Markers

The following are decision-making markers to determine the client's readiness to transition into the assessment and processing phases. These markers should be applied flexibly while accounting for capacity and tolerance fluctuations from session to session and moment to moment throughout the therapeutic process.

1. Some level of positive and negative affect tolerance. The client's overall capacity to be with emotional states without becoming dysregulated or shutting down supports reprocessing and indicates that the client may be ready to access traumagenic networks and stories.
2. Some capacity to shift between states. This creates a foundation for the client to manage affect in and in between reprocessing sessions.
3. Sufficient work has been done to reduce internal conflict for highly dissociative clients. Otherwise, polarized dissociative parts in a highly contentious environment could become exceedingly dysregulated or shut down during reprocessing. In addition, the parts should have

arrived at a consensus and agreement about moving into reprocessing and the memory to be addressed.

4. With highly defended clients, the clinician should have engaged in some level of negotiation with the client regarding their defenses. Having sufficiently explored and communicated with the client's self-protective system is recommended.

5. There should be sufficient safety and trust between the client and the clinician as well as among the multiple spaces surrounding the complex therapeutic work.

6. Many of the client's capacities are observable and visible in the tray and remain open to cues and information emerging moment-to-moment. Here are two case examples:

   a. A 16-year-old male created a world with a wall dividing the evil and the good worlds. In the evil world, some sheep are fearful and hiding. Three dragons accompany an evil man in the evil world, and two other dragons live in the good world. In the middle, a baby was hurt by the evil dragons but was rescued by the good dragons. A powerful creature with wings cares for the baby and defends him from the evil man and his dragons. Adaptive information is clearly observed despite the depiction of fear and activation and a mobilization response. The powerful winged creature taking care of the baby, the dragons living in the good side, and the mere existence of the good side represent the client's resources, the adaptive information, and the capacity to access supportive figures. Additionally, this client is able to remain present and in connection with his therapist while exploring the areas of the tray that challenge his regulatory threshold, providing another sign of readiness and the presence of integrative capacities. Remember that readiness does not mean the absence of symptoms but rather the presence of enough capacities for processing.

   b. A 14-year-old female client created a story of a town ruled by monsters. The monsters were extremely powerful, and no one could fight against them. A little girl was often hurt by the monsters that kept her prisoner. This girl was on her own, as the monsters kept their doings secret and had wounded and taken away the powers of the fairy, who was the little girl's only protector. The child had no escape, so she began eating her fear. This emerging story is overtaken by powerlessness and helplessness and demonstrates an absence of any supportive, protective, or helpful figures. Even the potential helpers were consumed in fear and defenselessness. Any suggestions on the part of the therapists about the little girl seeking help were received with hopelessness and a refusal to make even the smallest attempt to find shelter. Moreover, the child often closed

182   EMDR-Sandtray-based Therapy

the tray rapidly after creating it, indicating it was too scary. The information in the tray corroborated what was observed in this adolescent's life. She often reported feeling disempowered, hopeless, and helpless. She would shut down and disengage in the presence of even minor triggers. The mechanisms and strategies depicted in the tray provided valuable information to support decision-making in determining the client's readiness for trauma processing.

7. A fundamental decision to be made as clinician and client approach the assessment phase is related to the access route that will be used to enter the memory system holding the client's traumatic memories, as well as the rhythm and pace of the process. The standard EMDR treatment has a powerful portal into the memory systems, represented by the front door and the complete assessment phase. Through this portal, traumatic states of consciousness and the various levels of information processing are fully activated, unbounded, and without constraints. Standard EMDR therapy Phase 3 and the reprocessing phases that follow it are a direct entrance into the memory network. However, clients with reduced integrative capacities, resulting from developmental and complex trauma, may find this standard EMDR portal dysregulating and too challenging to access. Despite abundant preparation, trauma-related phobias may persist or a highly susceptible internal system can lose connection to present-day safety and become dysregulated. In these cases, EMDR–sandtray work can offer the sanctuary and vessel to hold space for the traumatic events while providing various levels of distance and multiple portals (implicit/explicit). Following the rhythm of the client's mind is pivotal, especially when moving into the reprocessing phases. When aspects of the mind are ready to be seen, and their voices are prepared to be heard, they will make themselves visible and known in the sand tray.

Staging: Optimizing Integrative Capacities

Before moving into reprocessing, especially when the client realizes and acknowledges the experience of trauma in the sand tray, the concept of "staging" is worth exploring. This is a construct and a conglomeration of strategies to optimize the client's integrative capacities. It is also about coconstructing a platform to support the client during reprocessing. The following are some factors to consider when staging and building the processing platform in the tray.

Who Will Be Present During the Reprocessing Session?

Especially with young children, the caregiver may be a companion during sessions when traumatic events will be reprocessed. This should be established beforehand so the clinician can adequately prepare the companion to make the session and the process more predictable. Let the companion know their role in the session. Usually, if the caregiver will be invited, the child requests it or agrees to the clinician's suggestion that the caregiver be present. The following are some reasons to invite the caregiver to the session:

- The caregiver provides support, increases safety, and elicits a greater level of grounding and presence in the client. They are also able to support the child during reprocessing by delivering interweaves, under the clinician's guidance.
- During the reprocessing phases, the caregiver can repair, mirror, validate, witness, and meet the needs of the character or the child represented in the tray.

As the caregiver enters the sacred space in the tray, where the child's mind can be reflected, witnessed, and seen, the caregiver and clinician have a fundamental responsibility to compassionately accompany the child in ways that repair previously ruptured states and attachment bonds. Therefore, the caregiver must understand how to support the child, what to expect, how the session will be structured, why it is structured that way, and the interventions that will be used. Special consideration should be given to the various interweaves in which the caregiver may participate. Interweaves that repair need extra attention.

For instance, if the child is reprocessing the actual traumatic event—the self is acknowledged in the tray—the caregiver may be invited to deliver an interweave in which they recognize and validate the hurts the child has endured. The caregiver might say:

> " I am sorry I was not there for you. What happened was not okay and hurt you deeply. I am now working on becoming the parent you need and supporting you in the way you deserve."

These forms of repair can be very powerful if the statements are truthful, heartfelt, and honest, which is why the caregiver's readiness to do this deep level of repair must be established. Explore these issues openly with the caregiver so the session can be adequately structured and so the clinician has a map to understand the interventions and interweaves that the caregiver can carry out as well as those that may be uncomfortable for them and counterproductive for the child.

Companions

Badenoch (2018) states that the core of trauma is not the event but the aloneness with it. Many children, adolescents, and adults have endured trauma alone and in emotional isolation, so we want to put every effort into setting up the sessions, especially the reprocessing ones, in ways that provide repair. Clinicians intentionally create a space for clients to feel supported, witnessed, and accompanied as they confront their shadows and inner storms. Adult clients may also want to have a companion in some of their sessions. They may choose a significant other, a partner, or an important family member. However, it is essential to openly explore and discuss how the presence of a chosen companion might support or hinder the process, such as by inhibiting the liberties of the mind to tell its story.

Resources

All the resources the client revealed and developed in the tray during the preparation phase can be brought to the tray (in resource areas) or set up in a separate tray (resource tray) that is in the vicinity of the one holding the space for the traumatic event (trauma tray). For instance, the team of companions described previously can now join the client and the client's representations of their inner assets and resources. "Resource areas" can be created in the tray to actively accompany the client through the inevitable turbulence they will encounter as they journey toward integration.

The first step in creating the platform for reprocessing before fully moving into the procedural steps of assessment phase is to create the space for the client's resources. You might say:

> ❝ Since we are visiting the memory of what happened to you, I wonder who and what you would like to bring with you (if you wish). Let's create the space for your companions, advisors, special powers, and anything else you want to bring. They may be with you inside the same tray, or you can create a separate tray for them.❞

The client then chooses the tray or trays that hold the resources and the trauma. Barriers and boundaries must be established if the two will coexist in the same tray unless the client requests there be no boundaries or barriers. Boundaries may be demarcated using fences, rocks, figures, and objects. Sometimes, boundaries may be represented by a river, sand moved to the sides creating open space, a line drawn in the sand, or a wide river devoid of sand. Regardless, the client chooses where and how the resources and the trauma will be.

Some clinicians may worry that resources could become associated with the trauma because if the negative elements of the traumatic event are placed in close proximity to the resources in the tray. If this is a concern for you, explore it with the client and invite them to place their resources in a separate tray, or with expanded boundaries if the client strongly prefers to work with only one tray.

If there are two separate trays, the client should choose the appropriate distance between them. However, especially when working with children or clients who may benefit from movement, encourage the client to set the two trays far enough apart that they can walk, jump, or dance between them. This may be especially helpful when working with children or adults presenting with inattentive or dissociative symptoms because the act of standing and walking can keep the client grounded in their bodies and the present.

Some of the resources that can be included in the resource areas or the resource tray include:

- A team of companions (relational resources)
- An animal helper
- A small representation of the safe/healing place
- Ancestral and generational strengths
- Symbols of mastery experiences
- Inner powers
- Spiritual or religious resources

For instance, the client may identify speaking up as one of their assets or intuition as one of the internal resources they possess. These assets can assist them when information processing stalls, and the clinician can use them to deliver interweaves.

Anchors and Anchoring

Trauma creates ruptures in the mind's natural rhythms of connection to time and space. Temporal biases occur when the client constantly reexperiences the past, seeing the present through the lenses of the past (F. Shapiro, 2001, 2018; Hensley, 2021). For clients who tend to move quickly out of their window of tolerance, anchoring them to the present creates a foundation of safety as we begin to activate the network in the assessment phase. Multiple types of anchors can be used adjunctively with EMDR–sandtray work.

Time Orientation. Take some time to orient the client to the present safety, and then invite them to select a figure (or figures) that represents it. The figure represents the knowing that the trauma is over, that it is not happening in the present, and that right now they are safe. This anchor is

186 EMDR-Sandtray-based Therapy

usually installed during the preparation phase and is often an integral ritual of every session.

Auditory, Olfactory, and Gustatory Anchors. Although the sandtray work inherently anchors the client in the present due to its dynamics and procedures such as standing, walking, and reaching out to choose and move figures, some clients may require additional anchoring. Some examples of olfactory anchoring include a scent associated with the felt sense of safety in the present. Auditory anchors, such as music or sounds associated with safety, may also be used. The sounds or music should be audible but not disrupt access to the traumatic event. Gum can be a great gustatory anchor that activates digestive juices and salivation, and movement of the mastication muscles stimulates ventral vagal activity. However, gum may not be appropriate for children who choke easily or have allergies.

Distance and Coverings

Although the tray already provides distance, some clients, especially those with a phobia related to their memory, will need a much greater separation from it. The client can observe the representations of the memory in the tray from a distance. Binoculars can be used when a client is unable to tolerate being close to the space that holds their memory. This approach is particularly helpful for children, allowing them to make visual contact with the trauma tray from a safe distance through the binoculars. Movement, as the client pendulates and shifts back and forth between a trauma tray and a resource tray, supports presence, groundedness, and a sense of control. This dynamic process fosters an empowering neural exercise by integrating states of trauma with those of safety and resilience. The building of the trauma tray and the assessment phase procedural steps may happen all at once or gradually.

FIGURE 6.1 **A sand world using coverings to obscure highly activating areas.**

FIGURE 6.2 **Containers for disturbing/activating material emerging in the sand world.**

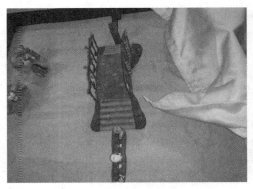

FIGURE 6.3 **A sand world holding space for resources on one side and disturbing material on the other. Solid coverings protect the client's mind from activating figures.**

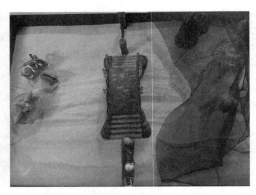

FIGURE 6.4 **A sand world holding space for resources on one side and disturbing material on the other. This client transitioned to using translucent coverings to have more contact with the activating figures.**

FIGURE 6.5 **A resource tray and a trauma tray using coverings for titration and gradual entrance into the trauma tray.**

Some clients may want to use tray coverings to hide the tray holding the traumatic event. This allows the client to observe the space holding the trauma while it is obscured by the fabric or to pendulate between lifting the covering for a few seconds and returning to the resource tray. Pendulation is a helpful technique for clients who are highly phobic of the memory despite robust stabilization. In-and-out strategies and pendulation protocols will be described later in this chapter.

Defenses and the Self-Protective System

To survive, the traumatized mind had to master the art of self-protection. The work with mechanisms of adaptation is interspersed throughout the eight phases of treatment. By the assessment phase, some level of work should have been done with these protective soldiers to obtain their permission to access the traumatic event. Defenses participate in the complex and multifaceted process of trauma integration. These mechanisms are not merely barriers, they are dynamic processes that can accompany the mind in preserving the delicate equilibrium between accessing traumagenic material and returning to safety, homeostasis, and protection when they are therapeutically welcomed.

As we approach the assessment phase, we intentionally embrace the intricate dance with these defenders. We invite the protector to be present while accessing and reprocessing the traumatic event. These protective parts can witness the process and express their concerns. The client's conscious and active involvement with their self-protective system facilitates processing, integration, and awareness. Protectors may be invited into the resource tray and can participate in deciding how the memory will be accessed as well as the pace, rhythm, and titration level. The client's protectors may agree to a slow pace or limited-time access to the memory. The staging process and the resources in the tray reassure the protective soldiers and give them a greater sense of control over the process.

Levels of Information Processing

The assessment phase is organized based on the established levels of distance from the traumatic event. Implicit access meets the mind in the "not me, not mine, not self" state of consciousness and remains in the refuge offered by the metaphor. The second and third levels use two forms of explicit access: one that can partially touch the neural network through the trigger, and one that is open to fully and overtly embracing the memory.

Implicit Access and the First Level of Distance: A Character-Driven Story

This portal is often used with children for whom nondirective and implicit stories that capture the child's inner battles and wounds become targets for processing. Trauma-related phobias, regardless of the gains achieved in the preparation phase, may persist, and the sand world can provide a back door into the traumatic events. In addition, play and the play metaphor may be some of the best and most developmentally appropriate ways of accessing traumatic events in young children. When using the stories created in the tray as targets, we are using the child's natural language, which inherently provides containment. However, we still arrive at this level of processing

Phase 3: Assessment **189**

intentionally and after making a conscious decision that is based on the child's overall capacities and level of stability.

For instance, a child may show significant symptoms but can shift states and is somewhat tolerant of affective data. They also have a nurturing and supportive environment that provides enough safety. This may be true of a resilient child in the foster system who demonstrates relational, regulatory, and homeostatic capacities while supported by a foster parent who is, overall, able to provide a safe relational environment, despite the inherent uncertainties of foster care. However, this child may still be somewhat phobic of the traumatic memories and, as yet, be unable to own them.

Alternatively, the case may be that the client's adverse events occurred at an age when explicit encoding capabilities were not fully developed. Attachment ruptures, the emotional unavailability of a caregiver, narcissistic wounds, role reversals, abuse at an early age, neglect, inconsistent care, and chronic misattunement, and so forth may remain below the client's awareness and out of their conscious mind's reach. These data may resurface only through reenactments, embodiments, and procedural and relational patterns. However, play themes and reenactments in the tray often show what the linear–verbal mind cannot express and acknowledge. When the decision is made to proceed with reprocessing, the assessment phase is set up with the world and the story the child created. The mind then tells its tales while in the refuge of the characters and avatars that will carry forward the untold story without the client having to own it. We meet the child in the "not me, not mine" space, allowing their mind to take shelter in the metaphor. For a child still holding on to an intense fear of a memory, this back door entrance provides asylum and a way to work around the phobia.

The process begins with an invitation to create a world using the procedural steps discussed in previous chapters. Once the world is complete, a short but sufficient exploration is completed before initiating the assessment phase's procedural steps. The main character becomes a central piece as it turns into the voice of the tray and the client's mind. The main avatar(s) is the direct storyteller and narrator of the story emerging in the tray.

Sometimes, the child may have some presence and ownership of the sand story. Although the story is not about them and they do not recognize themselves in the world, they may be able to identify the worst part of the world and even the emotions elicited in themself by the story. For example, they may express sadness as they witness the character's sadness in the tray. They may express anger while witnessing the characters get hurt in the tray. Accessing the emotions connected to the sand world explicitly and with ownership is achievable with clients who have cultivated an expanded capacity for tolerating affect. Keep in mind that the level of distance from the story may change from session to session, and even from moment to moment. If a client suddenly changes the distance, use reflective statements such as "I notice that your voice shifted and you said, 'This is me' when referring to the zebra. What should I call the zebra from this point on?" Stay with the level of distance established by the client, and dance with the shifts in consciousness and the movement from self to object and object to self. Remind the client that anything can happen in the tray, and they may shift and change as often as they desire.

After the world is created, the initial questions are intended to call forth a rather quick overview of what is emerging in the tray. Only a few minutes are allotted to the overview process to ensure plenty of time for reprocessing the world. Questions such as "I wonder if you can tell me what is happening in the world?" may suffice. However, if the answers are too vague, more specific questions should follow, such as "Can you tell me what is happening on this side? How does the main character see what is happening in the tray?" These questions should generate an overall idea of the story in the tray without eliciting copious details. Look for areas that show activation, conflict, relational dynamics, defenses, resources, emotions, polarizations, metaperceptions, and adaptive information. Once a general description of what is happening in the tray has been expressed, initiate the assessment phase and its procedural steps. Below is a comprehensive, step-by-step description of the initial implicit and nondirective world creation (Steps 1 through 5) and the assessment phase (Steps 6 through 12) using an implicit entrance into the traumagenic network.

Implicit and Nondirective World Creation and Exploration

Step 1: Invitation. Invite the child to create a world. You might say, "Let's begin by connecting with the sand tray and the miniatures. Let's invite your mind, your heart, and your body to participate. Let them guide you in choosing the figures." Give the child a basket for gathering miniatures.

Step 2: World Creation. Once the miniatures have been collected, invite the child to construct a world, story, or scene in the tray in any way they want. Remind them that anything is possible and anything they want can happen in the tray.

Step 3: World Completion. Ask whether the world feels complete or something needs to be changed, added, or removed.

Phase 3: Assessment   **191**

Step 4: Identify the Main Character. Invite the child to identify the main character and to indicate whether the child is part of the story. For example, "Are you in the story or world? Who are the main characters?"

Step 5: Tray Overview. Initiate a general exploration of the tray. You might ask, "What can you tell me about this world?" If the client does not offer sufficient information, use reflective statements, describe and acknowledge the silence while validating and normalizing it, or ask more specific questions. Once a general understanding of the tray is expressed, move into the procedural steps of the assessment phase.

The Assessment Procedural Steps

Step 6: Identify the Image. Begin exploring specific parts of the tray. Invite the client to reflect on the most important aspect of the world. You might say, "I wonder which part of the world [stands out/is more visible/is more important/is the yuckiest/is the worst part] for the [main character]."

You may also invite the child to be an active witness to the world. You may ask,

> " As you and [the main character] look at this story/world, what is the yuckiest part for both of you?"

It is important to stay within the level of distance established by the child. If the child is not in any way (active participant or witness) part of the story or world, stay with the character and direct all the questions to the character. For children who need a greater level of titration, you might ask,

> " What is the easiest part of the story? Which part of the world would [main character] like to focus on for now?"

Step 7: Identify the Negative Cognition. Invite the client to identify any negative cognitions they or the main character may have about the world. For example, "As you look at this story or world, what [mixed-up/negative thoughts] does the [main character] have about themselves now as they look at this part of the world?" Invite the client to represent the belief, if they choose to do so.

Step 8: Identify the Positive Cognition. Invite the client to identify the positive cognition they or the main character would like to have about themselves in connection to the part of the world that stands out. You may ask, "What is the [good/positive] thought the [main character] would like to have

192   EMDR-Sandtray-based Therapy

about themselves as they look at this part of the world or story?" Invite the client to represent the belief, if they choose to do so.

Step 9: Assess the Validity of the Positive Cognition. Introduce the client to the thought scale, and invite them to assess how true the positive thought from Step 8 feels. You might say:

> "Now we are going to use this cool thing called the *thought scale*. The thought scale helps kids check how true the good thought feels. Let me show you how it works. The thought scale has numbers that go from one to seven. The number one means that the good thought does not feel true, and the number seven means it feels very true. Let's practice using the thought scale with the good thought that [main character] picked. When [main character] looks at/connects to the part of the world that stands out [image identified in Step 6], how true do those words [thought identified in Step 8] feel to [you/the main character] now? Remember that one means it feels completely false, and seven means it feels completely true."

Sometimes, children are ready to play and work in the tray and the procedural steps of the assessment phase may seem lengthy to the child. In addition, as we actively work with the right hemisphere, procedures that draw primarily on left hemisphere functions, such as the validity of the positive cognition (VoC), may need to be skipped or introduced earlier during the preparation phase, so extensive time for explanation and practice can be minimized during the assessment phase.

Step 10: Identify the Emotions. Invite the client to assess their or the main character's emotions as they look at the tray. You might say, "When [main character] looks at/connects to [an image/part of the sand world identified in Step 6] and the words [a negative thought identified in Step 7], what feelings do they have now?" or "What feeling do you have as you watch/connect to [image identified in Step 6]?" Invite the client to represent emotions, if they choose to do so.

Step 11: Identify the Subjective Units of Disturbance. Invite the client to use the subjective units of disturbance (SUD) scale to assess their (or the main character's) level of disturbance. You might say, "How yucky/disturbing/bad/bothersome/upsetting does it feel, on a scale of 0 to 10?" or "How yucky/disturbing/bad/bothersome/upsetting does it feel for [main character], on a scale of 0 to 10?"

It is ideal to introduce the child to the SUD scale during the preparation phase so assessment time does not need to be used to explain and practice it. Additionally, it is recommended to use nonnumeric scales that align more closely with the symbolic nature of sandtray work. Measuring spoons and color palette strips that go from light to intense colors are playful ways of identifying the level of disturbance associated with a memory. Additionally, empty droppers (a drop) or spray bottles (a spray) may be used to express the level of disturbance (e.g., a drop of disturbance).

Step 12: Identify the Location of the Disturbance. Invite the client to assess where they or the main character feels the disturbance in their body. Have miniatures that the child can use in the tray to locate the disturbance in the body, such as a small "feeling finder" or "feeling detector." Use a figure, a magnifying glass, a small flashlight, or a wand to represent a feeling detector the child moves around their body searching for body sensations and disturbance. You might ask, "Where does [main character] feel it inside their body?" You might want to have a laser pen or small flashlight available so the child can point from a distance to an area in the tray or on the character where the disturbance is located.

Step 13: Prepare for Desensitization. Invite the client or main character to sit with the part of the sand world that stands out, along with their negative cognition, the associated feeling, and the place in their body where they experience it. Initiate rapid BLS/DAS as you begin the desensitization phase.

Explicit Access and the Second Level of Distance: A Story About a Current Worry or Difficulty

This level of information processing is utilized with clients who have already worked through several stories from the first level of distance and are beginning to recognize their triggers and current worries, or with clients who acknowledge their triggers but are unable to emotionally engage with the traumatic events. Peripheral reprocessing may be the only portal available for clients who still object to accessing the traumatic events, despite extensive preparation. Keep in mind that accessing the trigger may unintentionally activate the trauma memory and cause dysregulation and confusion for the client if they are phobic or not ready to fully acknowledge or access the memory. In addition, clinicians may use EMD strategies and go back to the target often to prevent the client from accessing associative channels that directly connect them to the actual memory of the traumatic events. Before beginning to reprocess triggers and recent events, the client's readiness and affect tolerance threshold must be determined using the previously described decision-making markers.

Even when initiating the reprocessing of peripheral targets, the client's readiness must be established first. The procedural steps for staging and creating the reprocessing platform to increase integrative capacities

194 EMDR-Sandtray-based Therapy

FIGURE 6.6 An older adolescent's resource tray, with her team of companions (her mother, father, boyfriend, younger brother). Her favorite character, Frodo Baggins, along with the part of her that is curious and loves animals, were also invited into the resource tray. In addition, her defenses and forms of self-protection (avoidance, manipulation, and control) joined to create the platform to support processing.

FIGURE 6.7 A resource area for the relational resources of an adult client. Ancestral and spiritual resources were included, while a painted stone symbolized their tendency to retreat into a fantasy world and disconnect from the present.

(Steps 1 and 2), world creation and exploration (Steps 3 through 6), and the assessment phase (Steps 7 through 14) using the second level of reprocessing are as follows.

Procedural Steps for Creating the Reprocessing Platform

Step 1: Staging. First, create a safe and protected space for the client and identify what they need to bring with them to visit a trigger or current worry/concern. You may ask,

Phase 3: Assessment   **195**

« Is there something you would like to bring with you as we visit this bothersome/triggering situation together? Do you need helpers, companions, advisors, special powers, the 'little self's' healing place, or anything else?"

Step 2: Resources. Set up the resource spots, a resource tray or a resource area within the world tray, and then invite helpers, companions, advisors, strengths and capacities, or special powers to come into the tray/area.

Procedural Steps for the World Creation and Exploration

Step 3: Invitation. Invite the client to connect with the sandtray miniatures. Invite their heart, mind, and body to participate. You might say, "Let your heart, mind, and body guide you in choosing the figures that will be your companions in creating the story/world that shows/represents what bothers/worries you right now."

Step 4: World Creation. Once the miniatures have been collected, invite the client to create a world, story, or scene with the miniatures chosen.

Step 5: World Completion. Ask whether the world feels complete or if something needs to be changed, added, or removed.

Step 6: Tray Overview. Invite the client to briefly tell you about the world, story, or memory.

Procedural Steps for the Assessment Phase

Step 7: Identify the Image. Begin exploring specific parts of the tray. Invite the client to reflect on the most important aspect of the world. You might say, "I wonder which part of the world stands out most or is the most [important/visible/disturbing/yuckiest/worst/most upsetting/bothersome]?" or "As you look at this [story/world/memory], what is the [most important/most disturbing/yuckiest/worst/most upsetting] part?" If necessary, you may instead ask the client to reflect on the easiest part of the tray, asking "What is the easiest part of the [memory/world/story]?" or "What part of this [world/memory] is easier to focus on now?"

Step 8: Identify the Negative Cognition. Invite the client to identify any negative cognitions they may have about themselves while connected to the world. You might ask, "As you look at the part of this story/world that stands out most, what [mixed-up/negative] thought, belief, or cognition do you

196   EMDR-Sandtray-based Therapy

have about yourself now?" or "What [mixed-up/negative] thought, belief, or cognition does the 'you' in the story hold about themselves and the 'you' in the sand world as they reflect on this part of the story?"

Sometimes, even when the client recognizes the story in the tray as their own, they may want to refer to the character in the tray in the third person. Once the cognition is identified, give the client the option to represent the negative cognition in the tray in whatever way it wants to exist in the sand world.

Step 9: Identify the Positive Cognition. Invite the client to identify the positive cognition they would like to have about themselves as they observe the part of the world that stands out most for them. You might ask, "What is the [good/positive] thought, cognition, or belief you or the 'you' in the [story/world/memory] would like to have about yourself or themself as you look at this part/side of the [story/world/memory]?" Once the cognition is identified, give the client the opportunity to represent the positive cognition in the tray.

Step 10: Assess the Validity of the Positive Cognition. Introduce the client to the thought scale and invite them to assess how true the positive thought/cognition from Step 9 feels. For children you might say, "Now we are going to use the thought scale. When you watch/observe [part/image identified in Step 9], how true does the positive cognition/good thought feel to you? Remember that one means it feels completely false, and seven means it feels completely true." For adults, omit the reference to the thought scale.

Step 11: Identify the Emotions. Invite the client to identify their emotions as they look/connect/watch/observe the tray. You might say, "When you look/connect/watch/observe [the image/part of the story in the tray identified in Step 7] and the words [repeat the negative thought/cognition identified in Step 8], what feelings do you have now?" Invite the client to represent the emotions they identify by choosing a figure and placing it in the tray, representing the emotion in any way it wants to be witnessed. The client may accept or reject this invitation.

Step 12: Assess the Subjective Units of Disturbance. Invite the client to use the SUD scale to assess their level of disturbance. You might say, "How [yucky/disturbing/bad] does it feel on a scale of 0 to 10, where 0 is no disturbance, or neutral, and 10 is the most disturbing?" For children, use nonnumeric scales, as previously suggested.

Step 13: Assess the Location of the Disturbance. Invite the client to assess where they feel the disturbance in their body. Have miniatures, such as the

Phase 3: Assessment   **197**

"feeling finder" or "feeling detector," that the client can use in the tray to locate the level of disturbance in the body. You might say, "I invite you use the 'feeling detector' and find where you feel this emotion in your body," or "Where do you feel this inside? Where is this sitting in your body?"

Step 14: Prepare for Desensitization. Invite the client to sit with the part of the sand world/memory that stands out, their negative cognition, the feeling, and the place they experience this in their body. You might say, "I would like you to take some time to be with this world/story/memory [repeat the part/image of the tray identified in Step 7], the mixed-up/negative thought/belief/cognition [repeat the negative thought/cognition identified in Step 8], and the feelings and where you are feeling them in your body and follow my fingers/the light/march/tap/brush." You may then begin the desensitization phase.

Explicit Access and the Third Level of Information Processing: A Story About the Actual Traumatic Event

When approached with self-awareness and an understanding of the temporal context in which the self exists, memory processing is a complex EMDR procedure encompassing cognitive, emotional, sensorimotor, generational, and social dimensions. It is a multifaceted journey we embark on to make sense of our temporal existence and identity. This level of processing is used with clients who demonstrate awareness and ownership of the traumatic experience and who can, finally, come face-to-face with the actual memory and the ghost from the past while remaining grounded in awareness of the "self."

At this level of processing, the client is encouraged to construct the story of the traumatic or adverse event in a way that best honors their current understanding of their experience. For the assessment phase of these clients, follow the procedural steps previously described, but refer to the actual memory and the client's self.

1. Start with staging and identifying what the client needs to bring on their visit to the memory. Set up the resource areas or resource tray to increase the client's access to strengths and support.
2. Invite the client to connect with the miniatures and select the figures that will accompany them in telling the story of what happened. Invite their mind, heart, and body to participate. You might say, "Let your body, mind, and heart guide you in choosing the figures that will be your companions in telling and creating the memory and the world that shows what happened to you."
3. Invite the client to create a world, story, or scene of the memory/experience with the miniatures selected.

198   EMDR-Sandtray-based Therapy

4. Follow the procedural steps outlined in the assessment phase addressing triggers and current worries.

Cognitions in the Tray

Sometimes, clients may be unable to identify the memory's cognitive aspects. If you are working with implicit memories, there may not be clearly identifiable negative and/or positive beliefs.

As we enter the assessment phase, a critical juncture arises where clinicians must decide whether to fully adhere to the procedure or to modify or omit certain steps. With some clients, especially children, it may be necessary to limit the number of questions used to assess cognitions at each of the three levels of distance. Cognitive elements may be out of reach for clients if the traumatic event(s) occurred when underdeveloped brain regions participated in encoding and consolidating the memories. In addition, many children do not have well-enough developed verbal capacities and cognitive literacy to answer complex questions that address clusters of cognitions along with a VoC scale. Often, children may access cognitive–affective aspects of the memory where embodied affects are intertwined with cognitive processes and body-based conditions in a single statement that is at the center of the affective storm caused by trauma. A child may identify the negative belief as "I am mad because he hit me" or "I am lonely, and no one wants to play with me" to represent the embodied affects that are embroiled with associated cognitions. Alternatively, a child without words may bring a figure, a movement, or a reenactment into the tray to represent the core embodied cognition that lies at the center of the sand world.

According to Siegel (2020),

> Information processing, sometimes called "cognition," may be within awareness, or it may not involve that subjective sense of knowing, of being conscious. As we have seen, information processing can be enacted and embodied, as well as extended beyond our bodies and embedded in our culture. (p. 56)

Cognitions, especially in children, may carry a strong emotional charge, be expressed through affect, or be embodied without the use of words. The central metaperception of the traumagenic system may be expressed through words, embodiments, or symbols. The clinician may simplify the procedural steps of assessment phase to make them developmentally appropriate. This decision should be intentional and based on the child's capacities, attention span, and the moment-to-moment context. Honoring the heart and procedures of EMDR therapy is important, but honoring the unique qualities of the client in each process is paramount.

Phase 3: Assessment   **199**

Assessment Phase: Working With Parts

Parts work may be incorporated into the assessment phase with clients who have an inner dissociative matrix and a compartmentalized sense of self. Even in the absence of compartmentalization and divisions in personality, clients with intricate internal configurations and high internal conflict may also benefit from parts work.

During the preparation phase, the client's system is mapped, and preliminary work is done to reduce internal conflict, orient parts in time and space, and ground the parts in the present safety. In the assessment phase, the adult, guiding self, or compassionate self and the story holders and keepers can be invited to tell their tales. While guided and accompanied by the adult/guiding self, the little self or the younger, vulnerable, or hurt self carrying the traumagenic story may come into the tray to tell their life accounts. The healing place and relational and individual resources are invited into the sand tray resource spots or into the resource tray. The client may choose a resource spot for their little self, their healing place, their adult/guiding/compassionate self, and other resources. From the safety of the healing place, the little self, younger self, or any part(s) can direct the story that unfolds in the sand tray.

Marie, a 10-year-old who lived in an orphanage during the first five years of her life, is ready to access a memory of trauma that took place at the orphanage. Workers physically abusing babies and children, including Marie, filled her mind. However, she had never told the story before. She had developed strong defenses that kept her pain, shame, and fear at bay. Parts work was initiated during the preparation phase, and the idea of multiplicity within appealed to Marie. She developed a relationship with her little hurt self and worked on differentiating this part from the bigger, older, and wiser self that knew that what had hurt her was over. However, the little self story keeper felt like those scary things that had happened were still part of her life. She agreed that she needed to help her little self and acknowledged that there were other sides of her that protected her from the pain, shame, and hurts. The first protector was avoidance, and the second was control.

Marie worked with her therapist on befriending and honoring these parts until they granted permission to work with the story keeper holding the traumatic experience (the little self). The child created a healing place for the little self in a tray with many relational resources, including companions of all kinds (animals, safe people, gods and goddesses, angels, etc.), food, shelter, toys, and everything this young part could wish for. These resources were installed and used to meet the needs of the hurt little self.

The clinician worked with Marie to assess her readiness for trauma processing, and Marie said the little self was ready to tell her story.

"What do the little self and you want to bring to the visit with this memory? Does she want to bring her healing place? Does she want her companions, food, toys, others? We want the little self to feel safe as she tells her story. Let's remind the little self that visiting the story does not mean it is happening again. It only means that the three storytellers—the mind, the heart, and the body—will work together to sort out the story this little self has been holding and carrying for you for some time."

Marie, supported by her therapist, created a safe and healing space for the little hurt self where numerous resources were available. The healing space provided Marie with a safe and nurturing environment to dialogue, interact, and build relationships with her inner parts and inner world. Within this space, the interaction unfolded, with the clinician serving as an intermediary. From this foundation of safety and comfort, the young part was able to share its story. Some parts were present to accompany and observe, while others chose to remain in the background, refraining from active participation.

The richness contained in the resource area supported Marie when information processing stalled and interweaves were necessary.

More than just the little self can be considered. Any part of the self that holds a story can come into the tray to tell its story while in the safety of the resource spots or the resource tray. The client's system selects the voice and the storyteller who will walk through the procedural steps of the assessment phase. Once again, the answers to the questions posed during the assessment phase may emerge nonverbally, through figures and avatars, or accompanied by the voices of the left brain.

Titration Continuum

EMDR–sandtray offers multiple entry points to the memory network that consider the client's capacities, affect tolerance, and presence. Each level of titration creates a space that may be highly bounded or limitless, giving the client restricted or full and open access to associative channels. The entry road is selected as the therapeutic process moves from the preparation phase to the reprocessing phase via the bridge of the assessment phase. Multiple authors have proposed gradual approaches to accessing traumagenic networks (Gómez, 2013; Gonzalez & Mosquera, 2012; Knipe, 2019) during EMDR treatment. Below, I present a titration continuum, which provides abundant possibilities for reprocessing while staying within the client's window of tolerance and integrative capacities.

Unbounded Access to Multiple Channels of Association

Clients engage with the memory and the self represented in the sand tray—explicitly, fully acknowledging their presence and the interplay of meaning within the process. During processing, they access unrestricted channels of association, allowing a free flow of cognitive, emotional, and somatic material. This depth of engagement is made possible by the client's cultivated capacity for affect tolerance, enabling them to explore and integrate these layers of experience with openness.

Segmentation of the Memory

Memories may be fractionated (Kluft, 1999) into smaller segments for processing. Before representing the memory in the sand tray, the clinician may invite the client to bring a fragment of the memory into the tray. Segmentation like this limits the amount of data the client accesses at one time. The assessment phase procedural steps are focused only on this kernel of information.

Clinicians may help clients segment a memory by using three trays with different sizes and sand colors:

1. A tray of a selected size and sand color harbors the most tolerated and least disturbing parts of the event.
2. A tray of a selected size and sand color that holds the segments of the memory that carry moderate turmoil.
3. A tray of a selected size and sand color holds the most distressing and challenging aspects of the memory system.

The clinician initiates the assessment phase with the least activating tray and invites the client to select figures that represent the most tolerable parts of the experience. Once this segment is reprocessed down to a SUD of zero, the client can transition into the next segment or tray, and so on. Once all the segments and trays are reprocessed down to zero disturbance, the client creates one sand world that contains the entire story/memory, which is then reprocessed down to a SUD of zero, and this step is followed by the installation phase (Phase 5) and body scan (Phase 6). This whole process often takes multiple sessions. This gradual entrance into the memory network works closely with the client's regulatory threshold.

Microprocessing

Clients with a narrow window of affect tolerance may benefit from integrating traumatic experiences in small, manageable increments, thus reducing the risk of becoming overwhelmed or dysregulated. This gentle and bounded therapeutic approach fosters a greater sense of safety and control.

Clients can work with negative but isolated and low-arousing experiences, such as those that are not part of the actual traumatic event. Sometimes, these titrated processing experiences allow the client and their inner systems to become familiar with EMDR-sandtray-based processing and give the clinician a sample of the client's processing style and capacities. The client may process something distant, such as a small, mildly disturbing trigger in their sandtray theme. A mildly disturbing segment may be selected from an implicit or an explicit tray.

Take, for instance, in one corner of the client's story tray is a dog who is upset because he cannot play with his favorite friend (implicit access). This story may be further segmented into the dog's emotions, behaviors, thoughts, and body sensations. The client's awareness would be directed to the segment associated with the lowest level of disturbance, congruent with their integrative capacities and window of tolerance. Mildly distressing segments may be found in their implicit sand worlds or elsewhere in the client's life.

To give another example, a teen may report minor annoyance associated with his sister changing the TV channel when he is watching his favorite movie. The teen may be invited to physicalize this mildly arousing incident in the tray. Once the incident is briefly explored, the clinician invites the client to focus on only one thought, emotion, or action while engaging in BLS/DAS (9 to 14 fast or medium-fast sets, increasing the speed as the client shows greater tolerance). Once the segment achieves an ecologically manageable SUDs level, the clinician can reassess the titration continuum to determine whether the client is ready to transition into reprocessing another segment or the full memory.

As a third example, a child creates an implicit world where a kitty has a birthday party but does not get to eat all the cake—it has to share with other cats. The child is invited to focus on just one small kernel of the story while engaging in BLS/DAS to reduce any charge and arousal associated with it.

Another example might involve an adult experiencing mild frustration from being stuck in traffic. They would be guided to focus on a small kernel of the arousal, carefully titrating the experience, while engaging in BLS/DAS and continuing the process until that portion of the arousal is fully resolved.

Pendulation

The concept of using pendulation strategies came from somatic therapies (Levine, 2015; Ogden et al., 2006). The Constant Installation of Present Orientation and Safety (CIPOS; Knipe, 2019)—one of the first published pendulation EMDR protocols—provides gradual and titrated exposure to the traumatic event while frequently returning to the client's connection to the present safety and desensitizing the phobia of the memory. Multiple pendulation protocols that promote a client's temporal orientation to a resource or to their present safety have been developed, such as "this was me then, and this is me now" and the resource pendulation protocol (Gómez, 2013, 2019), which I describe next.

This Was Me Then, and This Is Me Now. In this pendulation protocol, the client's temporal orientation alternates between the past and the present. It works best with memories of trauma that have already found some level of resolution in the present. If the present environment is equally traumatizing compared to the past, the clinician's focus should be on supporting the client in restoring some level of present safety. Two trays are created, one to hold the past and one to hold the present, and placed at sufficient distance to allow for movement, standing, walking, or (for children) dancing and jumping.

The client begins by creating the "This Is Me Now" tray, which serves as an anchor in the present, providing a foundation of safety and groundedness. This tray represents the here and now within the therapy room, reflecting changes in the client's life that have fostered greater safety, resolution, companionship, and empowerment. For instance, a client may now have new friends, the perpetrator may be in jail, and the client may have found a renewed sense of personal safety with family and friends. A new skill, knowing, or capacity may have been developed, and/or a developmental shift may have occurred: "I am older, taller, physically stronger now."

Once the now tray is complete, invite the client to select the trauma tray and the distance between the two trays. Traumatic material will surface at a pace the client can tolerate. Elements of the memory may emerge partially or completely hidden, covered, or buried to accommodate the client's moment-to-moment changes in affect tolerance. Some clients may build this "then" tray slowly and gradually, through multiple pendulation trips, while others will create it all at once. When the client returns to the now tray after visiting the then tray, take time to reorient the client to the present. You might say, "Can you tell me about what is in this world?" or follow up with questions such as "Are you older now? Is the person who hurt you away and unable to hurt you again? Do you now know things you did not know before? Do you have friends or a new relationship with your family?"

Once the client is fully oriented to the present safety, inquire about their affective states. You might say: "Let's take some time to [notice/observe] the 'now' tray and to notice how you feel now. Where does this feeling [land in your body/reside in you/hang out inside]?"

If the client's response signals comfortable and positive states, proceed with slow and short sets of BLS/DAS. Invite the client to travel toward the

Figure 1.1 A sand world of a mean farmer who keeps animals trapped in cages and abuses them. Near the farmer is a bull—an angry, silent bystander—witnessing the abuse. The bull is immobilized and unable to help his fellow animals.

Figure 1.2 A closer look at the mean farmer and the bull, witnessing the abuse of his friends and family in the sand world.

Figure 2.11 A mother stands beside a bridge, hoping to connect, while her daughter places a fence around her and between them. The mother freezes and stares at the child. A dragon holding a mirror focuses on itself, avoiding contact with others. The child, standing beside the dragon, turns her back on her mother.

Figure 3.4 An adult client creates a tray to connect with her anxiety. She places a figure of a ghost chasing a character on a bridge, representing the centrality of this emotion in her life. Around the bridge, she places different characters that represent her long relationship with anxiety: a monster depicts terror; a spiked dinosaur represents sharp body sensations; a lion and panther symbolize fierceness and heaviness; the lost man in the middle embodies a sense of powerlessness; and a Saint Bernard illustrates anxiety's protective forces.

Figure 3.8 A psychoeducational sand tray focused on the needs—such as water, food, light, companionship, protection, play, access to their feelings, and a home—of plants, animals, and people.

Figure 3.13 An adult client's timeline. It begins with experiences in her childhood, represented by a raging father (Hulk), a narcissistic mother (dragon with a mirror), and two older brothers who physically abused her (two boy characters with the client, who is under a rock). Her best friend died at the age of 12 (hippopotamus represents the best friend). Her dog was also killed when she was 13. At 23, she married a narcissistic and abusive man (bride and man with a straitjacket). Shortly thereafter, she developed an autoimmune disease (woman next to the eye). In the front of the tray, a figured labeled as happy is buried, a sad alien holds its heart, and the client is depicted as a bound and gagged character, representing her current symptoms.

Figure 4.1 In the middle of this tray, created by a 10-year-old client, a bridge depicts the client's frequent crossings into a safe, imaginary world. To endure the pain of her frequent surgeries, she often crosses this bridge represented in the tray from reality into a painless fantasy world where nature and loving fairies surround her. In her daily life, she frequently retreats into a disconnected world of fantasy when facing distress.

Figure 5.2 The caregiver's second representational tray. The younger self carries negative metaperceptions (dragon), emotions (ram), and somatic experiences of heaviness associated with parenting (rocks). The other figures represent the caregiver's wiser/guiding self as well as the relational and ancestral resources and assets.

Figure 7.3 A closer look at a resource area holding the safe and healing place of the client's story keeper.

Figure 7.5 The clinician uses an interweave to support the client in connecting to a resource. The client brings out a powerful wizard who confronts Medusa and protects the babies.

Figure 9.2 The resource tray of an adult and her inner dissociative system. Parts brought what they needed into the tray, including the level of containment and distance they needed to move into reprocessing phases.

Figure 11.2 The sand world from a complete C-GTEP session.

Figure 11.4 A caregiver's divided tray holds representations of the wiser/guiding self (right) and part/self that holds adversity, wounds, and trauma (left).

Figure 11.5 The Parenting Wheel in the tray: One caregiver's divided tray symbolizes the accordion and thermostat, using figures to represent emotions, thoughts, and body sensations. A movable bridge connects these elements, illustrating the pathway to regulated states and experiences of connection. The dresser is on the other.

Figure 11.7 A sand world representing a caregiver's full session of GPEP includes all the caregiver's resources alongside three identified moments of discord in the parent–child dynamics. Each moment is paired with a corresponding future template, designed to integrate the caregiver's strengths, regulatory tools, and relational capacities.

Figure 12.1 The sand world of Dora, an adult client enduring an autoimmune disease.

tray, and instruct them to spend some time observing the tray or even building and adding to it. Follow this with an invitation to go back to the now tray. After multiple tours back and forth, and as the client shows greater tolerance for being with their trauma memory, initiate BLS/DAS (9 to 16 medium to fast sets) while the client is in contact with the trauma (then) tray, and continue to pendulate into the now tray. A full session or longer may be necessary for the client to fully access the memory through the assessment phase and to move into the reprocessing phase. Pendulation sessions should end with the client oriented to the now tray, connected to present-day safety. Through the temporal pendulation of this protocol, the client's phobia is often reduced and their overall level of disturbance associated with the trauma memory decreases, which often allows the client full access to the memory network.

Resource Pendulation. This protocol has multiple similarities with the previous one. However, resource pendulation does not use temporal orientation; it focuses on grounding the client's connection to their resources. Two trays are utilized: one to hold space for the trauma memory and another to serve as a bastion for the client's most powerful resources. The resource tray is developed and created first, so that it can serve as an anchor to safety, empowerment, and companionship. Invite the client to identify and physicalize in the tray the resources that will accompany them, such as their safe place, healing place, team of companions, animal helper, personal strengths/special powers, and relational anchors. Once the tray is complete, identify affective and somatic states associated with it and, as long as the states are positive and comfortable to the client, provide slow and short sets of BLS/DAS.

Once the resource tray is created, invite the client to pick the miniatures to create the trauma world at the pace that best suits their system. When

FIGURE 6.8 **A tray providing space for the resources (right) and a tray holding the trauma (left) are positioned at a distance from each other.**

FIGURE 6.9 **Different colored stepping stones separate a resource tray from a tray holding trauma.**

FIGURE 6.10 **A tunnel—promoting movement, playfulness, maintain present awareness and social engagement—separates a resource tray and a tray holding trauma.**

the client has a narrow window of affect tolerance, it is essential that they be reassured that they are in control of how and how much time is dedicated to the trauma tray. For clients who are hesitant or highly phobic of the trauma memory, the process of building the trauma tray may take multiple pendulation trips to the resource tray to reanchor them in its safety, strength, and empowerment.

Once the client develops greater tolerance for witnessing and being with the trauma tray, provide BLS/DAS (6 to 16 medium- to fast-speed sets, depending on the client's affect tolerance). The session duration and timing should be adjusted to align with the client's regulatory and integrative capacities. The session should end with focus on the resource tray, where the client reconnects to their resources that promote homeostasis and safety.

CHAPTER 7

Phase 4: Desensitization

The desensitization phase, during which synthesis and assimilation of previously ruptured and fragmented memory elements are integrated, is one of the most complex phases of EMDR treatment. During this phase, the client's embodied mind travels through layers of autobiographical memory that exist in implicit and explicit forms. The client reconciles diverse states, weaving together layers of memories across their development into a continuous self-narrative (cognitive, emotional, and sensorimotor). The synthesis of memory contributes to the client's movement into a coherent, connected, and cohesive sense of self and identity. It also restructures the individual's relationships—with their experiences and with themself—as evolving entities through time and space. Information processing may occur in fluid and spontaneous or rigid and inflexible ways.

Unlike fluid processing (where information flows seamlessly), rigid processing is characterized by a client's tendency to get stuck in fixed thought, affect, and sensorimotor patterns. A tendency to be inflexible in processing hinders the mind's capacity to synthesize memories effectively, leading to difficulties in forming a coherent autobiographical narrative.

Based on the adult attachment interview (AAI; George et al., 1985), individuals with secure–autonomous states of mind in association with their attachment histories "have childhood memories (whether favorable or unfavorable) that are readily accessible and contained, and they are capable of discussing them in a coherent, cooperative manner" (Steele & Steele, 2008, p. 338). On the other hand, individuals with insecure states of mind tend to exhibit defensiveness during the AAI in response to any efforts to breach the inner wall that protects their life stories (Steele & Steele, 2008). Individuals exposed to early, chronic, and interpersonal trauma often present with challenges in affect regulation and information processing, such as difficulty maintaining a coherent relational discourse and a flexible flow of information processing. This may cause frequent instances of blocked processing in individuals exposed to developmental trauma. The clinician's use of interweaves and their close and attuned companionship are paramount for this population.

This chapter will address the desensitization phase of EMDR-sandtray-based treatment and its concomitants with the complex trauma population. The tray is a representational space where the client's mind is reflected while they dive into the roots of their current symptoms manifesting from the memories of trauma and adversity.

Memories play a fundamental role in identity formation. They are the building blocks of an individual's sense of self, shaping their relationships with others and with their past, present, and future. Autobiographical memory constructs a continuous narrative and stories of the self that helps the human mind maintain a coherent sense of conscious identity over time (Cozolino, 2014).

During the desensitization phase, the clinician and client are partners, cocreating new self-narratives and meanings for the client. These narratives are not solely cognitive but are deeply infused with affect. Cognitive, emotional, sensorimotor, and generational schemas are accessed, assimilated, and ultimately integrated using sandtray procedures throughout the eight phases of EMDR treatment, and more rapidly in Phase 4. The therapist attunes to the maps that emerge, moment-to-moment, from the client's embodied mind and supports the transformation of the client's old mental structures and inner representations associated with trauma. The client's mind travels within to face its ghosts from past traumas to understand, befriend, transform, and rearrange their relational dynamics. Death and rebirth coexist, inner material is released, and new adaptive information is linked to the tapestry of the trauma story. That said, transformation rarely comes without struggle. Emotions, sensations, and inner representations hidden in deep layers of the self make themselves visible. Protectors emerge with the intention of safeguarding and shielding the client from pain, often creating barriers and potential stagnation in the therapeutic process. These parts, rooted in survival and self-preservation, may resist change, reinforcing defenses that can limit access to deeper affect scripts.

During the desensitization phase, the inner journey moves to deeper corners, constituting the core and essence of EMDR therapy. The EMDR clinician remains attuned to the client so they can select interventions that can speed up or slow down the process as needed and can expand access to associative channels or intentionally contain them as needed. Clinicians, much like a mirror, can reflect and observe every movement, shift, conflict and every moment of obstruction and openness in the tray with attentive presence. The client can verbally report, but the tray and the miniatures

208 EMDR-Sandtray-based Therapy

are companions, storytellers, and reporters that illustrate the challenges and tribulations the client's embodied mind is experiencing.

According to van der Hart et al. (2019), trauma is the inability to integrate the implications of an event into the existing conceptions of oneself and the world. During the reprocessing phases (4–6), the ultimate goal is to promote and support the assimilation, synthesis, and integration of the various elements and forces at the core of the traumagenic network. However, the link between memory networks and the integration of the various implications of the memory may not happen spontaneously, so a more active approach from the clinician may be required. Because processing tends to become blocked more often in clients with reduced integrative capacities due to their extensive trauma histories, clinicians must possess an extensive repertoire of interweaves. Moreover, decision-making markers should already be in place that assist the clinician in selecting the most synchronic interweave possible when information processing stalls.

During the desensitization and reprocessing phases, the clinician navigates through a titration continuum that moves from unbounded access to associative channels to a contained and bounded-access approach.

Information Processing and the Titration Continuum

Information processing follows a stream that clients can access fully, or the clinician may intentionally modulate the flow to be congruous with the client's integrative capacities, homeostatic resources, and affect tolerance threshold. The clinician works on regulating the pace, rhythm, and timing while titrating the intensity to allow the client access to traumagenic material in manageable doses. The titration continuum during the reprocessing phases is fluid and dynamic, shifting moment to moment rather than adhering to a rigid or dichotomous structure as the client's integrative capacities and affect tolerance transition from times of expansion to periods of contraction.

Unbounded Access to Associative Channels

The client moves freely while tapping into a wide range of channels represented in the tray, such as emotions, metaperceptions, sensorimotor reactions and impulses, and other associated memories. Information flows into the tray at a pace that remains tolerable for the client, traveling into and out of consciousness as the process unfolds. This fluid exchange allows the tray to become a dynamic reflection of the client's inner world, unrestricted by any constraints imposed by the clinician. It honors the natural rhythm of the client's experience, creating a space for spontaneous exploration, expression, and processing.

Modulated Access to Associative Channels

Clients with a narrow window of tolerance and diminished integrative capacities could become overwhelmed, dysregulated, or highly dissociated when traumagenic information enters consciousness rapidly and abundantly. As a result, titrating and modulating its entrance will allow the client's mind to digest and gradually process what would otherwise be intolerable. The clinician may use EMD (F. Shapiro, 2001, 2018) and invite the client to connect with the part of the sand world that stands out (image) after each set of BLS/DAS (fast and short sets) alongside the negative cognition, and continue to redirect the client to this part of the tray.

Microprocessing

The clinician may redirect the client to one element of the world: a single emotion, thought/cognition, sensation, behavior, or element. Additionally, the clinician may invite the client to modulate the amount of affective material they can engage with and observe during processing. This intentional titration honors the client's capacity for emotional witnessing, fostering a sense of safety and agency while ensuring that the unfolding process remains within their window of tolerance. The client may symbolically engage and access a spoon, drop, or pinch of the image, emotion, sensation, cognition, or behavior.

Pendulation

The clinician may pendulate at any moment between distressing material and a resource, or between past traumatic experiences and the present, to help orient and ground the client in the safety of the here and now. This deliberate movement between challenge and support titrates trauma processing to align with the client's regulatory capacity.

Information Processing in the Tray

Processing in the tray allows the client and clinician to observe the representations of mental and embodied processes that occur as the trauma is metabolized. Each client will develop a unique relationship with the sand, tray, and collection of miniatures during reprocessing phases. Developmental variations are often evident in how clients process and in their mentalization and integrative styles.

For instance, children may continuously play and move figures in the sand while receiving BLS/DAS. This is often when the child's mind is most focused on the occurrences in the tray, and as such, it may be the best time to provide BLS/DAS. Older children may be able to engage in BLS/DAS while observing the sand story, then take a breath, and rearrange the tray to reflect the changes that have taken place within.

If you use tactile stimulation, you may use paint brushes or makeup brushes to provide BLS/DAS. Even adults may be receptive to the tactile experience of brushes, which does not require skin-to-skin contact with the clinician. You might invite the client to place their hands on each side of the tray and observe and connect to the sand world while you brush their hands. Have the client report what is unfolding between sets and, if they wish, physicalize it in the tray. Clients often follow a pattern of stopping, reporting, and modifying the tray to reflect what is emerging in their embodied minds. Language may or may not accompany every set, as the symbols in the tray already communicate the changes and reorganizations occurring in the client's inner world.

When the client arrives at the end of a channel, invite them to direct their attention to the entire sand world (going back to target in standard EMDR therapy), to notice what is happening in the tray now, and to try to access new channels of association.

As processing continues, a highly verbal client may disconnect from the tray and move to verbal-based therapy. In these cases, gently invite the client to notice if words or symbols better describe and honor their new inner reality. Clients may also reconnect to the tray and the miniature collection while continuing to invite their active verbal brain. Children may naturally stay connected to the world and story unfolding in the tray. However, adults, especially those who heavily rely on a verbally rich left brain, may quickly move away from contact with the symbolic world offered by the sand story.

There are many ways to help clients stay in close connection to the world of stories and symbols. To gently invite the client to reconnect to the sand world, you might say:

- I wonder how that would be represented in the tray.
- How would this exist or land in the tray?
- As you say [repeat their verbal revelations], what needs to happen in the tray to reflect/represent that?

If you are working with a child, you might say:

- I wonder if you can show me this in the tray.
- Let's represent that in the tray.

When the client gives verbal reports without representing them in the tray you might say:

Phase 4: Desensitization   **211**

- Let the figures accompany you and show in the tray what you are saying.
- Let your voice and words be seen in the tray.
- Let the figures in the tray tell your story.
- Let's witness/watch your words appear in the tray through the figures that call to you.

Another issue clinicians deal with during the desensitization phase is blocked processing. According to F. Shapiro (2018), information processing is blocked when two consecutive client responses show no movement, insight, change, or therapeutic gains. The client may be looping around the same issue and unable to resolve it, or the level of disturbance may persist and even increase. According to F. Shapiro, the first step is to change the speed, length, or type of BLS/DAS. However, an interweave may be necessary if this proves unsuccessful in reactivating information processing. If the clinician's intervention accomplishes its goal, information processing is restored.

Looping can manifest in various ways. It may manifest as a character that tries but fails to escape and that continues to experience terror and fear, or as a character that remains shot down and hopeless even after several sets of BLS/DAS. Looping may show up as lingering negative metaperceptions, such as: the character is bad, no one wants them because they are damaged, they have no choices, and they have to live this way forever. The surfacing of defenses can be another indication that looping is occurring: the story suddenly becomes very positive without real depth, avoidance appears in the form of responses such as "I do not know." The world in the tray may become flat, with the client reporting that nothing new is happening. These are all signs of stagnation, lack of fluid synthesis, and the presence of blocked processing. Uncertainty and ambiguity may arise with their associated void, especially during reprocessing phases, yet the clinician sits with the client in the relational space to embrace the unknown, sometimes in silence, sometimes verbally active.

The EMDR Interweave

An interweave is a clinician-guided intervention that supports memory integration when the flow of information processing is lost or compromised. The markers described above will guide decision-making, and yet, the clinician may still feel lost and stuck without an extensive repertoire of interweaves. The interweaves below are categorized based on the Interweave Systems model and its five domains and systems. Additional categories will be described based on their function, such as interweaves that modulate arousal by up- or down-regulating the client's system.

The Interweave Systems Model in EMDR–Sandtray

The interweave was designed by F. Shapiro (2001, 2018) to deliberately connect clinician-derived or clinician-elicited statements with client-generated material. When information processing is stalled despite the manipulation of BLS/DAS mechanics (speed, type, length, and direction), an interweave is warranted to restart the flow of information processing.

According to Gilson and Kaplan (2000), the interweave is one of the most challenging procedural steps of EMDR therapy for beginners to learn. However, it is also one of the most creative parts of the EMDR treatment. Interweaves are also coregulatory strategies that modulate arousal to maintain the client's affect within tolerable boundaries that support continued information processing. Preparing interweaves in advance will facilitate the process (F. Shapiro, 2018; Gómez, 2013, 2019).

Because of the complexity of choosing an interweave, it is crucial that clinicians have both a decision-making method and markers to guide them. The EMDR Systems Model (Gómez, 2019, 2023a) was developed to provide clinicians with a wider repertoire of interweaves and a decision-making guide. In this model, interweaves are organized into five categories:

1. Interweaves that work with the cognitive level of information processing and meaning-making.
2. Interweaves that work with the sensorimotor system and the body.
3. Interweaves that work with the self-protective system and defenses.
4. Interweaves that work with the emotional system.
5. Interweaves that work with the attachment system.

Markers in the Decision-Making Process

Being attentive to moments of rupture, obstruction, and stagnation during processing in the tray is pivotal. The clinician's mentalizing capacities play a fundamental role because they give meaning and guide the clinician's responses to what is unfolding in the moment. The following are markers to consider when selecting an interweave.

Plateaus of Information Processing. This first marker, developed by F. Shapiro (2018), references where the information processing is getting stuck: responsibility, safety, or power and control. The clinician carefully examines the plateau where information processing has stalled, gaining clarity on the specific point at which the flow of information has become stagnant. This insight optimizes their search for an interweave, allowing them to tailor the intervention in a way that reactivates and restores fluid processing, fostering memory integration and synthesis. For instance, a bullied rabbit brought flowers to her abuser, a large coyote. The child insisted on the rabbit's guilt. The clinician identified an interweave in the plateau of responsibility to support the rabbit in reorganizing the placement of accountability.

Levels of Information Processing: Cognitive, Emotional, and Sensorimotor. The second marker addresses the cognitive, emotional, and somatic levels of information processing that may occur in the tray. Is the information the client represents in the sand tray addressing thoughts, beliefs, and meta-perceptions mainly organized around higher cognitive capacities? Or are there emotions, urges, and impulses that signal affective, body-based information or truncated responses? The clinician may select an interweave in the same information processing level or move to another level.

As clinicians work actively with various levels of information processing, they also embrace the wisdom of the lower, middle, and higher brain, which work in synchrony and coordination to produce a coherent and cohesive experience of reality. However, trauma changes the balance and the capacities of these three brain regions to work in resonance and synchrony, resulting in diminished capacities for vertical and horizontal integration (Siegel, 2020). To actively promote both vertical and horizontal integration, clinicians must include in their repertoire interweaves that leverage the interconnected functions of the three brains. To restart information processing, clinicians should use interweaves that work directly with higher cognitive and mentalizing capacities and affective, somatic, and behavioral states. Many examples and categories of interweaves will be offered later in this chapter.

Hyperactivation and Hypoactivation. According to F. Shapiro (2018), clients may move too much into the past and begin to reexperience the traumatic event during processing, resulting in a state of hyperactivation and high arousal mediated by high sympathetic activation. On the other hand, clients may move into a state of hypoarousal, mediated by an activation of the parasympathetic dorsal vagal system that signals the client's movement into immobilization and shut down. Pushing the window of tolerance will be detrimental to clients in either of these extremes, thus interweaves that restore presence, modulate arousal, and reduce access to associative channels would be most appropriate.

We must assess whether the client is remaining within their window of tolerance or is approaching their threshold. A delicate balance must be maintained: sufficient connection to the traumatic material (within the client's window of tolerance) and enough grounding in the present safety.

When information processing stalls, we must investigate why: Is the

214   EMDR-Sandtray-based Therapy

client over-accessing and losing connection to the present? Is the client holding back and avoiding accessing the traumagenic memory due to trauma-related phobias and defenses? Based on the reason, the goal of the interweave will be to reduce and contain the associative channels that are overwhelming the client, to address the defenses, or to push the edges of the window of tolerance so the client can access more. When working with a dissociative system, parts may have different affect tolerance thresholds and thus the system must be consulted often to determine the best intervention.

Presence and Compartmentalization. Caution must be exercised when working with clients who present with a dissociative matrix. For these clients, the clinician needs to have worked with the inner system and the internal conflict during previous phases. Interweaves that seek communication with dissociative parts or self-states may be used. Anything emerging from new realizations promoted by the interweave is invited into the tray in representational form. This may include movement in the tray, characters exiting or entering the tray, information coming in, and information going out. Parts unblend inside the tray; they externalize and use symbols to tell their stories, emotions, and conflicts. If a conflict arises, it can be addressed and reprocessed through the symbols and avatars offered by the sand world. Interweaves that work with dissociative personality structures that honor the compartmentalized inner system may support coconsciousness and integration among parts.

Presence is another marker that guides the selection of an interweave. In clients with mild to moderate dissociation, spaciness and trance-like states may occur, especially children. Sometimes, the client may not notice that they are disengaged and detached from the experience. When the client begins to drift away, the clinician and the client need to work together collaboratively. The clinician should deliver interweaves that restore dual attention, guiding the client back into presence, connection, and relationship with themselves and their inner world. The clinician must support the client in reengaging with their inner world and their thoughts, emotions and sensorimotor responses, which are emerging in the client's mind and reflected in the tray. The tray, the miniatures, the sand, and the tray strategies become external regulators and modulators of arousal. For instance, the procedures that accompany the work in the sandtray—such as standing up to choose a new figure, touching the sand, and placing new figures in the tray—support presence and orientation to the present. However, dual attention may still be lost and compromised by over-accessing traumatic material. Clinicians should have a way to measure and communicate with the client about their current sense of presence (Gómez, 2013; Knipe, 2015; Mosquera, 2019).

Knipe (2014, 2019) developed the "back of the head scale" that allows the clinician and client to assess how much the client is grounded in the present. For the back of the head scale, the clinician asks the client to hold their arm at a 90-degree angle if they are well grounded and to move their arm toward the head as dual attention and connection to the present is lost.

You and your client may choose to use miniatures to represent different states and levels of presence. Invite the client to select three figures before or during the preparation phase: The first should symbolize full presence and awareness, the second should capture the felt sense of drifting away, and the third should embody a deeper level of disengagement from the present moment. Safety checks are effective interweaves that reorient and reground clients in the present moment. By reaffirming their safety in the here and now, these interventions help mitigate the dysregulation triggered by trauma memories, strengthening the client's capacity to differentiate past threats from present realities. When working with individuals with compartmentalized inner systems, the interweave may focus on increasing communication among parts or resolving a binary and polarized dynamic within the dissociative or ego-state system.

Systems. This marker aids in selecting interweaves based on five systems where information processing blockages may occur. These systems are (1) the cognitive and meaning-making system, (2) the sensorimotor system and the body, (3) the self-protective system, (4) the emotional system, and (5) the attachment system.

The systems serve as a guidepost, inviting a process of resonance and mentalization that informs the clinician's decision-making. This reflective process enables the clinician to more accurately identify and select the most effective interweave to support the restoration of disrupted information processing and facilitate integration.

The client may be missing information or may need support in mentalizing the memory, thus an interweave that invites higher cognitive capacities would be appropriate. Unmet needs and missing experiences may be at the core of blocked processing, so an interweave that works with the attachment system to support the client in fulfilling such longings will best assist the movement toward integration. A defense may impede the assimilation of an aspect of the memory, and the clinician may need to choose an interweave that works with the self-protective system.

Types of Interweaves

Interweaves That Work With the Higher Cognitive System

These interweaves use mindfulness, containment, mentalization, and education. As a result of acts of omission and missing experiences, the clinician may need to use interweaves that provide education and information that can be further synthesized and linked to the traumagenic network. EMDR therapy actively invites mindfulness and observation of what emerges from moment to moment. However, clinicians can use interweaves that more actively support the client in moving into a state of observation, curiosity, and presence. The following are examples of interweaves that capitalize on higher cognitive capacities.

Zoom-In and Zoom-Out Interweaves. These interweaves are intended to reduce or increase activation and access to the memory represented in the tray and to direct the client to connect with or distance themselves from data emerging in the sand story. When working with children, you may use playful instruments, like big glasses or binoculars, to make the zoom-in and zoom-out experience concrete and lively.

If a child is not connecting to an area of the tray that may have adaptive information or that may have activation that is not accessed spontaneously, invite them to zoom in or out. You might say:

> "I wonder if you could use the binoculars to look into the character's heart and see what they may be feeling."

To reduce the activation in the tray, you may invite the client to zoom out, so they can see and connect to the entire tray and the larger landscape associated with the memory/sand world. You may also invite them to search for a specific resource, support, help, or adaptive information. For instance, a princess drowning in a lake cannot find help nearby. The adolescent is invited to zoom out and search inside or outside the tray for someone or something that could help.

Interweaves That Access or Provide Adaptive Information

When information processing stalls and the client keeps looping because of missing experience and adaptive information, the clinician needs to fill in the gap. When using EMDR–sandtray, the adaptive information may be visible to the client and clinician or it may exist in a latent form that requires the clinician to question or use reflective statements for it to surface in the tray. If the information has emerged in the tray, it has entered the client's

Phase 4: Desensitization   **217**

field of consciousness, and BLS/DAS will continue to integrate it. You may ask questions such as:

> " I wonder if anyone or anything, inside or outside the tray (referring to the miniature collection), knows anything different or has a different perspective of what is happening."

If the new or adaptive perspective is not found, the clinician takes the next step of providing it. You might say:

> " I wonder if anyone or anything inside or outside the tray knows and can tell the [character] that [provide the information needed, such as children are not responsible for adult choices or that it is okay and normal to have feelings]."

For instance, Martin, 12, created a world in the tray where outlaws were attacking a village. A family pet attempted to fight against them but was overpowered by their strength. After that, the dog did not move, and the invaders repeatedly stated that he was a bad and weak dog for not defending his family (stuck point). Martin had been abused by a tall older man who overpowered him repetitively. The clinician's first step to ignite information processing was to reflect and describe what was emerging in the tray: "I see the dog tried fighting and defending the village and his family. The outlaws were larger and far more numerous (client's statement) and stronger compared to the size and the strength of the dog. He still tried."

Another step the clinician took was to see if the adaptive data was in the tray: "I wonder if anyone in the tray might see the dog and what he did differently? Is there anyone inside or outside the tray who may have a different view/opinion/perspective about the dog's actions?"

The mother in the tray had witnessed the dog's actions and said that the dog was very brave to face the outlaws. The client was invited to hold both perspectives.

If the adaptive information is absent, the clinician can provide it for the client. For instance, you might say:

> " I wonder if anyone inside or outside the tray knows that [character] did their best, considering it is smaller and younger than the [outlaws]. Who knows that the attacks to the village are the [invader]'s choice and responsibility?"

The child responded that the dog was brave for defending the family. The child continued to say that the dog did not want to move and was letting

218 EMDR-Sandtray-based Therapy

the outlaws do everything they wanted. At this point, the clinician delivered another interweave to bring adaptive information the client was not spontaneously connecting to:

> " I wonder if anyone inside or outside the tray knows that when we get really scared, we actually freeze. This is something that our bodies do to protect us, and by not moving, we actually save ourselves from further harm. The dog might be in freeze mode."

When Martin was abused, he did not defend himself, and according to his parents, he felt ashamed of his response. Questions about who could help the dog were later used as interweaves. Martin found other animals that went to rescue and fight against the outlaws for the dog. A potion against the outlaws was prepared in the tray, and the outlaws were finally defeated. BLS/DAS was used after each interweave; and at the end of the session, the dog and the other animals in the tray celebrated the triumph.

The Socratic Method. The Socratic method, originating with the Greek philosopher Socrates, remains a timeless tool for exploration, fostering self-awareness. Through iterative questioning, it delves deeper into inquiry, challenges assumptions, and cultivates a more nuanced and refined understanding. F. Shapiro (2001, 2018) introduced this method into EMDR therapy to support access to adaptive information that is not spontaneously arising and linking up. Interweaves utilizing the Socratic method can help clients gain insight into developmental gaps or limitations in their parents' abilities, fostering a deeper understanding of their experiences. Depending on the level of distance and the portal (implicit or explicit), questions are directed to the character or to the self. For instance, you might say:

> " Is the [character] a kid or an adult? Who is bigger, the [character] or the [perpetrator]? Whose hands are the ones making the bad choice or hurting the [character]? So, who is responsible?"

You may interact with the character by asking permission:

> " I wonder if we can ask the [character] if he is a child. Is the [perpetrator] a child or an adult? Do children know how to defend themselves, or they are just learning to do so? Adults should know that hurting others is not okay, so who is responsible for what is happening?"

Alex, a 37-year-old suffering from anxiety and exhaustion because of his busyness, could not find anything in his past that could explain why his schedule was always so busy and overwhelming. After sufficient preparation, the trigger of a heavy schedule was reprocessed in the tray. During reprocessing in the tray, Alex depicted himself chained to a computer, symbolizing the weight of his demanding schedule. Alex began to loop around overwhelming feelings and anxiety and a sense of powerlessness. Using interweaves based on the Socratic method, the clinician asked a series of questions:

"Alex, I wonder who makes the schedule."

Alex responded that it was him. The clinician asked him if he wanted to physicalize it in the tray.

"Who is keeping you trapped then, the schedule or the persona that makes it?"

Alex responded that he was his own jailkeeper. He then placed a cage in the tray and put himself inside it, symbolizing his feelings of confinement, and BLS/DAS was initiated. After taking a breath, Alex stated that other people pressured him to do things he did not want to do. Once again, he was invited to represent this in the tray. The clinician asked:

"What would happen to Alex if he did not meet the expectations that others placed on him?"

Alex then arranged several figures around him of people who would feel disappointed. BLS/DAS was applied. The clinician asked:

"What would happen if they are disappointed?"

Alex responded by moving the people away from him in the tray until he was alone. He then placed a fence around him, representing his loneliness and sense of abandonment.

Other potential questions include:

- Who Alex is loyal to, others or himself?
- What would happen if they leave?
- What gives them so much power over Alex?
- When did the fear of abandonment come into Alex's life?
- Where did Alex learn to expect abandonment?

How often and how many questions are asked depends on the context and the emerging data. Additionally, the questions should be interspersed with reflective statements and affective companionship.

I Am Curious or Confused. This type of interweave shares some similarities with interweaves based on the Socratic method. A question or a series of questions may be used to kindle the adaptive information. The clinician may express confusion or curiosity about the information emerging and unfolding in the tray.

For instance, if responsibility is placed in the wrong hands, the clinician might say:

> "I am confused. I thought the [perpetrator] was a grown-up, and the [character] was a kid and much smaller. How, then, is the [character] at fault?"

One boy, loyal to the perpetrator, created a tray where the main character was a big snake that was terrorizing and enjoying the suffering of the animals around her. The 8-year-old boy was very much allied with the snake and normalized her criminal and torturous behavior. When the clinician asked how the other animals felt, he said they were very scared. The clinician then asked how it was for the snake to know that others were afraid. He responded that the snake loved it and enjoyed the power she had. The clinician decided to use the curious interweave:

> "I am curious to know where the snake learned to enjoy suffering. She did not know about making others suffer when she was born into this world, so somewhere, the world gave her this. Can we ask her?"

Interweaves That Provide Temporal Orientation

This Was Me Then, and This is Me Now. As a result of trauma, consciousness may continue to exist in the past. Temporal integration and the reconnection to the present are often an important byproduct of integration. To aid clients in this endeavor, we may invite the representation of the "past self" and "the present self" to be in the tray when information processing stalls. You might say:

> "I wonder if you could pick a figure or figures that represent your past and present selves."

Phase 4: Desensitization **221**

Encourage the client to place the past self and the present self in opposite corners of the tray and then do BLS/DAS. For clients who use eye movement, you may use a light wand that invites eye movement from the past and present self. This interweave is often used in explicit processing where the past and the present can be delineated and differentiated in the tray.

Interweaves That Work With Polarizations and Binary States

Trauma moves the human mind into polarized states and divergent needs. Extreme and opposing feelings, thoughts, sensations, and behaviors manifest in numerous forms during reprocessing. Binary and rigid all-or-nothing terms, such as splits between entirely good and entirely bad without any shades of gray in between, may emerge in the tray without resolution. Clients may swing between intense affective states of loyalty and betrayal, love and hatred. They may oscillate between opposites. For instance, they may oscillate between overwhelming urges to dominate or submit, feelings of powerlessness, extremes of neediness and self-sufficiency, idealization and devaluation, aggression and submission, and a pull between seeking closeness and maintaining distance. Trauma may create uncertainty about identity, resulting in polarized self-states and self-perceptions. Individuals may pendulate between extreme senses of competence and defectiveness or grandiosity and worthlessness. When these polarized states emerge in the sand world with no movement toward resolution and integration, the clinician may use interweaves that bring awareness and representations of these divergent, binary states. A client may express love and anger toward their mother. Anger may remain hidden and appear alongside shame and guilt. Multiple states may long to find a resolution. Physicalization may be one of the first interweaves to use to allow the polarity to enter the field of consciousness. You might say:

> " Let's take some time to slow down to be with these emotions that coexist in you despite their being so opposite. These feelings/states/beliefs/sensations can arrive in the tray in any way that feels right for you."

If the client is a child, you might say:

> " I see that the [character] in your world feels happy but sad at the same time. Can we ask the [character] to hold both feelings and have figures in the tray to show these feelings? These feelings can show up in the tray in any way that feels okay to you."

The tray can hold multiple states; they may be physiological, emotional and affective, or cognitive and somatic. Let the client's embodied mind negotiate how they want these binary and divergent states to exist within. The

222 EMDR-Sandtray-based Therapy

client may realize that it is okay to be simultaneously sad about the loss of their wife, with whom they have many conflicts, and happy for the freedom they have without her.

Polarizations lead to internal conflict, which may arise during processing in the tray. Divergent states appear with different perspectives, ideas, emotions, and solutions. The physical representation of these inner dynamics begins the process of recognition, realization, and integration. One part may want to retaliate, while another wants to make peace with a character.

When using interweaves, clinicians begin by inviting representations of the internal conflict. The conflict needs to enter the conscious mind and the tray to be seen, expressed, experienced, and brought into the field of awareness. Interweaves that mediate different perspectives may be helpful when the internal conflict brings information processing to a halt. Initially, just the observation and representation in the tray will start a dialogue, and further questions, invitations for curiosity, and reflections will deepen awareness and expand meaning. In addition, the sand tray provides the space and containment for these conflicts to arise and exist in the physical world so the client's consciousness can dialogue with them. You might say:

- As you hold in the tray the different parts/sides of you/perspectives/ emotions/beliefs/impulses/self-states and their divergent/different perspectives, what happens/what do you want to see happening next? [follow with BLS/DAS]
- Are any of these sides/parts/perspectives in you and the tray willing to dialogue or be curious about each other? [follow with BLS/DAS]
- How is it for you to just sit with your own mind and see its multiple versions, ideas, and perspectives? [follow with BLS/DAS]

If the client is a child, polarities and discrepancies may appear in explicit and in implicit EMDR–sandtray processing. In that case, you might say:

- One side of the [character] loves his dad, and the other is afraid of him. Can we invite the [character] to see both sides? The love may show something different than the fear about the relationship with Dad. Maybe we can just watch closely, pay attention, and see what happens.
- Love and fear will guide different behaviors. Fear may signal the need for protection, while love may signal the need for connection from the hurtful yet, at times, loving father. We can love others and protect ourselves at the same time.

At times, clinicians may find it most effective to simply accompany the conflict or polarity with silent presence and nonverbal reflection.

Phase 4: Desensitization **223**

Interweaves That Work With the Body and the Sensorimotor System

During processing in the tray, truncated defensive responses often become activated without a path for completion. The actions that could not be executed during the traumatic event now push to find a path of expression. Passive and active defense responses take over the prefrontal cortex to promote survival (Bandler et al., 2000). Interweaves that actively work with the body and the autonomic nervous system support somatic release and completions through avatars as well as directly in the client's body. I will explore defensive responses that may arise in clients during processing in the sand tray, fostering a deeper understanding of how to support clients effectively while delivering EMDR-sandtray-therapy.

The Defense Cascade

Fight. When the body faces danger, a fight response is elicited and mobilized as the body prepares to defend itself. However, if the individual is not sufficiently equipped to fight the intruder, the body will respond differently: it will flee, freeze, or collapse. If this response was activated during the traumatic event, accessing the memory during the reprocessing phases in the tray often ignites a similar response. When the fight response is mobilized, characters may begin fighting in the tray, either successfully defeating the threat or surrendering and submitting.

According to Corrigan (2014, p. 140), "The obstruction of the fight response is often followed by a submit state." These are manifestations of entrenched defenses seeking completion. A thwarted fight response may become evident when the character conveys helplessness and an inability to defend themselves, despite repeated attempts to take action. Sometimes, the fight response manifests in the client's body both verbally and nonverbally. Demonstrations of anger and rage and reports of sensations in the upper body and upper extremities may signal the arrival of a fight response (Ogden & Fisher, 2015).

Fidgeting may also be a sign of sympathetic activation during reprocessing (Frewen & Lanius & Paulsen, 2015). If the mobilization of the sympathetic system is at the center of looping and blocked processing, clinicians may use interweaves to support the client in tracking their sensorimotor signals. Further interweaves may assist the client's embodied mind in completing the fight response and reestablishing social engagement.

Flight. According to Ogden & Fisher (2015), when the flight response is stimulated and mobilized, clients report emotions of fear, fright, and sensations in the lower extremities. Restlessness and movement of the client's lower body or a character in the tray trying to escape or run (even from emotions) may signal the presence of a flight response. The avatar in the sand may attempt to escape; however, an inability to do so may be at the core of blocked processing. Interweaves can support the repair of previously ruptured autonomic states by helping the character/client flee and regain freedom and homeostasis.

Activated Freeze, Fright, and Collapse. The activated freeze response is associated with high muscle tone. This is usually the very first response when a threat is detected and is followed by a full-blown fight-or-flight response (Corrigan, 2014). It has been exemplified as a deer-in-the-headlights response mediated by the sympathetic system. A client may exhibit signs of an activated freeze response and hypervigilance that is reflected in the behavior of the characters in their sand world. The client might begin frequently scanning the sand world for potential danger or become fixated on potential threats that emerge in the sand world, or the client may inspect the office/playroom often for signs of danger.

When fight-or-fight responses do not provide the solution to the present threat, and a fright response is activated, it is often accompanied by panic, dizziness, nausea, lightheadedness, tingling, and numbing (A. Schwartz, 2021). According to Schauer and Elbert (2010), there is a dual autonomic activation of both the sympathetic and parasympathetic systems. When the individual cannot resolve the threat successfully, they move into parasympathetic shutdown and collapse. Fright is an "in-between response" as the individual moves out of fight-or-flight responses into collapse.

Fright presents in the tray through characters that express and physicalize their fear and terror, and the movement toward submission and eventual collapse. The client may report nausea, lightheadedness, and numbness in different parts of the body, especially the facial muscles. Without a resolution, the client will move into the ultimate collapse, where they submit, surrender, and faint, losing complete control. The clinician's timely interventions and use of interweaves will prevent the client from collapsing and fainting.

A 54-year-old created a sand world representing an incident in which she woke up in the middle of a surgery and felt completely immobilized. As she started to process, she moved her facial muscles frequently and reported that her face, especially the area around her lips and cheeks, was getting numb. She also reported having nausea and lightheadedness. Despite the level of groundedness provided by the sandtray work and the previous work in the preparation phase, activation increased rapidly, flooding the client's system with terror as she stated that she could not escape or push the surgical team away. The clinician immediately used interweaves that modulated arousal, regulated the system, and restored connection to the present safety and social engagement. The client was invited to do a safety check and a 360-degree turn to reorient herself and recognize that this experience was in the past—not in the present. The client was also invited to reconnect to their resource tray and the figures that oriented her in time and space. The client spent time touching and holding these grounding figures and the sand until social engagement and presence were restored. In cases like this, interweaves that work with the sensorimotor system will help repair disrupted autonomic states.

Schauer and Elbert (2010) have identified other stages of trauma reactions mediated by the dorsal vagal complex, such as flag and faint, representing collapsed physiological states. The collapse response presents with low muscle tone and is accompanied by helplessness and hopelessness (Porges, 2017), parasympathetic dorsal shutdown and a state of collapse.

Clients may bring into the tray characters that give in, submit, and collapse. Unable to move or defend themselves, the characters succumb to the victimizer. Clients may also express verbal and nonverbal manifestations of collapse in their bodies—such as low muscle tone, lack of facial expression, emotional detachment, and disengagement. Clinicians must observe what transpires in the sand story and what is displayed nonverbally in the client's embodied mind. Dissociation may be present, and thus we must be attuned to even slight shifts in the client's physiological and affective states. the characters and the story in the tray may sometimes show dissociative states, disorientation, depersonalization, and the activation of the dissociative system.

A 17-year-old with a history of severe abuse created a world where a llama (the experiencing self) had a python around its body that did not let it move or escape. A fly remained above the llama's head, representing a part of the llama that was watching what was happening (the observing self). Consecutive sessions showed stories where depersonalization was often present in the sand worlds. Sometimes, a butterfly would go into magical places while a llama or a horse was experiencing abuse, attacks, and even death. Dissociative responses arising in the tray may be part of the memory. Sometimes, they indicate a present occurrence, wherein the client is drifting away and moving into a dissociative state in the current moment. Interweaves may be used to integrate the information carried by the observing self and the experiencing self. The clinician may invite the client to represent the sensory input of each part (the observing and the experiencing self-states) and then encourage parts to dialogue, through symbols, about their experience while involving the representations of the five senses to promote embodied integration.

The following interweaves work directly with the body and the sensorimotor system while using strategies borrowed from somatic therapies and the Polyvagal Theory.

226 EMDR-Sandtray-based Therapy

Interweaves That Modulate Arousal

These interweaves promote neuroregulation and allow the body to execute actions that could not be performed during the traumatic event.

Interweaves That Go Directly to the Body, Challenge Procedural Memory, and Execute New Actions. Clinicians work directly with the sandtray character or with the client's somatic intelligence when using interweaves that engage the body and sensorimotor system. The sand world dynamically activates states of somatic consciousness that change and move with the story. The avatar's movements and sensorimotor reactions may directly express the client's bodily states. Menus can help the client connect to the somatic material emerging through the character.

For instance, you might ask the following questions and follow each with BLS/DAS.

- I see that [character] is angry (client's report), and I wonder how the [character]'s body shows him that he is angry. Is the [character] feeling anger somewhere in his body, like in his head, arms, stomach, hands, legs, or feet?
- As the [character] watches the feelings in her arms, what do they feel like? Are they tight, heavy, light, shaky, or itchy? Does the sensation in her arms poke, hurt, or tingle? Let's notice/observe/watch.

You may invite the client to physicalize the sensation in the tray and follow up with BLS/DAS. Depending on the client's age, you might say:

- I wonder which figure would show or tell us about what the [character] feels in his tummy.
- I wonder which figure would represent what the character is experiencing.

If information processing is not flowing, you may invite the character to notice the movement their body longs to execute (Ogden et al., 2006; Ogden & Gómez, 2013). You might say:

> " As the [character] watches the feelings/sensations in their legs, are their legs getting ready or preparing to move? If so, what movement would the [character]'s legs like to make? Does their body want to kick, break free, run, escape, or just stay still?"

Sometimes, asking what the character wants to do while experiencing a tingly sensation or feeling may be enough. If the character wants to run

Phase 4: Desensitization   **227**

and escape, invite them to do so in the tray and continue with BLS/DAS. If the character wants to yell, scream, or make noises, invite them to do so and to physicalize the actions.

Educational interweaves may support the client in understanding and reconnecting to the natural rhythms of their body and nervous system. According to Porges (2017), people may become angry at their bodies and feel like their bodies failed or betrayed them. Misinformation may support states of guilt and shame because the body went into fight, flight, freeze, fright, or collapse. In these cases, you may use interweaves that foster a compassionate relationship with their embodied self:

- Your brain and body were trying to find the best way to help you get through what happened and survive it.
- Let's notice what happens as you watch/notice the work your body did to help you make it through and survive this experience.

Invite the client to represent peritraumatic resources, such as thoughts, emotions, sensations, and behaviors that occurred at the time of the trauma. You might say:

> ❝ Let's take a moment to reflect on the resources and strengths you used during this challenging moment and then bring them into the tray in the way that best honors you. You may have had a particular mindset, or maybe you moved, ran, pushed, fought, or froze. All these actions and thoughts played a crucial role in your survival."

If the client is open to experiencing self-compassion, you may use interweaves that invite compassion for the characters in the tray that carry their story.

Interweaves That Go From Object to Self

When the client experiences physiological activation to the point that it stalls processing, the clinician may use interweaves that go from object to self while preserving the protective layers of the metaphor. These interweaves actively use somatic interventions to support the release, reset, and recalibration of body-based states. You might say:

> ❝ I notice that your hand is tense as you share what is happening in the tray with [character]. Let's notice what is happening in your body now."

If you are working with a child, you can use the analogy of the storytellers:

228   EMDR-Sandtray-based Therapy

❝ I wonder if one of the storytellers is communicating something. May we pay attention? I wonder what happens in your body when you see the [character] being hurt. Do you notice any changes? Where do you feel this in your body?"

Once the client responds, follow with BLS/DAS. You may ask:

❝ Is this feeling or sensation in your body tight, chilly, shaky, itchy, pulsating, or does it tingle, poke, or hurt?"

The client and clinician can work together to create experiments that challenge procedural memory, that complete defenses, and execute new actions which could not be performed during the traumatic event (Ogden & Fisher, 2015; Ogden & Gómez, 2013).

Children may want to execute an action multiple times as they play, run, or push. Clinicians might use sword fights or pillow fights to assist the body in having the experience that was denied when the trauma took place. The child can fight using swords or pool noodles (Dion, 2018) while the clinician invites them to observe what emerges in the body as they complete such defensive actions. The clinician should follow with rapid BLS/DAS. Once the truncated defense is terminated and the client reports a sense of completion and fulfillment, invite the client to reconnect to the tray. You might say:

❝ As you look at the world in the tray now, what happens next?"

Interweaves That Use Mindfulness and Interoceptive Awareness

These sets of interweaves invite observation of what is and what emerges and unfolds in the tray and its story. You may introduce this interweave by saying:

- Let's sit with this a bit longer.
- Let's just observe what is happening to the [character].
- Let's see what happens if we visit what the [character] is feeling just a bit longer.

Depending on the client's age, you might also say:

- Let's watch without evaluating if this is good or bad. Just observe.
- Let's watch without thinking if this is good or bad. Just watch a bit longer.

Inviting mindfulness and observation supports the client's recruitment of biological systems organized around homeostasis instead of defenses.

According to Porges (2017), when we evaluate ourselves or a situation, we are already recruiting the biology of defense. Thus, creating a state of nonevaluation prevents the activation of the defense system. As a client's capacity for mindful awareness and observation grows, mindful interweaves may be used more often.

"Slowing down" and the "accordion technique" are powerful interweaves for use with clients of all ages, especially children. You can use an accordion or accordion-folded paper to demonstrate the process of stretching defensive reactions so these responses can be carefully observed and studied. You might say:

> ❝ When animals feel big feelings, they may want to fight or escape. Can we watch if the [character] wants to fight or escape?"

If the character wants to fight, you might say:

> ❝ When the [character] gets the 'fighting feeling,' where is it in their body? Can we stretch this feeling like an accordion to see it closer and slower?"

Continue with BLS/DAS. then you might say:

> ❝ I wonder if the [character] would like to know that this 'fighting feeling' is really their body working hard to help them survive."

Once the character can complete the truncated defense and return to safety and homeostasis, you might say:

> ❝ I wonder if anyone inside or outside the tray, or inside the [character] would like to let the body or the nervous system of the [character] know that this is all over and that they are safe."

The client may bring a new figure to interact with the avatar and to ground the character in the present safety. Moreover, this new knowing may be physicalized and followed with BLS/DAS:

> ❝ I wonder what figure would represent and remind the [character] that they are safe now. Let's place it in the tray."

While working with the body and defense responses, invite the client to observe and watch without judgment and to notice the incredible things the body can do. Especially if the client has moved from object to self, observing, slowing down, and stretching the experience while noticing and watching what is emerging can assist the client in bringing these biological responses to the field of consciousness and possibilities. EMDR clinicians should be active and intentional in bringing interweaves that support the goal of repatterning and recalibrating the autonomic nervous system.

Interweaves That Work With the Emotional System

Information processing may stall around overactivated, dysregulated, or inhibited emotional states. There are multiple ways by which emotional arousal can stall information processing. Two of them are:

- Emotions are overactivated, and the client shows hyperarousal in the tray and in themselves. Fear, anger, and rage may color the story and the world. Multiple conflicts and difficulties or terrifying stories often emerge simultaneously in the tray.
- Emotions are inhibited, denied, and avoided. The world quickly brings false positive states or pseudopositivity. Stagnation may occur in the tray due to activated defenses and trauma-related phobias.

Interweaves That Modulate Emotions. When emotions surface, the first step is to physicalize and give the feeling state a space to be seen, known, and witnessed in the tray. If the client's system has enough tolerance, then mindfully observing the emotion may create movement and jump-start processing. When the character and the story emerging in the tray are overwhelmed with emotions, invite the client to choose one area of the tray to focus on. Whether the client is processing implicitly or explicitly, you may invite them or the character to feel a small portion of the feeling. For example:

> " The [character] is feeling a big [feeling]. I wonder if we can invite the [character] to choose how much of this [feeling] they want to feel now. It may be only a pinch/drop or two."

At this point, you may want to offer the client a dropper, empty spray bottle, or measuring spoons so they or the character can decide how much of the emotion they are ready to feel, visit, or witness. Emotions can arrive in the tray hidden, half-covered, or completely visible. You can offer coverings or invite the client to bury the emotion that is not ready to be witnessed. An opaque fabric will provide full coverage, and the client can lift it slightly to have contact with the emotional state. See-through, sheer, translucent, and transparent fabrics offer multiple titration levels.

Phase 4: Desensitization **231**

Binoculars can be used to create a sense of distance. Client (especially children) may move as far away from the tray as possible and still connect to the emotions from that safe distance through the binoculars.

There are interweaves that can assist clients, especially children, "sit with" the emotional state. You may ask questions about the feeling's texture, color, and other features while the client physicalizes and closely observes the qualities of the feeling state. You might say:

> "I wonder, what is the color of the [character]'s feeling now? Is the feeling heavy or light? Old or new? Soft or rough? Pushing to come out or trying to hide inside?"

Pendulation interweaves invite access to disturbing material while titrating the process. The sand world is a landscape with multiple topographies and territories, some may be arid or rocky and filled with danger, while others may hold nourishment and resources. When information processing is blocked, identify the source of conflict, ambivalence, or stagnation and the area in the tray that holds the resources and adaptive information or utilize the resource tray that was previously created. Invite the client to move back and forth between the area associated with activation and the area holding the resources while engaging in BLS/DAS.

To modulate emotions, the clinician may need to support the client's access to the peritraumatic resources that already inhabit the trauma or the resource tray. Helpers from the resource tray may come to the trauma tray to save a character in danger. Nurturing figures in the trauma tray may provide the nourishment and protection that is needed. A feeling may be expressed and modulated through the body. For instance, emotions may have a sound or a voice and may be expressed through words, sounds, or movement. The clinician may validate, normalize, or deliver information about emotions. You might say:

> "I wonder if anyone or anything in or outside the tray knows that feelings are messengers. They are not good or bad. They just tell us stories."

If you are seeking specific information about the feeling, you might say:

> "I wonder if anyone in or outside the tray knows what this feeling has to say or what message/story this feeling has/is carrying?"

You may wonder aloud if the feeling is new or old and familiar. Once the information holder (character) is revealed, invite it to deliver the message.

232   EMDR-Sandtray-based Therapy

If a figure in the sand world knows that we all have the right to our emotions, that figure may convey this information to the character or area of the tray where the information is needed/missing.

When the feeling is hiding in the sand world, clinicians can assist the client in accessing it at an appropriate pace. Some clients, especially children, may bury or cover figures that represent feelings under sand or coverings. The figure representing the feeling may go in and out of hiding as the clinician invites observation and presence. What does the client need to be able to see and know to embrace the emotion? You might ask questions such as:

> ❝ Let's notice or search for what [character] in the tray needs for them to be able to visit/connect to this feeling. Does [character] need a companion and a helper? Does it need any special powers or strengths?"

Interweaves That Invite Emotions. Sometimes, emotions are hidden and remain repressed and unseen. Interweaves can be used to gently push the client's window of tolerance by inviting the emotion to be known and seen. You might say:

- I wonder what [character] is feeling as their [caregiver, friend, etc.] is leaving them?
- Does anyone inside or outside the tray know about the [character]'s feelings?

If the client is a child, you might say:

> ❝ It seems like the [character] may have lost their feelings. Sometimes, when we have big, big feelings, we hide them. Can we help [character] find their feelings?"

If a parent is present, invite them to help with the search. In preparation for lost feelings, the clinician should hide figures, feeling cards, or feeling faces in the office. The feelings search is an opportunity for movement and engagement and is especially helpful for children with dissociative tendencies or attention challenges.

Interweaves That Work With the Attachment System

Research has found a strong association between developmental trauma and attachment disruptions with primary attachment figures (Spinazzola et al., 2021). In developmental and complex trauma, one often finds that the caregiving system is/was abdicated and failed to adequately perform its

Phase 4: Desensitization   **233**

essential role of protection and bioemotional regulation. These caregiving deficiencies and acts of omission result in a cascade of insufficiencies, missing experiences, and unmet needs. The child may have been deprived of fundamental physical needs, such as food, safe housing, or healthcare. Clients with complex trauma may present with a history of early experiences that lacked emotional support, nurturance, consistent affection, validation, and appreciation. Processing in the tray often leads to the exploration of deep layers of vulnerabilities, where unmet needs exist. Sometimes, the longings and missing experiences will emerge spontaneously, acknowledged and recognized by the conscious mind, while other times they will remain hidden in layers of entrenched defenses and implicit memories. To coexist with these insufficiencies (or their legacies), individuals must make functional adaptations throughout their development.

Processing may stall due to an underlying unmet need that longs to be seen, witnessed, and fulfilled. Clinicians may use interweaves that repair, validate, accompany, nourish, and provide appreciation and affection. You might ask questions such as:

- I wonder what the [character] needs now, as they are alone in their house.
- I wonder what the [character] in the tray longs for at this moment.

Allow the client to connect with themselves and to find their need on their own. However, provide a menu of likely needs if difficulties arise or the client finds the task too challenging. Menus are especially useful for "needless" clients. A comprehensive list of needs is included in Appendix 2. Providing the client with a comprehensive list of needs may overwhelm them; instead, select the needs that seem most indicated by the client and offer just those to start. You might say:

> " I wonder if anyone outside or inside the tray would know what the [character] in the tray needs. Do they need protection or someone who could save them or fight for them? Do they need companionship or affection? Let's connect with the [character] and let them show you/us what they long for."

When feelings arise, it is often necessary to support the client in integrating the feeling by just being with the feelings first and identifying the need later. You might ask questions such as:

> " I wonder what the [character] needs while they are feeling sad and lonely. Let the [character] show you. Let the [character] tell you what they long for right now."

234   EMDR-Sandtray-based Therapy

FIGURE 7.1 **Sandtray need-fulfillment bottles and jars.**

If the client's parent or partner is present, they can actively participate and support the client in getting their needs met. If the character in the tray needs companionship, the next step is to inquire about how, what, and when. For example, you might say:

> "I wonder who the [character] wants to be loved by. How does the [character] want to be loved? Do they want to be hugged, rocked, or told they are loved?"

Invite the client to rearrange the tray to meet the character's needs. Once the need is met, or while the longing is being fulfilled, deliver BLS/DAS. If the client has difficulty connecting to the need, invite them to be curious:

> "I wonder if we can be curious together about what the [character] may need right now because [caregiver] left them alone."

Needs may be met playfully, by using empty spray bottles/salt shakers/miniature bottles. The clinician should label some bottles and shakers with common needs (e.g., love, compassion, joy) and have some unlabeled ones that can be marked in the moment, if unanticipated needs are identified. Once the need is identified, the client can spray or sprinkle the tray and character with what they need. Follow with BLS/DAS.

Working With Parents and Caregivers

Interweaves provided by parents under the clinician's guidance can be extremely powerful if the parent is ready and adequately prepared. Once the opportunity to deliver an interweave presents, the parent may support the child in meeting unmet needs and repairing and completing truncated responses. When characters need support and protection or have unmet needs in the tray, the parent can provide what is needed.

Monique, 7, created a world where a flower was lonely because other flowers did not like her. She repeatedly reported that "Lori-the-flower" was scared and lonely. Several sets of BLS/DAS were performed while Monique spent time with the flower's fear and loneliness. The clinician asked about what Lori-the-flower needed in this moment of loneliness and fear. The flower responded that she wished her flower mom was with her to hold her and protect her. Monique was invited to ask the flower who could be her mom, and Monique said that *her* mom could be Lori-the-flower's mom. Questions about how the flower wanted to be held and protected followed. Once the need, the who, and the how were clearly delineated, Monique's mother was invited to meet Lori-the-flower's needs in the sand world.

The parent may also be supported and guided to repair or fulfill a missing experience. For instance, the clinician might ask the parent:

> " Dad, I wonder if you think children are responsible for adult choices. I am going to invite you to connect your voice to your heart. From your heart, can you tell [character] that children do not hold responsibility for what adults choose?"

If the access of the memory is taking place explicitly, at the third level of processing where the self is recognized and acknowledged, the parent can speak, touch, sing to, and protect the figure that represents the child in the tray. Of course, you must always obtain the client's consent before inviting their parent to help the characters in the tray.

Andrew, a 6-year-old who spent most of his life in foster care, stated that the boy representing him in the tray had never had a birthday party. When asked what this boy in the tray wished and longed for, Andrew said he wanted a birthday party. The clinician invited Andrew to create in the tray whatever it was that he wanted to happen, and he was supported in having the party he always wanted. The child invited the foster parent and the clinician to the party, and they were both physicalized in the tray. The parent, clinician, and child sang songs and celebrated the child inside and outside the tray.

Working With Significant Others

Some clinicians who work with adults dismiss systemic work in the sand tray as being appropriate only for children. However, if clinicians and adult clients can get past the social conditioning of what adult therapy should be like, this work can also be profound for adults. The adult client may invite a trusted partner, a parent, or another close family member. Because of the nature of this work and how deeply it can reach into the layers of the self, clients should be encouraged to bring a safe, close, and trustworthy companion. Spouses and family members must be educated and prepared before accompanying the adult client. The safe and trusted companion can take an active role, under the therapist's guidance, to support the client in fulfilling unmet needs.

Sofia, a 32-year-old woman whose father rejected her even on his death bed, carried wounds of deep rejection. When attempting to reprocess memories associated with her father, she did not feel strong enough to visit and reprocess the memories. However, she had a safe and strong connection with her husband, who was aware of the work Sofia was doing in therapy and was eager to support and accompany her. Before scheduling a reprocessing session, the clinician met with Sofia and her husband to establish the husband's readiness to be present. The clinician addressed safety issues and provided clarification regarding the husband's role in therapy.

During the reprocessing session, Sofia's husband was mostly silent and just present. However, when information processing became stagnant after Sofia made contact with her father's rejection, the husband was invited to repair and support Sofia's hurt, younger self. When asked what this little girl needed, Sofia said she needed validation that she was lovable. The clinician asked who could provide this validation, and she responded that her husband and her adult self could do it. The clinician invited Sofia to tell her husband what her younger self in the tray needed to hear. Sofia's husband held the figure in the tray that represented him, and he and Sofia's wiser self approached the avatar of her younger self in the tray to nurture her. Together, they reminded her that she was loved and appreciated in the present and that her father was unable to show her love because of his wounds.

Interweaves That Work With Defenses and the Self-Protective System

Defensive structures emerging from trauma are complex and often play an important role in creating the sand world and in accessing traumagenic memories. Clinicians must remember that these forms of self-protection are intelligent adaptations to ensure survival. Due to the often rigid nature of these defenses, especially in adult clients, work with trauma-based forms of self-protection should be initiated during the early phases of EMDR-sandtray-based treatment to provide the foundation for processing. Then, the client and their defensive/protective parts will be prepared for and aware of the process during the reprocessing phases. During these phases, defenses and the self-protective system are often invited into the resource tray or resource areas to monitor and witness the session.

When a defense is suspected of stalling information processing, you may use an interweave that invites the protective part into the tray to voice its concerns. As challenging emotions or previously ruptured autonomic states emerge or safety is compromised, defenses activate previously develcped strategies for avoiding pain. However, these ruptures in safety during information processing give the clinician an opportunity to empower the client through interweaves that transition the client out of defenses and into ventral vagal states of connectedness, safety, and homeostasis. Protective/defensive parts (ego states or dissociative) are invited to express their needs and apprehensions in the tray. You might say:

> « I invite you to direct your attention to the tray, where your protectors are, and check if any of them have something to say or to show you (or to show to a character in the tray)."

Follow with BLS/DAS, and invite the client to notice what is emerging. Once the part communicates its concerns or reasons for its presence and activation, invite the client to represent the defensive part's apprehensions and needs in the way that honors those parts. Acknowledging the defense will open the door for the mechanisms of adaptation to be integrated. If the part expresses concern, inquire about what the client and this protector need to continue accessing the story that is emerging in the tray.

You may also invite the client to notice what the protector needs to let them (or the sand character) feel, express, voice, externalize, tell, know, realize, or continue processing the worlds. You might say:

> « I wonder, what does this part/protector need to feel more at ease and safe with the story unfolding in the tray?"

Interweaves That Restore Present Awareness and Dual Attention

According to F. Shapiro (2001, 2018), dual attention is essential for the assimilation and integration of memory. Despite the grounding forces of sandtray work, dissociative clients may still drift and disengage from the present safety. Using BLS/DAS that incorporates movement (especially for children and adolescents)—such as marching in front of the tray, engaging in bilateral dancing, like jumping from one foot to the other, or high knee marching—can keep the client engaged and in connection to their bodies. When hypoarousal, emotional detachment, and dissociation overtake information processing, clinicians may use the following interweaves to restore social engagement and presence.

Ask Questions. Be attuned and inquire, if possible, about what is emerging in the moment. This will give you more information about what is triggering the emotional response and disengagement from the present.

238   EMDR-Sandtray-based Therapy

Movement. Invite the client to move their body by standing up or using movement-based BLS/DAS.

Grounding. Increase engagement and relational presence and remind the client that you are right there. Here are some examples of what you might say:

- Let's remember that this is not happening now. We are just helping the storytellers sort it out.
- Let's look around and remember that right now, right here, this place is safe/okay (any term that is appropriate for the client that reminds them that the traumatic event is not occurring in the moment).
- Is there anyone hurting your right now? (If the answer is "no" you might reflected back by saying: Notice this awareness in the here and now; that there is nothing/no one hurting you right now.)

You may also invite the client to bring awareness to the part of the tray associated with safety or to touch or hold the figure(s) that supports their connection to the present safety.

Check Inside. Keep in mind that the state of threat may be generated internally, activating a neuroception of danger even in the present safety of the office and the therapeutic relationship. Invite the client to do an inside visit, check what is happening in their inner world, and represent it in the tray.

Reflection. Describe and use reflective communication. For example, you might say:

- I noticed that your eyes and voice got small as you held the [character]. Can we be curious together to see what is happening?
- If it feels safe to do so, you may represent your inner findings, in whatever way they want to be witnessed, in the tray. They may be buried, partly covered, or completely visible.

Sit With Uncertainty. If the client is not communicating or is becoming immobilized, use strategies such as movement or breathing to bring the ventral vagal system back online. Movement may need to be brought in slowly, such as moving just the hands, then the arms, legs, and so on. Use the best tools you have: yourself, the intonation of your voice, and your internal state. Learn to be in uncertainty and the unknown. Sometimes, despite how experienced we are, we may have moments of ambiguity. Sit with them, be in the moment.

Phase 4: Desensitization **239**

Relational Anchors. If you are using relational anchors, such as connecting feet with the client, remind the client you are there to hold space for them:

> "Can you feel my feet? Just remember I am right here holding you. I've got you."

You may invite the client to bring a figure(s) and hold it or place it in the tray that represents this knowing. If physical touch is utilized, the clinician must have obtained prior authorization and explicit consent at the time of its use.

Ask Before Continuing. The above strategies are intended to neuromodulate and restore the client's balance and homeostasis. Invite the client to check in with themself to see if it is okay to keep going and reconnect to the sand world.

Titration. You may ask the client to look at the tray and reconnect only with the side or part of the world that feels safe. Use coverings, and invite the client to choose the texture or kind of covering, such as transparent or opaque fabrics. The client can cover the side of the world that triggered the physiological and emotional activation that caused high mobilization or detachment. Continue reprocessing if the connection to the present safety and dual attention is restored and if the client feels safe and oriented enough to the present safety. Keep in mind that episodes of high activation, collapse, dissociation, and disengagement deserve thorough exploration to uncover and understand their underlying causes and the inner dynamics that generated them. If the client has a dissociative inner matrix, explore the internal processes and dissociative parts involved. The rest of the session may be dedicated to representing these dynamics in the tray while covering and moving the trauma tray aside. If the client has agreed to continue reprocessing, stay in the tray areas that are tolerable to the client, and assess whether the memory needs to be accessed using a greater level of titration.

Interweaves That Work With Generational Wounds

The human mind may be deeply injured in its early relational milieu, which may follow a generational wounding trajectory. Most clients receiving therapy bring not only wounds and burdens passed down from previous generations but also ancestral resources.

Joe, a 54-year-old with an extensive history of failed relationships, is depressed, anxious, and full of rage against women, especially his mother. When exploring the anger during one of his reprocessing sessions in the tray, Joe could not find the reason he was angry at his mother throughout

240 EMDR-Sandtray-based Therapy

his life, a rage he had transferred to his partners. When information processing stalled because of rage, the clinician asked Joe to trace his anger back to where it had begun. He placed the figure of his father raging against his mother in the tray, a typical scene throughout his childhood. The clinician used reflective communication and questions to expand meaning and invite mindfulness and curiosity:

> "I see how as a child you were the witness and story holder of your father's rage. Who does this anger belong to?"

Joe paused for some time and, without words, placed a big bag with bricks next to his father. He then said that the anger was his father's—and even his grandfather's anger, since Joe witnessed his grandfather have intense anger outbursts toward his grandmother. The grandfather was brought into the tray, carrying a bag of bricks. Joe sat with this new realization while receiving BLS/DAS. The clinician stayed in curiosity, observing the bag of bricks. Joe stated:

> "This is not my anger, and now I have choices about it."

The clinician responded, "Where do you want this anger to go?" Joe responded that he wanted to return the anger, so he moved the bags of bricks even closer to his father and grandfather and away from him. The clinician wondered how Joe wanted to return the anger, and he said that he wanted to speak to them. "Poppa and Dad, I'm realizing now that I've been carrying this rage that is not mine. In a loving way, I want to give this back to you. Now it is up to you to decide what you do with this, wherever you are (both had passed away). I am free now."

Joe reported an incredible sense of relief and peace. He felt that something very deep had transformed within him. He then brought a candle and a heart-shaped figure into the tray as symbols of this shift in his mental and embodied landscape.

Generational interweaves can be transformative and powerful in addressing deep-seated intergenerational traumas. You might ask questions such as:

- Whose feeling/belief/thought/behavior is that?
- How and from whom did you receive this emotion/belief/thought/ behavioral pattern?

Once the generational wound is found and acknowledged, a field of possibilities emerges to be and sit with its existence. You might ask:

Phase 4: Desensitization **241**

"How does it live in you? Where do you carry this in your body? Let's breathe with it, let it dance in and out of you/the character, and see what happens."

Clinicians may inquire about what the client wants to see happening next or where they want the wound to go. You might ask:

- What would you like to do with this discovery?
- What do you want to see happening next now that you are having this new realization?

If the client needs assistance, the clinician can provide menus. For example:

"Notice the impulse that arises in you/the character in the tray. Do you/the character feel compelled to release it, transform it, give it back, or hold on to it? Notice the urges in your body."

The sand world holds the space for these impulses to be represented, externalized, and moved to completion. The impulse is reprocessed and tracked until it finds its time and space as well as its release channel. The impulse may guide the client to hold on to part of the generational material or to release, transmute, transform, or return it. Some clients may want to create rituals in the tray to release the wound to the four elements, to a spiritual/religious entity, or to return it to previous generations. Often, clients opt for a group release wherein other generations are invited into the tray to let go or to heal previously ruptured relational bonds and thus break the cycle of transmission. Often, the compassion, freedom, love, and sense of connectedness and transformation that emerge from these sandtray rituals restore the individual's bioaffective rhythms and the resulting sense of continuity and belonging pave the way for future generations rooted in shared coherence, where individuals can thrive, grow, and realize their fullest potential together.

For clients with histories of colonization, migration, genocide, displacement, systemic discrimination, or marginalization, interweaves can provide validation and the restoration of generational rhythms that were disrupted or lost over time due to trauma. Throughout the use of generational and ancestral interweaves within EMDR-sandtray-based treatment, clients can acknowledge and process the trauma while celebrating traditional practices in the tray, allowing them to reconnect to their cultural identity. Clinicians may also integrate interweaves that assist clients in connecting with ancestral resources and strengths passed down to them through previous generations.

242   **EMDR-Sandtray-based Therapy**

These interweaves can be transformative when working with children, but they must be approached with great care and caution, as the wounding dynamics may still be unfolding within their current relational ecosystem. It is essential to consider hidden traumas, attachment ruptures, and the layered impact of racial disparities, particularly in multiracial and multi-ethnic families, where unique challenges and complexities arise. The intersection within the child's relational milieu, of diverse cultural identities, societal biases, and systemic inequities can create profound relational tensions, influencing the child's sense of belonging and safety.

In the systemic delivery of EMDR-sandtray-based treatment, the caregiver plays a pivotal role. Ideally, they are receiving individual or group treatment to address their own unresolved traumas and are actively participating in sessions with the child.

The child's clinician should collaborate with the parent to foster awareness and acknowledgment of relational dynamics that may be contributing to the child's wounding. With compassion and support, the parent is gently invited to actively engage in the child's reprocessing sessions, creating opportunities for healing and connection within the parent–child relationship. This approach emphasizes understanding and repair, empowering the parent to play a meaningful role in the child's therapeutic journey. The parent should be informed of the purpose of the reprocessing session and equipped to provide interweaves that can validate, acknowledge, and repair the relational ruptures.

Tara, a 9-year-old receiving treatment for severe health anxiety, lives with her overprotective mother, whose intense fears about illness and loss stem from the traumatic experience of losing her first baby. This profound loss has deeply influenced the mother's parenting, amplifying her anxiety about her children's health and safety. Tara's grandmother also suffered from anxiety around death and disease due to a severe illness she experienced as a child. Tara's mother came to understand that her daughter's anxiety was deeply intertwined with a generational story, rooted in her own unresolved trauma and fears surrounding illness, death, and the difficult experiences she had with her own mother, Tara's grandmother. Tara's clinician invited the mother to create a sand world—carefully planned in advance and tailored to be developmentally appropriate—that would share the generational story of how anxiety and fears around illness and death had traveled through multiple generations. This story aimed to help Tara understand her mother's experiences and the legacy of anxiety within their family, fostering insight and connection between them. During the reprocessing session, Tara's mother under the clinician's guidance use interweaves where she showed Tara how her "clouds" (representing the mother's trauma) of losing her child and growing up with a health-fearful

Phase 4: Desensitization   **243**

mother had given her the "big fear" that she had passed on to Tara. Tara and her mom physicalized and represented these fears in the tray while Tara received BLS/DAS. At the end of the third reprocessing session, Tara and her mother created a ritual in the tray in which they and all the prior generations that had carried health anxiety gave the fear back to the four elements. They also expressed and physicalized gratitude for the strength they received from previous generations who had to battle these fears.

Perfectionism, pressure to achieve, anxiety, depression, and beliefs such as "I am not good enough" may be the result of intergenerational trauma. Reprocessing these generational wounds with the child alone may be problematic because the parent and child may interpret this level of work as an attack against the parent. However, this work can be exceptionally transformative when the caregiver is a therapeutic partner and an active participant.

A Reprocessing Session in the Tray

FIGURE 7.2 A sand trauma world with resource areas. The client's younger storyteller is in her miniature safe and healing place alongside her team of companions; and from there, she tells the story of abuse from when she was in the orphanage.

FIGURE 7.3 A closer look at a resource area holding the safe and healing place of the client's story keeper.

FIGURE 7.4 **During reprocessing, Medusa (perpetrator) and her accomplices mistreat the babies in an orphanage. The babies are unable to escape and feel powerless.**

FIGURE 7.5 **The clinician uses an interweave to support the client in connecting to a resource. The client brings out a powerful wizard who confronts Medusa and protects the babies.**

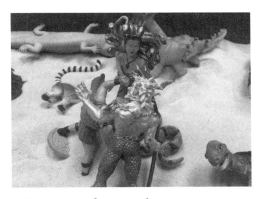

FIGURE 7.6 **After another set of BLS/DAS, the client brings out Hercules and several other protectors and defenders.**

FIGURE 7.7 **Medusa and her accomplices are defeated. The clinician continues BLS/DAS, and the client brings her inner story keeper (little hurt self) out to feel, see, and celebrate the act of triumph and the newly found sense of safety, freedom, and empowerment.**

General Procedural Steps of Phase 4: Desensitization

Step 1: Breathe and Notice

At the end of each BLS/DAS set, invite the client to breathe and reflect on what is happening in their embodied mind and in the tray. Remember to breathe with the client. Below are some examples of what you might say:

- Let's take a breath, let it go, or take a break.
- What happened/what do you notice? Show me in the tray what feels safe/appropriate to bring into the physical world or what you feel ready to witness.
- What is happening in the tray/world/story?
- I wonder what is unfolding in the tray.
- You may show it in the tray in the way that it wants to be witnessed.

Use the titration scale with the tray. Elements may be covered, buried, partially obscured, or completely visible.

Step 2: Physicalize

Some clients may proceed directly to representing in the tray without words, while others may first provide a verbal report. If the client moves into verbal reports, you might say:

> "I invite you to look at all the figures, connect with them, and see which one(s) represents [what the client is reporting verbally]. Is there anything you want to change, move, or arrange to represent/show the feeling/thought/sensation/impulse? Please remember that figures may come into or leave the tray. Things may change or stay the same."

Sometimes, clinicians may move into talk therapy and abandon the tray with highly verbal clients. Ask the client what form of communication best honors their longings at the moment, and proceed accordingly.

Step 3: End of a Channel

When information processing plateaus and the client reaches a state of realization; experiences comfortable, neutral, or positive emotions; and achieves insight into cognitive, affective, and somatic development, this is conceptualized as the end of an associative channel (F. Shapiro, 2018). The end of a channel becomes evident in the sand tray when the client's reflections on their unfolding sand story shift to adaptive, positive, or neutral themes for several consecutive responses. When there is no further movement or change, this

246   EMDR-Sandtray-based Therapy

signals the end of the channel and prompts the clinician to return to the original target to access a new associative channel and disturbance.

Step 4: Return to Target

In EMDR–sandtray, when we return to target, we redirect the client to the entire tray. This will support the client in accessing new channels of association that hold some disturbance. You might say:

"As you connect/notice/observe the entire world now, what happens?"

You may also ask the client to identify areas of the sand tray that still hold disturbances, conflicts, challenges, or "yucky stuff." Once an area is identified, invite the client to notice, observe, or just watch that area and see what happens. If the client reports new material verbally or symbolically through the miniatures, continue reprocessing with repeated cycles of BLS/DAS. It may be necessary to return to the entire tray several times during reprocessing before all channels are clear, then, use the SUD scale to determine the level of disturbance associated with the sand story.

When information processing stalls, it may be helpful to return to target (the entire tray). Stalled processing may manifest as the client consistently stating that nothing is happening or shifting focus to multiple issues that are distant or unrelated to the memory or sand world the client is processing. If going back to target does not jump-start processing, use an interweave.

Returning to target is only one of the many available interventions clinicians can turn to when information processing stalls. In cases of stagnation wherein the client shows signs of emotional dysregulation, returning to the entire tray may activate associative channels that hold greater disturbance and may further increase the client's level of arousal. In other cases, returning to the entire tray may restore the flow of information processing. What to do is a contextual clinical decision; it is highly dependent on the client's signals in the moment and on the overall clinical terrain.

Step 5: Check the SUD

Depending on the client's age, you may choose to use measuring spoons, droppers, spray bottles, or the numerical 0–10 scale to check the SUD. If the SUD is not 0: Invite the client to physicalize what is still disturbing, bothersome, or yucky. Once physicalized in the tray, do more sets of BLS/DAS.

Check for ecological soundness. When the client reports an SUD of 0, do one more set of BLS/DAS. If the response is still 0, proceed to Phase 5: Installation.

CHAPTER 8

Phases 5–8: Installation, Body Scan, Closure, Reevaluation, and Future Template

This phase offers space for the client to enhance and strengthen their adaptive networks and positive embodied beliefs. According to F. Shapiro (2018), positive cognition is a verbalization of the affect in connection to the traumatic experience. It is a felt belief that is highly charged in affect and radically embodied. Once the level of disturbance associated with the sand world is reduced, EMDR clinicians move to the installation phase.

Procedural Steps of Phase 5: Installation

Step 1: Check if the Positive Cognition Still Fits

Invite the client to connect with the sand world as it is now and notice if a new positive belief or good thought has emerged for the character if processing implicitly or the client if processing explicitly. Once the final positive cognition has been identified, invite it into the tray the way the client wants to witness and connect to it. The cognition may be verbalized or represented through symbols only. Modifying the language for the client's age, you might say:

> " Do you want this belief/thought/cognition to be visible in the tray? Let's find the figure(s) or the changes that need to occur in the tray to accommodate this new belief/good thought."

Step 2: Check the VoC

To check the validity of the positive cognition (VoC) in EMDR–sandtray with adult clients, the standard numeric VoC scale may be used; however, playful and nonnumeric scales may work better with children and some adolescents. Measuring spoons, droppers, and sprays may be used to identify the positive cognition's validity. You can also use spring toys that the

248

FIGURE 8.1 **Ruby's sand world, depicting obedience on one side and defiance of the queen's rules on the other side.**

child can stretch to show how true the positive cognition feels: the child can stretch an object to show how true the positive cognition feels to them. The size of a figure may represent how believable the positive cognition is in connection to the sand world. For instance, a big elephant can represent a fully believable cognition, whereas a small one can represent the a barely believable one. Ideally, your miniature collection will have various sizes of similar figures, such as elephants of many different sizes, that can be used to represent how believable the positive cognition is in connection to the sand world. You might say:

> " As you look at the world/memory/story in the tray and the positive cognition/good thought represented by [name, in the client's words, the figure or area representing the positive cognition], how true does this positive cognition/good thought feel to you now, on a scale of 1 to 7, where 1 is not true at all, and 7 feels really true?"

Step 3: Initiate BLS/DAS to Link the Positive Cognition With the Sand World

Invite the client to observe and witness the sand world or the memory along with the representation of the new positive belief/good thought, and initiate BLS/DAS.

Step 4: Enhance New Adaptive Material With BLS/DAS

Allow the augmentation of positive affect even after the client's VoC has reached a 7. Invite the client to physicalize these new positive and adaptive materials in the sand world so that the tray holds the new realizations and adaptive material emerging in the client's embodied mind.

Step 5: Invite Playfulness

Make the process playful by incorporating therapeutic embodiments that involve singing, dancing, and movement. For instance, a child may create a song with the positive cognition. The child may invite the clinician (and caregiver, if present) to sing as they remain connected to the tray and the representations of the positive cognition. Dancing or marching around the tray brings social engagement, the hybrid activation of the ventral vagal system, and sympathetic energy. This becomes a powerful neural exercise (Porges, 2017).

Phase 6 Overview: Body Scan

Embodiment, somatic processing, and somatic consciousness are interconnected concepts that underscore the body's role in healing the mind after trauma. Trauma is a psychobiological and embodied phenomenon that manifests physically and somatically. EMDR-sandtray-based treatment actively engages the profound mind–body connection, highlighting how trauma is deeply embedded in physical experiences. Throughout the eight phases, but especially during the body scan, EMDR–sandtray works to enhance interoceptive awareness, to track somatic markers, to help clients assimilate sensorimotor material linked to trauma, and to promote synthesis at a somatic level and restore the natural equilibrium of the client's body. The body scan aims to reconnect the individual to their bodily experience to further release, reset, recalibrate, assimilate, and ultimately integrate the embodied remnants left by trauma. The work in the sand tray activates body-based states through the avatars that implicitly or explicitly tap into the client's embodied mind in the sacred space offered by symbols. If navigating through the body scan phase implicitly, work with the somatic projections the client makes onto the character and direct your reflections and questions to the avatar that carries the sensorimotor load. You might say:

> " Let's invite the [character] to observe the entire world along with the good thought/positive cognition [repeat the positive cognition and the figure(s) representing it]. Let's ask them to check their body, starting from the head and all the way to their [paws or toes, depending on the character], and see if there are any feelings in their body. We are just looking at the important storyteller: the body."

Sensorimotor responses, which include sensations, urges, actions, and impulses, may enter the symbolic space of the sand tray through figures that rush in or slowly enter the sand world to represent the character's bodily states. Somatic consciousness, observation, and presence are invited as the client engages in BLS/DAS.

When processing explicitly, direct the inquiries and reflections to the client. You might say:

> **❝** I invite you to watch the entire world along with the positive cognition/belief/good thought [repeat the positive cognition and/or the figure(s) representing it]. Let's check in with an important storyteller: your body. Starting from your head and going all the way to your toes, let's check if there are any sensations in your body."

With young clients you may want to use the "feeling finder" (Gómez, 2013), which is a magnifying glass or a figure that the child can use to scan the body. Clients may also scan the character's body, providing some distance from activating somatic and embodied material.

If the client is an older adolescent or an adult, you might say:

> **❝** As you connect to the entire sand world and the positive cognition/belief or its symbol, let's notice and be curious about what emerges in your body from your head to your feet."

Going From Object to Self

If the client is processing implicitly, you may invite them to do a body scan as a witness to the sand story. It is inadvisable to activate the body if there is not enough time left in the session to also return the client to homeostasis (F. Shapiro, 2001, 2018). This clinical decision should be made based on the client's capacities and closeness to their own experiences. Some clients need refuge and distance from their inner world, which is offered by implicit processing. However, moving from object to self does not mean moving out of the metaphor. We continue to actively use the distance offered by the sand story and its avatars. You might say:

> **❝** I wonder if we can be curious together and find out what happens in your body as you witness/watch the [character]'s world."

Follow with BLS/DAS. When transitioning into an embodied state connected to the act of witnessing, it is possible to temporarily disconnect from the sand world. This allows the individual to fully engage with and inhabit their physical presence.

As somatic material arises in the tray, information processing may stall. The following are interventions and interweaves that work with body-based states:

Tracking Sensations. The clinician invites somatic consciousness and mindful observation of the sensation while tracking how and where the sensation is moving in the body. The clinician can provide menus such as:

> " As you watch what is happening in your body, let's check if the sensation is poking, tingling, buzzing, pulsating, or applying pressure. Is it pushing or hurting? Is it moving or staying still?"

Inviting Movement. The clinician may also invite movement by saying:

> " If what you feel in your [name the body part] was preparing your body to move, what would this part of your body like to do, and how would it like to move? Does it want to push, punch, break free, kick, or run?"

Invite the client to execute the movement, if possible, or to perform it in the tray. You may place a cushion in front of the client for pushing (Ogden & Fisher, 2015). If working with children, you may wrap toilet paper around their hands or their entire body so they can break free and feel the empowerment that comes with that. Follow with BLS/DAS, and execute these movements and actions as much as the client desires. Once the client completes their truncated responses and releases somatic energy, support them in reengaging and reconnecting to the tray. Repeat the body scan until balance and somatic equilibrium are restored as the client remains connected to the sand world and the memory.

Phase 7: Closure

Closure ensures the client's stability and safety. Every session must be appropriately closed to bring the client to homeostasis and emotional balance. Closure must happen in the tray and in the client's system, as they are closely interconnected. Flow and synchrony should continue as the session ends. Clients must experience the session's closure as a culmination of celebrated triumphs and adequately contained disturbances. Each session in which the client delves into painful experiences yet finishes in a place of safety, containment, and control supports them in reclaiming their sense of power and agency as each session becomes a victory over the legacy of their trauma. The client expands their capacities and learns that a wide range of emotions and affects can be experienced and, just like a journey, a safe return to balance and homeostasis is possible. These travels into the inner world, accompanied by the clinician, and adequate transitions back to emotional and somatic equilibrium retrain and repattern the client's nervous system. Each EMDR–sandtray session becomes a workout for the client's nervous system, which is learning that it is safe to feel and visit what hurts and longs to be integrated because there is a homecoming and a space to rest and distance themselves from their pain.

As the end of a session approaches, the EMDR–sandtray clinician works to find the most appropriate time to finalize the therapeutic encounter. Sometimes, especially when working in reprocessing phases with clients exposed to complex trauma, closure happens in the middle of high emotional turbulence in the tray and in the client's system. In these cases, the clinician must use interweaves to support the client in rapidly attaining balance before ending the session. Finding the right place in the process to announce the end of the reprocessing session is paramount. If the interweaves do not create the desired shift and restoration of information processing, then further work on containment and regulation will be necessary before closing the session.

The following are the steps for closing out an EMDR–sandtray session:

Step 1: Announce That It Is Time to End the Session

Let the client know that the time in the sand is ending. Remind them that each session is a small expedition in the larger journey toward healing. The voyage they embarked on in the session has come to an end.

Step 2: Close the Tray

Direct the client's attention to the tray and inquire about what must happen before the session ends. You might say:

> " Before we end our time together, I wonder if any voices in the tray still need to be heard. Is there anything that needs to happen in the tray before we go?"

Give the client time and an opportunity to rearrange the tray if needed. Sometimes, a character or the client in the sand world may be in danger. If the client does not make any changes, inquire about what is occurring in the tray using their language while giving them space to choose how to close it. For instance:

> " You said that the [perpetrator] was hurting the [character] in the tray, and I noticed that they are still in the [perpetrator]'s arms. Is this where they want to stay until our next meeting/Is this where you want them to stay until next time?"

Invite the client to rearrange the tray. Sometimes, you may offer the character(s) a safe haven in the office where they can remain safe until the following session. The client will choose from the places offered to house the character. Reassure the client that the character will remain safe in the office until the next session, when it can continue to tell its story. Allow the client to decide whether figures need to come out or come in. New figures may enter the tray at the end of the session, especially for protection. Remember that how the tray ends is ultimately up to the client, and remind the client that they are free to accept or decline any suggestions.

Step 3: Enhance Acts of Triumph

If resources, acts of triumph, realizations, and new knowings emerged during the work, especially reprocessing sessions, in the tray, take the opportunity to strengthen them with short and slow sets of BLS/DAS. Invite the client to notice what they want to take with them from what unfolded in the sand world. If the client has difficulty finding resources, you may use reflective communication and describe some of the assets and acts of triumph you observed. You might say:

> "As you look at the tray and the world you created, I wonder what you would like to take with you. Let's see if any resources or a new insight/awareness/understanding came your way."

If you are working with a child, you might say:

> "As you look at the tray and the world you created, I wonder what good/valuable/important stuff you want to take with you. I invite you to look for the goodies/treasures that came to you/character or a new understanding or feeling that came to you/character today. Let me know when you find them."

If the client does not report any findings, you might say:

> "I notice that [protector] helped the [character] that was struggling, and the [character] was [use the client's words to describe how the character felt, without interpreting] at the end. The [character] learned that others could help them and that they could survive and make it. I wonder if this is one of the goodies."

If the client resonates with the reflection, invite them to notice and witness the character's experience. Invite them to notice the feelings and the location in the character's body, and use slow and short sets of BLS/DAS to enhance the experience. Continue to direct the client to areas of the tray where they reported new awareness, insight, realizations, transformation, understanding, and movement.

254   EMDR-Sandtray-based Therapy

Step 4: Bring Parts of the Self to Safety and Containment

If you worked with parts (dissociative or ego states) during the session, they need to return to safety. The inner world must be contained before ending the session. Invite the client to look at the tray and return the parts of the self that were active to the safety of their inner home. Thank the client for allowing these parts to be seen/witnessed in the tray and honor the parts for their work. Refer to Chapter 9 for additional information about working with parts.

Step 5: Dismantle the Tray

In Chapter 2, this procedural step of sandtray therapy has been addressed from multiple angles.

Step 6: Allow Enough Time for Dismantling and Cleaning Up

The clinician must organize their time wisely when reprocessing in the sandtray. Sessions should not exceed 50 minutes because the last 10 minutes of the hour are essential for dismantling and cleaning to prepare the room and the tray for the next client. If your client has a slow tempo for selecting figures and reprocessing, consider scheduling 90-minute sessions for them, especially during the reprocessing phase. Having a small vacuum cleaner in the office will save you time. Cleaning is crucial for preventing the spread of disease.

Phase 8: Reevaluation

This is a fundamental phase in EMDR-sandtray-based treatment that is often overlooked. Reevaluation ensures the continuity of treatment and the reaccessing of the memory so it can be fully reprocessed and integrated (F. Shapiro, 2001, 2018). There are several levels of reevaluation that range from assessing changes, challenges, and improvements to reaccessing the memory and the sand world to the final reevaluation of treatment and goals when therapy is to be terminated.

General Reevaluation

This level of reevaluation frequently assesses treatment effects, enabling the clinician to make necessary adjustments for optimizing the treatment outcome.

- Check in with the client about any changes or occurrences between sessions, including improvements, new issues, or anything else that may have surfaced.

- Inquire about what has happened since the prior session. Are there any changes? Difficulties and challenges?
- If the client has faced challenges: How did the client handle challenges? Did they use regulatory strategies learned in therapy? If they did not, why not, or what happened as a result?

Target Specific Reevaluation

Reevaluation in the tray has multiple components, depending on the phase at which the prior session ended.

Target Specific Reevaluation: Implicit and First Level of Information Processing

If the client, often a child, is processing implicitly, reevaluation will continue to meet them at the same level. Some children like to continue with the same world, story, and characters, while others create diverse worlds with multiple avatars and stories. The child will craft a collection of sand stories, each representing a unique manifestation of the same embodied mind, despite each sand narrative's varying attributes and characteristics. The issues, challenges, and conflicts will emerge under different costumes and avatars, yet they speak about the same mind's journey.

When delivering the invitation to create a world, ask the client if they want to continue with the world they created previously or to start with something different. If the client proceeds to create a new sand world, follow the procedural steps of the assessment phase and move into the processing phases, as delineated in Chapters 6 and 7.

If the client wants to create a new world with a new story line, the clinician supports and affirms the client's autonomy and therapeutic path. In these cases, a new assessment phase will be necessary addressing and creating a baseline of the new sand world.

The reevaluation phase's procedural steps provide a structured pathway to re-enter the memory network, utilizing the procedural steps of the phase where the prior session was terminated. For example, if the client's session concluded in Phase 4, the corresponding procedural steps for that phase should be followed, such as:

1. Identify the area of the world that stands out for the character or the worst part (image).
2. Identify the character's emotions, and invite their physicalization in the tray using a titration continuum: covered/buried, half-covered, or completely visible.
3. Ask the main character about its SUD.

256 EMDR-Sandtray-based Therapy

4. Inquire about where the disturbance is located in the character's body.
5. Initiate BLS/DAS.

If the prior session ended with an incomplete installation phase (Phase 5), the positive cognition and the VoC are rechecked before initiating BLS/DAS. If the installation phase was terminated and the session ended with an incomplete body scan, leaving remnants of unassimilated and unintegrated trauma-related, body-based material, reaccess the sand world through the body scan (Phase 6). In this case, invite the client to connect to the sand world and the positive cognition while scanning the character's body and proceeding with BLS/DAS until the somatic remnants are integrated.

Case: Closure and Reevaluation Phases With Implicit and First Level of Information Processing

Sam, 12, came to therapy because of his oppositional behaviors. He had witnessed domestic violence in his home since he was 2 years old. After eight sessions dedicated to stabilization and preparation (Phase 2), Sam started to reprocess a world where crocodiles were hitting and enslaving swans. The main character was a swan that was running and trying to escape from a powerful crocodile. This sand world was filled with fear, powerlessness, and a lack of safety that overtook the world just as the session was approaching its end.

Closure. The clinician reflected on the fear and lack of safety in the world and invited the child to be curious about how he wanted to leave the world as they approached the end of the session. The child resonated with the world's dangers, so through interweaves, the clinician wondered about potential helpers, protectors, and ways to escape from the crocodiles—the swan had friends and escape routes and had experienced multiple acts of triumph during the session. Sam rearranged the world and placed the swan away from the crocodiles with its friends. Sam also represented the swan's strengths and capacity to run through rocks.

After witnessing the swan's strengths and acts of triumph, Sam reported feeling proud of the swan, safe, and happy, and he located these states in his stomach and heart. The clinician used slow and short sets of BLS/DAS to enhance Sam's affective and embodied experience. Sam chose to have the clinician dismantle the tray, so they moved it aside and practiced the container exercise that Sam had learned during the preparation phase. Sam also danced with air and played a ball game with his therapist. The clinician also did safety checks to orient Sam to the safety in the present moment and, through play and movement, activated social engagement.

Reevaluation. In the following session, Sam stated that he did not remember the prior world, and despite the therapist giving Sam a title and short overview of the world, he expressed a desire to start a new world.

In this new world, a killer spider lived next to a family with three boys. The spider would come to the house at night and inject the family with venom. The spider was big and powerful, and the family struggled to find a way out of the house where the spider ruled. Similar struggles, challenges, and conflicts unfolded under different characters and sand stories. Because Sam tended to get impatient and irritable with questions, the clinician conducted a brief assessment phase, focusing on fewer procedural steps, such as identifying just the image, the emotions, SUD, and location in the body. During reprocessing phases, Sam found help for the family and the three boys on his own. He brought in helpers that were bigger than the spider. In the end, one of the boys in the world kicked and killed the spider. Sam was able to mobilize resources and restore safety for the family and the three boys, returning to homeostasis more rapidly and without the clinician's assistance.

Target Specific Reevaluation: Explicit Information Processing

Begin by inviting the client to reconnect with the memory they processed in the previous session and externalize it in the tray. Then, encourage the client to select figures from the miniature collection to represent and accompany them in expressing how the event exists within them in the present moment. Once the memory is in the tray, invite the client to check if the world feels complete and to explore the tray before moving into the procedural steps of reevaluation phase. Once the actual memory has been accessed for the first time, maintaining continuity is essential to help the client move the experience that exists in their biology toward integration and adaptive resolution. If the client reports a strong urge to abandon the sand world being reprocessed, explore these urges because they may bring understanding and insight into the client's inner organization. Some of the potential underlying issues that could cause a client to oppose the reaccessing of a sand world from the previous session:

1. An increased level of activation in association with the traumatic experience and its concomitant cognitive, emotional, and sensorimotor schemas has upregulated the client's defenses, blocking access to their inner world and the memory.
2. Trauma-related phobias have increased their presence, pushing the client to abandon the sand world holding space for the memory. This can happen if reprocessing moved the client out of their affect tolerance threshold during the prior session.
3. The fear system has been activated, sending the client into a flight

response in which the client seeks distance from the distressing memory. This response, a deeply embedded survival strategy, serves the individual who is seeking solace in disengagement as a means of emotional preservation. This distancing strategy is a complex interplay between autonomic states and cognitive processes that underscores the intricate connection between the mind and the body in the face of trauma reprocessing. The client may not feel sufficiently safe in the therapeutic room, in the relationship with the clinician, or in the processing itself. The therapeutic relationship may need to be strengthened to hold a much safer relational space for the client during the deep states of vulnerability uncovered during reprocessing. The clinician may need to increase the level of titration used to enter the memory system.

4. The client doesn't understand the process, and EMDR treatment results in confusion about the therapeutic path. In these cases, it is best to reassess the underlying causes by inviting shared curiosity and exploring what is prompting the client to abandon the memory being reprocessed. Accessing another memory may take the client to the one they are phobic of or avoiding. There is profound richness, insight, and wisdom in the moments when the defense system is activated, highlighting its role of protection for the client. Clinicians should never enforce a procedural step if it overrides the client's needs. Instead, explore, accompany, coregulate, and coorganize the client's experience to support expansions in their field of consciousness. If the client's defenses become activated, explore and work compassionately with the protective and defensive states or parts in the sand tray. You may return to the preparation phase if it best serves the client, or you might need to further titrate the client's entry into the traumagenic networks.

5. The memory does not carry much disturbance or significance, so it becomes irrelevant to continue reprocessing it.

Future Template

The nuanced framework of EMDR treatment offers a three-pronged approach by empowering individuals to develop relationships with their past, present, and future. EMDR-sandtray-based therapy integrates the multifaceted dimensions of time and space that exist in the human experience. In EMDR treatment, the individual first embraces past traumatic memories to recontextualize and reorganize how they exist in the individual's embodied mind. Second, there is a present-focused reprocessing of activating stimuli (triggers) that as a result of secondary conditioning may hold disturbance on their own (F. Shapiro, 2018). Third, there is a future-oriented component that is designed to bring empowerment as the individual envisions the future with a new sense of hope, agency, and possibility. The temporal orientation and synthesis offered by the three-pronged approach provide a comprehensive therapeutic journey through which clients can weave their past, present, and future into a cohesive and integrated sense of self and a life narrative (cognitive, emotional, and somatic). At the same time, it helps develop a sense of temporal differentiation that transcends the constraints of past traumatic events and present triggers so clients can fully embrace the present. The future template is a vital prong in EMDR treatment. As the client looks toward the future, they can begin to embody their newly emerging sense of self, allowing them to engage in new and empowering actions. When working with the future template, the tray becomes the mind's playground where new thoughts and behaviors can be practiced. The client's embodied mind can now access a field of possibilities as it faces future challenges and battles.

Future Template Procedural Steps in the Tray

Step 1. Invite the client to connect to a future challenge (based on facing a previously triggering situation) and to pick figures from the miniature collection that can represent it.

Step 2. Invite the client to create a future world. If the client is an older adolescent or adult, you might say:

> I invite you to select the figures that will help you create a world in the tray representing the future where you are facing and dealing with [describe the trigger] in the way that truly honors you/supports your most authentic self/best supports you. Notice the qualities you have discovered in your new sense of self and identity. As you create this world, I invite you to include what you want to be doing or saying and how you act and feel. How are you managing/handling and responding to this situation?"

Once the client creates the future event in the tray, invite them to pick a figure(s) representing their positive cognition, if they want it physicalized in the tray.

If the client is a child, you might say:

- I invite you to pick the figures that will help you create a world in the future where you are facing/dealing with [describe the trigger]. Remember all the good stuff/things you have found out/discovered about yourself. As you create this world, I invite you to represent what you want to be doing and saying, as well as how you act and feel. In general, how are you handling this situation?

- Now that you have the future world, would you like to pick a figure or figures that represent or show in the tray the good thoughts you have/want to have about yourself as you look at this future world?

Follow with BLS/DAS unless the client reports a disturbance that does not decrease or resolve. If there is a disturbance, some "detective work" should be done to trace the turmoil and distress to where it began, which may lead to new unprocessed memory systems. New figures may represent the origin of this turmoil and be added to the sand world. The future distress may also be physicalized in the sand tray and reprocessed with Phases 3, 4, 5, and 6 in separate sessions.

Step 3: Install the Positive Cognition. Once the disturbance has subsided and positive, adaptive material begins to emerge more prominently, focus on installing the positive cognition (PC) until it feels fully believable to the client, reaches a VoC of 7 or a level of valence that is ecologically sound, and is accompanied by a sense of cognitive embodiment and connection to the positive cognition. Invite the client to reflect the enhanced positive affect through symbols in the tray, further anchoring the experience.

Step 4: Bringing Challenges. Once the positive cognition has reached ecological validity, invite the client to bring potential challenges into the tray. Invite the client to select figures to represent the trials that may appear as well as those that represent the client's potential responses. You might say:

> « I invite you now to think of a challenge/difficulty that may arise in this future situation, and let's create it in the tray."

Give the client time to connect and sit with the challenge.

> « How would you like to respond to this challenge? How would you like to act, think, feel? How would you like your body to feel? What would you like to do?"

Repeat Steps 3 and 4 until the client does not detect any disturbances.

The work described above may seem too technical at first to the newly trained EMDR–sandtray clinician. As you master the procedural steps, you will begin to dance with each step, and they will seem seamless and easy to navigate. This four-step future template process helps clients with complex trauma and dissociative tendencies start to develop a relationship

Phases 5–8: Installation, Body Scan, Closure, Reevaluation, and Future Template **261**

FIGURE 8.2 A sand world about the future template of an adult female client. In the future sand world, she faces narcissist men that tried to overpower her in the past (placed on the right side of the tray). After reprocessing the trigger she creates a future world where she is connected to her wiser self and the power within (on the left). She places a fence to depict her capacity to set boundaries and say no as well as the inner companions including her healthy anger.

with their future. Usually, their temporal orientation is skewed as a result of exposure to chronic traumatization. Creating a future world begins to set events on a temporal continuum while expanding the field of affective, cognitive, somatic and behavioral possibilities that the present and the future bring.

Some individuals are trapped by ghosts of the past or are hijacked by future anxieties. The future template provides the client with a framework to practice new skills, ways of being, and responses to the world in a forward-looking, actionable context. The tray is a safe space where the client's embodied mind can envision itself existing in a future that brings prospects and possibilities of mastery, empowerment, and personal agency. Standard EMDR and EMDR-sandtray-based therapy reset and restore the individual's relationships with time and space, which helps the individual become more firmly grounded in the present while drawing wisdom from the past and cultivating the potential of a more fulfilling future.

CHAPTER 9

Advanced Strategies During Reprocessing Phases With Complex Clients

The sand world serves as a field of possibilities, providing clients with a means to explore their intricate inner landscape. It also offers a refuge and an opportunity to access, explore, connect, and mentalize their inner experience. The addition of parts work to EMDR–sandtray provides clients with myriad opportunities to physicalize their inner system dynamics and conflicts in the tray during reprocessing. In severe cases that include strong divisions in the client's personality, comorbidities, and/or psychotic features, clinicians should exercise caution when determining whether a metaphor and symbol-based approach to trauma work is appropriate for the client.

Substantial work with the client's inner system should have been accomplished during the initial phases of treatment. As the client arrives to reprocessing phases, ego states or dissociative parts should share greater coconsciousness, increased capacities for communication, and improved conflict resolution. However, the system's readiness to access traumagenic material must be carefully assessed and established from moment to moment, as it can still change despite previous preparatory work. Multiple authors and scholars support a titrated and gradual entrance into the synaptic architecture that holds the dissociative matrix and traumagenic memories (Gonzalez & Mosquera, 2012; Steele et al., 2017; van der Hart et al., 2006; Fisher, 2017). Even though sandtray procedures and components provide distance, containment, and refuge to the compartmentalized mind during reprocessing phases, these clients may have responses that are unpredictable and volatile, requiring moment-to-moment tracking and adjustments to meet the client's requirements for safety.

Two levels of communication must be explored and assessed when working with clients experiencing dissociation during the reprocessing phases. They include communication between parts and self (intrapersonal) and communication between the inner world and the outer world (interpersonal). The capacity of clients with intricate internal dynamics to connect

263

and report on their inner experiences is often limited. This is compounded in children, depending on their verbal and cognitive developmental level, to the point that they cannot understand nor verbally report on what is emerging in their internal life. Clients living with fragmented identities or highly contended inner systems may not be open to sharing information with their clinician or their other parts. The greater the client's and their inner system's communication and regulation capacities, the more robust their integrative and processing capacities will be. The sandtray work offers these clients a vehicle of expression, through symbols and various levels of distance, especially as they approach traumatic memories.

The inner system has two access routes into memory networks:

1. **Implicit Portal:** This access route is gentle and is especially accessible to young clients who use play as their main language. Parts may emerge, hidden within the characters' costumes in the sand world, revealing themselves as the stories unfold.
2. **Explicit Portal:** This access route is used when the client's mind acknowledges the existence of traumatic experiences. Parts unblend into figures that represent inner dynamics and adverse experiences with or without the companionship of verbal narratives. Sometimes, parts unblend in the tray, protected by the symbol and metaphor without any words. Other times, rich verbal accounts and storytelling accompany the externalization of the inner system's experiences.

Readiness Markers

Openly and intentionally establishing the highly dissociative client's readiness to move into reprocessing is paramount. Sometimes, a client's increased stability may lead us to believe that they are prepared to begin trauma reprocessing. Readiness is convoluted and multilayered in the complex and dissociative population, and it changes from moment to moment with the client's shifting internal states and with external events. Micro- and macromovements into reprocessing trauma memories are integral to EMDR–sandtray work. The decision to advance into the reprocessing phases is not binary; it is a nuanced decision that considers the larger view of the client's clinical landscape and the context offered in the moment. Even after making a macrodecision to move into the reprocessing phases of EMDR–sandtray work, the clinician engages in moment-to-moment microdeterminations that depend on the client's ever-shifting internal experience. Before moving into the reprocessing phases of EMDR-sandtray-based therapy, clinicians should assess for the presence of the following markers of readiness in complex and dissociative clients:

1. Increased internal communication among parts and between the inner system and the client serves as a key benchmark, with progress indicated by parts being able to engage and dialogue even in the face of conflict
2. Reduction in inner conflict
3. Some level of temporal orientation within both of the parts and the system
4. Increased conflict resolution capacities for managing discrepancies if divergences arise among parts
5. Reduced inner dynamics that perpetuate wounding perpetrator-victim interactions (Mosquera, 2019; Paulsen, 2009)
6. Increased capacity to change state as a system, regulate activation, and tolerate affect (both positive and negative)
7. Increased capacity to discern between safety and danger and to tolerate states associated with safety
8. Increased coconsciousness among parts
9. Increased awareness of the differences between reality and fantasy
10. Increased awareness about inner and outer reality
11. Increased awareness between intrapersonal and interpersonal experiences
12. Increased capacity of the parents to be coregulators and coorganizers of the child's experience (for children)
13. Increased recognition and acknowledgment of traumatic experiences and decreased phobia of traumagenic memories
14. Evidence of strong therapeutic relationship, where client and therapist can enter the we-space to coregulate
15. Sufficient safety in the clinician–client relationship
16. Agreement from perpetrator-imitating parts to engage in trauma work/reprocessing (Mosquera, 2019; Steele et al., 2017; Paulsen & Golston, 2014)
17. Support from the adult/wise/bigger part or the part with the highest integrative capacities for trauma reprocessing (Steele et al., 2017)
18. Overall consensus in the inner system to reprocess traumatic memories (Paulsen, 2009; Steele et al., 2017)

When children or adolescents engage in "traumatic play" (Gil, 2017) with recurrent, constricted, and inflexible themes showing sadistic, highly aggressive, disorganized, and destructive sand worlds that rapidly provoke states of hyper or hypoarousal, it may be a sign that they are not ready to move into the reprocessing phases. This may also signal that there are dissociative parts that need more engagement to better prepare the inner system for trauma reprocessing.

Advanced Strategies During Reprocessing Phases With Complex Clients   265

Assessing Readiness

To assess the client's readiness, invite the client to create a world that illustrates their readiness to move into trauma reprocessing. Invite parts or ego states to share their viewpoints so the inner dialogue around trauma processing is visible in the tray. What concerns, opinions, and challenges do parts report to the client regarding bringing memories into the tray for synthesis and integration? Is there hesitation? Fear? Shame and guilt? Are there still strong defenses, avoidance, and phobic reactions surrounding the possibility of memory work?

You might invite the older/adult/wise/guiding self to direct the tray creation and to mediate communication among the parts. Several sand worlds are often created before reprocessing to explore who will be the story holders and storytellers during the reprocessing sessions and where the rest of the system will go while remaining contained, protected, and safe. The level of titration and the most suitable portals into the memory network may be discussed with the client and represented in the tray. Sometimes, one part or ego state may want to start with a small segment of the memory while another is ready to embrace the entire experience.

Many of the resources scattered throughout previous chapters can be used, such as the safe/healing place or the healing place for parts to remain while telling the story or observing and listening to the process. A part, while in connection to the "guiding self" or the "place within that knows or can manage most," may be a direct storyteller who is in charge of building the trauma tray, another part may be a silent witness that observes what is occurring in the tray. A part may listen without observing, and a part may be away from the tray, without any contact to the memory or the system during reprocessing. Once the tray is explored, decisions and agreements around accessing and reprocessing the trauma should be represented in the sand world.

Portals and Levels of Titration

The client's journey into their life stories is nuanced and intricate, involving multiple layers of decision-making. The level of titration should be determined collaboratively by the clinician and the client, based on the client's capacities. Therefore, the clinician and the client assess the inner system's readiness to tolerate trauma processing from moment to moment and select the best and most suitable portal into the traumagenic networks. This process demands careful consideration of the memory that will be reprocessed and the quantity and volume of the memory that will be addressed.

A memory may be reprocessed and unblended in the sand tray in full or segmented into smaller kernels of information. This determination should be made with the client and their system of parts or ego states. If the memory is broken down into smaller bits, the tray will hold the space for just a small segment of the memory, perhaps an image, sensation, emotion, thought, or belief extracted from a low-activating memory.

Another factor to consider when preparing to reprocess a trauma memory is the level of distance, physical and symbolic, the client needs from the traumatic event. Greater physical distance from the trauma may be created by placing the resource tray near the client and the trauma tray far away from the client. Physical distance provides clients an opportunity for movement, which is also a neural exercise. Clients, especially children, may use binoculars to watch the memory or segment from a distance and may travel between trays performing animal-like movements or dance moves. Symbolic distance is offered in the metaphor of implicit and nondirective worlds in the tray. Children and young adolescents often use this implicit level of distance, as do clients presenting with dissociation in my experience, because of the refuge it offers.

Along with titration, pendulation offers a gradual entrance into a memory. The client and their inner system may pendulate from the memory/trauma tray to a resource that can be set up in a separate tray, such as:

- The calm, safe, or healing place
- Companions, spiritual and religious figures, symbolic, relational, and intergenerational
- Temporal orienting tools that ground the client to the present safety or remind them that the traumatic event is over
- Resources that represent the period after the traumatic event when safety was restored and the client returned to a state of equilibrium (conclusion of the traumatic event)
- The safety of present time and awareness of the changes/transformations that have taken place in the client's life compared to the past when the traumatic event occurred (a sand world that represents "this is me now") (Gómez, 2013, 2019)

However, beyond these techniques and strategies, the clinician's close companionship, reflective presence, and coregulatory support represent the cornerstone of the therapeutic process as the client embarks on a journey of self-discovery and the synthesis of traumagenic networks.

Implicit and Nondirective Information Processing

Sandtray work with EMDR therapy provides clients, especially young clients, with an opportunity to experience implicit synthesis and integration of the memory. In the sand tray, children's emerging ego states and dissociative parts often unfold, protected by symbols and metaphors. The avatar's costume gives refuge to the inner system and its life stories. Depending on the child's integrative capacities, clinicians may move into implicit processing if markers for readiness are present. This level of distance (implicit) is often pursued by children who present with a cohesive sense of self that maintains continuity across various states of being.

Caution must be exercised while working with children who present with compartmentalized identities and who have been exposed to severe traumatization. It is important to highlight that even when processing implicitly, intrapersonal and interpersonal communication—whether verbal or symbolic—an awareness of what is occurring internally in response to the story unfolding in the tray must be present. There are some caveats to remember when working with implicit, nondirective sand worlds with highly dissociative children. Early and relational occurrences of trauma may remain in procedural memory and may not be transferred into a represented world or play theme (Vliegen et al., 2023). Thus, "it is only when children who have experienced complex trauma can be helped to process their traumatic memories at a symbolized and mentalized level that more adaptive functioning and development can emerge" (Vliegen et al., 2023, p. 38).

Generally, clients exposed to chronic traumatization did not receive the scaffolding to develop representational and meaning-making capacities. Therefore, when these children are reprocessing an incompletely and improperly processed memory, the clinician must take a more active stance, using interweaves that mirror, validate, and reflect accurately so the clients can connect to their inner experiences. These interweaves alone offer a restorative experience, as many of our clients received inadequate readings or no mirroring at all of their inner and outer realities. Ideally, the clinician's mind serves as a bridge between the client and their inner awareness.

According to Fonagy et al. (2002),

> The child needs an adult or older child who will "play along," so that the child can see his fantasy or idea represented in the adult's mind, reintroject this, and use it as a representation of his own thinking. . . . The child's mental state must be represented sufficiently clearly and accurately for the child to recognize it, yet sufficiently playfully for the child not to be overwhelmed by its realness. (p. 324)

As Fonagy et al. compellingly describe, pretend-mode states are decoupled from reality, which allows the child to experience their inner landscape while maintaining a safe distance. However, other authors have cautioned against fully embracing fantasy when working with children who cannot differentiate between fantasy and reality. According to Merckelbach et al. (2005), being fantasy-prone coupled with trauma may predispose individuals to develop dissociation. Bagamasbad and Levin (2023) found that dissociation strongly correlates with fantasy proneness. However, other authors have reported robust empirical evidence supporting the hypothesis that trauma causes dissociation (Dalenberg et al., 2012). According to Dalenberg et al., there is minimal evidence to support the hypothesis that the relationship between dissociation and trauma is attributable to fantasy proneness. Some authors question the potential consequences of treating fantasy-prone dissociative children with metaphors. According to Silberg (2022), engaging in symbolic and fantasy play may be counter-therapeutic when the dissociative child is highly enmeshed in their fantasy world.

Typically, children between the ages of 2 and 4 begin to notice and distinguish discrepancies between their own internal states and the outside world. The secure caregiver then provides the scaffolding the child needs to develop connection with and differentiation from their inner and outer worlds (Fonagy et al., 2002). In chronically traumatized children, the inner and outer reality become indistinguishable, resulting in a significant lack of trust in their inner reality. Thus, the fantasy world becomes the default mode for the child experiencing dissociation (Fonagy et al., 2002).

We need to investigate whether the issue of utilizing symbol-based play with children that dissociate is related to the engagement in symbolic play or the absence of an external coregulator and coorganizer of experience who can accurately mirror and reflect the client's inner experience. When the clinician (and, ideally, the parent) serves as the anchor and bridge, gently grounding and connecting the client to reality and realization, the client's inner system of parts can find themselves reflected in the mind and the thoughtful reflections of the clinician (and parent, if present). One might wonder if this is an all-or-nothing decision regarding how to approach the use of symbol and metaphor-based methodologies with children exposed to chronic traumatization prone to fantasy. Instead, the decision may depend on how we deliver these forms of treatment, with the clinician serving as the anchor and bridge to reality.

Keep in mind that the clinician, throughout the eight phases of treatment, support the highly traumatized and dissociative client in gradually and gently differentiating the inner and outer worlds and reality from fantasy and interpersonal from intrapersonal experiences. For many chilcren exposed to trauma, pretend play is the only portal through which they can access their inner world. Thus, pretend play may, for these children, be a prerequisite for mental processing. In pretend play, "toys or persons can be used as if they were something or someone else and be part of imaginary stories which help to master and process experiences" (Vliegen et al., 2023, p. 33). For many children, trauma took away their freedom and capacity to engage in play, so the initial approach to EMDR-sandtray-based treatment should prioritize the restoration and reestablishment of the natural biological rhythms associated with play so that development can resume.

Another issue connected to implicit (as well as explicit) and metaphor-based processing is rumination. When processing within the context of children's play in the sand, rumination can manifest as repetitive, rigid, and obsessive reenactments, and it can hinder the rhythm and flow of information processing in the tray. However, the clinician's and caregiver's presence, attunement, mentalization, regulation, and reflective functions support children in restoring information processing so states that continue to exist, such as repetitive thoughts, emotions, and actions, can finally be resolved and synthesized.

Clinicians must use caution when moving into the reprocessing phases without the acknowledgment of the client's inner system and without systematic and strategic work to prepare dissociative parts to access memories of trauma, even implicitly. When processing in "pretend mode" and metaphor, even when the sand world is decoupled from real events, the highly dissociative client may move rapidly into a rigid access of traumagenic data without resolution and into activation of dissociative parts without a clear path back to safety and homeostasis. Before processing trauma, parts should have an intrapersonal and interpersonal pathway of communication, even when the system chooses to process an implicit and nondirective story. In all cases, the client and clinician should have a route into the inner system to maintain checks and balances during the synthesis and integration of memory.

During the reprocessing phases, the clinician continues to use interventions (interweaves) to bridge the connection between the self and the inner system of parts. You might say:

> " As you notice the [character] in fear, what happens within you, their witness? How are the different sides/parts of you feeling about/noticing/responding to the sand world/the character's emotions?"

This interweave can gently move the client into the self and the system of parts while preserving the metaphor and its protective forces.

270   EMDR-Sandtray-based Therapy

Sometimes, the client may have disclosed that a character is actually a part but still continue to process implicitly. In that case, you might say:

" Could you ask this part of you if it still needs to be the [character] in this world or if it is ready to show itself? It is okay if this part still needs the [character] to hold space for it, and it is okay if it is ready to be seen/witnessed/known."

Continue to use a titration continuum and to offer the client's parts various levels of visibility: buried, half-seen, behind or under the character, or completely visible.

Working With the Inner System of Parts in the Sand

This chapter cannot sufficiently address the complexities of working with dissociative parts in the sand tray. The topic is extensive and intricate, requiring a level of exploration and dedication that goes beyond the chapter's scope. However, I intend to provide an overview of what is possible in the tray when working with complex trauma and dissociation. Before one can address dissociative parts and ego states in the tray, one must have a model that guides the therapeutic work.

According to Putnam (1997), trauma disrupts one's metacognitive ability to integrate information and knowledge across different behavioral states. Dissociative alterations in identity represent a differential accessibility to autobiographical memory and the development of a state-dependent sense of self (Putnam, 1997). Each part is a story keeper that holds the client's disowned life story. Steele et al. (2017) eloquently state that parts are "psychobiological representations of what cannot yet be realized" (p. 28). According to F. Shapiro (2018), the dissociative structure of the individual represents insufficiently processed information, configured during earlier experiences, that exist in the brain in state-specific forms.

Approaching dissociative parts as separate persons and, on the contrary, discounting, dismissing, and denying the client's subjective experience of having separate selves are both counterproductive (Kluft, 2006).

The clinician should be mindful of how they engage and interact with dissociative parts, honoring the system while simultaneously supporting realization and integration. It is crucial to honor the client's version of integration and what aligns with and respects their system of parts.

During EMDR-sandtray-based therapy, the clinician accompanies the client as they expand their field of awareness and realizations at a pace and rhythm they establish so their autobiographical story and sense of identity can be owned, assimilated, and integrated.

There are moments when direct communication with a dissociative part is necessary during reprocessing or when the parts request contact with the clinician. However, even if the communication occurs only with one part, the clinician explores the inner relational environment surrounding the part, as it seeks direct contact with the therapist, while increasing the client's mentalization. What prompted this part to refuse/avoid/not pursue communication with other parts or the client's wiser/guiding/adult self? What is this part seeking, and what unmet needs are behind this request? Does this part hold power and control over the system? What does it need at the moment? What is this part doing for the inner system? These questions serve as interweaves that expand the client's field of realization and awareness. As a field of possibilities, sandtray work gives parts and the self-system a blank canvas where they can unblend and physicalize their concerns, thoughts, emotions, conflicts, and potential resources as they embark on the synthesis of memory and, ultimately, identity. As they arise in the client's conscious or implicit awareness, double binds, polarizations, and conflicts are also reflected in symbols added to or acting in the tray. The clinician invites the client to represent in the tray any inner divisions they notice to promote realizations, inner connectedness, and coconsciousness.

In the client's psyche and its representation in the sand tray, multiple story keepers and parts may emerge.

Young and Child Parts

These parts are often anxious, fearful, in distress (Fisher, 2017), and stuck in action systems of defense (attachment cry, flight, fight, freeze, fright, flag, or faint) (Steele et al., 2017). These parts may be easily triggered and often hold stories of trauma. Child parts are likely to hold unclaimed and, at times, repudiated unmet attachment needs.

Unfulfilled longings may be identified, represented, and satisfied in the sand world. Parts that exist on both sides of a polarity may show up to represent their lack of acceptance of other parts, their stories, and especially their needs. Often, inner caregivers participate in nourishing and containing these young parts in the tray.

During reprocessing phases, invite curiosity about what keeps these parts at a much younger developmental stage. Are there stories/memories that can be depicted and symbolized in the tray to unburden them? Temporal orientation is often necessary for these clients as is exploring and depicting the motives, experiences, and stories that keep them from growing up and developing. Interweaves may invite the system to be and sit in the tray with the disclaimed need of these young parts.

In the tray, nourishment, love, protection, companionship, and play are represented while the client and their system allow this information to enter

272 EMDR-Sandtray-based Therapy

awareness. What happens as a result? Are there polarizations that need to be represented in the tray? One part may find a need childish and disgusting, while others may hold acceptance for it. Invite the polarity into the tray so these discrepancies can continue to expand the client's consciousness and promote the assimilation and integration of memory and identity.

Perpetrator-Imitating Parts

These parts often emerge when one has endured frightening experiences of severe abuse (Mosquera, 2019) by important relational figures that become imprinted and represented in the client's embodied mind. According to Steele et al. (2017), these parts reenact traumatic memories using the perpetrator's perspective. They protect the client from shame by attacking the self, holding the intolerable memories of trauma, and reenacting dynamics of abuse in the inner system. In the tray, these perpetrator-parts may show up as implicit characters that abuse, kill, and torture, or they may show up as acknowledged abusers and oppressors. However, underneath the avatar resides the wounded, burdened, and tormented inner child (Paulsen, 2009). The work in the tray supports identity differentiation so the client can distinguish their true self from the internalized perpetrator and realize that

FIGURE 9.1 An adult client represents in the tray her compartmentalized inner system. On the left side, two very critical and hostile parts are depicted by the man in a trench coat and the shaming queen. A flying owl represents a side of her that depersonalizes when emotionally activated, and next to that are two young parts that are often fearful and who carry many memories of abuse. Freddy Krueger (man in striped shirt) depicts a perpetrator-imitating part that harms the body and, while active, has attempted suicide. Wonder Woman is the part that functions in daily life, often overdoing and taking on multiple responsibilities. The last part is a highly sexualized teen.

FIGURE 9.2 **The resource tray of an adult and her inner dissociative system. Parts brought what they needed into the tray, including the level of containment and distance they needed to move into reprocessing phases.**

this part that emulates the perpetrator is a defense rather than a manifestation of their true self and identity.

During the initial phases of treatment, the safe place and the team of companions for the young parts are created in the tray so they can be internalized and generate boundaries and protection from the perpetrator-imitating parts, thereby preventing the reenactment of abusive dynamics. Before moving into the reprocessing phases, the therapist must foster stronger communication with perpetrator-imitating parts to contain and rearrange dynamics that perpetuate and reenact the trauma suffered in the hands of the actual perpetrator. If these dynamics stall processing, the clinician could use interweaves that restore safety, differentiate identity, and provide compassion and temporal orientation.

Differentiation. Sandtray-based interweaves that support the client in differentiating their identity from the perpetrator include:

- No one is born knowing ways to hurt others, so how or where did this part of you learn to [describe what the part is doing to hurt others]? Did this part witness someone do this to others or to themselves?
- To learn these hurting tactics, this part of you must have witnessed or been the recipient of them.
- I would like to invite you to look underneath the figure representing this part of you in the tray and see if the hurt self is actually somewhere deep underneath that part.
- Is it possible that this part of you is carrying all the memories and stories from what [perpetrator] did to you, and it is actually trying to help you? This part may be holding the story so you do not have to carry painful and terrifying stories/memories or remember what happened to you.

- I invite you to bring this new knowing and understanding into the sand world in the way that you and your inner system are ready to witness it.

Compassion. This sandtray-based interweave supports the client in cultivating compassion:

> " Let's take a moment to just sit and witness the tray and what is emerging. It is hard to see this part's actions and realize that this part has been carrying some of the most challenging experiences in order to protect you, even though these protective efforts hurt you and others."

When the client is ready to see the perpetrator-imitating part through the lens of compassion, invite it, and follow with BLS/DAS.

Reenactments During Reprocessing and Realization. While the client is processing memories, or kernels of memories, a perpetrator-imitating part may engage in abusive actions and reenactments toward another part, especially the young parts, and this may stall processing. When this happens, you could offer these reflections:

- I wonder if you can check with the part and story holder of the perpetrator's stories and memories.
- What is triggering these actions? How is this part trying to protect, and how and what is it trying to protect?
- How did this part come into your life? How did it come to do its job in the way it does? Was it always this way?
- Sometimes, the hurtful act is an act of storytelling. It may be this part's way of telling the story of what happened or what was done to them.
- Maybe this part can tell the story in the tray.
- Is the system ready? Do the parts that are present know what happened?

The story may emerge without words and be protected through symbols, reducing unwanted activation while giving these parts an entry point to tell their stories.

Temporal Orientation. This sandtray-based interweave helps ground the client in the present. You might say:

Advanced Strategies During Reprocessing Phases With Complex Clients **275**

- Let's take a look at the figure in the tray representing the part that is [perpetrator]. How old is this part of you? Let's represent it in the tray (if appropriate). If this part was [perpetrator] who hurt you so much, he would be much older now and would be living in another country and not here with you.
- What would help this part to know that what [perpetrator] did is over and that you are safe now?

Validation and Reflections. This sandtray-based interweave supports the client in reflecting and validating the work their parts do. You might say:

> " It must be a lot of work to be angry and ensure that all the parts inside are properly aligned."

Additionally, parts affected by the actions of perpetrator-imitating parts need validation and compassion.

Hostile and Aggressive Parts

These parts often emerge after exposure to aggressive and abusive environments as well as experiences of invalidation and betrayal (Steele et al., 2017). These parts may express rage and exercise a punitive-controlling strategy that emerged because the child had to coexist with a caregiver who simultaneously activated attachment and defense systems. Autonomic states provide the space where inner parts exist as they are held in state-dependent form. Hostile, critical, and blaming parts, which are often looking for a fight, carry a sensitized and unintegrated pattern of sympathetic fight responses that frequently become activated during processing. When these parts show up in the tray to change the flow of information processing, use reflective statements and invite the physicalizations of long-held patterns of compartmentalized cognitive, affective, and somatic schemas. When did these story keepers come into the client's life? When, where, and from whom did they acquire this way of being, thinking, feeling, relating, and acting? The depictive process through sandtray representations and their symbolic reflections can solidify and make the stories and old messages these parts carry even more real. The underlying shame and rage can be carried by avatars that gently bring this information into consciousness and help build autonomic awareness.

The clinician delivering EMDR–sandtray supports the client's connection to the place of knowing within (able to see or manage) or empowers the client's "guiding self" to emerge as the mediator and leader of the system. This allows for greater differentiation greater differentiation, mentalization, temporal organization, and rearrangement of the client's relationship with time and space, realizations, and coconsciousness. The sandtray work provides acknowledgment, and the symbols themselves offer an act of recognition to the inner system while assimilating and integrating material, with or without words. The sand worlds will provide information about how the client is internally organized from moment to moment and how they relate to themselves and their system of parts while processing.

Explicit Information Processing: Setting Up the Landscape

Explicit processing can begin once the inner system has agreed on the following:

- The memory that will be accessed
- Which parts will participate during trauma processing sessions, and how will they participate (some parts will be fully present, while others will be half-present or present at a distance)
- The level of titration and the access route into the memory
- The number of trays that will be used and what each will hold (e.g., trauma tray, resource tray, safe place tray, healing place, safety tray)
- The size and color of sand of each tray

While in connection with their inner system, the client begins to create their resource tray(s) to expand their sense of safety and containment and to raise their integrative capacities for processing. The client's parts, or ego states, are invited to bring their own resources and whatever they need to feel comfortable visiting/accessing the memory of trauma. The resource trays are created first to anchor the inner system. Once the healing place has been created, the part doing the storytelling may decide to direct the creation of the trauma tray from the safe refuge of this healing place.

FIGURE 9.3 **The client prepares the tray to receive a traumatic story by creating areas where resources and supportive parts are present. Some parts face the area where the trauma will be represented, while others face away, their backs turned.**

Parts can choose multiple levels of distance, from direct participation in the trauma tray to complete absence, remaining in their safe harbors. For some parts, being present yet having some level of distance from the trauma memory can reduce the chances of becoming flooded and overwhelmed by what is unfolding in the trauma tray. Some parts may choose to be under the sand, under a character, or under other coverings.

The client may choose to use only one tray to hold both the resource areas and the space for the trauma (or a kernel of it) to be represented. In this case, the client may use dividers, such as fences, doors, rocks, or any other figures that can hold boundaries in the tray. Defensive and protective parts are invited to monitor the process from within the tray because clinicians may find it easier to access, through interweaves, protectors who become activated if these parts are already represented in the tray. For instance, an avoidant part, stuck in the flight response, may be placed in the resource or trauma tray to monitor the sand world containing the traumagenic memory. Negotiations with this part should have preceded trauma work and reprocessing, even if only at an implicit level. Once the resource tray or resource areas are completed, parts select the areas they will occupy during reprocessing so the client can create the trauma tray based on the level of titration agreed upon. Additionally, an imaginary or physically represented container (maybe a separate tray) may remain open and near the client to provide containment and modulate arousal as needed.

Once the resource tray or area has been created, encourage the client, while maintaining connection to their inner system of parts, to notice if the resource tray feels complete. You might say:

> ❝ Does this world that holds all the different parts of you along with your resources feel complete and sufficient to support you when we visit/access the memory (or small kernels)? Can you check within to see if the tray(s) feels complete?❞

If the client is a child, you might say:

> ❝ I invite you to check inside with all the different sides/colors/parts of you and see if this tray has everything that you and each side of you need to visit the memory of the hurtful/bothersome thing that happened.❞

A part that does not want to be seen may be invited to create a fort in the tray, where it can remain hidden and unseen.

Once the client's inner system is adequately resourced and there is enough agreement among parts about moving into reprocessing phases, the client is invited to tell the story in the tray at a pace that feels appropriate to the client. The client's "guiding self" can direct and accompany the part(s) that holds the memory to monitor the creation of the story from the comfort of the healing or safe place.

Titration and pendulation strategies and protocols covered in Chapters 6 and 7 can be used with complex trauma clients. The client can access a kernel of the memory. The memory, in part or as a whole, may be covered by a piece of fabric that the client can lift or shift to reveal only parts of the memory as they pendulate from the resource tray to the traumatic memory tray. When working with children, movement can be incorporated to keep the client present and engaged. Movement-based BLS/DAS may be used, for instance, by saying:

> "Let's go to the other tray like a [horsey] or a [rabbit]. Which [animal] would you prefer?"

If the client chooses to or can only access the memory in segments, which may be organized around chronology or level of disturbance, multiple trays and sand colors might be used (Gómez, 2013). The clinician may use EMDR recent event protocols to process each segment in its tray before bringing all the segments of the memory together into a single tray so the client can synthesize and process any remaining disturbances. If the client is embracing the full memory, it is advisable to start working with mildly disturbing events and move into high-intensity events only after the client's integrative capacities have been tested and observed through multiple processing sessions.

Sarah, a 13-year-old with four identified dissociative parts, came to therapy because of self-harming behaviors and suicidal thoughts. During the preparation phases, communication within the system was increased as was coconsciousness among the parts. *Mad*, a teen part, was the first to enter the sand tray. Sarah stated that Mad hated everybody and wanted to hurt this body that she did not recognize as her own. *Cloudy* was a 4-year-old, fearful part that held many memories of neglect and abuse at the hands of her biological father. *Sunny*, a very young part, was pleasing, submissive, and compliant and carried the memories of the abuse and a defensive strategy of submission. *Katherine* was a 24-year-old part that took care of the young parts and had been with Sarah since she was very young to supply the care and nourishment that Sarah lacked in her life. Sarah did extensive work connecting to her inner system while her therapist accompanied her, providing coregulation, mirroring, and presence. The therapist remained open and engaged in frequent reflections to support Sarah in connecting and developing a relationship with her compartmentalized mind. Extensive work was also done with Sarah's mother: the clinician modeled how to coregulate and coorganize experience so Sarah's mother could learn to mirror the nuances and often disorganized information that inhabited Sarah's mind.

After extensive work in the initial phases of EMDR-sandtray-based treatment, Sarah's episodes of self-harm and suicidal ideations declined significantly. Sarah's interoceptive awareness and capacities expanded as she developed clear communication pathways with her therapist and between her guiding self and her inner system of parts. Sarah learned to do frequent inside visits and inner meetings to resolve internal conflicts. Sarah remained conflicted, torn between her dissociative parts. At times, she leaned toward Mad and Sunny, who were eager to share their story. Yet, other times, she aligned with Cloudy, who remained paralyzed by fear at the thought of disclosing her own. Sarah was invited to create a tray of her inner system's parts and their concerns, opinions, feelings, and thoughts related to visiting the memories of abuse. In the tray, Cloudy represented her fear of the experience occurring again if they even thought about it. Despite having done work around temporal orientation with Cloudy, it was clear she was still in trauma time. Further trauma reprocessing was delayed until Sarah and her part Cloudy could work on the phobic reactions to the traumatic event while actively addressing temporal orientation in the tray. Sarah, while remaining connected to her inner system and especially to Cloudy, created a sand world with the theme of "this is me now" and another of "that was me then." After several sessions of work on orienting Sarah and her inner system to the present safety, Cloudy was ready to be with Sarah to visit the memories of adversity. Sarah and her inner system agreed to start with a small kernel of the smallest and least frightening experience of the trauma. This time, the entire system was on board and well-resourced overall.

Information Processing With Complex Internal Systems

For the most part, the clinician supports part–self communication (R. Schwartz, 1995, 2021; Schwartz & Sweezy, 2020), unless a part insists on direct communication with the therapists or stalls information processing and does not respond to the client's requests to communicate. However, it is worth exploring what is prompting this part to seek direct communication with the therapist and what is happening in the communication channel between the client's guiding self and the part responsible for blocking the flow of processing. In response to blocked information processing, the clinician should use decision-making markers described in Chapter 7.

One of the most important procedural steps of EMDR therapy is the interweave, as it closely accompanies the client during the delicate and intricate phenomena of memory integration. Considering the close connection between trauma and disorganized attachment in the emergence of dissociation (Liotti, 2017; Farina et al., 2019) and the frequently diminished mentalizing and metacognitive capacities of individuals exposed to chronic trauma (Fonagy et al., 2002), the flow and coherence of memory processing is often affected by disruptions in information processing. Therefore, clinicians must be well-versed in the delivery of interweaves and must possess a vast repertoire of interventions that can aid clients when the flow of processing halts.

Interweaves That Work With the Body and the Sensorimotor System

When information processing stalls, the clinician may use interweaves that work directly with the body to challenge its procedural memory, to get it to execute new actions, and to support completions and synthesis. Some dissociative parts and ego states are organized around motivational systems of defense (van der Hart et al., 2006; Steele et al., 2017) and carry the burdens of unintegrated defenses and patterns of autonomic activation. Additionally, the self-system holds somatic as much as affective and cognitive stories of truncated defensive actions that have not yet been integrated into a coherent and cohesive sense of self. "The unexpressed call for help, the inability to run, or the thwarted need to push away a perpetrator are held in our soma" (A. Schwartz, 2024, p. 162). It is crucial that the EMDR clinician to work with body-based memory and have a rich repertoire of interweaves. The following are some examples of body-based interweaves that work with the inner system.

Fight-or-Flight Response. The self-system or a part may carry an unintegrated fight-or-flight response. During processing, affective and somatic indicators of a part carrying defensive actions and urges may surface in the sand tray and within the client's inner experience. An interweave would invite the client to focus their awareness on the urges and to represent them in the tray. For example:

> *"* As you notice these sensations in your/the character's body, how do you want this information to be represented in the tray? How has your inner world been carrying this information/sensation? What part of you carries/holds (or has been carrying/holding) this information/sensation/urge for you?"

Advanced Strategies During Reprocessing Phases With Complex Clients

You may invite the part holding the fight-or-flight response to come to the forefront, if it feels safe to do so:

> "I wonder if you could invite the part of you holding the [name the response (e.g., anger, fear, desire to fight/flee)]. What happens as you become more aware of this side of you? What happens in your body as you notice/become aware of what this part of you brings? How is it for this part of you to carry this sensory or somatic load/sensation/information? What happens for you and your inner system as you become aware of what this part of you has been carrying/holding/doing for you?"

Give the client the opportunity to physicalize in the tray what is emerging, and provide BLS/DAS. You might say:

> "As you and this side of you watch the story it has carried for you, what is happening in your body? What sensations are unfolding for you? Does this sensation poke, throb, or tingle? Does it push or grab? Does it expand or contract? Can we invite you and the story holder to watch?"

Once again, continue BLS/DAS. Remember that each question represents an interweave, so you may start just with one question or reflection followed by BLS/DAS. You may also invite movement by saying:

> "As you and this story holder within watch these sensations in your body, what movement would the body like to execute? Let the body and this part of you show you the movements and urges it has been carrying for you in the body. Let's stay close to the body, if it feels safe enough, and let it show you and this part of you how it wants to move."

You may use reflections, such as:

- As the sand world moves and changes and your awareness moves with it, your [describe movement (e.g., hands move more rapidly)].
- The [character] became [describe body (e.g., motionless and still)]. . . just like *your* body.
- I see the [describe body (e.g., stillness)] of the [character]'s body. They are [name emotion (e.g., angry)] and [describe the urge reported by the client (e.g., wants to move and fight)], yet they [describe what the client reports is suppressing the behavior (e.g., does not want to hurt the other character)]. It is a big dilemma for the [character] as they hold the tension and energy of [repeat the body descriptor (e.g., stillness)] and [repeat the emotion (e.g., anger)] in their body. (Reflective interweave.)

282 EMDR-Sandtray-based Therapy

For clients exposed to complex trauma, the process of connecting with the body often needs to be carefully titrated. Rapidly or fully accessing trauma rooted in body memory can lead to dysregulation or further constriction of emotional expression. A pendulation interweave can gently directing the client to move between two somatic states: one that supports safety and serves as an anchor, and one rooted in trauma (Levine, 2015). Both states are invited to be in the tray in a way that honors the client.

If processing implicitly, moving from object to self can activate neuro-platforms, which can then be recalibrated and integrated using EMDR procedures. You might say:

> ❝ As you watch what is happening to the [character], your body gets [the client's report of the physical manifestation (e.g., tense and jittery)]. May I invite you to slow down a bit to watch? Let's have an inside visit and see what is happening next as you track this [repeat the physical manifestation (e.g., tension)]."

The clinician may also invite the client to discharge pent-up affective energy held inside body-based memory carefully, in small quantities, akin to slowly opening a shaken soda bottle to release the pressure without letting it erupt wildly. If a part is holding the bottled-up energy, that part may be accompanied by resources in the sand tray and the system of parts. As the client and inner system witness and track the body as it executes empowering actions, apply BLS/DAS. A young client may want to run while connecting to a part holding a flight response. After the child has run, invite them to observe their actions and triumphs while staying connected to their body.

Interweaves That Titrate

These interweaves modulate arousal while titrating moment-to-moment access to associative channels. You might say:

> ❝ As you remain connected to your inner world and all sides of you, let's notice how much of this experience seems appropriate to see/feel/know/witness right now."

The level of titration may change depending on how the client's affective states transform as well as how their tolerance threshold and integrative capacities change. At any point, the symbols in the tray may be buried or covered and accessed only in small segments.

Advanced Strategies During Reprocessing Phases With Complex Clients **283**

Titrated Mindfulness.
- Let's sit with this a bit longer.
- Let's just observe what is happening.
- Let's see what happens if you notice this pinch/drop/spoon of [name the feeling] a bit longer.
- Let's just watch without evaluating or judging. Just observe.

By inviting the client to step into a neutral space, we support them in recruiting biological systems for homeostasis rather than defense. According to Porges (2017), when we evaluate ourselves or a situation, we are already recruiting the biology of defense. The state of nonevaluation does not promote or activate the defensive system. Invite the client to just watch the information in the tray and the figures representing the associative channel. Mindfulness should also be titrated and used gradually because a client presenting with dissociation may find it initially challenging. However, as the client's capacity for mindful awareness and observation expands, mindful interweaves may be used more often.

Expansion and Constriction. Pendulation is an important concept of somatic experiencing, which refers to the biological rhythm of contraction and expansion during the resolution of implicit traumatic memories (Levine, 2015). Clients with complex trauma often feel trapped in overwhelming sensations that they fear, echoing the experiences of their trauma. These sensations can become persistent reminders of their past, reinforcing feelings of vulnerability and disconnecting them from their present sense of safety and control. This cycle can hinder their ability to trust their bodies and the therapeutic process, emphasizing the importance of carefully paced, compassionate interventions that gradually build tolerance and foster a sense of empowerment. There are multiple ways that pendulation has been used throughout this volume, especially during discussions of reprocessing sessions. The accordion technique (Gómez, 2021b) is used to carefully observe the stretching and contracting of [emotional/somatic] states. If a part holds the fight/flight response and it is activated during trauma reprocessing, the primary story holders—supported by the guiding self—are encouraged to use the accordion technique to observe and engage with the energy burden these parts have carried on behalf of the client. You might say:

> "All mammals, when they are in danger or feel big/strong feelings, may want to fight or escape. Can we watch if the [character, part of you] in the sand world wants to fight or escape?"

If the fight response is selected, you might say:

> " When the [character, part of you] gets the 'fighting feeling,' where is it in their/your body? Let's take your accordion and expand this sensation in your body. Notice how it moves or stays still. Now, when you are ready, let's watch it contract. If this is okay with you and your inside world, just watch it dance in and through you. Remember that it just represents a biological/natural rhythm that was activated to keep you alive and help you survive. This is your body's best attempt to survive, and this part has been holding this story for you for years."

Follow with BLS/DAS. If the client is a child processing implicitly, you might say:

- I wonder if the [character, part of you] knows that this 'fighting feeling' is really the [character, part of you]'s body doing its best to help him survive.
- Let's keep stretching and shrinking this sensation/feeling.

When the opportunity opens up, we can invite compassion and even love for what the body and the nervous system did to maximize survival and the part that has been carrying this strategy on behalf of the client. In addition, the client or a companion/helper may be invited to speak to the body and nervous system of the character that represents the defensive response.

Temporal Orientation. These interweaves support the client in orienting their nervous system to the present and in restoring dual attention during processing.

- I wonder if your inner system/group/family knows this experience is over?
- Is there anyone inside or outside the tray that could reassure this part (and your entire system) of you that this is over and that it is now safe?

The client may bring a new figure to interact with the part in the tray and ground the part/character in the present safety. This new knowing may also be physicalized in the tray:

> " I wonder which figure would represent and remind the part/character that they are safe (use the most appropriate word for the client) now/ there is more safety now. Let's place it in the tray."

Advanced Strategies During Reprocessing Phases With Complex Clients   **285**

BLS/DAS should follow. To restore dual attention and reground the client to their present safety, you might say:

> ❬ I invite you/part of you to look around and notice where you are. You may touch the sand or the figure that reminds you where you are now and how this experience (trauma) is not happening now."

Interweaves That Work With the Emotional System

Information processing may stall around emotional states due to over-activation or difficulty accessing them. Parts that minimize, deny, and avoid arise in the tray of the well-defended client. There are various ways in which access to associative channels linked to emotions can become restricted:

- Parts are overactivated, and the client shows hyperarousal or hypoarousal in the tray and in themselves. Fear, anger, and rage may color the story and the world. Multiple conflicts and difficulties or terrifying stories emerge simultaneously in the tray.
- Emotions are covertly present, which may signal defensive and protective parts.

Parts that carry emotions may enter the tray as they want to be witnessed. If enough tolerance is present in the client's system, then mindfully watching and observing the emotion may create movement and jump-start processing. You may invite the client or the character to feel only a small portion of the feeling:

> ❬ The [character, part of you] is feeling a big [name the feeling]. I wonder if we can invite the [character, part of you] to choose how much of this [feeling] they/you want to feel. It may be only a drop or two of [feeling]."

You may bring a dropper, a small empty spray bottle, or measuring spoons so the client/part or character can choose and express how much of the emotion they are open to feeling.

There are interweaves that can assist the client/part in *sitting with* the emotional state. You may ask questions about the feeling's texture, color, and other qualities while the client physicalizes and closely observes the feeling state. You might say:

- I wonder which season best represents the feeling you/this part of you is having right now. What is the weather like inside this feeling: sunny, stormy, windy, rainy, snowy, or cloudy? Let's find a way to cre-

285 EMDR-Sandtray-based Therapy

ate space in the tray, find figures, or create movement to help you and your inner system be with this part that holds the [feeling].

- How is it for the rest of your inner system to witness this feeling?"

You might also ask questions regarding the feeling's texture. You might say:

- Is the feeling heavy or light? Is it pushing to come out or trying to hide? Is it rough or soft?

Once the feeling is characterized, invite the client, the client's inner system, or a part to represent it in the tray. Apply BLS/DAS while the client focuses on the information emerging in the tray. Remind the client, as necessary, that everything in the tray may come in as it wishes to show up: buried, half-seen, covered, or completely visible. The client should have access to various coverings of different transparencies and should choose one that aligns with how much they can tolerate the emotions represented in the tray. The transparency of the fabric covering the client selects—from opaque to translucent—offers different levels of titration tailored to the client's needs. These coverings allow the client to shield the emotion while still maintaining some level of visibility and connection to it.

Support from the resource tray may be brought in to assist the client's inner system or part with any given emotional state. Helpers may come to save the character in terror, or nurturing figures may provide the nourishment needed. The emotional state may be expressed through the body; for instance, the emotions may have a sound or voice. The sand or the figures may move to represent the sound, the words, and the texture of this feeling. Once this is accomplished, follow with BLS/DAS.

Psychoeducation can be provided about emotions and body sensations. The client's feelings can be validated and normalized. As clinicians, we may wonder out loud if the client's feeling is old and familiar or brand new. We may think out loud and search for what or who holds the adaptive data in the client's inner system or in the tray. When the feeling is "hiding" in the tray and the story, clinicians can support the client's self-system access it at an appropriate pace. Some clients, especially children, may bury figures under the sand. Even verbally reflecting that the feeling or the figure is buried may direct the client's conscious awareness to that area of the tray. Invite curiosity as an intervention if information processing stagnates. What does the client or part need to be able to see, know, and embrace the emotion? Companionship? Strength or another quality or capacity? You might ask questions such as:

" Let's notice or search for what this part—or your entire internal system in the tray—needs to be able to visit/witness/access this feeling. Does it need a companion and a helper? Or any special powers and strengths?"

Menus may be provided as the client's inner system or part searches for the underlying need. Once information processing is restored, the clinician stays out of the way (F. Shapiro, 2018) and allows spontaneous processing to continue. It is essential to emphasize the active support and companionship needed by clients presenting with complex trauma and dissociation—due to their difficulties in mentalization, affect regulation, and integrative capacities—during EMDR–sandtray processing.

Interweaves That Invite Emotions

Sometimes, emotions are hidden and may remain unseen and repressed. Pushing the edges of the window of tolerance nudges the client to expand their field of consciousness, which promotes greater integration and realization. Reflecting and wondering out loud about the denied feeling in the tray puts the spotlight onto emotional states. You might say:

- Does anyone in or outside the tray know about the emotions this part/ entire inner system has been carrying for you?
- I wonder if this part—or your entire inner system—has any contact with its feelings or if it may have lost that contact. Sometimes, when we have challenging feelings, we may have to hide them because they are too big, heavy, or difficult.

Pendulating in the Sand World. Notice the geography of the tray. If the client or part reports disruptions in information processing in an area of the tray that is overflowing with challenging emotions, identify the area of the tray that holds the resources and adaptive information. Invite the client to move back and forth between these two areas and to notice what is emerging while engaging in BLS/DAS. The clinician may also invite the client and their self-system to pendulate and to zoom in or out from areas of the sand world.

Interweaves That Work With the Attachment System

Underneath every traumatic event, especially if it took place with an important attachment figure, are missing experiences and parts that hold unmet needs. This may be why a part is rooted in an earlier phase of development. These regressive states, held by a dissociative part, may be tied to developmental wounds and defensive attachment strategies. Recognizing, validating, and fulfilling these needs during the reprocessing phases with

288   EMDR-Sandtray-based Therapy

dissociative clients will be fundamental to the process of restoring the natural rhythms of development and allowing these parts to move forward in their growth. Sometimes, the need will emerge spontaneously in the sand world, and the client will be able to identify and verbalize it on their own. Often, however, the need will remain hidden in layers of entrenched defenses and implicit memory.

Parts in the self-system may exist at the two extremes of the spectrum. Some parts may be needless and oblivious to their deepest longings, while others may be needy and overwhelmed with confusing and unclear needs that never seem to get fulfilled. Because trauma has colored their deepest longings, these parts are often unable to ask for what they really want, which leaves them with the experience of emptiness and powerlessness. The clinician uses interweaves that repair, validate, accompany, and nourish while working within the client's system's intimacy threshold. The work in the tray lends itself to fulfilling the missing experiences as the miniature collection joins the client's inner system in fulfilling their longings. You may want to say:

- I wonder what the [character, part of you] needs as they stand alone by the corner.
- I wonder what the little [character, part of you] in the tray longs for at this moment.

Because individuals exposed to neglect and attachment injuries did not have their needs reflected on and contingently fulfilled, they are likely unable to mentalize their needs and thus require need menus to choose from. Appendix B includes a comprehensive list of needs that you can use with clients based on your knowledge and understanding of their clinical landscape. The list is not meant to be presented in its entirety: a long menu of needs may overwhelm clients with a narrow threshold of intimacy and low capacity for connectedness as well as clients who are already inundated with simultaneous longings. Instead, select from the list needs that seem most relevant to the client at the moment. Clinicians should maintain a grounding presence and not overextend their emotional expressions of support or step into a rescuing role that may overactivate an already taxed attachment system.

Initially, you may reflect on or wonder about the underlying need. However, if difficulties arise or if identifying the need appears challenging for the client, provide a menu. You might say:

“ I wonder if we can be curious about what the [character/part of you] in the tray needs. Do they need protection or someone who could save them or hold them? Do they need support, nourishment, or companionship? Let's connect with the [character, part of you] in the sand world and let them show you what they long for at this moment."

If the client is experiencing a big and challenging emotion, invite the client to see what the underlying need is. Every emotion has a message and a need. After the emotion has been addressed and accessed, acknowledge the need. You might say:

> " I wonder what the part under the [character] or the [character] needs while they are feeling [name the feeling]. Let the [character] show you. Let the [character] tell you what they long for right now."

Polarized Self-States. Oaklander (2007) emphasizes the importance of working with polarities within the client's environment. The splits in the relational milieu are internalized, forming binary and rigid states. The human experience is one of divisions, fissures, and divergences. Each person's subjective reality is diversely colored; meaning, we can be simultaneously angry and in love with the same person. Trauma exposes an individual to ruptures and environmental inconsistencies that become internalized in the psyche. The resulting dysfunctional and misaligned relational milieu occupies space in the inner system of individuals exposed to complex traumatization. Abuse at the hands of a caregiver, for instance, exposes the child to divergent and incompatible models of the caregiver, who engages in violent and cruel behaviors while simultaneously fostering love and care. The perpetrator who grooms the child with attention, gifts, and connection while engaging in wounding exchanges also promotes the formation of incongruent and conflicting self-states that create a landscape of internal discord. These polarities are often preserved into adulthood—sometimes for a lifetime.

Each therapeutic approach conceptualizes and addresses the presence of polarizations in unique ways. Gestalt therapy, for instance, uses the chair technique, where two opposing views or states can communicate and be validated. The two-hand interweave in standard EMDR invites the opposing views into the client's hands (R. Shapiro, 2016). In EMDR–sandtray, the tray and miniature collection unblend and physicalize competing self-states so they can enter the client's field of awareness and their mind can begin to realize, synthesize, and eventually integrate them or it can just come to terms with their coexistence. The opposing self-states and divergent dissociative parts may sometimes be responsible for halting information processing. When the internal conflict keeps the client looping, a first step may be to invite these polarities into a representational level under the guise of an avatar. Each polarity, or conflicted part, is invited to unblend in the sand world at opposite sides of the sand tray. The further exaggeration

290   EMDR-Sandtray-based Therapy

and separation of the polarized parts can give the client enough distance to explore them (Oaklander, 2007).

A frequent conflict in the traumatized psyche is between "knowing" and "not knowing," which often develops into extreme conflict in dissociative clients (Steele et al., 2017). One part may be receptive and ready to disclose emotions and the haunting memories of trauma, while another is highly invested in keeping these stories hidden. Instead of resolving the conflict for the client, the clinician meets the client with curiosity in the neutral space offered by the sand world, where two divergent states can coexist and thereby enter the client's consciousness.

Navigating Through the Reprocessing Phases

Although not all parts participate in the reprocessing sessions, at some point, the entire system is invited to join the trauma tray or the resource tray or one of the resource areas so they can observe or listen to the client telling the story. Often, parts that did not participate are gathered once all the parts that did participate report a 0 level of disturbance, or a level that is appropriate and aligned with the client's current life circumstances and capacity. The parts that have not yet participated may enter the tray all at once or one at a time (depending on the system's integrative and regulatory capacities) until each part can participate while the client (storyteller or adult/wise self) goes over the story in the tray. Once all parts report no disturbance associated with the memory or kernel of the experience, move into the installation and body scan phases.

CHAPTER 10

The Therapeutic Relationship and the Intersubjective Field

The therapeutic relationship is considered one of the most important agents of change in treatment (Cozolino, 2017; Schore, 2011). As the external coregulator, coorganizer of experience, and cocreator of meaning, the clinician witnesses and accompanies the client's mind as it embarks on a journey of self-discovery that takes it into its deepest vulnerabilities.

> As sandtray witnesses, we have great knowledge of child development, psychotherapy, play, and the sandtray process. Yet our abilities to be with the child inside the play, while honoring what is coming forth and facilitating the emergence of meaning, may be the more useful skill set. (Rae, 2013, p. 143)

In EMDR-sandtray-based therapy, presence, synchronicity, coherence, resonance, and contingency are only some of the capacities that clinicians embody.

The clinician, through EMDR–sandtray models and procedures, accompanies the client in entering (through the work in the sand and the therapeutic relationship) into internal working models and synaptic systems from early developmental stages, facilitating the reorganization, linkage, and integration of disowned and fragmented embodied mental structures with higher-order conscious frameworks. "The flow of states within the dyadic system (client–therapist) is allowed to achieve increasing degrees of complexity as the individuals themselves achieve increasingly coherent states" (Siegel, 2020, p. 409). This reciprocal and dyadic regulating system expands adaptive information processing and modulates its flow, which is internalized in the client's mind.

To accomplish such a profound task, the clinician mentalizes the client, holding the client's mind in their mind and providing a safe relational space that promotes social engagement and corrective experiences of mirroring and co-homeostasis. The clinician's mirroring and reflective words and behaviors that are congruent with the client's state are, in turn, internalized and represented in the client's embodied consciousness (Fonagy et al., 2002). The client can then, as they find their mind accurately reflected and regulated by the clinician's mind, begin to differentiate between inner and outer reality, interpersonal and intrapersonal experiences, as well as fantasy and actual reality.

Traumatic stress in early childhood appears to be associated with emotional dysregulation and constriction and deficits in affective mentalization (Frewen & Lanius, 2015). According to Fonagy et al. (2002), attachment relationships grant the intersubjective basis for developing mentalizing capacity. In the absence of secure attachment and in the presence of trauma, the capacity to mentalize and hold an awareness of both one's own mind and the mind of the other is diminished. When the clinician's biology is organized around survival, their responses to the client are nuanced by defenses, which moves them out of social engagement and coregulation. If the clinician's memory networks holding traumagenic material become fully activated, it may influence the clinician's decisions, potentially clouding their ability to accurately mentalize and make meaning about their clients. The client–therapist relational milieu serves as the space that harbors mutual engagement, allowing for the healing of deep-seated wounds and the reorganization of self-narratives (cognitive, affective, and sensorimotor).

However, the therapeutic space can also become a place of contention, overtaken by reenactments of unresolved and unhealed trauma, either implicitly or explicitly. These reenactments may manifest as overidentification with the client, frustration, withdrawal, or a need to rescue the client. A therapist overwhelmed by a client's dysregulated emotions or trauma disclosures may nonconsiously withdraw or become distant. A therapist with unresolved attachment wounds may perceive a client's independence as rejection or detachment, responding with frustration or overinvolvement. These reenactments can challenge the safety of the therapeutic relationship. They can potentially recreate early relational dysfunctional and wounding dynamics, necessitating a careful and sensitive approach from the therapist to navigate and address these relational undercurrents. These dynamics underscore the complexity of human relationships and the fundamental need for clinicians to engage in ongoing self-exploration and self-observation.

Motivational Systems and the Therapeutic Relationship

Motivational systems are passed on evolutionarily and originate primarily in subcortical regions of the brain (Liotti, 2017; Liotti & Gilbert, 2011; Panksepp & Biven, 2012). Motivational systems engender distinctive types of affective consciousness and behavioral goals organized to ensure survival and prosocial behaviors. Authors have organized innate motivational systems into categories (e.g., Panksepp, 1998; Panksepp & Biven, 2012; Liotti, 2017; Steele, 2022):

- Seeking (expectancy and curiosity; guides anticipatory learning, seeking things in the world, exploration)
- Care (nurturance; display of supportive behaviors)
- Fear (anxiety)
- Rage (anger)
- Panic/grief (sadness)
- Play (social joy)
- Lust (sexual excitement)

Steele (2021) proposed nine categories of multimotivational systems:

1. Attachment (security and safety)
2. Caregiving (response to separation cry)
3. Panic/loss (panic at loss of connection)
4. Collaboration/cooperation
5. Competition/ranking
6. Sexuality (organized by lust, sexual excitement)
7. Play (organized by joy, exploration, and social connection)
8. Defense (flight, fight, freeze, and faint)
9. Predation (organized to kill or injure another)

The growth and maturation of these systems is highly affected by development, attachment experiences, and interpersonal trauma. These motivational/action systems may become inhibited, overactivated, or maladaptively combined due to trauma and disorganized attachment (Liotti, 2017). Some systems are foundational and primarily oriented toward survival, reflecting early evolutionary stages. In contrast, others are evolved, encompassing complex prosocial behaviors and supporting advanced neocortical functions (van der Hart et al., 2006; Steele, 2021). The therapeutic encounters between the clinician and the client are often nuanced by reenactments mediated by motivational systems.

According to Steele (2021), clinicians can actively use and shift into prosocial systems that promote regulation. For instance, in response to a client with an overactive competitive ranking system, exerting high levels of control over the therapeutic process, the clinician may pivot to activate the play and collaboration system to increase connection to their social engagement. There is a constant interplay between the motivational systems of the client and the therapist in a dynamic and complex process by which they influence and modify each other. These reciprocal interactions encompass a vast spectrum of biopsychosocial factors.

A client with early exposure to trauma and neglect may present with an overactivated attachment system. This client may expect the clinician to fulfill their deep needs for love, acceptance, and connection, which is taxing on the clinician's caregiving system. However, when the clinician has trauma and attachment injuries and also presents with imbalances in motivational systems, the therapeutic relationship can become even more complex. These imbalances may influence the therapist's responses and interactions, which may exacerbate relational reenactments of trauma with their clients. The clinician must work to ensure that the therapeutic space remains safe and constructive for both the client and the therapist. However, relationships can be quite challenging for individuals exposed to complex traumatization. According to Steele (2021):

> The therapeutic relationship is meant to be a vehicle of repair and connection, yet relationship is the very experience that causes the most suffering and pain to clients. . . . The closer and more vulnerable the relationship, the more likely activation of defense will deactivate or delimit attachment in many clients. (p. 91)

A therapist's well-intentioned efforts to form a relationship with the client may become a source of activation to the client. The clinician must be prepared to challenge trauma-formed relational templates and to embrace the healing journey, which will be nuanced by moments of rupture and repair.

Now, considering that motivational systems play a critical role in shaping the dynamics of the therapeutic relationship, let's explore how these systems influence and actively participate in the therapeutic encounter. By examining the ways motivational systems drive behaviors, shape relational patterns, and respond to safety or threat, we can better understand their impact on the therapeutic process and the paths they open toward connection, healing, and growth.

A Highly Activated Ranking/Competition System

A clinician who holds a highly activated competition and ranking system may nonconsciously leverage the therapeutic process and the client to go along with their interpretations and suggestions. This clinician may impose, often unknowingly, their interpretations of the data unfolding in the sand world or may begin reprocessing trauma before the client demonstrates clear signs of readiness, making therapeutic decisions that appease the clinician's rhythms rather than the client's. Conversely, a clinician may engage in power struggles with a highly competitive client, which may result in premature termination of treatment.

For highly submissive clients with inhibited competition systems, these experiences may be reenacting their previous dysfunctional and wounding relational transactions.

An Overactive or Abdicated Caregiving System

The drive to care is one that we all carry in our biology, yet it may become dysregulated or inhibited due to trauma and disorganized attachment. Clinicians with a highly activated caregiving system may be exceedingly focused on rescuing and caring for their client while feeling overly responsible for their client's emotions and therapeutic outcomes.

When working in the sand with complex trauma cases, a clinician with a highly active caregiving system may tend to suggest strategies and engage in therapeutic practices that rescue, nurture, and support characters that are in some kind of need or distress while assuming a great deal of responsibility for the client's states of distress. This therapist may also overstimulate the client's attachment cry, potentially creating greater dysregulation of the attachment system that is already taxed by exposure to chronic relational ruptures. The client may become highly dependent on the clinician and relinquish their sense of agency. When clinicians recognize these motivational tendencies, they must move into self-compassion, curiosity, self-observation, and mentalization of the client's responses as well as their own.

Conversely, a clinician with a relinquished caregiving system may become hopeless and helpless with a complex client who is not showing any signs of improvement, despite the clinician's hard work. This may result in an abdicated care system that withdraws care and support and ultimately disengages from the client, recreating the client's previous relational dynamics nuanced by abandonment and emotional distance. If this happens, the clinician must work on moving into a place where they can see the client through the eyes of possibility, hope, and empowerment while maintaining a state of compassion for their clients and themselves. A clinician's abdicated or overactive caregiving tendencies can only reenact previously wounding relational dynamics, perseverating a client's relational templates of insecurity.

The Overactive Defense System

The effects of trauma often manifest as a cascade of overactivated and sensitized defenses—such as fight, flight, freeze, or faint—that deeply influence an individual's ability to engage in relationships, including the therapeutic

296   EMDR-Sandtray-based Therapy

one. The clinician may move quickly into fight-mediated states, such as criticism, anger, or hostility, in response to a highly aggressive client or a violent sand world, or the clinician may take a "flight" and avoidant stance when the sand world content overwhelms their system or activates their unprocessed trauma. A therapist who is recruiting the biology of defense and survival misreads and misinterprets the client's intersubjective cues and demonstrates depleted mentalizing states. This clinician's appraisals of their client's states and needs may be shadowed by their own biologically entrenched defenses, hindering mentalization and therapeutic decision-making.

The Overactive Sexuality/Lust System

Multiple systems may exist in a state of dysregulation or be maladaptively combined in individuals of any age who have a history of chronic traumatization and disorganized attachment. For instance, the client who did not receive security in their attachment and relational/emotional nourishment and who only experienced "connectedness" through incidents of sexual abuse may present with dysfunctionally blended sexuality and attachment systems. In these cases, the client may pursue their attachment needs through the sexuality system, becoming flirtatious and sexualized during sessions or creating sand worlds with highly and overtly sexual content. Clinicians with an overly activated motivational system of sexuality as a result of their own trauma may be in danger of crossing ethical and moral boundaries and recreating traumagenic and abusive relational dynamics with their clients.

The Attachment System: The Clinician and the Client

The attachment system of clients exposed to early and chronic traumatization involving primary relational figures is often either disorganized (Liotti, 2017), anxious, and overactivated or inhibited and avoidant. Clinicians should explore and observe how the client's attachment system operates and what early experiences shaped it so they may strategically address and work with the attachment system to support healing and reorganize the client's internal working models and synaptic systems. Similarly, clinicians are encouraged to embark on their own journey of self-exploration and to travel within to understand their own attachment tendencies and strategies and how these influence their therapeutic encounters. For individuals exposed to complex traumatization (both client and clinician), connectedness and relational closeness are often associated with danger, abandonment, enmeshment, or pain. The attachment system is multilayered, nuanced with dilemmas and polarizations, and delicate yet fundamental in the therapeutic and intersubjective relationship between the client and the therapist. Early attachment experiences profoundly shape the mental landscapes of the individual seeking therapy as well as the therapist delivering the care.

Bowlby (1988) suggested that the therapist would become a temporary attachment figure for the client who needs consistency, reliability, and trust so the client can safely work on developing a relationship with their inner experiences and self. The therapist becomes a secure base for the client so that the client's mind can be explored and reflected on while diving into vulnerable spaces and layers of pain. However, the coconstruction of relational safety in therapeutic relationships is nuanced by ruptures, chaos, and turmoil as the client's internal working models are challenged by the clinician's attempts to form a therapeutic relationship. In complex trauma cases, closeness and relational safety become simultaneously a source of relief and distress (Fisher, 2017). In individuals with developmental trauma, relational connectedness activates painful yearnings that, sustained by the fear of abandonment, may become obsessive demands on the therapist (Fisher, 2017).

In the pursuit of creating a relational bond with the client, the clinician may overfocus on the attachment system, unintentionally moving the client into dependency, dysregulation of the attachment cry, or disengagement (Steele, 2021). The therapist's best attempts to create safety and attunement may evoke painful memories of trauma and attachment ruptures (Fisher, 2017), overactivating the attachment system and the defensive attachment cry. Having the theoretical constructs around the treatment of complex traumatization does not ensure that one has the inner space and capacity to support a highly demanding and traumatized client; the clinician needs to have traveled into themselves. "How we come to understand others is directly related to our awareness of our own internal states" (Siegel, 2020, p. 251). As such, ongoing inner exploration and increased self-awareness will significantly aid clinicians who work with client experiencing complex traumatization.

This chapter underscores the importance of the clinician cultivating awareness around how their own attachment system functions and how it influences the therapeutic milieu and their decision-making. The AAI (George et al., 1985) demonstrated that how individuals come to integrate early attachment experiences influences and predicts the pattern of attachment caregivers will later form with their own children. How, then, do the organization and integration of internal working models and their relational representations in the therapist's mind influence the therapeutic field and treatment delivery (e.g., EMDR–sandtray therapy)? How does the inner organization of the therapist's life story influence their capacity to accurately reflect the client and to create therapeutic coherence and safety?

One study shows that clients with a secure attachment to their psychotherapist show greater in-session exploration (Mallinckrodt et al., 2005). According to John Bowlby (1988), when individuals feel scared, ill, or in danger, they naturally exhibit attachment behaviors to elicit caregiving responses from others. The nature of the care they receive is influenced by the attachment styles of the individual in need and the caregiver. How the client gives cues to the clinician and how they are received and responded to is influenced by how the client and the clinician have been shaped by relational experiences. Research is still needed to fully understand how the clinician's attachment style and representations affect the therapist–client relationship, specifically when using EMDR and sandtray-based therapies. Therapists and clients with anxious/preoccupied attachment and who find enmeshment familiar and secure may develop symbiotic relationships in their pursuit of therapeutic connection. Avoidant and dismissive dyads may find comfort in detachment; while disorganized and unresolved clinician–client dyads may have relationships characterized by frequent incidences of communication and attachment ruptures, crises, and emotional dysregulation.

Adult individuals characterized in the AAI as having a dismissive state of mind regarding attachment experiences present with an attachment-related strategy of disengagement and deactivation of their attachment needs; they tend to be rejecting and distant at times when others exhibit the greatest need for connection. According to Cundy (2019), clinicians with avoidant and dismissive propensities are more inclined to be non-reciprocal, unattuned, and unemphatic, and to minimize negative experiences while interpreting them positively. The dismissive clinician may withdraw when the client needs their presence, be biased toward left-brain logical strategies, and may disconnect from affective states and direct the client away from their emotions.

In contrast, adults with attachment preoccupation may present with a highly activated attachment system, leaning toward enmeshment in their relationships. Their narratives may reflect a preoccupation with early experiences of attachment, often marked by an intense focus on or entanglement with those relationships. Therapists with these internal representations may be more eager to rescue their clients and to form a relationship with their clients that seems more familiar, colored by enmeshment (Cundy, 2017). Clinicians with unresolved trauma and disorganization in their states of mind regarding their attachment history may present with significant deficits in mentalization, affect regulation, and reciprocity in their responses. They may misread and inadequately mirror and reflect the client's mind and their sand worlds. Their deficits in self-regulation impact their capacity to engage in coregulatory processes with their clients. They may move into deep states of shame when clients do not progress as they make the client's failure theirs.

Some studies indicate higher levels of aggression post treatment in children with disruptive behavioral disorder diagnosis associated with higher levels of therapists preoccupied attachment style (Muratori et al., 2017). However, others have found that the clinician's capacity for emotional regulation mediates their attachment style; that is, while the clinician has functioning capacities for emotion regulation, their attachment style does not impact the clinician's capacity to establish a therapeutic alliance and bond (Ruiz-Aranda et al., 2021). Based on these findings, the development of affect regulation is an essential element of the therapist's journey toward growth and expansion. This topic is extensive and merits much greater exploration, but the intent of this chapter is to expand awareness of and kindle interest in the fundamental role of the therapist's self in the client's therapeutic growth and healing.

Dyadic and Shared Biological States

As clinicians, our internal experiences are visible to the client's mind. According to Cozolino (2020), our viscera are automatically linked to our facial expressions, which give others information about our internal states. As the clinician observes the client's face and body and emerging sand worlds, the clinician's mirror neurons create, within the clinician's mind and body, an inner representation of what the client feels and shares. These inner representations and how they are internalized are also influenced by the clinician's synaptic systems that hold traumatic and relational information. Each of us sees the present through the lenses of the past (F. Shapiro, 2018). The human mind interprets and perceives others through the prism of its own experiences—both adaptive and maladaptive—along with its inherent biases and subjectivities. It employs this amalgamation of data to formulate conclusions and construct intricate representations of others. Cozolino (2020) brings up the concept of the "bipersonal field," referring to how the clinician's and client's conscious and nonconscious minds link and communicate during each therapeutic encounter. Cozolino further emphasizes that "the therapeutic relationship is influenced by the therapist's unconscious wishes, needs, and unresolved traumas as well as training, strategies, and conscious intentions" (Cozolino, 2020, p. 118).

Furthermore, a clinician's personal ideology; belief system; religion; racial, social, and ethnic group; and sexual orientation may have exposed them to experiences that have shaped their ways of seeing and interpreting the world. This embodied information may not be conscious, remaining buried in the implicit, nonconscious mind. According to Levine (2015),

300 EMDR-Sandtray-based Therapy

survival reactions, which appear during times of distress, represent the deepest and most compelling form of memory because it overrides the implicit and explicit memory. When working with individuals affected by trauma, the therapist's internal working models and memory systems can become activated and move the therapist out of social engagement and into survival mode.

The Polyvagal Theory, developed by Steve Porges, enhances our understanding of the autonomic nervous system's role in the therapeutic relationship and in the client's emotional and social functioning. The autonomic nervous system is a nuanced feedback system that involves bidirectional communication between the brain and other organs with the ultimate goal of attaining homeostasis (Porges, 2017). Traumagenic synaptic networks do not exist in isolation; they are deeply connected to the viscera and autonomic states. The autonomic nervous system has afferent and efferent fibers that travel between the brain and the internal organs, with 80% going from the viscera to the brain stem (Porges, 2017). The visceral afferent (sensory) pathways operate as an intricate surveillance system, relaying data to the brain stem's regulatory centers. This ongoing communication ensures continuous updates and precise modulation of the body's physiological states. The visceral efferent (motor) pathways represent a top-down system that provides output to the organs that supports homeostasis (Porges, 2011, 2021).

In the biperson field and the we-space, the client's nervous system constantly interacts with the therapist's, each deeply influencing the other. The client's surveillance systems continuously scan for signs of danger and safety in the therapeutic relationship. When this dance of autonomic states is made conscious, it becomes an asset to the therapeutic process and the clinician's decision-making. However, when both the client and clinician become nonconsciously trapped in dysfunctional patterns of autonomic states, it is detrimental to therapeutic process. Sand worlds—with their covert or overt affect, cognitions, and sensorimotor schemas—connect with the "biperson" field and its shared autonomic states. The sand world, engaging and sharing the phenomenological space of the client and the therapist, becomes an integral part of the intersubjective matrix, creating a triadic blend of entities that serves the client's healing and their return to themself.

The attuned clinician uses passive and active pathways to repair, contain, and regulate previously disrupted autonomic states, to recruit the social engagement system, and to transition into a vagal state (Porges, 2021). When employing passive pathways of neuroception, the therapist conveys safety cues by leveraging their own social engagement system. Facial expressions, voice intonation, and the therapist's grounded and attuned presence signal safety to the client's nervous system, increasing the client's social engagement. The flow by which these states enter the client's nervous system is regulated and titrated by the clinician's autonomic nervous system, as needed, based on the intricate and often ambivalent relationship individuals affected by chronic traumatization have with physiological states of safety.

The clinician's biology may be recruited for protection or survival and move into defensive strategies, such as overdoing, overworking, rescuing, and evading boundaries or, conversely, becoming unresponsive, emotionally distant, critical, shaming, rejecting, and frequently misattuned to the client's needs. When defenses and early mechanisms of adaptation are enlisted during therapy sessions, a cascade of biobehavioral states in the clinician's system become activated, and they may clash with the client's. Clients and clinicians may use the same defenses, such as avoidance, perfectionism, dissociation, control, pleasing, manipulation, idealization, and so forth. A clinician's need for control may cause the clinician to guide the session to where they want to go and not to the places the client's mind longs to visit. Similarly, a therapist's desire for perfection may cause them to push their client to work harder and move at a pace that is not in sync with the client's rhythms. Clinicians may avoid addressing challenging emotions, may move into reprocessing phases, may evade accessing traumatic material, all due to their own current adverse life experiences or personal turmoil. Therapists may push themselves to work long hours, which may affect their energy levels and, in some cases, their capacity to stay present and actively accompany the client. Clients with complex clinical presentations and/or dissociative inner systems may stretch the clinician's regulatory capacities and push them out of their window of affect tolerance.

The therapeutic process is as messy as our human existence. Thus, it involves recognizing and embracing moments of turmoil and humanity, which are intrinsic to the journey of healing and self-discovery. We clinicians must not walk this path alone. We need the support and companionship of consultants, supervisors, and colleagues who can aid our decision-making and therapeutic growth. The therapist's awareness of self is constantly evolving, transforming, and growing. The most challenging moments in therapy are often the most conducive to personal and professional development.

Acknowledging the assets and resources clinicians bring is crucial. These can include their empathy, mentalizing capacities, lived experiences, and even their own journey of healing. When they actively recognize and consciously engage these strengths, they become powerful tools to deepen therapeutic connection, foster safety, and facilitate clients' growth. By becoming aware of the richness we hold within, we can consciously and intentionally use it therapeutically. An ongoing journey toward self-recognition and self-knowing can support a stronger and safer therapeutic environment.

Humility in the Process

The early overfocus on pursuing the most adherence to the EMDR model at times resulted in the rigid use of procedural steps while abandoning variables specifically associated with the therapist's capacity to create a collaborative therapeutic environment and engage in intentional moment-to-moment decision-making and introspective practices.

Sandtray and EMDR work can access deep layers of a client's inner world, inviting profound vulnerability as clients journey through the heights and depths of human experience. Witnessing this level of work can reach into the unseen layers of the clinician's mind. At times, it may be uncomfortable to move into uncertainty and the unknown. The openness to embark on our own conscious journey, demands profound humility and the recognition that none of us have all the answers. The therapeutic work also requires that clinicians cultivate awareness of their inherent biases and how these can impact therapeutic directions and decisions. Biases may be present at the outset, during selects made when building the miniatures collection and the setup of the physical space for the EMDR–sandtray work. We clinicians should strive not for perfection but for the recognition of our humanity. We should remain open and willing to see and repair the ruptures that result from unrecognized biases and implicit oppressive practices.

As we clinicians become more comfortable with our inner worlds and interoceptive states, we also become more comfortable with being with and sitting with the visible and palpable as well as the subtle dynamics in the therapeutic encounter. Homeyer and Lyles (2022) state that the most sensitive therapy focuses on being rather than doing. To that end, we must embrace an ongoing practice of traveling into the self and the space of being and knowing within.

Learning About the Clinician's Mind: The Therapeutic Home

This section is dedicated to practical sandtray exercises that help the clinician expand awareness. The first exercise is the therapeutic home, which is intended to direct you back into yourself.

Imagine your mind as a house where therapeutic strategies, approaches, your belief system, your affective landscape, and your identities often intersect. You may have one house, or you may have multiple houses to accommodate a more intricate process. The houses and parts of the house may be represented in one tray with multiple divisions or several sand worlds to represent and give life to your inner home. You may use one main therapeutic approach with multiple adjunct methodologies and theoretical models or multiple treatment modalities.

Basement

The basement symbolizes and holds space for your own story; life experiences; belief system; autonomic patterns or activations that are most familiar and potentially sensitized; deep-rooted states of mind; and physiologic states connected to early attachment experiences, ideology, religious beliefs, biases, and cultural, racial, gender, ethnic, and sexual orientation. Select a designated space in the tray and miniatures to represent this information, allowing for flexibility as it may occupy either an entire tray or just a section, depending on the need.

First Floor

You may now choose the space in the tray and miniatures to represent the first floor of your house. The first floor holds the theoretical models that guide your clinical practice, which may be myriad: attachment theory, Polyvagal Theory, AIP model, structural dissociation theory, and so forth. Many clinicians practicing EMDR or sandtray–based therapies have been trained under multiple theories, models, and therapeutic principles that actively influence their therapeutic decisions and meaning-making.

Second Floor

Choose an area in the tray and figures to represent the second floor of your house. The second floor holds space for the specific treatment approaches and strategies, procedural steps, and how-to's of the approaches that closely guide your practice. Often, multiple approaches, strategies, and models are not integrated into one home. Instead, you may operate between multiple homes that hold different, and sometimes divergent, procedural steps and therapeutic approaches. How do you negotiate the movement between homes? How do you decide to enter one house and not the other with a particular client? Is there a movement where clinicians travel from multiple homes at once in the therapeutic process with one single client?

Sometimes, we may fall into the trap of accumulating techniques and using them randomly or without intention and awareness of the context offered by the therapeutic moment. A clinician may have multiple homes that house approaches such as play therapy, sandtray therapy, EMDR therapy, cognitive behavioral therapy, and sensorimotor psychotherapy. The integration of multiple approaches that often happens in the therapy room, sometimes without the therapist's conscious awareness, must be brought to the surface so that it can exist in the field of consciousness, where inten-

304   EMDR-Sandtray-based Therapy

tional decision-making can occur. The clinician who lives in only one house often has to negotiate how different views and approaches can coexist in one house. Intentional, mindful, and conscious decision-making comes from knowing one's "home," which will ensure that therapeutic choices are not random acts.

Transtheoretical and multimodal use of EMDR-sandtray-based therapy incorporates multiple theories that complement the AIP model: attachment theory, Polyvagal Theory, structural dissociation theory, interpersonal neurobiology, mentalization theory, gestalt theory, and sandtray theory, among others. It also brings important elements, constructs, and strategies from other approaches: somatic therapies, polyvagal-based interventions, parts work, gestalt, ego states, and play therapy.

Creating your inner home may take multiple sessions, so make time to be with yourself and the companionship of the miniatures collection and the safe space offered by the tray. Take time to sit and be with the information emerging. Reflect on new findings and previous knowings as you come face-to-face with yourself. Practice self-compassion and acceptance as you encounter realizations that bring pain or shame. Embrace the human that exists beyond your profession.

Sandtray Strategies and Exercises for Clinicians

Mindfulness

The next time you are with a client, begin the session by noticing the impulses, urges, and tendencies that this client awakens in you and how your body communicates these responses. Wonder what it is about this client or the information unfolding in the tray that created this movement of energy in you. Is your impulse to be open or to close down? To approach or distance from what the client is sharing? To engage or disengage? To protect and defend yourself? To rescue and protect the client? To move away or to move closer? Is your therapeutic decision influenced by the client's need to distance from something disturbing or is it influenced more by your own needs to move away? Is there an identifiable emotion arising in you? How does it communicate its arrival to you? When this emotion lands in you, how is your body receiving it? These conscious observations will provide invaluable data about your autonomic and therapeutic tendencies, which may vary from client to client, as each client will kindle your autonomic nervous system in a unique way. Schedule some time to create a sand world about this experience for yourself. Let the information reach new heights of awareness. Moments of expansion often feel uncomfortable. Represent all of your emerging affective states. Give yourself time to take the experiences in and let them exist in the representational realm until you are ready to bring your understanding into the verbal world.

Nondirective and Implicit Trays for Clinicians

Create a series of nondirective trays through multiple sessions where you can closely dialogue with your own mind and see its reflection in the tray. Select the figures you are drawn to, and create sand worlds as you please. Spend time with your creations, and sit compassionately with what emerges as you explore and witness them. Become curious about the avatars in your stories and the relational dances in the trays. Let the sand worlds serve as your mirrors and companions as you mindfully and fully present observe your inner world.

Your Refuge

Create your refuge, safe place, or protective place. Invite your protective, nurturing, and supportive resources into the space furnished by the tray. Keep a picture of these resources nearby, so you can return to it between sessions for strength, solitude, and refuge. Create it with care and compassion for yourself. Spend time with it, and notice the emotions that emerge and how and where they arrive in your body. If the emotions are comfortable, use slow and short sets of BLS/DAS on yourself.

Your Companions

Create a team of companions in the tray. They are the ones by your side when you fully embody the therapist in you. Bring in animals, nature entities, characters, superheroes and heroines, to represent religious or spiritual figures, family and friends, teachers, and anyone else who helps you stay centered and connected to your most authentic self. Spend time with your team to make sure they are the right companions. It is better to avoid bringing in companions that are connected to your trauma, unless you have processed the trauma completely and can now fully connect with it without becoming emotionally dysregulated. Notice the emotions that arise and how your body responds to this sand world. When your emotions are comfortable enough, use slow and short sets of BLS/DAS.

Defenses

Take some time to reflect on your protectors and defenses. What self-protective mechanisms come to your aid when you feel activated during the therapeutic process? Reflect on your most challenging clients and the moments when you have felt tension and distress in the therapy room/playroom as a result of your client's sandtray work. Spend time with the miniature collection, choose those that represent your self-protectors, and give them a voice. Is it avoidance and emotional distance? Is it the need to escape and move the client out of the affective state emerging in the moment? Is it control and the need to have everything figured out? Is it dissociation and disengagement? Is it the need to rescue the client so you do not have to see them suffer? Is it perfectionism and trying too hard to always be the best clinician so you can avoid shame and feeling not good enough? Sit compassionately and in a neutral space with these protectors for some time. Remember that they represent former survival strategies, originally adaptive and supportive in helping you navigate challenges. Take time to understand each protector and to find compassion and gratitude for them all. Slow down and notice how they enter your mind during your clinical practice. What are they protecting you from? What job are they doing for you in your office? Take some time to represent all your findings in the sand tray. If it resonates with you, connect with gratitude and compassion within yourself, and bring these protectors into the tray. As they enter your field of awareness, a conscious and transformative relationship can emerge. During critical decision moments in the therapy room, you can gently invite these protectors to step aside while honoring and recognizing their best intentions. Bring figures in the tray that represent how you will work with your self-protective system and how they can support your therapeutic work with your clients.

My Most Challenging and Easiest-to-Work-With Clients

I invite you to divide a tray in half, or use two trays. Reflect on the clients you have found most challenging and those you have most enjoyed working with. In separate areas of the tray(s), represent what made the difficult ones challenging and the enjoyable ones rewarding. What makes these clients challenging or fun to work with? What personality and behavioral characteristics are taxing for you? Which characteristics do you find most desirable? Physicalize the answers to all these questions in the tray(s). Sit with the tray(s), notice your responses, and then represent them. Do you see differences in how you respond or how your self-protective system operates with each of them? What is the most demanding client doing that pushes your window of tolerance and stretches your regulatory capacities? What makes it easy to work with your favorite clients? Take time to hold both sand worlds, each representing unique aspects within you. Observe these differences and embrace them without judgment. Take some time to reflect on what you need in order to manage your most arduous clients. Hold yourself and your client with compassion. Notice what these clients bring up in you, and consider that they may be activating unhealed and unresolved trauma. Determine whether you need a companion that can walk with you to reprocess these memories, and seek support as needed.

Represent what you uncover in the trays in the way you want to witness them. Use the container exercise described in Chapter 2 if needed.

Meeting the Therapist in You

This work will support you to connect with the helper in you and with all the gifts and assets you bring into the world. Create a tray with the title "The Therapist in Me." Connect to the collection of figures, and select the ones that represent the helper in you. What gifts and assets do you see in your inner helper/healer? What does the therapist in you bring into your life and into the lives of others? Take time to be with this important side of you. As you spend time with it, notice the emotions and body sensations that emerge and physicalize them in the tray. Can you reach inside and find gratitude? How do you want to express gratitude in the tray? Take a pause, then notice what the therapist in you needs. Do they need more space, rest, or time to get to know themself? Do they need to know it is okay to set boundaries? Do they know it is okay to be more open or close emotionally in their work with clients? Do they need more connection with other clinicians in the form of support, consultation, or companionship? Represent these needs in the tray and connect with how they can be acknowledged, recognized, and eventually met. When you are ready to leave the tray, take the time to honor yourself with compassion and self-appreciation. Select a figure that will be your companion and the voice that will remind you to take care of yourself and to live in self-love and compassion. This figure will not return to your collection (unless you change it)—place it near you in your office.

At the end of these activities, use the container exercise, and place any disturbing material inside the container. You may also need to use breathing exercises or movement if these activities have been highly activating. It is essential for clinicians to acknowledge the importance of doing their inner work and to seek support within their community.

As we clinicians recognize our subjective presence in the therapy room, we can begin to acknowledge that our energy, patterns of autonomic activation, and therapeutic home influence our perceptions and understanding of the client's story, their therapeutic goals, and the approaches and strategies we select. Just as we make a commitment to our profession and to our clients, we must also to make a pledge to ourselves to remain centered and connected to our most authentic selves. At the same time, we must stay open to observing, noticing, exploring, and working through our biases, injuries, and defensive strategies. By doing this, we open our hearts to compassion, acceptance, and humility in our roles as clinicians and helpers.

308   EMDR-Sandtray-based Therapy

CHAPTER 11

Group EMDR-Sandtray-based Therapy

This chapter highlights the potential for optimizing and enhancing institutional and private practice resources for clients affected by complex traumatization while leveraging the strength and advantages offered by therapeutic work in group settings. Group work in the tray can take various forms and be offered to families, couples, caregivers, children, or other groups. The work may be performed following one of multiple EMDR-based protocols or may take a more open approach, using standard procedural steps and the eight phases of EMDR-sandtray-based treatment in group settings. Group work may be directed and focused on stabilization and resourcing, or it may be directed and centered on trauma reprocessing. Because this topic is extensive and its possibilities are endless, only some approaches and protocols using EMDR and sandtray techniques will be addressed in depth in this chapter; others will be mentioned briefly.

The mental health crisis that developed in the wake of the COVID-19 pandemic is straining community mental health resources. In the past decade, the number of people forcibly displaced has also increased exponentially worldwide (UNHCR, 2022), demanding a paradigm shift of new and expanded formats for treatment delivery that allow therapists to adapt their methodologies to better suit the demands and needs of the population they serve. The inclusion of group and systemic work actively recognizes that individuals exist not in isolation but as part of a larger interconnected system. By acknowledging and leveraging this reciprocal influence, clinicians can facilitate more effective healing processes and on a much broader scale.

Offering group work as part of a clinician's services can reduce waiting times and enable mental health providers, agencies, and facilities to serve more people. Maxfield (2021) differentiates between low- and high-intensity EMDR treatment. High-intensity treatment consists of an individualized, resource reach and comprehensive treatment. Low-intensity

309

treatment involves limited coverage, a brief preparation phase, and is delivered through a group approach. The essential task when both options are available is to rigorously evaluate clients to discern which will benefit from group therapy settings and which have pronounced symptom severity, warranting comprehensive and intensive therapeutic interventions. Even when selecting group work as the treatment modality, the level of intensity can vary and exists along a continuum. For some clients, group therapy alone may prove sufficient, while others may need individual and comprehensive treatment or a combination of individual and group therapy.

Children and adolescents benefit greatly in their healing process when their caregivers build greater capacities for self-regulation, coregulation, emotional attunement, and mentalization by participating in standard EMDR, EMDR-sandtray-based psychoeducation, or rerocessing groups. (Gómez, 2019, 2023b; Urdaneta Melo & Triana, 2024).

Some organizational formats for the delivery of EMDR-sandtray-based group treatment include:

1. Short-term group treatment for the child, adolescent, or adult, including a resource phase and low-intensity processing. Clients with single-incident trauma and high integrative and regulatory capacities may benefit from this approach.
2. Extended group treatment with comprehensive stabilization and preparation phases and longer protocolized group reprocessing for clients across development.
3. Systemic delivery, involving EMDR group resourcing and reprocessing with families and couples.
4. Extended group treatment, for children or adolescents, with parallel resource and psychoeducation focused EMDR group work for the client's caregiver(s) or partner(s).
5. A combination of individual, systemic, and group EMDR treatment for clients across the lifespan with parallel and extended group treatment for caregivers/partners, including extensive group and individual EMDR resourcing and reprocessing.

There is a number of group EMDR protocols, such as the EMDR group traumatic episode protocol (GTEP) from Elan Shapiro (2014, 2024), the EMDR integrative group treatment protocol (IGTP) from Ignacio Jarero (Jarero et al., 2008), and the EMDR group protocol for children (GPC) from Korkmazlar et al. (2018). Multiple studies support the effectiveness of EMDR group protocols in treating a variety of emotional issues (Artigas et al., 2014; Moench & Billsten, 2021; Jarero et al., 2018; Korkmazlar et al., 2018) across development, cultures, and diverse populations (Harris et al., 2018).

Sandtray therapy in group settings has also been validated by multiple studies (Lee et al., 2018; Lee et al., 2023) and found to be effective with various populations (Flahive & Ray, 2007; Shen & Armstrong, 2008)

EMDR and sandtray therapy have been used with families and groups of caregivers and children (Gómez, 2024a; Lyles, 2021). Further research is needed to support the practice-based evidence that supports the effectiveness and efficiency of EMDR–sandtray in groups. This chapter seeks to kindle the interest in studying the power of EMDR-sandtray-based group work.

Group Traumatic Episode Protocol in the Tray

GTEP, developed by Elan Shapiro (2014, 2024), is based on the EMDR Recent Traumatic Episode Protocol (R-TEP) (Shapiro & Laub, 2008). The GTEP protocol has been extensively researched and effectively administered to various groups, including refugees (Lehnung et al., 2017; Yurtsever et al., 2018), humanitarian workers (Papanikolopoulos et al., 2021), workplace trauma survivors (Tsouvelas et al., 2019a), victims of intimate partner violence (Tsouvelous et al., 2019b), natural and man-made disaster survivors, medical personnel, and first responders (Moench & Billsten, 2021; Williams, 2022; Johanson et al., 2021; Smith, 2012; Farrell et al., 2023). However, GTEP and sandtray therapy are new delivery routes that bring new possibilities and explore a new dimension of group work for clinicians who are already trained in standard GTEP. GTEP in the sand tray may be used with clients, across the lifespan, who have experienced complex trauma and who already possess regulatory and integrative capacities. Additionally, it may be delivered to the caregivers/partners of clients who have been exposed to chronic traumatization and are receiving individualized and comprehensive treatment. GTEP in the tray may also be used with couples, families, and caregiver–child dyads as an adjunct to comprehensive treatment or as a stand-alone approach, especially for single-incident or shared trauma.

A significant distinction between conventional EMDR therapy and the GTEP protocol is the latter's emphasis on all constituents of the trauma episode rather than on the seminal trauma alone. The trauma episode encompasses the seminal trauma along with all ensuing experiences and developments, extending even to future anticipations and anxieties that might originate from it.

The sand world and its symbols accompany each individual and the group in creating and accessing resources with which to craft and build the safety net each mind needs for reprocessing trauma. GTEP can be a stand-alone treatment or it may be used as part of more comprehensive group and individual work. However, before using GTEP protocols, clinicians must attend a formal training. Worksheets, manuals, and step-by-step directions are usually provided to attendees so they are well-prepared to guide and accompany their clients. When delivering GTEP in the sand, the treatment space needs to be relatively large. The group size might be small because the sand trays and miniatures will occupy a significant amount of space and clinicians may not have the infrastructure (the number of sandtrays and figures) to accommodate a large number of clients.

Readiness for EMDR group reprocessing must be discussed and established prior to accessing traumagenic material, and should be based on the client's history, preferences, capacity to regulate and change state, behavioral fitness to work collaboratively with other group members, presence, and capacity to access and report on inner data. To this end, the clinician should, during the initial intake, guide the client to practice the state change strategies and protocols such as the four elements (E. Shapiro & Laub, 2008) and the safe place, taking before and after measurements, to establish the client's ability to move out of activation into a regulated state. The state change procedure, the client's psychosocial history, and the administration of other standardized assessments provide important information that should be used to determine if the client can benefit from GTEP or if they require a more comprehensive and in-depth treatment. Overall, GTEP is appropriate for individuals with low to moderate symptomatology who have experienced trauma. Clients with acute symptoms, complex trauma, severe dissociation, pervasive emotional dysregulation, current self-harm behaviors, or active suicidal ideations will need a comprehensive approach to EMDR-sandtray-based therapy. However, group work may be an adjunct approach to increasing the client's stability and capacities.

The GTEP combined with sandtray procedures is an adaptation from Gómez (2022b), initially developed for children and later extended to apply to adults and adolescent groups. To deliver GTEP in the tray, clinicians must create an appropriate and safe space to accommodate groups, including a robust miniatures collection, a sufficiently large space, and trays for each group member. A therapeutic contract should be created to make the process predictable and to support the client's ability to make an informed decision to participate (see E. Shapiro, 2024, for detailed information on GTEP procedures). Clinicians will need to determine what size group they can accommodate, the age range of the participants, and the number of sessions the group is expected to attend as well as the prospective clients' behavioral fitness (especially when some clients present with low frustration tolerance, poor boundaries with other group members, and/or highly aggressive behaviors) and needs regarding mobility and medical and physical issues.

Intake Meeting and Screening

GTEP–sandtray may be delivered to existing or new clients after a thorough intake. The length of the initial intake will depend on the population to be served. For instance, refugees may only be available to attend a limited number of sessions. In this case, the intake should be precise and focused on readiness for group work and how the group work aligns with the individual's needs and therapeutic objectives.

Preparation

Group members usually sit around a table during sessions. They are given a tray in which dividers, such as rocks or fences, are used to create separate sections in the work tray. Group rules and boundaries are established to create a safe and supportive environment. Participants are encouraged to share resources and positive experiences while keeping private any material that may produce negative affect, as group members may be working on either the same or different traumatic episodes. In cases where families or groups have experienced the same traumatic episode, members may mutually agree to share traumatic information. Depending on the group size, the clinician may enlist a cotherapist to assist clients who need further support or regulation. According to E. Shapiro (2024), in standard GTEP, "the worksheet serves as a visual–spatial metacommunication that has the Trauma Episode enveloped with present, past, and future resources" (pp. 25–27). Due to their symbolic and metaphorical nature, miniatures and the sand space provide clients with a vast and rich medium for communication and feedback. The tray and figures enhance visual and symbolic understanding and provide distance, containment, and the opportunity for individual and collective minds to dialogue with themselves and each other.

Various forms of BLS/DAS are used, depending on the individuals' devel-

FIGURE 11.1 **The sandtray version of the GTEP work tray.**

opmental stage and whether group members are enhancing resources (BLS/DAS using a slower tempo) or reprocessing traumatic memories (faster BLS/DAS). When reprocessing, self-administered eye movement (EM) is recommended (E. Shapiro, 2024). However, it may be challenging for children to engage in self-administered EM. When using the tray, the following options are available:

- **For adults and older adolescents:** The individual may (1) drum with one hand or both while following the hand(s) with their eyes, (2) implement the butterfly hug or gorilla beats, (3) march while standing or sitting, (4) the clinician may attach and secure buzzers to each side of the tray by using Velcro on both the buzzers and the sides of the tray. This allows the client who is unable to engage in EM or prefers tactile stimulation to hold the tappers in each hand comfortably.
- **For children and adolescents:** The client may (1) drum while using the sand tray corners (some clients may be able to follow the drumming with their eyes), (2) march or move bilaterally around or in front of the sandtray, (3) do the butterfly hug.

The GTEP clinician should orient the group members, so they know what to expect and how to use the sand tray and the miniatures collection. Each group member is then instructed to create their individual GTEP work tray using the following four steps.

Step 1. Invite group members to practice the four elements, to physicalize their safe place in the tray using the miniatures collection, and to measure their pre and post stress level. They may use numbers; however, symbols and figures can also represent the distress level in the tray. Gems and rocks of multiple colors can also depict various levels of distress (a red stone may represent high disturbance, while a yellow stone may depict low distress).

Step 2. Once group members have practiced the four elements and safe place, direct them to move into step two and the area inside the tray that holds the space to access the beginning of the traumatic episode. Invite each group member to represent and physicalize the memory in the section of the work tray, then rate its level of distress and disturbance.

Step 3. Guide the group members to bring their attention to the section of the tray where they represent a memory associated with positive affect, where they felt whole, centered, and good. Deliver BLS/DAS once the group has identified the emotions (if they are comfortable and positive) and how they inhabit the body.

314 EMDR-Sandtray-based Therapy

Step 4. Invite the group to identify and represent in their individual trays their positive metaperceptions—the embodied cognitions they each would like to have while envisioning the traumatic episode in the future. They might represent these cognitive schemas envisioned in the future by using figures.

Step 5. The traumatic episode is accessed using a titrated approach, retrieving only one segment at a time and using longer and faster sets of eye movements (E. Shapiro, 2024). The group is guided to do a Google search/scan and find a point of disturbance (PoD), within the traumatic episode. The Google search/scan segments the episode into smaller fragments that can be assimilated without overwhelming the individual's system. Once identified, each group member uses a figure to depict the disturbing and activating segment (the PoD) and the SUDs associated with it, then the clinician delivers BLS/DAS at a faster pace and for a longer duration (20–30 seconds). After each set of BLS/DAS, the clinician directs the group members to observe and connect to any images, thoughts, feelings and body sensations or anything else they are noticing. SUD levels should be checked after the third, sixth, and ninth sets of BLS/DAS. The procedural steps of GTEP intentionally limit the activation of associative channels by not inviting the client to amplify the process and share their experiences with the group. Additionally, GTEP is procedurally organized to prevent vicarious traumatization of other group members. The goal of GTEP is not necessarily to bring the level of disturbance down to zero (even though it may be ideal) but to reduce it to its lowest possible intensity, thereby bringing some relief and stability to the individual suffering the legacy of trauma. Usually, three points of disturbance are accessed and reprocessed in one session. Additional PoDs are reprocessed depending on the number of sessions contracted with group members. Gems, rocks, and figures may be used to represent the changes occurring as the PoDs are reprocessed.

Step 6. After reprocessing three points of disturbance, the group members are directed to bring up the entire episode and rate its level of distress and disturbance. Once again, numbers or symbols may be used to represent the amount of disturbance experienced while holding the entire episode in mind in the sand tray. Clinicians can use this feedback to determine if group members need additional group or individual sessions. If a client's level of disturbance is still high at the end of the session or if they appear dysregulated or dissociated, the clinician should ensure the client's stability and use additional resources to support their return to homeostasis and emotional balance. Then, the clinician should reassess the appropriateness of group work for this client and consider inviting the client to individual and more comprehensive treatment.

INSTALLATION OF THE POSITIVE COGNITION.

Group members are directed back to the area of the tray that holds space for the positive metaperceptions linked to the traumatic episode. The most salient positive cognitions that are represented in the sand tray are installed and enhanced using BLS/DAS.

Step 7. The four elements protocol and a container exercise are used to bring the group back to homeostasis.

Step 8. Clinicians should follow up to ensure the safety of all the group members and to determine whether the group needs additional group sessions and whether any members need individual therapy.

Children Group Traumatic Episode Protocol

Children Group Traumatic Episode Protocol (C-GTEP; adapted by Gómez, 2022b) is based on GTEP. It has a short lifespan and was developed during the COVID-19 pandemic and subsequent mental health crisis. One of the C-GTEP delivery formats is in the sand tray. This powerful group-based therapeutic format actively uses the sand tray and miniature collection with children (Gómez, 2024). C-GTEP is a low-intensity protocol with numerous built-in resources and a titrated approach to accessing traumatic episodes. It is intended to promote stabilization and to reduce disturbance without strong activation and mobilization of traumagenic networks beyond the client's regulatory threshold. It is classified as a low-intensity treatment for use with children who have sufficient regulatory capacities, grounding in reality, and present safety.

Phase 1

During Phase 1, the clinician assesses the child's readiness to undergo treatment with C-GTEP by collecting their history and evaluating their behavioral capacity to be part of a group. Children who demonstrate severe traumatization and dissociation or acute and significant emotional dysregulation, aggressiveness, and pervasive difficulties interacting with other children in a group setting should instead receive individual, resource-rich, comprehensive, and systemic standard EMDR treatment.

Mental health agencies, residential treatment facilities, clinics, and schools may benefit from incorporating group work for children who do not need extensive stabilization and who show some capacity for emotional regulation. Moreover, institutionalized children affected by complex traumatization might be able to benefit from C-GTEP–sandtray because of their contained environment, such as residential treatment agencies. The use

316   EMDR-Sandtray-based Therapy

of group approaches can enhance and optimize a mental health clinic's resources, since the demand for mental health services often exceeds their capacities and the number of available clinicians.

During the initial phase of C-GTEP, the clinician should meet with caregivers to gather history and with the child to explore their regulatory capacities using the container protocol (Gómez, 2022b). This protocol includes taking pre- and post-measurements, using a 0 to 10 scale of distress (SUD) or a represented and symbol-based measure. Symbolic representations of distress levels will look different for different individuals; for example, one child might select a giraffe to represent calm and a long snake to represent intense distress, whereas another client might select a mountain lion to represent regulation and a tornado to express strong disturbance. When implementing the C-GTEP sandtray container protocol, the container may be physicalized using a small side tray or a bucket/box next to each group member, and the group should be invited to place miniatures that represent disturbing and intolerable material into the physical container. Children who show capacity to shift states may be invited to attend C-GTEP work; children who struggle with shifting states may be further assessed and/or referred to individual and comprehensive standard or EMDR-sandtray-based treatment.

Phase 2: C-GTEP Preparation Phase

The sand tray becomes the space to harbor and contain the therapeutic group work of children. It also holds the space for resources, and traumatic material to be physicalized in the sand through miniatures.

As described in the GTEP protocol at the beginning of the chapter, the C-GTEP work tray is created first by adding dividers, fences, and rocks to the sand tray. Stabilization strategies and resources are interspersed with the access of the traumatic episode. C-GTEP has several built-in resources: the team of companions (a relational resource incorporated by Gómez, 2021b, 2024), the four elements, the safe place, the positive memory, and the positive cognitions. One of the differences between C-GTEP and GTEP is the language used to meet the child's verbal communication capacities. Instead of discussing the four elements, we invite the "awesome four": earth, air, water, and light. Instead of using Google search/scan, we invite children to do "detective work" and find a "bothering spot." Instead of a positive cognition, children find "good thoughts."

Children may use coverings with their tray when the physical representation of the trauma or PoD is distracting or too activating to the child.

Every step of the C-GTEP in the sand tray is accompanied by the richness of the miniatures, the sand tray, and the natural movement of sandtray play. The C-GTEP session is terminated with music, songs, and play to

FIGURE 11.2 **The sand world from a complete C-GTEP session.**

bring the group back to homeostasis and honor the work they have done alongside their acts of triumph which may the completion of a visit to the kernels of the traumatic episode. Children are invited to share the positive experiences and resources in their sand worlds, but they are asked to keep their "challenging" and "hurtful stuff" private because each child may be working on a different type of traumatic episode. This practice is meant to prevent other group members from being vicariously traumatized and to avoid the further activation of traumagenic data. However, group members are informed that when needed, they can share in a separate space their concerns or disturbing material with one of the therapist.

C-GTEP and sandtray may be scaled up in institutions with large spaces, enough trays, and a miniature collection abundant enough to accommodate the increased number of participants. Refugees and other large groups of people affected by trauma may use the beach as their tray and items from nature as figures to externalize and represent their resources and trauma. C-GTEP in the sand highlights the power of play by illuminating how play [holds/increases/augments] the children's ability to focus, engage, and remain interested throughout the process. Children with mild dissociation or attention difficulties may benefit from C-GTEP in the sand because the kinesthetic forces of the tray, the miniatures, and the movement of sandtray work cultivate the child's social engagement. C-GTEP–sandtray can be administered as a stand-alone intervention over one, two, or more sessions or integrated into a more comprehensive treatment process that includes additional sessions dedicated to preparation, enhancing the children's homeostatic repertoire, and reprocessing.

C-GTEP Combined With Extended Preparation

C-GTEP includes extensive built-in resources to accompany titrated and low-intensity trauma reprocessing. However, some clients may benefit from or require additional stabilization sessions before they are ready for C-GTEP–sandtray.

A separate and more extensive safe place protocol may be used before implementing the C-GTEP. Each child will have their own sand tray, which provides a contained and secure space for the safe place to be created. Their team of companions can be extended using the steps mentioned in Chapter 3. Each group member is invited to create their own team of companions in their tray. A group tray and only one or two figures may be used to physicalize the minor disturbance (one of the procedural steps of the safe place protocol) to avoid the need for each child to use two trays. The figure(s) or the shared group tray can be positioned at a distance so group members can use movement—walking, dancing, or doing an animal walk adds a playful element and a neural exercise to the process—to reach the minor disturbance. Invite the children to move back and forth between the minor disturbance outside the tray and the tray containing the safe place and its associated affect.

A creative and effective stabilization strategy that can be used alongside C-GTEP is selecting an "animal helper." In this process, each group member selects an animal to accompany them throughout their healing journey. The animal helper is physicalized near the individual tray or in a shared tray where all the animals can coexist. If an animal chosen by a group member creates discomfort for someone else, adjustments should be made. For instance, to establish boundaries and minimize triggers, all animals can be kept within their respective client's tray.

The multifactor model of preparation addressed in prior chapters offers multiple roads and potential resources that can be crafted in the sand in individual or group settings. Affect tolerance activities, such as feeling parties, and meeting and exploring affective states exercises work well with groups. Children are invited to physicalize a feeling or feelings they would like to visit in the tray. Each child may visit a different feeling, or the group may agree on which feelings to invite into a collective tray. Group members sit with and visit the guest feeling in the tray while bringing in figures that represent what unfolds in their mind, heart, and body as they allow the visitor to enter their inner world. Each group member may choose how much—a drop, a spoon, a bucket, or a spray—of the feeling is invited into the tray and into their inner world. Once the visit is complete, children share their experiences and continue to use figures to represent their insights and inner occurrences in the sand world. Children may label or name their

Group EMDR-Sandtray-based Therapy **319**

emotions, body sensations, and cognitions. However, these inner experiences may remain solely in the symbolic and metaphorical world.

The clinicians and institutions offering group EMDR-sandtray-based treatment to children must determine the number of group sessions, the number of participants, the length of each session, the age range of the clients, the group's main objective, the characteristics and needs of the group members, and how to create a relationally safe environment. Inclusion and exclusion criteria should be established. Many of these groups operate as closed groups, meaning participation is limited to those who join from the first session, with no new members allowed once the group has started. Because group sandtray-based EMDR requires a greater amount of supplies and space, four to six members may be the group size limit. Choose a length of the session that is appropriate for the participants' ages. As you design your treatment plan, consider that children aged 5 to 7 would likely benefit from the accompaniment of a caregiver, who can support them while they engage in BLS/DAS, help them follow instructions, and generally keep them engaged.

EMDR-Sandtray-based Group Therapy for Caregivers

Many of the symptoms children present with are the result of generational wounds. In many instances, these symptoms represent the child's best attempts to elicit care from a caregiving system that is or was either collapsed and abdicated or in a constant state of mobilization and sympathetic activation. Group work can encompass and support the healing of intergenerational trauma, and a combination of group and individual treatment may optimize resources, time, and the benefits that organically come from group work. Companionship, normalization, and validation are just a few benefits of using EMDR-based groups. Various formats may be used with caregivers, from resource groups to reprocessing groups.

EMDR-sandtray-based groups may focus on:

1. The development of emotional regulation capacities, affect tolerance, and state change strategies and protocols, such as the safe place, the team of companions, and the capacity to be with and tolerate a wide range of affective states. Parenting groups focused on emotional regulation may invite caregivers to create their own healing place where they bring figures to represent a place of calmness, companionship, belonging, and safety. This tray can provide the physical and safe space for clinicians to deliver the RDI protocol, whereby each caregiver works through challenging situations with their children by developing resources and envisioning a future full of competency and empowerment.

2. Embodied psychoeducation to support the caregiver in becoming the child's external psychobiological coregulator, organizer of experience, cocreator of meaning, and reflective companion.
3. The reprocessing of parenting episodes or events that move the caregiver out of connection, coregulation, reciprocity, and mentalization into survival and self-preservation. The GTEP delivered in the sand tray supports caregivers in reprocessing traumagenic memories that are activated by their child's behaviors.

Group Parenting Empowerment Protocol and the Parenting Wheel

The group parenting empowerment protocol (GPEP) paired with the parenting wheel (PW; Gómez, 2022a) is a combination of protocols influenced by the structure of the GTEP protocol, developed by Elan Shapiro (2014, 2024), and by the RDI protocol, developed by Korn and Leeds (2002). The PW, created by Gómez (2021b), is organized to enhance caregivers' self-regulatory and coregulatory skills by providing resources that empower them to parent from their adult/wise/guiding self while increasing their capacity for playfulness, connectedness, reciprocity, and mirroring. The GPEP and the PW both use an approach that supports conscious, reflective, contingent, and synchronic parenting, fostering deeper emotional attunement, promoting secure attachment, and encouraging adaptive responses to children's needs in the context of their unique developmental and relational experiences (Gómez, 2022a).

The tray, used individually or in group settings, becomes a mirror that holds the safe space for caregivers to explore themselves in their caregiving role.

The inclusion of caregivers within a child's treatment—whether a comprehensive individualized treatment or a group approach—is designed to embrace the sometimes vulnerable but resilient caregiving system. Incorporating parallel group work with caregivers concurrently with the individual treatment of their children can be a powerful strategy for healing. Caregivers should be included and invited to be actively involved in a generational healing journey with their children. EMDR–sandtray work in groups gives each embodied mind—accompanied by the collective—a vehicle of expression and an instrument of change and transformation. The PW and GPEP intend to shift caregiving paradigms and foster a deeper nurturing and healing bond between caregivers and their children.

GTEP–sandtray and GPEP are often used in combination with caregivers, which provide the caregivers with extensive caregiving-focused resources and a profound understanding of their children's needs. With expanded connection to self- and coregulatory capacities, the caregiver can begin reprocessing parenting-related episodes to reduce the activations that interfere with their role as the wiser, bigger, guiding and soothing force. For many caregivers, the initial group approach becomes the portal and a stepping stone to in-depth and comprehensive individual processing, which may be necessary for the most traumatized caregivers.

GPEP and PW Phase 1

A thorough psychosocial history of the caregiver is obtained to determine which track might offer the greatest benefits to the child and their relational system: (1) comprehensive individual and systemic treatment, including individual treatment for caregivers, (2) a combination of group and individual treatment for both the child and the caregiver, or (3) group treatment for the child as well as for the caregiver. How much the caregiver is involved will depend on multiple factors, such as the caregiver's willingness to participate and the client's need for the caregiver to be an active therapeutic partner. Unless the child's symptoms are isolated incidents that are unrelated to their relational ecosystem, attachment ruptures, or family and caregiver–child dynamics, most children's treatment should involve the caregiver in some capacity.

FIGURE 11.3 **The seven elements of the parenting wheel.**

Constanza Rodríguez Ramírez - Editorial designer. Dresser icon made by dDara from http://www.flaticon.com. Jump rope icon made by Freepik from http://www.flaticon.com. Mirror icon made by Nikita Golubev from http://www.flaticon.com.

The delivery of the PW begins with segmented psychoeducation in the tray (Gómez, 2019, 2021b), using metaphors, stories, and analogies that capitalize on the wisdom and capacities of the right brain. Each session may focus on one or more elements and resources of the PW, with these components gradually accumulating and increasing in complexity as the sessions progress. Each element of the PW is represented and explored within individual trays created by each group member. In some cases, this process is followed by the enhancement and installation of resources, as well as the integration of new insights and realizations. Depending on the number of caregivers in one group, sessions may last from one to two hours. Clinicians may schedule short sessions and allocate one to each area, resource, and element of the PW, or they may address combinations of them in longer group sessions.

Group sandtray strategies that incorporate exploration of the seven areas of the PW will be described next.

1. My Bigger, Wiser Self, Inner Guide. This part of the parenting wheel is designed to help caregivers connect with their older, wiser, compassionate, guiding, and most capable self (the one that holds the space for generational assets). It also helps them differentiate how they feel and act when they are parenting from this guiding and compassionate self from how they feel and behave when their younger, vulnerable parts that carry generational wounds and trauma are active. These trauma-formed self-states often hijack the caregiver's best intentions to connect, coregulate, and meet their child's needs. These story keepers hold traumagenic memory networks that the child's behavior frequently activates, becoming the lens through which the caregiver sees, feels, and gives meaning to the child's attempts to elicit care. According to Lyles (2021), "The goal of healing emotional and relational wounds becomes substantially more attainable when caregivers also come to view children's trauma responses as adaptive and protective" (p. 75).

In the group, caregivers are invited to select their individual tray and create two spaces, separated by fences or dividers. Next, each member is invited to create a world dedicated to their wiser, adult, guiding, and most compassionate and capable self in one of the two spaces in the tray. Invite them to represent their wiser/guiding self's characteristics, when this self is most available, how they know they are connected to it, how this self feels, what thoughts accompany it, how their bodies feel and act while connected to the wiser self, and how they relate to their child while this self is guiding the caregiver's parenting.

Once the caregivers connect to the wiser/guiding and most compassionate self, invite them to notice their emotions and body sensations

FIGURE 11.4 A caregiver's divided tray holds representations of the wiser/guiding self (right) and part/self that holds adversity, wounds, and trauma (left).

before engaging in slow and short sets of BLS/DAS. Once the caregivers are grounded in connection to their wiser/guiding selves, you may direct their attention to the other space in the tray and ask them to connect to moments of contention and conflict that occurred because their wounded warriors and hurt story keepers influenced their parenting behavior. This level of work in the tray allows the caregivers to connect and dialogue with their wise/guiding self and the part that carries the wounds and traumas they accrued over their lives. Invite the caregivers to carefully notice how the trauma-formed self-states and the wiser/guiding self occupy their minds, hearts, and bodies. What is different when one or the others inhabit spaces within? What cognitive, affective, and somatic patterns accompany each self? How do they see, feel, and respond to their children when they are connected to the wiser/guiding self compared to when they are connected to the one holding their life burdens? Invite the caregiver to journey inward, fostering compassion (when ready) for the part of themselves that has endured trauma and adversity. This work will often take an entire session, after which, caregivers are encouraged to remain mindful and observant of when the adult/wise self is guiding their interactions with their children and when the hurt self is in charge. Group members can share their experiences to validate and normalize the intricacies and profound challenges of parenthood.

2. My Thermostat and My Accordion. This part of the PW represents the heart of coregulation and the vital role of being the external psychobiological regulator of the child's system (Schore, 2019). Similar to a thermostat modulating the temperature, the caregiver has the fundamental role of regulating the child's shifting physiological states. In fact, caregivers and children concurrently alter each other's states of consciousness from moment to moment (Putnam, 1997). Invite the caregivers to reflect on their inner thermostat and how it operates when the child presents with "emotional heat" or "emotional coldness." Invite the caregivers to create a sand world with all the nuances of parenting while assuming the role of an external thermostat and bioemotional regulator of their child's physiological and affective states. Ask the caregivers to explore how they embody this fundamental role while remaining connected to their adult/wise/guiding self that will support the development of the child's own thermostat. Afterward, invite caregivers to share their experiences with the group.

The accordion is used to represent one's affect tolerance and one's capacity to accompany others as they experience a wide range of affective states. Having a high affect tolerance enables both the child and the caregiver to navigate and embrace diverse emotions. Some caregivers nonconsciously restrict or unintentionally dysregulate their children's affective and physiological states. For instance, a caregiver with a dismissing state of mind, who uses avoidance as a primary strategy to deal with challenging emotions, may limit their child to existing within a controlled and restricted range of emotions. Conversely, a caregiver with preoccupied tendencies may exacerbate the intensity of their child's emotional and autonomic states and increase their dysregulation. Invite caregivers to envision and represent a wide range of emotions with the fluidity of musical notes or dance steps. The accordion represents the natural rhythms of expansion and contraction of emotions, which is aligned with the pulsation of life and energy. The accordion—or any other similar and applicable musical instrument selected by group members—can remind them to join the child in recognizing and acknowledging their embodied affective states while, at times, sitting in stillness and being with or engaging in the dance of coregulation and movement. Caregivers add symbols to the sand world to represent tolerable emotions as well as those they avoid or exacerbate. How do the caregivers relate to their emotions and their child's emotions? Do they constrict or further activate emotions? What impulses and body sensations are awakened by the child's emotions or needs? Once the sand world is complete, invite group members to share their experiences.

3. My Dresser. The caregiver's internal dresser supports the labor of organizing the child's experience. Caregivers are not only external coregulators but also coorganizers of experience (Gómez, 2021b). As coorganizers, they take the information emerging from their children moment-to-moment and reflect it. When doing laundry, one takes a disorganized mixture of clothes, classifies and sorts them, and then neatly places them inside the dresser's drawers; similarly, the coorganizing caregiver takes the child's emotional messiness and gently brings understanding, organization, and order to the child's mind. The child and the caregiver cocreate meaning as the child participates actively in understanding how each moment unfolds. Invite

FIGURE 11.5 **The Parenting Wheel in the tray:** One caregiver's divided tray symbolizes the accordion and thermostat, using figures to represent emotions, thoughts, and body sensations. A movable bridge connects these elements, illustrating the pathway to regulated states and experiences of connection. The dresser is on the other.

caregivers to conjure situations and moments that need organization and coregulation, then to physicalize them in the tray. With each new realization and understanding, the clinician invites the group to remain observant and connected to what is unfolding. How are these realizations settling within? What emotions, thoughts, and bodily states emerge? When the moments of inner knowing awaken comfortable, regulated, and positive emotions, the clinician may invite the group to engage in slow, short BLS/DAS by drumming on the corners of the tray, doing the butterfly hug, or marching.

4. My Mirror. Caregivers are mirrors for their children, since children do not yet have the capacity to know and see themselves. This mirroring initially occurs in the caregiver–child relational space. Children first begin to understand their own internal states when their primary attachment figures reflect and mirror their inner experiences. The mind seeks to find itself in the mind of another to validate its existence. This complex concept is brought into the concrete world using the mirror analogy. Invite group members to create in the tray worlds that represent moments of mirroring.

The clinician can accompany the members with questions that deepen the experience, such as:

- What do you see in your child that they need to know?
- What do they feel? What do they need?
- How do you usually mirror their experience?

Sometimes, this activity is an eye-opener that brings awareness to how mirroring and reflective communication build a strong and healthy sense of self and the lack thereof dims the light of the child's inner world. Clinicians may wish to use reflective statements in addition to or instead of questions so the caregivers can experience what it feels like to be mirrored, seen, and known by another. Group members may take turns mirroring each other and representing these profound experiences in their sand worlds.

5. My Inner Sun. These are inner companions on the parenting journey that are often forgotten in the habitual busyness of life. The analogy of the sun, the rainbow, and the clouds sheds light for caregivers on how their trauma can insidiously undermine their heartfelt intentions to express love to their children and fully savor the mutual delight of their shared existence. Explain to the group that the sun and the rainbow represent the human capacity to experience love for others, especially our children; however, the emotion of love, which is the crux and essence of our human voyage, is often affected by lifelong conditionings and trauma. Next, share that the clouds represent the traumagenic memory networks that become activated, covering the sun and the fundamental essence of love and its myriad forms of expression. It is quite puzzling how the emotion that moves humanity and is at the center of its existence may remain buried in expectations, conditionings, defenses, and lifelong pain and trauma.

During the group work, invite caregivers to choose symbols and figures representing this love and to create a world of their histories and relationships with love. How has love been passed from generation to generation? Where does love want to go in this generation? How is it being expressed and experienced at home by the children? What are the clouds that stand between the caregiver's subjective experience of love and their behavioral expression of love to others?

Invite the caregivers to let rainbows remind them that joy and compassion can emerge even after a stormy experience with their children. The rainbow is a symbol of repair. Guide caregivers to bring into the tray symbols that represent the power of repair while normalizing the fact that moments of rupture occur in all human relationships. However, the emergence of the rainbow after the storm is paramount to coconstructing caregiver–child relational safety.

6. My Playful Self. Play is an innate biological motivational system (Panksepp & Biven, 2012). Play fundamentally shapes the social brain (Cozolino, 2014), and it is a primary need of children. Unfortunately, the modern world has removed the time that was often allocated to play and, with that, its profound benefits. Invite caregivers to create a tray depicting their history and relationship with play. How have their life stories shaped how they play with the next generation? How can they reconnect with their playful forces and energy? What are the cognitive, emotional, and somatic barriers to engaging in play states? How can this dynamic and playful drive influence and impact their children? How can they increase playtime?

7. My Shield and My Boundaries. This component of the wheel is dedicated to protection, containment, and limit-setting. In this part of the PW, care-

Group EMDR-Sandtray-based Therapy   **327**

givers create sand worlds where they can explore their capacity to contain, say no when needed and appropriate, and establish boundaries. Invite the group members to create an individual tray depicting their history and current relationship with boundaries. Are their boundaries absent or overly rigid and stern? How can they use boundaries (their shields) for protection from others—including their children. What behaviors and actions require strong limits? When are negotiable and soft boundaries appropriate? Which part of the caregiver is setting the limit: the adult/wise self or the one holding the hurts and emotional injuries?

Clinicians then enhance new insights and realizations that are associated with comfortable and positive emotional experiences with BLS/DAS. Invite caregivers to take pictures of their tray so they can keep it with them and access it as needed.

GPEP

Once the parenting wheel process is complete, the GPEP protocol may be used in one or two sessions of two hours each. The sand tray is organized to accommodate the procedural steps of GPEP using rocks, fences, or any other dividers.

Step 1. Caregivers are invited to enter the sand world with the four elements (Shapiro & Laub, 2008) and the safe place represented in the tray.

Step 2. Group members create their own team of companions, composed of family members, friends, fantasy figures, superheroes, story and book characters, other helpful people, animals and pets, nature items, and safe mem-

FIGURE 11.6 **GPEP Step 2: Relational resources.**

bers of their support system. The tray is a safe space for their companions to emerge and act as a source of empowerment. Invite the caregivers to identify their emotions and bodily sensations. Caregivers may use the butterfly hug, drumming, or even marching while using self-administered short and slow sets of BLS/DAS once they have reached a positive and regulated emotional state resulting from the connection to their team of companions.

Step 3. Guide caregivers to access their personal, ancestral, and parenting assets and resources. Invite the group members to physicalize them in the tray, and follow with the installation of the positive affective states connected to them.

Step 4. Invite caregivers to identify and physicalize positive metaperceptions, positive embodied cognitions, and affirmations that will accompany them when they interact with their children. Support the group members in finding the most potent and empowering metaperceptions that will most effectively enhance their parenting and their connection to their resources. Invite the caregivers to physicalize these positive thoughts in the tray to access the power of symbols to penetrate the implicit and nonconscious mind.

Google Search and the Future Template (Steps 5, 6, 7, and 8). These steps are essential and are repeated four or more times. **Step 5** begins by inviting the caregiver(s) to engage in a "Google search/scan" (Shapiro & Laub, 2008) as a metaphorical tool to explore moments of strife and discord in the caregiver–child dynamic that currently feel unmanageable and challenge the caregiver's regulatory capacities. **Step 6** involves guiding each caregiver to represent these future encounters (identified in Step 5) in the tray. This includes envisioning their responses to their children while drawing on both their personal resources and the skills developed through the Parenting Wheel.

Some resources focus on fostering **self-regulation**, such as the four elements, the safe place, the team of companions, personal strengths, and positive, empowering metaperceptions. These tools help caregivers maintain internal balance and regulation in the face of challenges.

Other resources are designed to enhance **coregulation** and **parenting capacities**, supporting caregivers as they engage with their children in a way that expands their **cohomeostatic capacities**—the ability to maintain shared psychobiological equilibrium within the caregiver–child dynamic. Tools from the PW like the wiser and guiding self, the thermostat, the accordion, the dresser, the mirror, the sun and rainbow, the playful self, and the shield and boundaries serve to strengthen the caregiver's **coregulatory threshold**,

Group EMDR-Sandtray-based Therapy   **329**

FIGURE 11.7 A sand world representing a caregiver's full session of GPEP includes all the caregiver's resources alongside three identified moments of discord in the parent–child dynamics. Each moment is paired with a corresponding future template, designed to integrate the caregiver's strengths, regulatory tools, and relational capacities.

allowing them to respond with greater flexibility, patience, reciprocity, and emotional attunement. These resources foster an environment where both caregiver and child can thrive, even in moments of discord or stress.

Once the represented future template is created in the tray, group members are invited to sit with this represented scenario, taking time to notice their emotional and bodily responses. If the future template evokes positive, empowering, and comfortable emotions for all caregivers, they are guided to engage in brief, slow sets of BLS/DAS to deepen their connection to the physicalized scenario.

Caregivers are to access and identify additional parenting-focused future templates (aligned with Steps 7 and 8, as well as additional iterations if time allows) and to rehearse and practice them in the sand tray. This process helps create and explore various possible relational interactions with their children, expanding their capacities to respond contingently and effectively.

The GPEP protocol is playful and accessible, making use of the evocative power of images, symbols, and metaphors represented through the miniature collection. While GPEP harnesses this symbolic richness, it remains easy to understand and implement, offering a seamless blend of creativity and transformative practice.

EMDR-Sandtray-based Group Work With Families

Sandtray strategies and procedures can be used with EMDR-based protocols with families and dyads or triads. The treatment goal is the best guide for how to organize family sessions. Sometimes, the goal is to resource and bring greater emotional balance to the whole family; other times, the goal is to process disturbing material to reduce the mutual activation of unhealed trauma. It is important to remember that "treating a child's trauma in a systemic manner allows for more comprehensive healing, and restoration in all members of the system" (Lyles, 2021, p. 76). The number of sessions and length of each session will depend on the number of family members and their ages. For instance, if the sessions include young children, special accommodations should be implemented to ensure that the work is developmentally appropriate. If sessions involve processing trauma shared by the entire family, then it may be appropriate to work with the caregivers first before processing as a group so caregivers can assist younger family members if needed. In cases of families with children, the C-GTEP can be delivered to the entire family, or a combination of C-GTEP and GTEP can be used.

GPEP may be adapted for families, couples, teachers, and groups when the focus is on expanding access to relational resources. School clinicians can support teachers in becoming a secure base and external coregulators and coorganizers of their students to facilitate learning. Couples' therapists can also adjust GPEP for groups of couples.

When working with families, EMDR–sandtray clinicians must spend time creating a relationally safe environment for all the members of the family. This may be challenging if family members—or the individual receiving individual services—distrust the family and feel disenfranchised by others in the family system. Families may also bring a wide range of entrenched defensive strategies that may stagnate the therapeutic process if not acknowledged and worked through. In some cases, the tray can hold the space for family members to represent their "soldiers" and mechanisms of survival, such as avoidance, control, perfectionism, and manipulation. Trauma-related phobias may also interfere with or block family work by keeping members at bay from their inner world and unable to share their challenges, emotions, and deepest needs. When generational defenses are present, it is essential to gently support the family in bringing them into consciousness. Segmented psychoeducation can prompt the family to identify and physicalize in the tray what they do within the family and in the sessions to avoid pain or uncomfortable emotions or what they do when they do not feel safe.

To increase relational safety within the family, group work may commence with each member creating a tray or cocreating one with the family around safety. The tray may be divided into three spaces using fences or rocks. Once the tray is divided, family members are guided to select figures that represent how safe they feel (1) externally and physically in the family, (2) relationally with all the family members, and (3) internally with their inner worlds. The next step is for group members to select miniatures that represent what they need to feel safe physically, relationally, and internally.

EMDR-sandtray-based family work can be used during any or all of the eight phases of EMDR treatment. If used during the initial phases, the focus is on exploring the relational choreographies of the family and understanding the individual client within their relational ecosystem. A lot can be learned from observing these dynamics, and these findings will inform the organization of the eight phases. Several sandtray activities can be used to expand the therapist' knowledge and understanding of the clinical and relational landscape of the family or the individual within their relational context:

1. A world about the family's assets and strengths
2. A world about the family's challenges
3. A tray divided into three, using fences, rocks, or something else: the first area populated with the family's resources and strengths; the second depicts their main issues; and the third holds their resources and strengths and how these may be used in potential solutions to address conflicts within the family

Each tray/section is explored and discussed within the family. These activities may involve a tray for each family member or one tray that the entire family cocreates together.

4. Each individual is invited to create a world titled "This is me in my family," depicting how each member experiences themselves within the family. What role do they play? How do they feel in the family? Which

FIGURE 11.8 **A single tray cocreated during a family session. The left side holds the family's assets; the middle holds their problems and challenges; and the right holds their solution.**

longings are met, and which need to be seen, acknowledged, known, and fulfilled? What issues are they struggling with within the family? What resources exist in the family and in each member? Are these resources being used? What facilitates their use, and what hinders it?

5. Family "trees" can be coconstructed in a shared tray. The caregivers may start by depicting their story in the tray, and then each member contributes elements known to them, inserting and providing their own perspective on the story. When moments of disagreement arise, all perspectives should be represented in the tray so the family can work through these polarized states. Points of agreement, concord, and harmony, as well as moments of compromise and flexibility, are also represented in the tray.

6. Genograms can unfold in the tray rather beautifully as symbols and figures actively represent the family members' relational dynamics and the quality of their bonds and affiliations. Each family member is invited to physicalize themselves in a shared tray, followed by representation of relational dynamics. Resources and challenges that live within each family bond are physicalized and witnessed, making their existence real in the outer world so each member can dialogue with what exists within and with what lives in the relational space of the family.

Families may participate in sessions directed to increase individual and systemic capacities. One clinician will be dedicated to working with the family and building resources while other clinicians may deliver individual sessions to some of the family members. State change resources and protocols, such as the safe place, team of companions, personal assets, and RDI, provide scaffolding to the family and to each individual. Even though the family works together, they each work with their own tray and resources that may be shared with the rest of the family.

Nondirective worlds can bring information that is often delivered through the nonconscious and implicit mind. The family is invited to collect the miniatures that call to them without any agenda. Then, they are prompted to create together a group world or a story, in any way they desire, in a shared tray. These implicit stories provide distance for the family members to explore and verbalize issues, challenges, and conflicts that otherwise would be overwhelming. The manner in which the family constructs the sand world will offer valuable insights into their relational dynamics. Observe how they negotiate and make decisions regarding figures and story elements, which may reveal rooted relational patterns. Notice how they handle conflict and what method they use to resolve it. Do they approach challenges with flexibility and willingness to adapt, or do they display rigidity and resistance to change? Observe areas of cohesion,

Group EMDR-Sandtray-based Therapy **333**

strength, or tension. Family members may ask questions or be invited to reflect on what they cocreated in the tray. Members are invited to stay with the metaphors and symbols unless the family decides to move the sand story into an explicit world. The story that is unfolding gives the family members opportunities to contribute to their collective world and reflect both as individuals and as a system. The clinician will observe how the family coconstructs the sand story, who leads and who is relegated, and what movement, shade, and color each family member gives to the story. Engaging young families in nondirective and implicit play in the tray allows the children to express themselves freely and naturally, fostering better communication and understanding within the family. Resources may emerge for individuals and the system through symbols and avatars that the EMDR–sandtray family clinician can enhance with BLS/DAS. Throughout the use of sandtray strategies within EMDR treatment, the EMDR clinician remains observant, connected, attuned, and open to receiving the signals and information emerging from the collective minds of the group. Facial expressions and nonverbal communication are as valuable as verbal communications. In the delicate tapestry of familial therapy in the tray, establishing a foundation of safety is paramount. Families thrive in environments where trust and security are woven into the therapeutic sessions. When families feel secure, they can engage in meaningful interactions that are crucial to fostering emotional growth and resilience. Relational dynamics unfold as the family tells its story, while the clinician remains open and responsive, providing feedback, reflections, and boundaries for containment and respect. It is most helpful for clinicians to remain curious and compassionate as they witness how the relational and generational stories are revealed. Who leads, and who is denied their space and voice? What is addressed and strongly voiced, and what is not expressed? All information is invited into the tray and represented so each individual and the family as a whole can dialogue with it.

Processing With Families

During the processing phases, the tray is an invaluable asset and companion when engaging with families and dyads. The healing potential of play in the sand tray confronts and challenges the effects of trauma (Lyles, 2021). Through play and the use of symbols, family members process traumatic experiences in a nonthreatening way, gradually rebuilding a sense of safety and trust in themselves and their relational milieu.

However, when working with families exposed to complex trauma and presenting with acute symptomatology, the family's capacities for processing must be carefully established. The group protocols and other treatment formats using EMDR–sandtray are recommended for families with some level of stability, integrative capacity, and the behavioral and emotional capacity to sustain and participate in EMDR-sandtray-based family therapy. Comprehensive, high-intensity, and individual treatment is often more suitable for clients on the severe side of the symptomatology spectrum.

All the protocols addressed and covered earlier in this chapter can be adapted to working with families. The number of sessions a family needs will vary and depend on the treatment goals for the family and its individual members. The family, as a collective at this stage and as a result of previous work, possesses greater cohesiveness and the ability to accompany each other as they embark on processing sessions. Family members may work on individual or collective experiences of adversity or trauma. After participating in multiple group sessions dedicated to resource building, family members often become better equipped to support one another as they navigate their emotional landscapes and shared experiences.

Case

Alex, a 7-year-old boy who was adopted at age 5, has displayed severe anger outbursts since his adoption, causing his family to become hypervigilant and fearful of his reactions. He has been abusive to the family pets. Both caregivers reported substantial exposure to trauma and losses throughout their lives, and yet they were resistant and opposed to receiving any kind of therapy for themselves.

The parents accepted the invitation to attend parenting group sessions focused exclusively on resource development using EMDR and sandtray approaches. The clinician initiated sessions with Alex and parallel sessions with both caregivers to address parenting issues. The clinician working with Alex mixed systemic, dyadic, and individual sessions where EMDR–sandtray was often used within a comprehensive approach.

The caregivers worked with the PW and GPEP sandtray for nine sessions, increasing their regulatory, relational, and parenting capacities. After seven months, Alex had made significant progress. The family then began family sessions to learn the PW and the GPEP together. These approaches were adapted to meet the developmental needs of Alex and his two teenage brothers. They also participated in GTEP–sandtray and reprocessed episodes associated with family conflicts and frequent fights that ended in physical and emotional wounding.

Each family member worked through their own episode despite sharing a similar theme. The family received four sessions of GTEP–sandtray and reported a significant reduction in disturbance associated with their selected episodes.

In the last session, the family created a communal tray where they communicated their shared experiences through symbols and verbal accounts of their group experience. This exercise fostered deeper understanding and connection among the family members. Alex continued his individual sessions, which supplemented his group work, throughout the parallel family process.

The family therapist maintained constant communication with Alex's therapists to provide adequate companionship. Alex's mother chose to undergo individual and comprehensive treatment after recognizing, through the group work, the benefits and potentialities of embracing her life story, which was marked by exposure to complex trauma.

A team approach and the use of multiple methodologies to EMDR therapy along with sandtray therapy made a substantial difference in the lives of Alex and his family.

CHAPTER 12

Special Populations and Considerations in the Application of EMDR-Sandtray-based Therapy

Sandtray therapeutic work lends itself, with incredible flexibility, to be used with a wide range of issues across the lifespan. However, each population has special and unique needs and characteristics that must be accommodated with flexibility and acknowledgment. The clinician's understanding of the challenges and tribulations that are unique to each client will contribute to a positive treatment outcome. In this chapter, we will review adaptations and special considerations when working with multiple issues and populations, as well as how to work with diversity and use antioppressive practices in the tray.

Attachment Wounds

Attachment injuries lay at the core of human existence and human suffering. Even when other forms of trauma are present, attachment wounds frequently coexist, adding another layer of complexity. The human mind needs other minds in its journey toward realizing wholeness, consciousness, and the awareness of its own existence. Acts of omission force the mind to journey alone and in isolation because all the mind has to construct itself with is its own subjective experience of pain, abandonment, and emptiness. On the other hand, wounds may be inflicted by acts of commission that occur during crucial stages of maturation and growth of the child's biological systems. As a result, acts of commission and omission tint the experiences of the wounded self, profoundly shaping its perception and responses to the present. These neural networks, formed through a multitude of daily experiences with unavailable or wounding caregivers, exert a significant influence on the shaping of the individual's mind. As a result, the processing of core, and rooted attachment traumas with EMDR–

337

sandtray may be, in some cases, lengthy and convoluted. These memory networks have complex and intricate layers that extend into myriad symptoms and relational issues that are brought into the therapeutic process.

Clients with attachment wounds often present with lingering and unfulfilled needs that haunt them. Sandtray work provides a refuge to the mind seeking healing and completion alongside EMDR and sandtray as potent treatment methods. In the tray, emotions emerge, sometimes rambunctiously and sometimes quietly and somber or dull in color. These clients, of all ages, bring courage, strength, and resiliency as well as entrenched forms of survival and adaptation. The clinician's mind becomes a fellow traveler who journeys and explores the deep layers of the client's self. The clinician structures the eight phases of treatment to facilitate correction and repair. The following considerations are essential for implementing EMDR-sandtray-based treatment with clients exposed to attachment ruptures and wounds.

Phase 1

When working with clients exposed to attachment injuries, the trays may be nondirective or may have a theme that focuses on early childhood or on current relational dynamics, which very likely connect to early relational patterns and internal working models. The client may be invited to create a tray focused on their relationship with their needs, emotions, or themself as well as their current struggles and challenges. Figures come into the tray to represent the voices of deep needs, longings, emotions, and relational templates marked by caregiving insufficiencies. Clinicians may explore attachment injuries through affect scans to invite the mind to travel to earlier experiences where the deficiencies occurred. If the client is an adult, you might say:

- Let's sit with this longing just a bit longer. Notice if there is a feeling connected to this need and how your body responds to this need and its emotions.
- Let's spend some time here.
- How is this need/emotion speaking to you now? How intense or visible is it to you? How have you related to it throughout your life?
- Connect long enough to it, and then let's journey through your life to see where this need/feeling came to you. When did it become this intense/invisible? What about this need/feeling keeps you focused on it? When did this need/emotion become invisible to you?
- What did others, especially important caregiving figures, do about this need? Did you express it? Did the important people in your life notice it? How did they respond to it? Did they see it? Did they acknowledge it? Did they fulfill it?

- Let's bring this information into the tray. Let's have the figures show what you see, what you feel, and everything unfolding in your inner world right now.
- Let the sand tray be your mind's mirror. Arrange it whatever way you are ready to see, witness, and interact with it, and leave aside (or cover) what feels too big, challenging, or painful.

If you are working with children, modify the language as follows:

- Let's visit with this need just a bit longer and notice if there is a feeling that goes with this need and how your body responds to this need and its feelings.
- Let's spend some time here.
- Now, let's travel back to your life to see when this need came to you.
- (Children can put on a cape and fly around the tray as they travel to visit the past.)
- What did others do about this stuff you needed? Did you express/ show/say something about it?
- Did the important people in your life notice it? What did they do about it?
- I invite you to find figures to represent and show what you see, what you feel, and everything that is happening inside. If something feels too big, yucky, and difficult, put it aside or cover/bury/hide it.

Needs and emotions are strong access routes into attachment injuries and attachment resources as well as into current relational tendencies and templates. Embodied metaperceptions associated with defectiveness, unworthiness, or being unlovable are also portals into early wounding experiences in the client's relational ecosystem. Positive and adaptive experiences can often be retrieved and linked to secure affective dialogues with significant attachment figures, who continue to serve as powerful biological neuroregulators. These relational and personal assets can be enhanced with BLS/DAS. Past generations did not leave only injuries but also assets and strengths. Often, the injury and the strength coexist, and the strength may actually be in the injury. As the client embraces the injury, the source of expansion emerges.

Phase 2: Preparation

Parts work incorporated into EMDR–sandtray gives the client the space for inner storytellers carrying attachment injuries to be seen, known, and witnessed. The sand avatars open a field of possibilities for the client to develop a relationship with these wounded parts. The clinician may invite the hurt younger self or little self that carries the early wounds into the field represented in the sand tray. The needs and emotions may come to the surface through symbols and representations that give light, air, and wings to the inner world. The vulnerable young parts can tell their stories, longings, and missing experiences. Clients can physicalize their relational tendencies. How do they navigate relationships? What strategies do they use: approach or distance and avoidance? What do they do in response to separations and ruptures? What emotions, impulses, and urges emerge? This explicit portal into relational internal working models unfolds in the tray and the physical realm, allowing them to enter the client's field of awareness. Implicit portals are often more accessible to children. Relational dynamics among characters often represent nonconscious relational templates that can be explored while protected by the distance offered by the sand world.

Reprocessing Phases

Profound and substantial transformations often emerge in clients following the comprehensive processing and integration of their deep-seated attachment wounds and the reorganization of internal working models and self-representations.

Multiple interweaves, addressed in prior chapters, are useful with this population, especially interweaves that promote attachment completions of deeply ruptured bonds and the repatterning of accompanying autonomic states. Often, breaches in the affective dialogue with important attachment figures remain deeply buried underneath nonconscious and implicit memories (Lyons-Ruth et al., 2006). As such, the clinician should use a gradual and titrated approach to enter these memory systems during processing. Resources should surround the client so they can now find adaptive ways of satisfying what was once unseen and unfulfilled. Repair interweaves that validate, mirror, reassure, and meet the deep needs for connection, acceptance, appreciation, and, ultimately, love are used throughout reprocessing sessions. The client may invite characters, mirror holders through which the embodied mind can experience and see itself in delight and compassion.

The clinician uses passive and active pathways (Porges, 2017) to activate neural mechanisms associated with homeostasis and safety. Passive pathways recruit the social engagement system, through cues of safety that come from the physical and therapeutic relational ecosystem, and do not require conscious awareness. The clinician intuitively uses voice intonation, compassionate stand, eye contact, and so forth to down-regulate defenses and bring homeostasis to the client's biology (Porges, 2017). During processing, the clinician remains open, curious, and compassionately present to gently challenge the client's internal working models of insecurity, distrust, and shame. This mutual cocreation of relational safety

340   EMDR-Sandtray-based Therapy

during processing strongly contributes to reorganizing insecure relational templates. The clinician also works with the client's companions, such as the caregivers (in the case of children), who become active therapeutic partners during processing. The clinician guides and supports the caregivers to deliver interweaves that repair previously ruptured attachment experiences and autonomic states in the tray and through the emerging stories. The caregiver may sing lullabies, rock, soothe, and fulfill needs that emerge through sandtray characters. The caregiver may repair previous ruptures verbally and symbolically and may accompany the child and the characters when they are distressed.

Grief and Loss Issues

Grief is a multifaceted and nuanced phenomenon that extends to almost all levels and shades of the human experience, especially when it coexists with complex and developmental trauma. The work in the tray using EMDR therapy validates, normalizes, depathologizes, and deshames the mourner. The griever can connect with the deep shadow of loss and its profound opportunities for expansion and healing. EMDR–sandtray provides and holds a safe and sacred space for the grieving mind to find acceptance and the possibility of restructuring their inner world to harbor the loss of the object.

> From an attachment point of view, we will see that the goal of grief work does not involve detachment from the loved one. Rather, the goal is a reorganization, a transformation of the relationship that accommodates the reality of the death and results in the development of a continuing bond. (Solomon, 2024, p. 79)

The ultimate goal of treatment is not to take away the natural emotions that arise in response to the loss of a loved object but to facilitate the grieving process toward assimilation of the loss and rearranging relationships to the lost object. Love and pain often coexist, and the loss of a loved object can radically change the inner landscape of the human mind. Grief is an affective experience embedded in every incident of trauma, adversity, and loss that the human mind experiences across the lifespan and, as such, is present in most EMDR–sandtray sessions.

As we work with grief, we also work with the attachment system. We are hardwired to attach and to love, and as a result, we are bound to grieve the loss of the object. There is also grief in attachment ruptures. According to Bowlby (1988), the child experiences an emotional loss when they cannot connect affectively to their primary attachment figures. Repetitive

Special Populations and Considerations **341**

ruptures in the caregiver–child affective dialogue result in frequent experiences of emotional abandonment and loss.

Reprocessing Phases

A vast spectrum of grief themes may be summoned to the surface and represented in the tray while in the presence of the client's resources. Clients may be invited to craft sand worlds on the following themes:

- **Loss of a loved one:** Miscarriage, illness
- **Loss of identity:** Career change, role change
- **Loss of a relationship:** Divorce, separation, breakup
- **Unresolved issues with the deceased:** Victim perpetrator dynamics with the deceased, unspoken wounding acts
- **Health-related loss:** Chronic illness, moment of diagnosis, disability, changes in the body, symptoms
- **Loss of an experience or developmental stage:** Innocence, developmental experiences, periods of happiness, the person they used to be, the loss of a feeling, a capacity, a belief
- **Loss of employment:** Retirement, financial loss
- **Loss of property:** Natural disasters and loss of a home, eviction
- **Loss of one's home country and culture:** Cultural identity loss
- **Loss of dreams and expectations:** Struggling to achieve or continue a long-held career goal

Often, as trauma moves toward integration, grief becomes open and visible. The grief that was once buried is now revealed so it can be embraced with solemn dignity and profound acceptance. Processing grief is often a painful encounter that ultimately brings freedom to the mind that mourns. For instance, Marie, a 35-year-old with severe early trauma, finds herself in deep pain and mourning for the childhood she did not have after processing the extensive episodes of physical abuse at the hands of her caregivers. She expressed profound sadness for the innocent little girl who received so little from life when she needed it the most.

Various mentalizing styles and states of mind will influence how individuals process losses in the tray and how they grieve. In addition, each metacognitive processing tendency will require a different approach from the clinician. The adult client with dismissing states of mind may use avoidance as a primary strategy to deal with grief and may remain on the periphery of affective content. In response, the clinician gently and compassionately pushes the edges of the client's window of tolerance, gradually facilitating and encouraging the avoidant mind to release its defensive adaptations, fostering a shift into a more open state of awareness.

The preoccupied client will circle and loop around the grieving process, coming back over and over again—at times obsessively—to the mourning of a lost object. The clinician becomes a grounding rope, consistently available and reliably present, providing constant anchoring amid the client's turbulent internal conflict.

The adult with unresolved states of mind and experiences of traumatic loss may present with lapses in their sand world and in their verbal discourse around the lost object. They may bring in characters representing loved ones who have passed away as if they were alive. The clinician delivering EMDR–sandtray honors the states of consciousness in which the client's mind exists and meets them there in compassion, promoting the movement the client is ready for and providing coregulation and a titrated entrance into the space where mourning can take place.

During processing, the clinician meets the grieving mind's natural rhythms of expansion and contraction. Mourners may pendulate between grieving and distancing or contracting. This phenomenon may occur during processing, as the client may naturally retrieve and find refuge as they shift into a different image, thought, emotion, or sensation. The clinician follows and accompanies the client as they navigate through the "in" and "out" dance of grieving and distancing, spiraling down into deeper and more profound layers of grief and awareness. The clinician and the miniatures collection accompany the grieving client in stillness and, at times, in commotion, agitation, and turmoil.

When the pain that accompanies grief shows up, it can be externalized in the sand world. The client is invited to be with and sit with the shadows of grief, allowing the moment to unfold, with the companionship of the clinician or other "helpers." The mind that experienced the loss in aloneness now receives the companionship, support, validation, and mirroring that was absent. The clinician guides the client through interweaves in the tray during processing phases, providing corrective experiences to the grieving mind. Needs and longings are identified and fulfilled, and words that had remained trapped and hidden can now be expressed through symbols and words. Clients of all ages are invited to physicalize the reunion with their loved ones, with their younger bodies, or with their younger selves so they can say or do what could not be said or done before. Unfinished business with a loved one or lost object can be addressed in the tray. What does your loved one need to hear/know/see from you? Are there words, stories, or messages that you need to deliver? What could not be communicated before can now unfold and emerge through the voices emerging from the tray. The client may speak, interact, and be with the lost capacity, body function, ability, or stage of life as it exists in the physical and symbolic world offered by sandtray work.

Special Populations and Considerations **343**

Clients can benefit from interweaves that invite and support the completion of previously ruptured bonds with departed persons. In the tray, the client can navigate unresolved matters with the lost object, allowing for emotional healing and the opportunity to honor their memory by finding closure and peace within. Through this transformative experience, clients can continue to cherish the legacy of the lost object and can rearrange their relationship with their loved ones. Individuals who lost their previous health or a bodily function can rearrange their relationship with their body. This reconfiguration involves the acknowledgment of the loss while embracing novel ways of functioning and connecting to their body. It is a profound and ongoing process of establishing a new connection to themself, embracing a new sense of identity, and finding hope and new meaning as they face change.

Case 1

Andrew, a 47-year-old male client, had lost his father. While reprocessing the memory of his father's death, Andrew realized that he had been carrying resentment because of his father's addiction to alcohol and his father's emotional absence throughout his childhood. Andrew represented his father's addictions and associated behaviors and his disengagement using miniature bottles and cigarettes. He also placed his father's figure far away from his younger, vulnerable self. He used heavy and giant dinosaurs to represent his old emotions toward his father that he never had the opportunity to express.

As Andrew spent time noticing these dinosaurs, a deep sense of grief overtook the sand world. He brought crystals to represent his deep pain associated with the desire to have a different father. At the same time, Andrew remembered moments of connection and play and his father's hard work to pay for his education. These emotions—pain, grief, and gratitude—coexisted, emerging in both his mind and the sand world.

After several sets of BLS/DAS, Andrew connected with his anger, which took over the stage in Andrew's mind. The clinician invited Andrew to physicalize it in the tray, to notice how he wanted this information to exist in the tray, and to reflect on what had emerged.

> "What do you want to be visible in the tray that your mind is ready to see, witness, and know, and what needs to take a step back?"

Andrew chose an angry bird to represent his rage, making it completely open and visible, while a dove depicting gratitude, joy, and grief remained buried. As he continued to reprocess and his anger dissipated, he expressed the desire to uncover the figures representing joy, gratitude, and grief. He

344   EMDR-Sandtray-based Therapy

started by removing some of the sand, making them somewhat visible. As BLS/DAS continued, grief took the front seat and became completely open, seen, and visible. Andrew brought in more crystals to represent the immensity of his pain, not only for the loss of his father but for the missing experiences that came with having a father with addictions. He also grieved the loss of his childhood and what he did not have but he wished he did.

The clinician reflected his pain and wondered out loud what he needed. Andrew answered that he wished he could have a conversation with his father to tell him how he felt. The clinician wondered if this could happen in the tray. Andrew brought in a figure to represent his older father, another to represent his present adult self, and a third to symbolize his hurt self. While the clinician delivered BLS/DAS, Andrew verbally and symbolically told his father all he needed to say through the figures. He reported a sense of relief and completion.

Without anger, Andrew stepped more fully into mourning his father's death. Grief and mourning are nuanced with myriad layers that are often not accessed through linear work. During reprocessing sessions in the tray, clients like Andrew may go from accessing traces of pain and grief to fragments of rage and anger and later return to grief. The process may be circular, reminiscent of a spiral, with each access point into the grief landscape offering a new portal to deeper layers of grief, expansion, and integration.

Case 2

Julian, 7, had lost his brother in an accident. In the tray, he created a world representing the sudden departure of his brother. When asked through an interweave what he needed to say or do that he did not get to say or do before his brother's death, Julian stated that he never told his brother how much he loved him.

The clinician reminded Julian that anything was possible in the sand world and that if he wanted to express anything to his brother, the tray could give him the space and opportunity to do so. Julian's brother had loved dragonflies, so Julian created a corner in the tray filled with dragonflies, flowers, and a river. He brought a figure representing his brother to this special corner and told him multiple times how much he missed him and loved him.

BLS/DAS followed while Julian verbally and symbolically expressed his love to his brother and added more flowers to the tray. At the end of the session, Julian asked for a picture of the dragonfly and the special place where he could talk to his brother and keep him close to his heart. The therapist reminded Julian that he could express his love to his brother anywhere and anytime he needed.

Special Populations and Considerations **345**

FIGURE 12.1 **The sand world of Dora, an adult client enduring an autoimmune disease.**

Case 3

Dora, a 35-year-old woman with an autoimmune disease, lived in constant pain. She frequently grieved for her younger body and her previous life without this chronic illness and pain. In the sand tray, she reprocessed the memory of her diagnosis and everything that surrounded this life-changing event. When grief entered her mind and the tray, deep pain emerged, accompanied by tears, which she represented with small rocks. Dora physicalized her younger and her present body with its challenges and difficulties. In the tray, they dialogued, hugged, and cried together.

As an interweave, the clinician invited Dora to search for the much older future self and to be curious about what wisdom she would bring to the two selves currently in the tray. The three women, existing in different temporal realms and chronologies, had the space to dialogue and reflect on life, grief, and pain. Realizations about their existence, aging, health, and more were exchanged while engaging in BLS/DAS.

Deep grieving emerged as they all embraced the changes life had brought to their body. Fire, representing strength, and a pond, symbolizing the vortex of universal energy, became the center for these women. Dora realized that she had choices in her treatment and could make lifestyle changes to reduce her current limitations. She placed bridges and doors in the sand world to represent life possibilities and her entrance into acceptance.

Implicit Information Processing and Grief

Grief issues also surface in implicit worlds as the characters mourn the death, illness, or disappearance of another. The clinician accompanies the avatars in their pain and sadness or unresolved issues.

Kaitlyn, a 6-year-old living in foster care after both of her caregivers went to prison, created a sand world where a chameleon had lost all of her colors after her caregivers had gone to jail. Kaitlyn placed the chameleon in a lonely corner without friends, family, or colors. The tray was empty, mirroring Kaitlyn's life. As Kaitlyn reprocessed this implicit world, the chameleon expressed her desire to find her colors but could only find one, which represented her sadness.

Kaitlyn's foster mother and the therapist sat in companionship with the chameleon and her sadness. The clinician offered her reflective and compassionate presence while Kaitlyn's mind battled with the absence of her caregivers and the deep loneliness of her heart. Eventually, the chameleon realized that she could invite her teacher, foster mother, and younger sister to join her as she was recovering traces and small kernels of her embodied colors.

The clinician used interweaves to support Kaitlyn in expanding the rainbow of feelings that existed within the chameleon. Kaitlyn brought in a new, much bigger chameleon that could carry more colors. This chameleon and her addition of colorful gems, while simultaneously holding precious moments and memories of joy with her chameleon caregivers and the other chameleons in her life, symbolized her openness and her capacity to experience sadness in the tray. The chameleon and her story became the bridge into Kaitlyn's grief and the portal to new relational possibilities with herself and with others.

Culture

Throughout the eight phases of treatment, clinicians must consider the intersectionality of cultural identities and how they impact and shape the grieving mind. Clinicians may invite the client to create a sand world about their cultural beliefs, traditions, and conditionings surrounding death, dying, and loss.

Cultural humility and curiosity will aid the clinician as they remain open to exploring and reflecting the client's mind as they embark on a journey to discover how they are internally furnished and shaped to face loss. What did they learn early in their lives about loss/death/dying? What meaning do they attach to the experience of loss? How does the client's religion or spiritual beliefs influence their perceptions, beliefs, emotions, and actions? What cultural and ancestral traditions exist around loss/death/dying? What cultural resources does the client bring? What information have other generations passed on to the client around death/dying/loss/grieving? These explorations in the tray can be enriching and transformative.

Abuse Issues

Experiences of abuse can surface in the sand world through explicit and directive trays or through implicit and nondirective worlds. The abuse may have a direct entrance into the tray; it may come in uninvited, surprising the storyteller's mind. It may slip in to a world where the self is not yet acknowledged or into one where it is explicitly recognized.

The abusive acts that occur in the sand world are as important as how the relational ecosystem responds and reacts to them. A bird may be mistreated and hurt in the tray while no one sees or acknowledges the abuse, meaning the abuse remains invisible to the other characters in the tray. Other times, characters in the sand world may fight fiercely, defending the vulnerable character and successfully returning it to safety. At times, the relational milieu may turn against the victim through criticism and abandonment, and at other times, it may shower the victim with love, empowerment, and protection.

It takes incredible courage from mental health practitioners to be the witnesses of such horrendous acts that unblend in the tray from individuals exposed to chronic traumatization and abuse. As witnesses, we are, undeniably, deeply touched and at times vicariously traumatized. Yet, we are also transformed and expanded by walking the often rowdy, turbulent, and painful roads of healing with our clients.

As Kathy Steele (2009) so deeply and profoundly states:

> As I walk, making this road, I have the strangest feeling that my heart has simultaneously diminished and expanded. And if this journey, which has both given and taken, be not entirely good, it is most certainly genuine and honest. It is a real and present encounter with each other and our self. (p. 11)

Attachment to the Perpetrator

The consequences of abuse—especially abuse perpetrated during sensitive periods of development by important attachment figures—are multidimensional and long-lasting. A constellation of underlying forces, involving power differentials and relational betrayal dynamics, coexists between victims and perpetrators. The bond with the perpetrator can inhabit a complex inner architecture, often emerging in a dissociative system marked by deep internal rifts where the inner perpetrator is experienced as the actual offender. Victim–perpetrator allegiances can also exist within a system of ego states.

Understanding the perpetrator and their motivational systems can support the clinician's discernment in terms of the type of the client's internalized aggression and idealized perpetrator. Rage, predatory aggression, and social dominance aggression are biologically mediated forms of aggression that have been identified as neurobiologically distinct (Panksepp & Beaven, 2013). These differing forms of aggression can have unique ramifications on the victim, particularly at various stages of development. Aggression may be calculated or impulsive, and it may be coupled with rage, anger (emotional and affective), or pleasure (predatory). It may be directed to punish, injure, compete, overpower/dominate, or attain pleasure.

Victim–perpetrator dynamics are complex and multilayered phenomena that involve the activation of innate motivational systems. These inborn action systems, when impacted by trauma and disorganized attachment, may become inhibited, overactivated, or maladaptively combined (Liotti, 2017; Liotti & Gilbert, 2011):

> The abuser–abused relationship is not only characterized by unbearable mental pain inflicted by the abuser to the abused: it is also a disorder in the complex dynamics between the multiple innate dispositions that allow human relatedness to proceed along healthy pathways. (Liotti, 2018, p. 68)

Aggression intended to attain obedience, such as spanking, may have different consequences compared to other forms of aggression because it activates other systems beyond defense. This kind of aggression is different from predatory aggression, which is directed at injuring the victim. Children who grow up in secure relational ecosystems and appropriate experiences of coregulation have smooth and balanced transitions between motivational systems, and they respond adequately to environmental changes and demands. However, children exposed to abuse perpetrated by important attachment figures may present with activation and shifts between systems that are maladaptively linked (Liotti, 2017). For instance, a child with experiences of sexual abuse perpetrated by a caregiver may pursue attachment system goals through the sexuality system (instead of the attachment system), which has been prematurely and repetitively activated. The child exposed to abuse nuanced by domination may inhibit or overactivate the ranking/domination system, moving the child to perpetual submission or a controlling/punitive strategy.

Special Populations and Considerations   **349**

Several authors suggest that these motivational systems become the basis for the emergence of dissociative self-states (Liotti, 2018; Steele et al., 2017; Steele, 2021; van der Hart et al., 2006).

When the primary caregiver is simultaneously a source of fear and of protection, the child becomes entangled in a paradoxical situation. The caregiver, indispensable for the child's survival, protection, and emotional regulation, is also the source of fear and abuse, creating a profound and inescapable conflict (Farina et al., 2019). These dynamics may surface in sand worlds where the character assuming the caregiver role is abusive and loving at the same time or where the abuser is also the caregiver.

Implicit Access. In children, the alliance to wounding figures often emerges implicitly in the tray, hiding behind characters, which provides distance from the client's mind so they may see these trauma bonds without having to consciously own them. Implicit work in the tray allows the child to expose hidden dilemmas and to explore the complex dynamic that led them to move toward self-betrayal and allegiance to the perpetrator. Attachment theory (Bowlby, 1988) has helped us understand the intricacies of the internal representational system in which the human mind creates mental representations of the relational dynamics with important attachment figures. These internal working models and inner representational systems function as a foundation for the development of a sense of self and identity across time. The attachment figure, with their good or bad characteristics, becomes part of the child's inner representational system and thus is embedded in the tapestry of the child's identity and sense of self.

Morgan, a 12-year-old in foster care with a history of severe physical abuse at the hands of her biological mother, created a sand story in which Nemo and Pluto lived in a divided world. On one side of the tray, there was a witch who trapped them both in a cage while surrounded by ghosts and evil characters. The witch possessed a powerful eye that could see and know all, which kept Nemo and Pluto in a state of fear and hypervigilance. On the other side, the same witch—a much nicer one—cared for the two characters.

When allegiance to the perpetrator arises implicitly in the tray, it may take many forms. The child may create repetitive sand world themes of perpetrator–victim dynamics in which the perpetrator is almighty. Sometimes, the main character and the child's preferred figure is the perpetrator, whom the child supports, admires, and offers boundless loyalty, representing an inexorable bond. The ego state or the dissociative parts holding the alliance and imitating the perpetrator may be explicitly acknowledged and unblended from the inner system into the sand world. This route is more often observed in older children, adolescents, and adults.

FIGURE 12.2 An implicit sand world of a 13-year-old where a powerful perpetrator enslaves vulnerable animals while a young ghost has no choice but to submit and please him. Dragons, scorpions, and a dinosaur protect and serve the authoritarian abuser. A powerful force gives the perpetrator infinite power. This sand world depicts the client's internalizations of power imbalances and perpetrator–victim dynamics resulting from severe abuse.

When the figure representing the internalized perpetrator shows up in the tray, the clinician meets it with curiosity and compassion because these parts only represent the client's best attempt to adapt and survive the often horrendous and wounding relationship with their oppressors.

What actions is the perpetrator executing? Are they aware of the wounding they produce? How do they feel about these actions and their victim's responses? How long have they been hurting others? Where did they learn to hurt others? How do they choose their victims? Do they feel any remorse? What are they getting out of their actions—pleasure, power, a sense of control? Does the perpetrator feel rage, competitiveness, or pleasure?

How is it, for the animals or people who are close to or live with the perpetrating character, to witness, know, or be the perpetrator's direct victims? Are there characters in the tray that do not see, know, nor speak about the perpetrator and their actions? Is there secrecy, fear of telling, or fear of knowing what the perpetrating character is doing? Are there characters that cover up the perpetrator's actions?

How is the victim responding? Are they fighting, trying to escape, hopeless, helpless, or collapsed? What strategies do they use—submission, dissociation, pleasing? Clinicians should be attentive to and explore how aggression and abuse occur in the sand world. Is the aggression defensive, offensive, competitive, or predatory? Is the abuse or aggression calculated or impulsive? Is it coupled with rage and anger, or is it linked to pleasure?

Clinicians may also go from object to self, if appropriate and tolerable by the client, and invite curiosity. You might say:

"How is it for you to witness the [perpetrator] killing all the [characters]? How is it for you to see their suffering?"

The answers to these questions will give you a better sense of the type of perpetrator the child has internalized and a much deeper understanding of how the client relates to their inner oppressors.

The clinician uses reflective statements, inviting curiosity about the occurrences in the sand tray as well as segmented psychoeducation that builds bridges to the adaptive network and connection to self. The clinician's reflective statements and questions support the client's return to the ruptured inner realities to mend them and realize them while accessing consciousness and connecting to the place within that is whole and unbreakable.

Dissociation, at its core, represents separation and disengagement from self, identity, and any intolerable part of the mind's experience, which may become extensive and pervasive in cases of severe dissociation. Fundamentally, treatment should seek to reestablish a relationship with self and the wholeness within. As Jamie Marich (2023) so eloquently states:

> When there is a breakdown in communication or a fissure between the different aspects of us working together and learning from each other, dissociation may be present. And once we notice that dissociation is present, we can challenge ourselves to reconnect with our inherent wholeness. (p. 12)

In the tray, the client may encounter what is perceived as divided and ruptured as well as the full spectrum of their innate integrity and the unblemished aspects within.

Use reflective communication to describe the relational ecosystem that exists implicitly in the sand:

- The [character] in the tray feels broken (client report), yet they are still whole enough to be aware of the broken pieces. I wonder if they can hold these two places together as they coexist within him.
- I notice the big [perpetrator]'s pleasure as they attack the little [character]. I am also aware of the [character]'s fear and pain and the ones watching without hope. They are all part of the same story.
- I watch the little [character] give up after their fights did not help them escape. I notice their fear and pain and see that they serve the big [perpetrator] (client report) as a way to survive.

- Little and baby [characters] do not know how to hurt others unless they have been hurt themselves or have seen others being hurt. I wonder if the big [perpetrator] remembers how they learned to hurt others.

Issues of accountability are addressed only when the client shows readiness. Trying prematurely to place the responsibility in the hands of the perpetrator may further activate perpetrator-imitating parts or ego states and those holding loyalty and allegiance to the oppressor. Often, the victim carries the responsibility in the dysfunctional victim–victimizer relational dynamic. Bring shared curiosity into the therapy room. You might say:

“ I wonder if we can be curious together about who is responsible for the actions of the big [perpetrator]? What do other characters in the tray see, think, and believe about who is responsible? Are there differences of opinion in the tray?”

These divergences in the tray may indicate the presence of internal conflict that usually surrounds these tumultuous relationships. The clinician works on bringing out these polarities so they can be seen, felt, and known by a mind that opposes owning these realities. The companion consistently remains reciprocal, attuned, and coherent, creating a space that invites the client to bring these divergent realities to the surface and physicalize them in the tray, thereby validating the client's subjective experience. Use reflective statements, such as:

- I can see now how the little [character] is struggling between wanting to be close to the big [perpetrator] and wanting to run away from.
- It must be really confusing for the little [character] to live with a big [perpetrator] who takes care of them but also hurts and scares them.
- Going away from the scary feelings caused by what the big [perpetrator] is doing is how the little [character] found a way to survive and make it through something so difficult and painful. I wonder if little [character] needs to know that we all go away in our minds when we have to go through very scary things. They are doing all they can to survive.

In the representation process and the internalization of attachment figures, the child's sense of identity and self may be entangled with the perpetrator's, requiring differentiation of the self from the perpetrator's identity. You might say:

“ I see the big [perpetrator], and I also see the little [character]. They might live together, yet they are two different [characters] with different thoughts, feelings, actions, and bodies. When little [characters] are hurt by important [characters] in their lives, they may feel confused about who they are. Even when the [perpetrator] makes the little [character] hurt others, they are still not the same [characters]."

For children who experienced sexual abuse accompanied by pleasure coupled with fear and other emotions, such as disgust, the enduring burden of shame and guilt and the pervasive and overwhelming sense of responsibility becomes a relentless torment. This profound anguish shapes their thoughts, emotions, sensations, actions, and ultimately their sense of self.

When these elements of self-blame emerge in the sand world, they are received with compassion. Through interweaves, clinicians support the client by validating the body's natural response and how the experience caused deeply confusing feelings. A wide range of emotions are invited into the tray as they coexist in turmoil. They come into the sand world in the way that the client's mind is ready to witness them.

Explicit Access. When accessing perpetrator loyalty explicitly, the clinician uses reflective statements and questions directed to the client and their ego states or their dissociative parts that emerge in the sand world. Perpetrator-imitating parts/ego states may recreate victim–perpetrator dynamics in the inner world that may be recreated in the tray. When these dynamics are physicalized, the client's embodied mind can witness, interact with, and dialogue with the parts involved and the dynamics.

To deepen the experience, invite the client to slow down time—for children, to go into slow-motion time—to just observe this new way of seeing, feeling, knowing, or understanding the issue. During the initial phases of treatment, clients may be invited to breathe in this new piece of information that has entered their field of consciousness while remaining connected to the figures that embody them. However, as the client moves into the reprocessing phases, questions like those described above, and reflective statements, serve as powerful interweaves, followed by BLS/DAS.

Reflective and descriptive statements and curious questions continue to move the client into deeper layers of understanding, which have the potential to dim and attenuate the conflict among parts as the parts find ways to resolve their differences or to compromise and accept their discrepancies.

> " As you connect to the side of you that is loyal to the [perpetrator] and the one that is angered by them, what do you notice? what happens as they recognize each other's existence? How is it for them to know that there is diversity within you? Are they open to finding ways to coexist and compromise?"

Physicalize any agreements or ways in which these opposing parts can negotiate and cooperate, even if they are just small attempts. See Chapter 9 for additional recommendations for work with perpetrator-imitating parts with EMDR–sandtray.

Dysfunctional Positive Affect

Both positive and negative affect can be processed and integrated in EMDR therapy (Knipe, 2019) and sandtray therapy. Dysfunctional positive affect (DPA) is a psychological defense held by an ego state or a dissociative part. The individual shifts away from the pain and suffering to overfocus on what brings pleasure and positive emotions. DPA may surface from various sources, such as the coexistence of pain and pleasure in traumatic events like sexual abuse and the grooming process. On the other hand, strong positive memories, or fragments of them, may become an escape route when confronted with memories associated with negative affect.

One of the issues many clinicians find staggering is the positive emotions and affect that some individuals may have experienced with sexual abuse. The assessment and reprocessing phases assume the presence of disturbance, so how do we respond when the abuse is seen through a positive lens?

In sexually abused individuals, DPA quite often emerges in the grooming process and the sexual pleasure and attention the victim may have experienced during the abuse. For children living in relationally and emotionally impoverished environments, the grooming process showers them with attention, gifts, and a false sense of appreciation, acceptance, and connection. When the child has been deprived of fundamental attachment needs, the grooming process and the abuse itself become their only source of connection. The associated emotions connected to the abuse are colored by DPA.

It is worth clarifying that dysfunctional does not imply pathological, as these affective responses simply signal the child's best attempt to attain homeostasis and to survive the abuse and its inner legacies. The tray opens up the space to materialize distortions, dissonances, and polarizations as well as peritraumatic resources in association with the abuse. If the client acknowledges the abuse, the reprocessing of the memory may be initiated with an SUD of 0.

Interweaves may be necessary to bring curiosity and clarity to the complexities of what the client was exposed to and what they endured to survive and navigate through the experience. Accompany the client as they remain under the protection of defensive armor, gently probing the hidden and painful aspects of their journey while collaboratively and gradually uncovering the underbelly of their experience. Meet the client in the protections offered by positive affect, gently peeling back the layers and guiding the client toward the profound realization of what happened. Wonder aloud about the presence of other emotions, thoughts, sensations, urges, and impulses. Start with a reflective statement that gradually expands their field of awareness. As the client awakens lost fragments of their experience, the clinician may ask questions while preserving the distance established by the client's mind (implicit or explicit). You might say:

- The little [character] in the sand world says they are happy, and yet their adult, older, bigger [perpetrator] is taking them away and doing things to them while asking them not to tell.
- Can we be curious together about other feelings the little [character] may hold? Do they hold feelings that no one knows? Are they hiding feelings from themself?
- I wonder if anyone inside or outside of the tray can see, feel, or notice something different about what [character] is doing?
- In the sand story, the [perpetrator] gave you presents, yet on the other side, they do things to you and your body.
- I am feeling quite confused. I wonder if anyone inside or outside may feel the same way?
- Can we be curious together about your age and the [perpetrator]'s age? I see a child and an adult, and the adult is doing things to the child's body. How does this resonate with you? How is it for you to witness what the [perpetrator] did to you in the sand world?
- Can a child of that age make choices about being touched in the way the [perpetrator] touched you?
- Can we be curious together? I wonder, how is it for the you in the tray to get all the gifts and attention, and then have the [perpetrator] do unsafe things to you that should never be done with children?
- I am feeling a bit confused. The [character] is saying that the [perpetrator] is safe and nice, but then the [perpetrator] does unsafe things that should never be done to a little [character].

Drops of information and education may be used to teach the client or the avatar about grooming. You might say:

- [Perpetrators] have a way of convincing little [characters] that what they do, or are about to do, is good and right for the little [character]. They may start by being nice, giving gifts, and offering lots of attention. This is very confusing because little [characters] trust and believe in others. I wonder how [characters] inside or outside the tray receive what I am saying. How is it for the little [character] to know this?"

356   EMDR-Sandtray-based Therapy

Sometimes, in extreme cases, the client may reject any questions or remarks from the clinician in reference to the wounding aspects of the abuse or the perpetrator. This response provides information about the strength of the trauma bond with the perpetrator. Before doing this work, a thorough exploration should be conducted to determine if it is safe to initiate work around allocating responsibility and awakening the remnants of negative affect in association with the perpetrator and the abuse.

If the perpetrator is an attachment figure and a decision maker, there is a high likelihood that therapy will be discontinued, and/or the child may remain utterly loyal to their oppressor, as their lives and survival depend solely on the abuser. If the perpetrator does not have contact or power over the child, the nonoffending caregiver should give consent to initiate this delicate work, or the clinician should explore an adult client's readiness.

The strength of the DPA associated with memories of abuse will depend on the level of intimacy and closeness the individual developed with the perpetrator. Maintain a pace and rhythm that allows the mind to discover these realities at its own pace. Facing the truth of betrayal is incredibly laborious and agonizing, especially if the perpetrator is a primary and trusted attachment figure. Make sure you uncover the veil the mind has harnessed for protection slowly and gradually, especially with highly dissociative clients, in which case involving the dissociative matrix and the perpetrator-imitating parts will be paramount. Extensive work, some of which was addressed in Chapter 9, needs to precede any reprocessing around memories of abuse. The internal dissociative system is a delicate and yet resilient ecosystem, into which the clinician accompanies the client, entering with the utmost respect and care. Additionally, clinicians must have expertise in treating and working with compartmentalized inner systems.

In the tray, dynamics that surrounded the abuse and disclosure may surface. The silence and betrayal of other friends, family members, and caregivers around the abuse may be a source of confusion, rage, fear, and shame.

Sometimes, reprocessing with a client whose mind focuses only on the positive may start with an SUD of 0. As stated by Knipe (2015, 2019), sometimes the point of entry into the dysfunctional memory network may be an idealization defense that contains positive affect. The memory network in itself is a mixture of cognitive, emotional, and somatic data and the mind's defenses. The synaptic connections that hold disturbing material remain buried and inaccessible under defensive layers that move the mind, almost automatically, into a positive realm (Knipe, 2015). These positive distortions may be the only accessible portal to the traumagenic memory network. As the reprocessing begins to progress, the client's level of disturbance may increase, and this can activate other defensive strategies. If the defenses have been explored and brought to the surface, interweaves can be used that invite the client to see, notice, and acknowledge the defensive strategy. The clinician may use interweaves that negotiate with these defensive parts so the client can see, feel, and know what they need when they are ready.

In some cases, the defense itself may need to be processed separately. Invite the client to create a world dedicated to the defensive part that finds refuge in positive memories, thoughts, or actions. Processing these defenses can weaken the emotional investment in the idealized image (Knipe, 2015, 2019), opening a space for the disturbing data to reveal itself to the mind and enter the field of consciousness.

Jenny, a 37-year-old woman, was sexually abused by her neighbor when she was 4 years old. After she disclosed the abuse, her mother stopped the visits with the neighbor but never spoke to Jenny about what happened. The issue was never addressed, and the events were completely buried. The abuse continued for several years after the disclosure, yet in therapy, Jenny spoke only of the fun times she had with her neighbor. She stated that he made her feel special, pretty, important, appreciated, and seen— emotions that contrasted sharply with how her family, especially her caregivers, made her feel.

During the preparation phase, extensive work was done, and multiple trays were created to hold Jenny's strategies, such as avoidance and selective focusing (focusing on the parts of the memory/sand world that are positive or turning negative material into something positive). During the reprocessing phases, Jenny was invited to create a tray about her experience with her neighbor that was initially colored by DPA. Jenny invited her defenses into her resource tray so they could monitor and remain in contact with her mechanisms of adaptation.

Once the tray was complete, the clinician invited Jenny to evaluate whether her two protectors—avoidance and selective focusing—had influenced the making of the world. Jenny was asked to look within and see if there were occurrences, thoughts, or emotions that were different from the ones already unblended into the tray. Jenny acknowledged the presence of her strategies and was invited to compassionately ask them to step aside temporarily so she could access her inner world and emotions.

Jenny brought in additional figures to show the actual abuse but did not connect emotionally to the miniatures or the story they represented. She reported no disturbance associated with this memory and could not find a negative belief. Initially, Jenny focused on how important and special she felt with the neighbor and how much her own mother worshipped him. The clinician asked questions/interweaves to support Jenny in tapping into the unintegrated and covert emotions associated with the abuse.

358 EMDR-Sandtray-based Therapy

❝ I wonder if the little you in the tray is aware of what is happening on the other side of the tray (the side holding the story of the abuse)?”

Jenny reported that she did not want to see that side. The clinician offered titration possibilities, such as using coverings or burying parts of the memory under the sand and uncovering them when she felt ready to witness and know them. The DPA, with its protective armor, was accessed and reprocessed first.

❝ Let's get a figure that represents how much she does not want to see that side of the tray.”

Once Jenny tapped into the protective forces of the DPA, BLS/DAS followed and continued for some time, until consciousness began to penetrate the defensive and self-protective walls, gradually uncovering the full spectrum of the experience. In a similar situation, you might say:

- What would happen if she saw/knew what is happening on that side of the tray? Is there anyone else, in or outside the tray, who knows or who can see what is happening?
- How much she does not want to know/feel? Let's bring in a figure(s) that shows it.
- What does she need in order for her to know?
- What needs to happen for her to move to the other side of the tray and see/know?

Other questions and reflective statements may be offered, based on the client's responses. Inviting the client to see, know, notice, observe, and use mindfulness can assist their mind in integrating complex polarities such as knowing and not knowing. For example, two figures may be placed on opposite sides of the tray, allowing the client to move their gaze back and forth, observing the divergences and splits that come from not knowing and knowing.

A titrated approach may be used. The figure representing the client's younger self in the tray can gradually jump into the side of the story that holds the disturbance and move in and out while using the resource tray. Eventually, clients begin to realize that the grooming was also a betrayal, which can be more painful than the abuse itself.

Culture, Diversity, and Antioppressive Practices

The EMDR–sandtray therapist must demonstrate a commitment to self-evaluation and self-reflection (Tervalon & Murray-García, 1998) as well as

Special Populations and Considerations   **359**

FIGURE 12.3 **Representations of the racial, religious, ethnic, and gender identity of an adult client. Generational and historical trauma, as well as ancestral assets and resources, are also represented.**

cultural humility and responsiveness. It is essential to acknowledge that we will never know every aspect of a client's cultural, gender, and religious history. Nonetheless, we must remain committed to understanding, inquiring, exploring, and learning new ways of relating to one another as well as unlearning unhelpful ones. The decision-making process during diagnosis, prognosis, and treatment planning should be guided and supported by equitable and nondiscriminatory practices, avoiding prejudice and stereotypes (Ridley, 2005).

Humility, flexibility, and an openness to explore our own cultural, racial, gender, religious, and ethnic biases should inform the therapeutic encounter. The invisible—and visible—privileges of EMDR and sandtray clinicians must be realized and acknowledged. The clinician's education level; social and economic status; racial, ethnic, and gender group; and "professional seat" may provide sources of privilege. Many authors have called for clinicians to commit to fixing power imbalances (Tervalon & Murray-García, 1998). This begins by acknowledging and recognizing that each person brings something valuable, unique, and distinctive while remaining open to learning from what clients bring. Entering the therapeutic relationship with cultural humility while remaining open to moment-to-moment changes in the client's inner world and relationship with their cultural identities is foundational to the EMDR–sandtray journey.

Individual, collective, historic, and generational traumas are frequently interweaved and intricately connected. The color of our skin, our language, our ethnic background, our gender, our immigration status, and our sexual orientation are core elements that form our identity. Often, they are dismissed and overlooked in the therapeutic process unless they are the client's direct issue. Even when these elements of identity are not reported to be the main issue in therapy, they are always intricately connected to the client's concerns. Clinicians are responsible for inquiring about such experiences and providing space for the client to decide whether they want to address these issues and work through them in the EMDR–sandtray.

For instance, a client may be invited to create a world with the theme of "my identity," which includes race, gender, ethnicity, religion, and gender identity. Because these elements of identity may be quite complex for some clients, the client may be invited to create a separate tray for each part of their identity. When exploring the tray, the clinician should inquire about what the client needs to feel safe in relationship with another human who is of a different racial, gender, religious, or ethnic group. This can help create a strong relational safety between the client and the therapist.

Special Considerations in the Delivery of EMDR–Sandtray Therapy

Phase 1. The miniatures collection should represent various racial, social, ethnic, and gender groups. If figures with these variations are difficult to locate, you may need to find places where specific figures can be manufactured.

A strong therapeutic alliance and safe space are paramount for the client to freely and openly explore these issues. The clinician should engage in a compassionate exploration of the client's racial, gender, cultural, ethnic, and legal (for undocumented clients, like refugees) experiences in the tray. With immigrants, experiences such as leaving one's home country, entering a new country, political and social marginalization, and learning a new language can be brought into the tray. Many of these experiences hold polarities, pain, and grief as well as courage and strength. Their experiences are a source of distress but also a source of pride. These experiences are targets and resources and what Yosso (2005) calls "navigational capital."

Phase 2. When working on developing resources in the tray, enhance dreams, aspirations for the future, acts of triumph, and mastery experiences, such as linguistic skills, literacy, and capacities for navigating through marginalizing institutions. Acknowledging the client's reality—whether explicit or implicit—is paramount. For example, a little rabbit may exist in the tray among a group of dogs that are a different color. The clinician may ask how the rabbit feels being in a group where everyone looks different from them and has a different color of fur. You might ask:

- How do other characters react or respond to having a rabbit among them?
- How does the rabbit respond? How do they feel free? What do they need?

Special Populations and Considerations **361**

The clinician validates the rabbit's experience and accompanying feelings and may identify some of these sand worlds created around multiple identities as potential targets for implicit processing.

During the preparation phase, explore and identify cultural or religious traditions that bring the client a sense of well-being or rituals that can enhance their experiences in the tray. For instance, before reprocessing in the tray, some clients may want to have a prayer or time for chanting or smudging to prepare themselves.

Clients who have been raised or live in oppressive environments may become accustomed to others making decisions on their behalf. Sometimes, clinicians may unknowingly become complicit in oppressive practices by pushing clients to go at a rhythm that may feel overwhelming or that moves into the reprocessing phases without sufficient readiness. Clients with histories of attachment ruptures may not speak up because of a fear of being abandoned by the therapist. These oppressive practices may perseverate self-abandonment, self-betrayal, and internalized oppression. Notice the client's rhythm in the tray and honor it as you cocreate greater levels of safety and connectedness while gently challenging rigid forms of self-protection and defenses created to promote survival. However, we must honor the protective stance of clients facing oppression and marginalization.

It is also essential to inquire about the client's preferred pronouns of she/he/they and how they wish for you to refer to the figures and characters in the tray. This consideration is significant for individuals with dissociative identities or those experiencing compartmentalization within their sense of self who identify as plural or may refer to themselves in the plural form. Acknowledging and respecting client's and their figures' chosen pronouns and the way they conceptualize themselves is crucial in honoring their identity and ensuring a supportive and affirming therapeutic environment (Marich, 2023). Similarly, transgender and nonbinary clients and clients with a wide range of gender expressions may have a preferred pronoun that may or may not extend to the sand characters. Be curious, and ask the client for their preferences, knowing that preferences may change.

Reprocessing Phases. The client's affective expressions are deeply shaped by their relational and cultural environment and how the client deals with emotions, needs, painful experiences, and grief. As a result, some clients may show only subtle signs of emotional expressions even when they feel overwhelmed, while others may express significant dysregulation even under low emotional intensity. Do not assume that large expressions of emotions indicate dysregulated states. Establish an open and safe channel of communication to more easily determine the intensity of the client's

362   EMDR-Sandtray-based Therapy

emotional states and how these states relate to the client's emotional tolerance threshold and integrative capacities.

Keep in mind the presence of oppressive cognitions that acknowledge historic, ongoing, and internalized oppression. The tray may harbor the client's anticipatory anxieties and fears as they navigate through institutional marginalization. Clients may process internalized oppressive experiences to move toward empowerment, while still acknowledging the ongoing presence of racism, marginalization, and discriminatory societal practices. In some cases, the client's level of disturbance may not reach zero because they have to live with societal and institutionalized forms of "isms" in their lives.

After processing memories of trauma as well as their triggers, create a future template in the tray. While constructing the future, the client anticipates the forthcoming challenges brought up by their racial, cultural, ethnic, religious, gender, and sexual affiliations. Figures will support the client in embracing realized and newly discovered strengths and resources that can accompany them as they continue to face life challenges and tribulations in the future.

Collective and historic trauma can be processed in the tray. Past generations may be invited into the trauma tray and/or resource tray to accompany the client. The shared experiences of generations bring the client a sense of companionship while deshaming and depathologizing their pain and suffering from the traumas inflicted by society and its institutions on past and present generations. This process becomes a generational voyage from which the individual can borrow from the strengths and assets of past generations.

The client's intersectionality of identities is also a source of empowerment, resilience, and strength, which become protective layers when moving into reprocessing phases. The client's cultural, racial, ethnic, gender, and religious background may play a role when selecting resources and identifying emotions and needs. For instance, some emotions are celebrated in one culture but rejected in others. Examples include pride, a sense of self based on individualism or collectivism, or the belief that an individual's sense of self-worth is dependent on validation and definition by the collective. Invite curiosity so the client can sit with how culture, society, and institutions have shaped their relationship with themselves and their inner world.

Invite the client to be with these learned ways of being. How is it for them? What do these ways of being bring up cognitively, emotionally, and somatically?

Invite the client to bring these inner voices, shaped by cultural experiences, into the tray. This allows them to enter their field of consciousness and begin repatterning old autonomic states formed through trauma—ancestral, ethnic, racial, gender-based, and more. Are there cultural practices, traditions, and beliefs that have caused harm and trauma? Does the client want to continue to nurture such traditions? Are conflicting feelings arising? Invite the client to represent any polarities in the tray to hold them together or separate them, as their mind wishes, while engaging in BLS/DAS.

Addictions

The mind impacted by trauma often seeks refuge in addictive behaviors and substances, finding a temporary sense of safety. Yet, trauma and addiction are deeply intertwined, emerging and evolving within the relational, social, and historical tapestry that shapes the addicted mind. "Many addictive disorders begin, and then continue, because the addictive behavior contains or prevents the emergence of disturbing feelings and/or memories" (Knipe, 2019, p. 12). The field of addiction research is not unified, and there are numerous perspectives and theories that attempt to explain and understand what makes an individual susceptible to developing addictions. Some researchers and authors believe genetic and biological etiological factors play a central role, while others firmly consider environmental and relational factors are the defining elements. "Addictions are not individual choices in their origins, nor are they determined by genes, but they are manifestations of multi-generational, social, and familial processing" (Maté, 2011, p. 19). Adverse childhood experiences (ACEs) corroborate this assertion, showing that adverse experiences before age 18 were highly correlated to addictive behaviors later in life (Felitti et al., 1998).

Often, addiction becomes the individual's attempt to coexist with pain and inner turbulence or to fulfill deep longings that are often connected to unmet attachment needs. Such dependencies never truly nor consistently satisfy the most profound longings for connection, relational safety, acceptance, appreciation, protection, belonging, and love. This sends the individual into a voyage of self-betrayal and self-abandonment. According to Maté (2011), addictions become the best remedy and strategy to maximize survival and deal with emptiness and pain. Addictions are not abruptly formed; they are the product of lifelong occurrences and interpersonal and intrapersonal processes. They speak about the journeys of hardship, adversity, and desperation that prompt the individual to find shelter and refuge in addictive behaviors, objects, and substances.

Considering the complexity and multitude of co-occurring clinical symptomatology and conditions, addiction is an extensive topic that requires a much deeper exploration than what this chapter can offer. However, this section aims to explore the potential of EMDR-sandtray-based therapy for clients dealing with addictions. It is worth highlighting that standard EMDR or EMDR-sandtray-based treatment is delivered within a comprehensive treatment that includes an interdisciplinary team such as medical care, support groups, family, and group therapy.

Special Considerations

Phase 1. As described in previous chapters, one of the most important goals in any treatment is creating relational safety from the moment we meet the client. Additionally, the clinician focuses on increasing the client's integrative capacities and access to resources. The following are some specific strategies that may be used in the EMDR–sandtray; however, each activity or strategy must be a coherent and cohesive part of a comprehensive treatment, guided by intentional decision-making.

- The client may create a world in the tray about the history of their addiction. Where and when did it start? What triggers it? What maintains it? What impulses and urges are associated with it? How does it protect them? What positive affect is elicited?
- Figures representing the addictive behaviors can tell the story using a shame- and pathology-free approach.

Addictions often take root in childhood, with the seeds of dependency quietly germinating long before their explicit emergence in an individual's life. This journey begins early, simmering beneath the surface until it ultimately manifests in its full, undeniable presence. Each adverse and traumatic experience that accumulates contributes to a growing story that culminates in long-lasting dependencies and addictions. Thus, the client can unblend their life story in the sand world.

Depending on the client, substantial preparation and stabilization are needed before clinicians can cultivate awareness and invite the client's mind to sit at the table with their addiction. Medically based and supervised interventions may be necessary for some clients (Marich & Dansiger, 2022), so clinicians working with this subset of the population should be well-versed in the field of addictions. Medical providers may need to be involved if complications related to withdrawal symptoms arise (Marich & Dansiger, 2022). Thus, the clinician delivering EMDR–sandtray with a client confronting addiction is often part of a much larger interdisciplinary team.

What is accessed during the initial phases of treatment when using only

Special Populations and Considerations **365**

the forces of the linear left brain will be limited, because the information that remains in the implicit mind, below the client's awareness, may not make itself known to the clinician. Defenses may govern the client's mental landscape, making it difficult to get the full story. However, the worlds created in the tray can offer a portal to access deeper layers of the client's inner world that lie at the core of their addictions. Implicit and explicit worlds invite the client to create stories with specific themes that can give the symbol-guided, somatically and emotionally connected right brain a voice and a space to tell its story. Timelines and genograms in the tray can provide abundant information about generational wounds underneath addictions and generational addictions.

The work in the tray may give a client with addictions a safe space for self-expression and self-discovery. Often, EMDR work and sandtray are combined with other approaches and interventions that may be individual or systemic, such as mindfulness, 12-step programs, other expressive arts therapies, support and psychoeducation groups. This work is delicate and should be done with care, to avoid stripping the client too quickly or too soon of their self-protective armors.

Many experts in the addiction field have recommended that clinicians thoroughly evaluate the client's readiness to change, their support system, and the probability that they will relapse (Marich & Dansiger, 2022; Abel & O'Brien, 2010). To this end:

- Clients may be invited to create a readiness tray dedicated to the variables that can support them through the process of change and to represent their disposition, and keenness to do the work necessary.
- The client may create a tray devoted to their goals for therapy, which may involve partial or full sobriety.

Another tray can be created to embody a supportive recovery environment, providing a foundation that nurtures resilience and empowers the client as they prepare to navigate the complex, intricate, and multifaceted journey of embracing change.

Phase 2. In the tray, affect tolerance can be organically expanded by being with or sitting with what is emerging in the sand world. This work is essential because the mind grappling with addiction is caught in a relentless cycle of attempting to escape the pain and profound emptiness it so often experiences. When emotions or disturbances arise in the tray, invitations to be with these feelings, while in the companionship of the clinician, will be paramount. Validation, witnessing, companionship, and presence are essential. You might say:

366 EMDR-Sandtray-based Therapy

- I can see how challenging this is. Let's try to sit with this emotion, or just a drop of it, for a bit longer without pushing it away.
- These feelings are messengers and storytellers. Let's see what they hold for you.
- I am right here with you and this drop of [sadness].
- I've got you right here. Let's stay with this just a bit longer.
- I see and feel how challenging this is!
- Let's breathe with this emotion and dance with it as it goes in and out of you.
- How much of this feeling is appropriate/safe to hold or visit now? A drop or a spoonful?

The reconciliation of the dissonance between the overpowering urge to engage in addictive behaviors or take substances and awareness of their self-destructive consequences often remains elusive in the mind that struggles with addictions. The sand tray provides the space to unblend both, the addiction and its lifelong consequences, so the client can begin a process of reconciliation and integration. Triggers and the DPA often associated with addictions (Knipe, 2019) can be represented in the sand. However, how EMDR-sandtray-based therapy is delivered depends on the client's goals, integrative capacities, and readiness for change alongside the coordination with other mental health professionals to provide coherent and cohesive treatment.

The most important element of preparation—especially in clients who present with comorbid PTSD, dissociation, and severe symptoms—is not its duration but how it is organized and composed. An overemphasis on state-change protocols and self-regulation to the detriment of nurturing coregulatory processes, cocreating safety in the therapeutic relationship, and enhancing affect tolerance and integrative capacities can lead to unnecessarily long preparation periods. It is crucial that clients—especially those affected by trauma and addictions—develop the capacity to tolerate and engage with the activation, as this is a crucial factor in their ability to navigate and access the traumagenic network. Without affect tolerance, individuals may experience persistent states of dysregulated hyperarousal or hypoarousal or oscillation between the two (Hill, 2015).

Two approaches in the field of addictions and EMDR therapy have been established that can be combined and integrated (Markus & Hornsveld, 2017):

Trauma-Focused EMDR. The main emphasis of this approach is to clear underlying trauma or adversity and comorbid PTSD.

Addiction-Focused EMDR. The focus of this approach is on the mitigation and processing of addiction-related memories, addiction-related symptoms, emotions, cravings, memories of dysfunctional positive affect, fear of relapse, and more (Markus & Hornsveld, 2017). Several EMDR-based protocols have been developed for urge reduction, such as the desensitization of triggers and urge responses protocol (Popky, 2009), the feeling state addiction protocol (Miller, 2010), and the craving reduction protocol (Hase et al., 2008; Hase, 2010).

Dysfunctional positive affect–based work and protocols can be successfully used in the tray. For instance, in the craving reduction protocol, the "addiction memory" is reprocessed. This memory remains below awareness and is implicitly encoded in the brain in association with addiction-specific and associated memory (Hase et al., 2008; Hase, 2009).

The memory of the positive affect experienced after using the substance or engaging in the addictive behavior and the craving to engage in it again is powerful and often nonconscious. According to Knipe (2015, 2019), when the individual consumes the addictive substance or engages in the addictive behavior, it provides relief that results in a charged positive affective experience, which continues to reinforce the addiction. This subsequently develops into an idealization of this addictive object/behavior because it helps the individual avoid the pain and suffering connected to their underlying trauma.

Knipe (2015) developed the level of positive affect method in which the client is invited to target the original memory, where idealization first occurred, and to process the dysfunctional level of positive affect that maintains the defense. The addiction behavior and the dysfunctional positive affect can be represented in the tray, giving the mind a clear view of its own illusions, longings, and struggles. It is important to highlight that how, where, and when we use protocols within the eight phases of treatment in the sandtray should be guided by mindful and intentional decision-making as well as case conceptualization.

Often, addictions are associated with intense internal conflicts in which one part of the self is highly committed to maintaining the addictive substance or behaviors, and other parts feel shame, guilt, and anger and do not want the addiction. These parts can be unblended and invited to make themselves known in the tray where they can enter the client's field of consciousness so the client's mind can dialogue with it. With the use of EMDR procedural steps and sandtray, clinicians can guide processes to reduce urges and increase inner system integration. Knipe (2015, 2019) conceptualizes addictions as defensive and dysfunctional idealizations in which the individual overvalues the positive emotional experience the addictive object generates, and the addictive object then becomes a shield that protects the individual from unwanted negative affect. The tray and the miniatures collection become tools the mind can maneuver to tell its story and unmask defensive and dysfunctional idealizations.

368   EMDR-Sandtray-based Therapy

Clinicians can use a myriad of resources in the tray, such as the safe place, the team of companions, positive memories and mastery experiences, and the RDI protocol, where specific resources are installed to support the client in managing addiction-specific triggers.

Reprocessing Phases. Multiple authors have brought attention to the powerful role that trauma plays in the development of addictions. These memories of adversity and attachment traumas can be created and reprocessed in the tray. Distance and titration are frequent companions of the reprocessing sessions of individuals battling addictions and their co-occurring conditions, such as PTSD and dissociation. When accessing memories of trauma, the client may choose to enter them implicitly or explicitly. Sometimes, clients may want to create their story in the third person and assign a character to represent them when these memories are too activating. Many of the protocols described in prior chapters that titrate and pendulate may be used when the client's mind becomes overwhelmed by traumagenic memories and their associated affect.

Clinicians should have items that depict addictions, such as miniature alcohol bottles, gaming items, and cigarettes. You may want to keep these items in a plastic bin that you bring out for the clients who need them.

There are multiple and multifaceted portals into the addicted mind. Sometimes, a clinician will start with urge reduction protocols or processing and desensitizing defenses before addressing traumas. Other times, the underlying trauma is processed in the tray using implicit or explicit access routes. In this case, a resource tray or resource areas in the main tray can accompany the client while they access the deep pain and suffering brought on by the addiction and underlying traumas. Pendulation and titration protocols described in prior chapters may offer a progressive entrance into the memories. When working with clients who show greater capacities and support systems, going directly into the traumas would be recommended and a trauma focused–EMDR approach may be used. Regardless of the approach, ample preparation and stabilization should be provided before entering the realm of trauma.

Virtual EMDR-Sandtray-based Therapy

During and after the COVID pandemic, telehealth and online sites proliferated and became more popular in the market. Much of the work covered throughout this book can be accessed successfully online or through virtual sandtray applications. Although the physical relationship with the sand tray, sand, miniature collection, and clinician in person cannot be replaced by online work, digital venues are a good alternative for clients who are unable to attend in-person psychotherapy.

When working with children, especially younger ones, presence is paramount. However, online work offers some advantages:

1. Clients who cannot drive or have limited mobility can still benefit from using EMDR–sandtray through digital applications.
2. Some clients may open up quicker while in the safety of their homes and with their pets and loved ones nearby, resulting in meaningful therapeutic work.
3. Children and adolescents are computer-savvy and enjoy working with digital applications. They quickly learn to use and play with these apps.
4. Attendance may be easier, reducing the number of no-shows and cancellations. Working online may also facilitate access to caregivers.
5. Clients who cannot tolerate contact with sand or miniatures due to concerns about germs may find the digital format easier to navigate, even when attending therapy in person.

Conversely, working online does present some challenges:

6. It is more challenging to visually access the tray and the client's facial and nonverbal expressions. This can reduce access to feedback channels that aid the in-person clinician in moment-to-moment decision-making and thereby impact therapeutic data collection and use. This challenge has a greater impact when reprocessing traumagenic material with EMDR-sandtray-based therapy, when the need for access to the tray and the client's nonverbal expressions is crucial.
7. Several of the EMDR–sandtray strategies and protocols require two trays, especially when working with clients with whom extensive titration, which requires more than one tray, is important for entering into memories of trauma. This is challenging, and impossible for some clients to accomplish online. Only clients with sufficient computer skills can manage to have two windows open with the digital app, which can become cumbersome and intrusive to the process.
8. Clients living in small spaces may worry that others can hear them in their sessions, which can inhibit the client and hinder their process.
9. Changes in bandwidth and internet connection may interrupt sessions. This is not only disruptive but may disconnect the therapist from the client during critical periods when the client may need assistance, especially during reprocessing phases.

When using EMDR–sandtray online, the following areas require advance preparation:

10. Clinicians need to practice using the app so they can train clients to use it. Providing, before the sessions, a training video or using demonstration videos from the app developers will be helpful for clients. If working with a client who has limited time, consider using the website http://onlinesandtray.com, developed by Dr. Karen Fried, which does not require prior practice. In general, clients should be familiar with the session/process format (app or website) before the session. On the other hand, learning to use the tray with the clinician's guidance may be therapeutic and help build rapport, especially with children.

11. Some apps, like https://simplysandplay.com, require clients to share their desktops. Others, like https://www.virtualsandtray.org, provide a link for the client to join the therapist in the tray.

12. The butterfly hug, drumming, marching, and even eye movement can be used during online EMDR–sandtray work. Clinicians should practice these forms of BLS/DAS in advance. When doing eye movement, invite the client to place sticky notes on both sides of the computer and move their eyes back and forth between them. This is one of the best ways of inviting eye movement because it causes the client to pass their gaze over the sand world. It is ideal to use BLS/DAS forms that keep the client engaged with and connected to the tray. When working with children, especially those under six, tactile stimulation may be the easiest and preferred form of BLS/DAS. The butterfly hug, drumming, and marching allow the child to remain intimately connected to what is unfolding in the tray.

13. Caregivers may be invited to the child's sessions, but this should be an intentional decision the child fully agrees with. The presence of the caregiver should be discussed with the child. In some cases, the child may request it; in others, the therapist may suggest it and leave it up to the child to decide. The caregiver may be invited to provide a greater sense of safety, to support the development of resources, to help the child during target identification sessions, to help the young child navigate through the sandtray app, and to provide interweaves, under the clinician's direction and support. The caregiver can also provide the BLS/DAS under the direction of the clinician, especially when working with younger children.

14. Clinicians should communicate with older clients and caregivers about how to create a safe and secure environment that is protected from interruptions and intrusions, which is especially important when processing memories of trauma in the tray. Boundaries must be established with siblings, family members, neighbors, and pets prior to the session.

the child or adult may choose to have a pet in the session if the pet offers a sense of safety and security.

In general, online EMDR–sandtray can be delivered successfully, helping clients of all ages who would otherwise be unable to benefit from these powerful interventions and methods.

Neurodiversity

This section will offer some key tips and affirming practices for delivering EMDR-sandtray-based therapy with neurodivergent clients. It will not dive deeply into the subject because neurodiversity is broad and complex.

According to Grant (2024),

> Neurodivergence is the term for people whose brains function differently in one or more ways than is considered standard or typical. Neurodivergence refers to any structured, consistent way that brains work differently for a group of people than they do for the majority of others. (p. 2)

Neurodiversity encompasses and is used within the context of autism spectrum disorder, developmental conditions such as ADHD, learning and cognitive disabilities, and giftedness. Neurodivergent individuals across the lifespan display an extensive continuum of strengths, needs, challenges, and symptoms. This diverse range encompasses a variety of cognitive, emotional, sensorimotor, and social attributes, equally and uniquely influenced by each individual's neurological makeup. The diversity in people's experiences necessitates a nuanced and flexible approach to delivering EMDR-sandtray-based treatment that acknowledges that neurodivergence exists on a multifaceted spectrum.

Neurodiverse individuals are at a much higher risk of experiencing interpersonal trauma compared to neurotypical individuals (Webb et al., 2024). Rumball (2019) reports that individuals on the autism spectrum experience high rates of early trauma exposure. Neurodivergent individuals—especially those on the autism spectrum—often encounter restrictions, bullying, and therapeutic strategies that impose ways of being and behaving that conflict with their natural biological inclinations. Their needs, symptoms, and characteristics, as well as how they perceive and relate to the world, may become a source of trauma. This is compounded by how others relate and respond to them and their specific needs and challenges.

Their typically high dependence on their caregiver combined with differences in communication, lack of sensory or social filters, and hyper- and hyporeactivity to stimuli may challenge caregivers beyond their regulatory threshold. This may activate the caregiver's traumagenic networks and move them out of coregulation and into self-preservation and survival, resulting in insufficient and potentially traumatizing relational experiences.

Mental health professionals are challenged to differentiate between trauma-related symptomatology and those associated with the client's specific neurodivergent diagnosis. At times, the social and mental health systems may ignore the legacy of trauma in these individuals, attributing every symptom to their neurodivergent status, and resulting in therapeutic approaches that do not address or recognize the individuals' experiences of trauma and adversity.

Kalisch et al. (2023) conducted a literature review to evaluate different therapeutic approaches for neurodivergent children. They found that multiple articles recommended play-based, interactive, creative, and sensory as well as visual and pictorial tools with the neurodivergent population. Additionally, several articles recommended language modifications and adaptations to the structure of the sessions that make sure the process is predictable and provides breaks, the session length is shortened, and emotional data is gradually introduced (Kalisch et al., 2023). Kalisc et al. (2023) found that the literature favored therapeutic approaches that relied less heavily on verbal skills or high cognitive loads. Additionally, the involvement of the caregiver was emphasized throughout the literature. It is noteworthy that most of the therapeutic approaches that were implemented included EMDR therapy, trauma-focused CBT, attachment-based therapies like Theraplay and child–caregiver psychotherapy, and art and symbolic play, such as child-centered play therapy.

EMDR–Sandtray

Working with this population in the tray should be guided by a deep knowledge and understanding of the nuances of providing treatment to neurodiverse individuals and consider the specific characteristics, diagnosis, and clinical symptoms of each individual. Clinicians must operate not with a deficit-focused but a strength-based approach to support the individual to connect with their capacities and assets while bringing recognition to their needs and challenges.

It is worth noting that some neurodivergent individuals present with nervous system and brain patterns similar to those emerging from exposure to developmental and complex trauma. Trauma, adversity, and attachment injuries affect how each individual moves through various stages of development. Maturation and growth are both influenced and at times thwarted by the experiences of trauma throughout the lifespan. Attention, information processing (cognitive, emotional, and sensorimotor), and relational challenges are often present in neurodivergent individuals and individuals exposed to trauma. For instance, children experiencing anxiety as a result of trauma may be inattentive, hyperactive, and have a low frustration tolerance threshold—which is also observed in children diagnosed with ADHD. When the child's development is impacted and affected by trauma, especially chronic and pervasive trauma, the developmental pathways and milestones are thwarted, resulting in symptoms that transpire cognitively, emotionally, behaviorally, relationally, and somatically.

In addition, when trauma coexists with neurodevelopmental diagnosis and symptomatology, the impact on the individual's development is much greater. Remember that sandtray work combined with EMDR therapy is not for everyone, so clients should not be forced into it even when we believe it could be favorable.

Working in the Sand Tray During the Preparation Phases

The following are special issues regarding EMDR–sandtray use with neurodiverse clients:

Sensory Engagement. To accommodate the client's integrative capacities and regulatory threshold, consider and work around their differences in communication, fixations, and hyper- and hyporeactivity to stimulus as well as any lack of sensory filters (Grant, 2024). Sessions may be shortened or broken down into manageable, predictable parts.

Some children with sensory integration and sensitivity issues may find the sand overstimulating or may be averse to it. Grains (e.g., rice, quinoa) or beans (e.g., garbanzo, red, pinto) or other small particles may offer a different texture for the tray and sensory-stimulating alternative. The work in the tray provides a nonverbal, safe, and sensory-rich environment that facilitates regulatory processes through sensory modulating strategies, offering the opportunity to adjust stimulation by either dimming or increasing it to meet the individual's needs. To work on relationship development, Grant (2024) suggests a playful intervention in the tray where "one person makes a hand cup, and the other person fills it with sand" (p. 88). This activity invites togetherness with the clinician and/or the caregiver. Grant also recommends playing a game of uncovering each other's hands, especially with caregivers. The child hides their hands under the sand, and the caregiver finds them and gently removes the sand. These resources, if associated with positive and comfortable states, may be enhanced with BLS/DAS. Before using any BLS/DAS strategies, the client should be acquainted with the different forms and select the one that feels comfortable for them.

374   EMDR-Sandtray-based Therapy

Mobility Issues. Mobility issues may impact a client's capacity to engage in the dance with the tray and the miniatures collection. Clients may have challenges with standing, reaching out, grabbing figures, and/or placing figures in the tray as well as with using apps that require computer, cognitive, and/or other motor capacities. Clinicians may offer to help the client, particularly with reaching for figures on the shelves and accessing the miniature collection, ensuring the process remains supportive and collaborative. Discuss assistive options with each client to determine the best way to support their work.

Building Relational Bridges. Connection with others may be challenging for children on the autism spectrum, even in the tray. Sometimes, objects may dominate the tray's landscape instead of people. The clinician may need to take a more active role in supporting the client in naming and bringing people and relationships into the tray.

In his extensive work with this population, Robert Jason Grant (2017) recommends helping the client pick figures by using questions and reflective statements that can aid them. For instance, to help a child pick a father, the clinician may ask, "What does your father like? Does he like to [e.g., read the newspaper]?" and then point to a figure that represents this characteristic.

Neurodiverse clients may also use the sand tray as a space to represent social scenarios and create moment-to-moment sequences of relational interactions to explore dynamics and potential responses. These scenarios can serve as a future template that may be enhanced with BLS/DAS.

Connecting to Themselves and Their Inner World. As previously described, clients may be invited to bury and then find figures that concretely represent their feelings, needs, likes and dislikes, memories, or anything that is important to them. Once again, it is of paramount importance that any exploration of cognitive, emotional, or somatic data be titrated and gradual to avoid further flooding a system that is already overwhelmed by sensory input. Two trays may be used, so the client can walk from one to the other while impersonating animals or engaging in movements such as marching, running, or dancing. It is important to keep the client's capacities, abilities, and resources as well as their challenges and needs in mind when selecting strategies and using the sand tray and the miniatures collection. If the client has mobility issues, movement-based activities may not be appropriate.

The client may create timelines in the sand world to promote developmental continuity and a sense of self across time and space. This is import-

Special Populations and Considerations **375**

ant for helping clients develop relationships with themselves, their identity, and their unique ways of being in the world.

Communication. Verbal communication may be challenging for some neurodiverse clients. The clinician will rely on observations of what unfolds in the sand world. When needed, the clinician becomes the voice of the client and may give sounds or a voice to the characters and avatars emerging in the tray. However, the physical act of placing figures in the sand supports the client in externalizing, communicating, and forming a relationship with their internal experience.

Gifted Children. Gifted children can greatly benefit from EMDR-sandtray-based therapy. Some may initially reject this level of work because they consider it childish. This resistance may be part of the injury they carry, as many struggle with high and long-term expectations from caregivers, family, teachers, and even friends due to their advanced abilities. They may experience feelings of shame or inadequacy if they are not performing at their highest level and may find playing in the sand tray childish.

To address this, therapists must exercise patience and perseverance and provide segmented psychoeducation. Explaining that there are two ways of knowing and interacting with the world—through the right and left modes of the brain—can help demystify the process. Teaching these clients the science behind the sandtray method may help reduce stigma and make the therapeutic process more acceptable and effective for gifted clients across development.

Reprocessing Phases. Individuals on the autism spectrum sometimes struggle with metaphors and symbols, since they often rely on a literal, concrete way of knowing the world.

Belen, a 13-year-old diagnosed as being on the autism spectrum (level 1), came to therapy to work on her phobia of bugs. She created resources in the tray and began to bring her experiences with bugs into her sand worlds. The miniatures collection gave her an opportunity to interact with unanimated bugs so she could process and desensitize her phobia.

Identifying the ancillary memories related to her phobia was the most challenging aspect of her treatment. Despite her ability to create worlds filled with bugs, additional support was necessary to help Belen connect her past experiences to her present fear. She wondered how seemingly unrelated past events could be linked to her phobia.

When Belen's caregivers divorced, they shared custody, and Belen had to split her time between homes. Her father's house had a bug infestation, and Belen began to associate her visits to her father's home, which were marked

376   EMDR-Sandtray-based Therapy

by a strained relationship and a sense of insecurity, with the presence of bugs. This was a time of overwhelming stress for Belen, which also contributed to the development of the phobia.

To help Belen understand the connection, the clinician showed her pictures of the brain and how memories are stored, linked up, and activated. The clinician cocreated with Belen a sand timeline showing the connection between the past experiences and her current fears. One tray held the present phobia, and a second tray provided the space for her past experiences. The visual and sensory representations in the trays supported Belen in understanding her phobia. At the end of treatment, Belen was able to tolerate bugs without experiencing terror.

EMDR-sandtray-based treatment must be tailored to the client's neurodevelopment, capacities, and needs. According to Grant (2017), tracking and reflective statements can be beneficial when working in the tray. You might say:

- You just moved the [character] to the other side of the tray.
- That made you [scared/upset].

Clinicians need to use affirming practices and remain open to the unique ways each mind processes information. They should avoid imposing limitations or expectations of attaining a 0 SUD level during reprocessing or identifying a negative belief with specific requirements and characteristics established in EMDR standard treatment. Additionally, some clients may need shorter reprocessing segments or breaks between segments. The titration continuum, addressed throughout this book, can serve as a foundation for maintaining the client's activation within a manageable and tolerable threshold. Pendulation strategies/protocols and segmenting the memory into small fragments may facilitate the accessing of traumagenic memories, keeping the client within their window of affect tolerance.

Conclusions

In closing, this book invites us to embrace the profound complexities of the mind shaped by chronic traumatization through an integrative and comprehensive approach—one that honors both the verbal and linear processes alongside the rich, symbolic dimensions of the mind. EMDR-sandtray-based therapy works actively with the brain's bihemispheric structure. It expands the therapeutic lens beyond traditional verbal approaches, integrating nonverbal and symbol-based portals that access the layered depths of memory and meaning hidden beneath symptoms. EMDR-sandtray-based therapy is nested within the power of a multimodal and transtheoretical approach, weaving together diverse frameworks to enrich the clinician's understanding of the treatment of complex trauma and dissociation while preserving the essence, principles, and transformative power of EMDR therapy. This approach seamlessly integrates the rich, symbolic depth of sandtray therapy with the transformative principles of EMDR therapy, forming a dynamic and comprehensive therapeutic framework. By integrating EMDR therapy with this creative and symbolic modality, we unlock new possibilities for healing across developmental stages, offering clients dynamic pathways to restructure their relationship with their stories, sense of self, and others, and opening the door to transformative change.

Considering the complexities of human experience, many aspects remain yet to be fully explored through research, and EMDR-sandtray-based therapy is no exception. While further scientific inquiry is essential to deepen our understanding, the powerful outcomes observed in clinical practice provide compelling practice-based evidence of its effectiveness.

To bridge the gap, it is imperative that research efforts align with and validate what is observed in clinical practice. Rigorous studies can substantiate the efficacy of EMDR-sandtray-based therapy and offer valuable insights into optimizing its delivery. Such research will enable clinicians to refine their methods, ensuring that this innovative approach continues to evolve and meet clients' diverse needs in even more effective ways.

APPENDIX 1

Classifications and miniature groups recommended by various authors (Homeyer & Sweeney, 2017, 2023; Rae, 2013; Smith, 2012).

Human Figures

    a. Adults: Male, female, and gender fluid figures of various ages and ethnicities
    b. Children of different ages and ethnicities
    c. Babies: newborns or infants
    d. Elders
    e. Individuals from various historical eras

Emotional Figures

    a. Figures showing different emotions
    b. Figures in various postures, such as standing, sitting, kneeling, laying down, fighting, sleeping, crawling, walking.

Professions

    a. First responders
    b. Teachers
    c. Medical and mental health professionals
    d. Construction workers, farmers, and business people
    e. Hobbies
    f. Drivers, pilots
    g. Lawyers

Life Experiences

    a. Birth, baptism, graduation, marriage, death
    b. Sports

Animals

    a. Prehistoric animals (e.g., dinosaurs)
    b. Domesticated and farm animals
    c. Wild animals
    d. Bugs and insects

e. Reptiles

f. Fish and water animals

g. Birds

Shadow and Horror Figures

a. Monsters, ghosts, skeletons, zombies

b. Figures representing anxiety, depression, fear, or negative thoughts

c. Death and dying symbols (e.g., tombs, coffins, sick people and animals)

Authority Figures

a. Judges, queens, kings, captains, and soldiers

b. Authority figures from diverse cultural backgrounds

c. Ancestors

Victims and Perpetrators

a. Aggressors, oppressors; figures with weapons or in aggressive postures

b. Vulnerable and injured figures

Religious and Spiritual Symbols

a. Gods, goddesses, priests, pastors, angels, monks, nuns

b. Symbols from different religious and spiritual backgrounds, such as deities, halos, prayer flags, menorahs, and crosses.

Fantasy and Magical Figures

a. Fairies, unicorns, knights, princesses

b. Wizards, dragons, witches, mermaids

Buildings and Houses

a. Castles, homes, schools, hospitals, churches, temples, mosques, synagogues

Furniture

a. Chairs, sofas, beds, tables

b. Cradles, desks

Vehicles of Transportation

a. Cars, trains, airplanes, bicycles

b. Boats, scooters, buses

Natural Elements

    a. Trees, rivers, lakes, ponds, mountains

    b. Clouds, sun, moon

    c. Flowers, bushes, plants

    d. Volcanoes, rocks, caves, rainbows

Medical

    a. Band-Aids, syringes, thermometers, ambulance

    b. Pill bottles, pills, and capsules

Weapons

    a. Shields, bows and arrows, guns, swords

    b. Missiles

Bridges and Pathways

    a. Tunnels, roads

    b. Bridges, staircases

Food and Drink

    a. Food items, such as bread, vegetables, fruit

    b. Healthy and unhealthy food

    c. Food for babies, children, and adults

    d. Utensils, plates, cups, glasses

Fences and Dividers

    a. Wooden/metal fences

    b. Stone walls

    c. Bricks

    d. Hedges and bushes

    e. Gates and doors

Play Items

    a. Toys for children across development

    b. Teddy bears, dolls, toy, cars, balls, baby rattles, building blocks

Abstract Items

    a. Spheres

    b. Amorphous shapes

    c. Clay lumps

Gender-Affirmative and Gender-Fluid Figures (Stitts, 2020)

    a. Masculine-presenting girls

    b. Feminine-presenting boys

    c. Transgender and nonbinary representations of people

Figures That Nurture

    a. Baby bottles, blankets, musical boxes, hearts, birthday cakes, gifts, cribs, rocking chairs, toys, stuffed animals, books

Signs and Symbols

    a. Stop sign, traffic, light, arrows

    b. Peace, love, and connection symbols

    c. Hearts

Containers and Boundaries

    a. Cages, boxes, walls, doors, gates

    b. Containers of various sizes and shapes and small bottles filled with colored sand with special powers, fairy dust, and more

Conflict and War

    a. Battlefields, trenches, prisons

    b. Dungeons, fortresses, ruins

Safe Places

    a. Shelters, sanctuaries

    b. Nests, warm and cozy homes

Clothing

    a. Shoes, hats, bags

    b. Masks, armor, jewelry

Tools and Instruments

    a. Hammers, sewing kit

    b. Paint brushes, musical instruments

APPENDIX 2

The categories of needs outlined by Maslow provide a valuable framework, and I have expanded upon them to encompass a broader understanding of human needs. However, the process of addressing these needs does not necessarily adhere to the specific sequence or hierarchy in which they were originally categorized by Maslow. Instead, the approach is tailored to align with the unique experiences, priorities, and developmental pathways of the individual, allowing for greater flexibility and responsiveness to their personal context.

Love and Belonging

- To have friends
- To be held when I feel safe
- To receive safe and nurturing touch
- To have someone I can trust
- To have someone I can feel safe with
- To feel connected
- To feel that I belong
- To feel understood
- To feel that my needs matter
- To feel that I matter
- To feel that I am important
- To feel loved
- To be held and loved when I'm not feeling well
- To have the right to my feelings
- To have someone help me feel that my feelings are okay
- To have someone help me with challenging feelings
- To have someone mirror me
- To have someone show me parts/aspects/sides of me
- To be loved, even when I have made a mistake
- To have someone help me feel proud of myself
- To have someone teach me with patience

Physiological Needs

- To breathe and get air (breathing)
- To get water
- To be fed and get food
- To have shelter or a place to live
- To have clothing
- To have a place to sleep
- To have someone safe help me fall asleep
- To be cared for when I get hurt

Safety and Security Needs

- To feel safe and secure
- To be protected
- To have someone look out for my safety and protection
- To have someone fight for me
- To have someone stand up for me
- To have someone by my side as I stand up for myself

Self-Worth Needs

- To feel respected
- To have someone help me feel that I have rights
- To be seen
- To have someone interested in knowing me
- To have the freedom to express what I feel and need
- To have the freedom to be me

Cognitive Needs

- To know what I want/need to know
- To explore the world
- To be curious
- To have someone help me understand
- To have someone explain when I'm confused
- To have someone help me organize and understand what is happening inside me

Self-Actualization Needs

- To grow as an individual
- To grow as part of a group
- To be supported in achieving my goals and dreams

Emotional Needs

- To receive affection
- To have someone who can accompany me as I connect with/visit my feelings
- To have happy and comfortable feelings
- To have a companion when I have uncomfortable/comfortable feelings
- To have emotional support
- To receive compassion
- To have someone who makes me feel that my feelings are okay, no matter how big they are

Play Needs

- To have time to play
- To have someone to play with
- To have someone who can join me and have fun
- To have someone sing to me to help me fall asleep
- To have someone celebrate my birthday

APPENDIX 3

Sand World Exploration	
Summary	
Cognitive Data	
Emotional Data	
Sensorimotor Data	
Neural Tendencies: Areas of heat and activation (sympathetic mobilization)	
Neural Tendencies: Areas of collapse, immobility, and shutdown (dorsal immobilization)	
Attachment Tendencies and Relational Patterns: Preoccupation and anxiety, disengagement and avoidance, and disorganization and dysregulation/affective constriction	
Relational Dynamics: Sources of conflict and disengagement (separation, loneliness)	
Approach Versus Distancing, Autonomy Versus Dependency, Power and Powerlessness Tendencies	
Defenses and Self-Protective Strategies	
Polarizations	
Areas Where Adaptive Information and Resources Exist	
Regulatory Capacities: How characters relate to their emotions	
Regulatory Capacities: How characters relate to their needs	
Actions and Urges	
Grief and Loss	
Intersubjective Field	
Capacities and Realizations	
Acts of Triumph	

386

APPENDIX 4
EMDR–Sandtray Session Summary

Name: _____ Date:___/___/___

Reevaluation (changes/challenges/progress): _____

_____

EMDR–sandtray phase: 1 2 3 4 5 6 7 8

Preparation (resources/protocols): _____

_____

Implicit resources: _____

_____

Explicit resources: _____

_____

Assessment and processing phases: Implicit ( ) Explicit ( )

Resource tray/areas: _____

_____

Memory (trauma tray, sand world, theme):

_____

_____

_____

Main and other characters:

_____

_____

_____

Initial negative cognition (verbal or symbolic): _____

Initial PC (verbal or symbolic): _____

Initial SUDs: 0 1 2 3 4 5 6 7 8 9 10 Nonnumeric value: _____

Final SUDs: 0 1 2 3 4 5 6 7 8 9 10 Nonnumeric value: _____

Was the memory processed to completion? ( ) Yes ( ) No

Phase 5: PC _____

Final VoC: 1 2 3 4 5 6 7

Phase 6 completed: ( ) Yes ( ) No

Areas of blocked processing: _____

_____

387

Interweaves used: _____

_____

_____

Relevant issues that surfaced in the tray: _____

_____

Relational dynamics: _____

Neural tendencies: _____

Defenses: _____

Cognitive data: _____

Emotional data: _____

Sensorimotor data: _____

Resources: _____

Needs: _____

Urges and actions (truncated and completed): _____

Capacities: _____

Polarizations: _____

Closure strategies: _____

Additional comments/data:

_____

_____

_____

_____

_____

_____

REFERENCES

Abel, N. J., & O'Brien, J. M. (2010). EMDR treatment of comorbid PTSD and alcohol dependence: A case example. *Journal of EMDR Practice and Research, 4*(2), 50–59. https://doi.org/10.1891/1933-3196.4.2.50

Amaya-Jackson, L., & DeRosa, R. R. (2007). Treatment considerations for clinicians in applying evidence-based practice to complex presentations in child trauma. *Journal of Traumatic Stress, 20*(4), 379–390. https://doi.org/10.1002/jts.20266

American Psychiatric Association. (2022). *Diagnostic and statistical manual of mental disorders: DSM-5-TR* (5th ed., rev.). American Psychiatric Association Publishing.

Angeles Tornero, M. D. L., & Capella, C. (2017). Change during psychotherapy through sand play tray in children that have been sexually abused. *Frontiers in Psychology, 8*, 617. https://doi.org/10.3389/fpsyg.2017.00617

Artigas, L., & Jarero, I. (2014). *The butterfly hug method for bilateral stimulation.* EMDR Foundation. https://emdrfoundation.org/toolkit/butterfly-hug.pdf

Artigas, L., Jarero, I., Alcalá, N., & Cano, T. L. (2014). The EMDR integrative group treatment protocol (IGTP). In M. Luber (Ed.), *Implementing EMDR early mental health interventions for man-made and natural disasters: Models, scripted protocols, and summary sheets* (pp. 237–244). Springer Publishing Company.

Badenoch, B. (2008). *Being a brain-wise therapist: A practical guide to interpersonal neurobiology.* W. W. Norton & Company.

Badenoch, B. (2018). *The heart of trauma: Healing the embodied brain in the context of relationships.* W. W. Norton & Company.

Bagamasbad, A., & Levin, R. (2023). Fantasy and consciousness. *Psychology of Consciousness: Theory, Research, and Practice, OnlineFirst,* 1–12.

Bandler, R., Keay, K. A., Floyd, N., & Price, J. (2000). Central circuits mediating patterned autonomic activity during active vs. passive emotional coping. *Brain Research Bulletin, 53*(1), 95–104. https://doi.org/10.1016/s0361-9230(00)00313-0

Barron, I. G., Bourgaize, C., Lempertz, D., Swinden, C., & Darker-Smith, S. (2019). Eye movement desensitization reprocessing for children and adolescents with posttraumatic stress disorder: A systematic narrative review. *Journal of EMDR Practice and Research, 13*(4), 270–283. https://doi.org/10.1891/1933-3196.13.4.270

Bowlby, J. (1988). *A secure base: Parent–child attachment and healthy human development.* Basic Books.

California Evidence-Based Clearinghouse for Child Welfare. (2006). *Eye movement desensitization and reprocessing (EMDR) [trauma treatment - client-level interventions (child & adolescent)].* https://cebc4cw.org/program/eye-movement-desensitization-and-reprocessing

Chen, R., Gillespie, A., Zhao, Y., Xi, Y., Ren, Y., & McLean, L. (2018). The efficacy of eye movement desensitization and reprocessing in children and adults who have experienced complex childhood trauma: A systematic review of randomized controlled trials. *Frontiers in Psychology, 9*, 534. https://doi.org/10.3389/fpsyg.2018.00534

Corrigan, F. M. (2014). Defense responses: Frozen, suppressed, truncated, obstructed, and malfunctioning. In U. F. Lanius, S. L. Paulsen, & F. M. Corrigan (Eds.), *Neurobiology and treatment of traumatic dissociation: Toward an embodied self* (pp. 131–152). Springer Publishing Company.

Courtois, C. A. (2004). Complex trauma, complex reactions: Assessment and treatment. *Psychotherapy: Theory, Research, Practice, Training, 41*(4), 412–425. https://doi.org/10.1037/0033-3204.41.4.412

Courtois, C. A., & Ford, J. D. (2013). *Treatment of complex trauma: A sequenced, relationship-based approach.* Guilford Press.

Cozolino, L. (2014). *The neuroscience of human relationships: Attachment and the developing social brain* (2nd ed). W. W. Norton & Company.

Cozolino, L. (2017). *The neuroscience of psychotherapy: Healing the social brain* (3rd ed.). W. W. Norton & Company.

Cundy, L. (Ed.). (2017). *Anxiously attached: Understanding and working with preoccupied attachment.* Routledge.

Cundy, L. (Ed.). (2019). *Attachment and the defense against intimacy: Understanding and working with avoidant attachment, self-hatred, and shame.* Routledge.

Cyr, C., Dubois-Comtois, K., Paquette, D., Lopez, L., & Bigras, M. (2020). An attachment-based parental capacity assessment to orient decision-making in child protection cases: A randomized control trial. *Child Maltreatment, 27*(1), 66–77. https://doi.org/10.1177/1077559520967995

Dana, D. (2023). *Polyvagal practices: Anchoring the self in safety.* W. W. Norton & Company.

Danylchuk, L. S., & Connors, K. J. (2024). *Treating complex trauma and dissociation: A practical guide to navigating therapeutic challenges* (2nd ed.). Routledge.

Dalenberg, C. J., Brand, B. L., Gleaves, D. H., Dorahy, M. J., Loewenstein, R. J., Cardeña, E., Frewen, P. A., Carlson, E. B., & Spiegel, D. (2012). Evaluation of the evidence for the trauma and fantasy models of dissociation. *Psychological bulletin, 138*(3), 550–588. https://doi.org/10.1037/a0027447

Department of Veterans Affairs & Department of Defense. (2023). *VA/DoD clinical practice guideline for management of posttraumatic stress disorder and acute stress disorder.* U.S. Government Printing Office. https://www.healthquality.va.gov/guidelines/MH/ptsd/

Dion, L. (2018). *Aggression in play therapy: A neurobiological approach for integrating intensity.* W. W. Norton & Company.

Dispenza, J. (2007). *Evolve your brain: The science of changing your mind.* Health Communications, Inc.

Farina, B., Liotti, M., & Imperatori, C. (2019). The role of attachment trauma and disintegrative pathogenic processes in the traumatic-dissociative dimension. *Frontiers in Psychology, 10*, 933. https://doi.org/10.3389/fpsyg.2019.00933

Farrell, D., Moran, J., Zat, Z., Miller, P. W., Knibbs, L., Papanikolopoulos, P., Prattos, T., McGowan, I., McLaughlin, D., Barron, I., Mattheß, C., & Kiernan, M. D. (2023). Group early intervention eye movement desensitization and reprocessing therapy as a video-conference psychotherapy with frontline/emergency workers in response to the COVID-19 pandemic in the treatment of post-traumatic stress disorder and moral injury—An RCT study. *Frontiers in Psychology, 14*, 1129912. https://doi.org/10.3389/fpsyg.2023.1129912

Felitti, V. J., Anda, R. F., Nordenberg, D., Williamson, D. F., Spitz, A. M., Edwards, V., Koss, M. P., & Marks, J. S. (1998). Relationship of childhood abuse and household dysfunction to many of the leading causes of death in adults: The Adverse Childhood Experiences (ACE) Study. *American Journal of Preventive Medicine, 14*(4), 245–258. https://doi.org/10.1016/s0749-3797(98)00017-8

Fisher, J. (2017). *Healing the fragmented selves of trauma survivors: Overcoming internal self-alienation.* Routledge.

Flahive, M.-h. W., & Ray, D. (2007). Effect of group sandtray therapy with preadolescents. *The Journal for Specialists in Group Work, 32*(4), 362–382. https://doi.org/10.1080/01933920701476706

Fonagy, P., Gergely, G., Jurist, E. L., & Target, M. (2002). *Affect regulation, mentalization, and the development of the self.* Other Press.

Fonagy, P., Luyten, P., Allison, E., & Campbell, C. (2019). Mentalizing, epistemic trust and the phenomenology of psychotherapy. *Psychopathology, 52*(2), 94–103. https://doi.org/10.1159/000501526

Ford, J. D. (2021). Polyvictimization and developmental trauma in childhood. *European Journal of Psychotraumatology, 12*https://doi.org/10.1080/20008198.2020.1866394

Forgash, C., & Copeley, M. (Eds.). (2008). *Healing the heart of trauma and dissociation with EMDR and ego state therapy.* Springer Publishing Company.

Fraser, G. A. (2003). Fraser's "dissociative table technique" revisited, revised: A strategy for working with ego states in dissociative disorders and ego-state therapy. *Journal of Trauma & Dissociation, 4*(4), 5–28. https://doi.org/10.1300/J229v04n04_02

Frewen, P., & Lanius, R. (2015). *Healing the traumatized self: Consciousness, neuroscience, treatment.* W. W. Norton & Company.

George, C., Kaplan, N., & Main, M. (1985). The adult attachment interview [Unpublished manuscript]. University of California at Berkeley.

Germer, C. K. (2013). Mindfulness: What is it? What does it matter? In C. K. Germer, R. D. Siegel, & P. R. Fulton (Eds.), *Mindfulness and psychotherapy* (2nd ed., pp. 2–35). The Guilford Press.

Gil, E. (2017). *Posttraumatic play in children: What clinicians need to know.* Guilford Press.

Gilson, G., & Kaplan, S. (2000). *The therapeutic interweave in EMDR: Before and beyond: A manual for EMDR trained clinicians.* Ginger Gilson and Sandra Kaplan.

Gómez, A. M. (2013). *EMDR therapy and adjunct approaches with children: Complex trauma, attachment, and dissociation.* Springer Publishing Company.

Gómez, A. M. (2018). *Stories and storytellers: The thinking mind, the heart and the body: A book for children about healing and EMDR therapy.* Agate Books.

Gómez, A. M. (2019a). *Let's have a visit with our feelings: Therapeutic cards that work with the self-protective system of children affected by trauma.* Agate Books.

Gómez, A. M. (2019b). The world of stories and symbols: The EMDR-sandtray protocol. *Go With That Magazine, 24*(1), 35–39. https://emdria.org/course/the-world-of-stories-and-symbols-an-introduction-to-the-emdr-sandtray-protocol-with-complex-and-developmental-trauma

Gómez, A. M. (2021a). Dissociation in children: A multimodal approach to EMDR therapy. *Go With That magazine, 26*(4), 17–25. https://emdria.org/magazine/emdr-therapy-and-dissociation

Gómez, A. M. (2021b). *The parenting wheel training manual* [Unpublished manuscript].

Gómez, A. M. (2022a). *The EMDR group parent empowerment protocol (GPEP) training manual* [Unpublished manuscript].

Gómez, A. M. (2022b). *The journey of the butterfly G-TEP with children* [Unpublished work book]. https://www.anaGómez.org/the-journey-of-the-butterfly-gtep-with-children/

Gómez, A. M. (2023a). *EMDR therapy basic training manual* [Unpublished manuscript].

Gómez, A. M. (2023b, January). *EMDR parent–child & attachment specialist intensive program.* Agate Institute. https://agateinstitute.org/emdr-parent–child-attachment-specialist-intensive-program/

Gómez, A. M. (2023c). *My helpers and protectors: Therapeutic cards that work with the self-protective system of children affected by trauma.* Agate Books.

Gómez, A. M. (2024a). *The journey of the butterfly: G-TEP with children.* In R. Morrow Robinson & S. Kemal Kaptan (Eds.), *EMDR group therapy: Emerging principles and protocols to treat trauma and beyond* (pp. 139–148). Springer Publishing Company.

Gómez, A. M. (2024b). *The visitor: A book about pain, defenses and love.* Agate Books.

Gómez, A. M. & Paulsen, S. (2016). *All the colors of me: My first book about dissociation.* Agate Books.

Gómez, A., & Shapiro, F. (2012). EMDR therapy with children: Journey into wholeness. *Child & Family Professional Journal, 15*(3), 20–30.

Gonzalez, A., & Mosquera, D. (2012). *EMDR and dissociation: The progressive approach.* Amazon Imprint.

Grant, R. J. (2017). *AutPlay therapy for children and adolescents on the autism spectrum: A behavioral play-based approach* (3rd ed.). Routledge.

Grant, R. J. (2024). *Play interventions for neurodivergent children and adolescents: Promoting growth, empowerment, and affirming practices* (2nd ed.). Routledge.

Greenwald, R. (1999). *Eye movement desensitization and reprocessing (EMDR) in child and adolescent psychotherapy.* Jason Aronson.

Harris, H., Urdaneta, V., Triana, V., Vo, C. S., Walden, D., & Myers, D. (2018). A pilot study with Spanish-speaking Latina survivors of domestic violence comparing EMDR & TF-CBT group interventions. *Open Journal of Social Sciences, 6*(11), 203–222. https://doi.org/10.4236/jss.2018.611015

Hase, M. (2010). CraveEx: An EMDR approach to treat substance abuse and addiction. In M. Luber (Ed.), *Eye movement desensitization and reprocessing (EMDR) scripted protocols: Special populations* (pp. 467–488). Springer Publishing Company.

Hase, M., Schallmayer, S., & Sack, M. (2008). EMDR reprocessing of the addiction memory: Pretreatment, posttreatment, and 1-month follow-up. *Journal of EMDR Practice and Research, 2*(3), 170–179. https://doi.org/10.1891/1933-3196.2.3.170

Hensley, B. J. (2021). *An EMDR therapy primer* (3rd ed.). Springer Publishing Company.

Herman, J. L. (1992). Complex PTSD: A syndrome in survivors of prolonged and repeated trauma. *Journal of Traumatic Stress, 5*(3), 377–391. https://doi.org/10.1002/jts.2490050305

Herman, J. L. (2022). *Trauma and recovery: The aftermath of violence—From domestic abuse to political terror.* Basic Books. (Original work published 1992)

Hill, D. (2015). *Affect regulation theory: A clinical model.* W. W. Norton & Company.

Hill, D. (2021). Dysregulation and its impact on states of consciousness. In D. J. Siegel, A. Schore, & L. Cozolino (Eds.), *Interpersonal neurobiology and clinical practice* (pp. 169–194). W. W. Norton & Company.

Holmes, T., & Holmes, L. (2007). *Parts work: An illustrated guide to your inner life* (4th ed.). Winged Heart Press.

Homeyer, L. E., & Lyles, M. N. (2022). *Advanced sandtray therapy: Digging deeper into clinical practice.* Routledge.

Homeyer, L. E., & Sweeney, D. S. (2017). *Sandtray therapy: A practical manual* (3rd ed.). Routledge.

Homeyer, L. E., & Sweeney, D. S. (2023). *Sandtray therapy: A practical manual* (4th ed.). Routledge.

Hughes, D. A., Golding, K. S., & Hudson, J. (2019). *Healing relational trauma with attachment-focused interventions: Dyadic developmental psychotherapy with children and families.* W. W. Norton & Company.

Hurston, Z. N. (1942). *Dust tracks on a road: An autobiography.* J. B. Lippincott.

International Society for the Study of Dissociation. (2004). Guidelines for the evaluation and treatment of dissociative symptoms in children and adolescents. *Journal of Trauma and Dissociation, 5*(3), 119–150. https://doi.org/10.1300/J229v05n03_09

International Society for the Study of Dissociation Taskforce. (In press). Guidelines for the evaluation and treatment of dissociative symptoms in children and adolescents. *Journal of Trauma and Dissociation.*

Jang, M., Choi, Y., Lee, S., Lee, Y., & Cho, E. (2019). The effect of sandplay therapy on the PTSD symptoms and resilience of street children in Uganda. *Journal of Symbols & Sandplay Therapy, 10*(2), 37–55. https://doi.org/10.12964/jsst.19009

Jarero, I., Artigas, L., Montero, M., & López, L. (2008). The EMDR integrative group treatment protocol: Application with child victims of a mass disaster. *Journal of EMDR Practice and Research, 2*(2), 97–105. https://doi.org/10.1891/1933-3196.2.2.97

Jarero, I., Givaudan, M., & Osorio, A. (2018). Randomized controlled trial on the provision of the EMDR integrative group treatment protocol adapted for ongoing traumatic stress to female patients with cancer-related posttraumatic stress disorder symptoms. *Journal of EMDR Practice and Research, 12*(3), 94–104. https://doi.org/10.1891/1933-3196.12.3.94

Johanson, E., Tamblyn, W., Pratt, E., Payne, D., & Page, S. (2021). Adapting a trauma pathway within an improving access to psychological therapy (IAPT) service in the context of increased demand and severe acute respiratory syndrome coronavirus 2 (COVID-19). *EMDR Therapy Quarterly, 3*(1), 1–12.

Jung, C. G. (1969). *The archetypes and the collective unconscious* (R. F. C. Hull, Trans.). Princeton University Press. (Original work published 1934–1955)

Kalff, D. M. (2003). *Sandplay: A psychotherapeutic approach to the psyche* (B. A. Turner, Ed.). Temenos Press. (Original work published 1980)

Kalisch, L. A., Lawrence, K. A, Baud, J., Spencer-Smith, M., & Ure, A. (2023). Therapeutic supports for neurodiverse children who have experienced interpersonal trauma: A scoping review. *Review Journal of Autism and Developmental Disorders.* https://doi.org/10.1007/s40489-023-00363-9

Karadag, M., Gokcen, C., & Sarp, A. S. (2019. EMDR therapy in children and adolescents who have post-traumatic stress disorder: A six-week follow-up study. *International Journal of Psychiatry in Clinical Practice, 24*(1), 77–82. https://doi.org/10.1080/13651501.2019.1682171

Kern Popejoy, E., Perryman, K., & Broadwater, A. (2020). Processing military combat trauma through sandtray therapy: A phenomenological study. *Journal of Creativity in Mental Health, 16*(2), 196–211. https://doi.org/10.1080/15401383.2020.1761499

Kestly, T. A. (2014). *The interpersonal neurobiology of play: Brain-building interventions for emotional well-being.* W. W. Norton & Company.

Kluft, R. P. (1999). Current issues in dissociative identity disorder. *Journal of Practical Psychiatry and Behavioral Health, 5,* 3–19.

Kluft, R. P. (2006). Dealing with alters: A pragmatic clinical perspective. *Psychiatric Clinics of North America, 29*(1), 281–304. https://doi.org/10.1016/j.psc.2005.10.010

Knipe, J. (2015). *EMDR toolbox: Theory and treatment of complex PTSD and dissociation.* Springer Publishing Company.

Knipe, J. (2019). *EMDR toolbox: Theory and treatment of complex PTSD and dissociation* (2nd ed.). Springer Publishing Company.

Korkmazlar, Ü., Bozkurt, B., Tan, D., Devrim, E., & Kulca, Y. A. (2018, June 29–July 1). *The EMDR group protocol for children, adolescent and caregivers.* 19th EMDR Europe Conference, Strasbourg, France.

Korn, D. L., & Leeds, A. M. (2002). Preliminary evidence of efficacy for EMDR resource development and installation in the stabilization phase of treatment of complex posttraumatic stress disorder. *Journal of Clinical Psychology, 58*(12), 1465–1487. https://doi.org/10.1002/jclp.10099

Lanius, U. F., & Paulsen, S. L. (2014). Towards an embodied self: EMDR and somatic interventions. In U. F. Lanius, S. L. Paulsen, & F. M. Corrigan (Eds.), *Neurobiology and treatment of traumatic dissociation: Toward an embodied self* (pp. 123–140). Springer Publishing Company.

Lee, G. M., Johari, K. S. K., Mahmud, Z., & Jamaludin, L. (2018). The impact of sandtray therapy in group counseling towards children's self-esteem. *International Journal of Academic Research in Business and Social Sciences, 8*(4), 1019–1030. http://dx.doi.org/10.6007/IJARBSS/v8-i4/4132

Lee, S., Kwak, H. J., Ahn, U. K., Kim, K. M., & Lim, M.-H. (2023). Effect of group sand play therapy on psychopathologies of adolescents with delinquent behaviors. *Medicine, 102*(40), e35445. https://doi.org/10.1097/MD.0000000000035445

Lehnung, M., Shapiro, E., Schreiber, M., & Hofmann, A. (2017). Evaluating the EMDR group traumatic episode protocol with refugees: A field study. *Journal of EMDR Practice and Research, 11*(3), 129–138. https://doi.org/10.1891/1933-3196.11.3.129

Levine, P. A. (2015). *Trauma and memory: Brain and body in a search for the living past: A practical guide for understanding and working with traumatic memory.* North Atlantic Books.

Lieberman, M. D. (2013). *Social: Why Our Brains Are Wired to Connect.* Crown Publishers.

Liotti, G. (1992). Disorganized/disoriented attachment in the etiology of the dissociative disorders. *Dissociation: Progress in the Dissociative Disorders, 5*(4), 196–204.

Liotti, G. (2004). Trauma, dissociation, and disorganized attachment: Three strands of a single braid. *Psychotherapy: Theory, Research, Practice, Training, 41*(4), 472–486. https://doi.org/10.1037/0033-3204.41.4.472

Liotti, G. (2009). Attachment and dissociation. In P. F. Dell & J. A. O'Neil (Eds.), *Dissociation and the dissociative disorders: DSM-V and beyond* (pp. 53–65). Routledge.

Liotti, G. (2017). Conflicts between motivational systems related to attachment trauma: Key to understanding the intra-family relationship between abused children and their abusers. *Journal of Trauma & Dissociation, 18*(3), 304–318. https://doi.org/10.1080/15299732.2017.1295392

Liotti, G. (2018). Conflicts between motivational systems related to attachment trauma: Key to understanding the intra-family relationship between abused children and their abusers. In W. Middleton, A. Sach, & M. J. Dorahy (Eds.), *The abused and the abuser: Victim–perpetrator dynamics* (pp. 62–75). Routledge.

Liotti, G., & Gilbert, P. (2011). Mentalizing, motivation, and social mentalities: Theoretical considerations and implications for psychotherapy. *Psychology and Psychotherapy: Theory, Research and Practice, 84*(1), 9–25. https://doi.org/10.1348/147608310X520094

Lipscomb, A., & Ashley, W. (2021). A critical analysis of the utilization of eye movement desensitization and reprocessing (EMDR) psychotherapy with African American clients. *Journal of Human Services: Training, Research, and Practice, 7*(1), Article 3. https://scholarworks.sfasu.edu/jhstrp/vol7/iss1/3

Lowenfeld, M. (1993). *Understanding children's sandplay: Lowenfeld's world technique.* Margaret Lowenfeld Trust.

Lyles, M. (2021). Room for everyone: EMDR and family-based play therapy in the sandtray. In A. Beckley-Forest & A. Monaco (Eds.), *EMDR with children in the play therapy room: An integrated approach* (pp. 75–108). Springer Publishing Company.

Lyons-Ruth, K., & Jacobvitz, D. (2008). Attachment disorganization: Genetic factors, parenting contexts, and developmental transformation from infancy to adulthood. In J. Cassidy & P. R. Shaver (Eds.), *Handbook of attachment: Theory, research, and clinical applications* (2nd ed., pp. 666–697). Guilford Press.

Lyons-Ruth, K., Dutra, L., Schuder, M. R., & Bianchi, I. (2006). From infant attachment disorganization to adult dissociation: Relational adaptations or traumatic experiences? *Psychiatric Clinics of North America, 29*(1), 63–86. https://doi.org/10.1016/j.psc.2005.10.011

Mallinckrodt, B., Porter, M. J., & Kivlighan, D. M., Jr. (2005). Client attachment to therapist, depth of in-session exploration, and object relations in brief psychotherapy. *Psychotherapy: Theory, Research, Practice, Training, 42*(1), 85–100. https://doi.org/10.1037/0033-3204.42.1.85

Manfield, P. (2010). *Dyadic resourcing: Creating a foundation for processing trauma.* CreateSpace Independent Publishing Platform.

Mann, D. (2021). *Gestalt therapy: 100 key points and techniques* (2nd ed.). Routledge.

Manzoni, M., Fernandez, I., Bertella, S., Tizzoni, F., Gazzola, E., Molteni, M., & Nobile, M. (2021). Eye movement desensitization and reprocessing: The state of the art of efficacy in children and adolescent with post traumatic stress disorder. *Journal of Affective Disorders, 282*, 340–347. https://doi.org/10.1016/j.jad.2020.12.088

Marich, J. (2023). *Dissociation made simple: A stigma-free guide to embracing your dissociative mind and navigating daily life.* North Atlantic Books.

Marich, J., & Dansiger, S. (2022). *Healing addiction with EMDR therapy: A trauma-focused guide.* Springer Publishing Company.

Markus, W., & Hornsveld, H. K. (2017). EMDR interventions in addiction. *Journal of EMDR Practice and Research, 11*(1), 3–29. https://doi.org/10.1891/1933-3196.11.1.3

Martin, K. M. (2012). How to use Fraser's dissociative table technique to access and work with emotional parts of the personality. *Journal of EMDR Practice and Research, 6*(4), 179–186. https://doi.org/10.1891/1933-3196.6.4.179

Maté, G. (2011). *Close encounters with addiction*. Central Recovery Press (CRP).

Maxfield, L. (2019). A clinician's guide to the efficacy of EMDR therapy. *Journal of EMDR Practice and Research, 13*(4), 239–246. https://doi.org/10.1891/1933-3196.13.4.239

Maxfield, L. (2021). Low-intensity interventions and EMDR therapy. *Journal of EMDR Practice and Research, 15*(2), 1–13. https://doi.org/10.1891/EMDR-D-21-00009

Merckelbach, H., à Campo, J., Hardy, S., & Giesbrecht, T. (2005). Dissociation and fantasy proneness in psychiatric patients: a preliminary study. *Comprehensive psychiatry, 46*(3), 181–185. https://doi.org/10.1016/j.comppsych.2004.08.001

Miller, R. (2010). The feeling-state theory of impulse-control disorders and the impulse-control disorder protocol. *Traumatology, 16*(3), 2–10. https://doi.org/10.1177/1534765610365912

Moench, J., & Billsten, O. (2021). Randomized controlled trial: Self-care traumatic episode protocol (STEP), computerized EMDR treatment of COVID-19 related stress. *Journal of EMDR Practice and Research*. https://doi.org/10.1891/EMDR-D-20-00047

Mosquera, D. (2019). *Working with voices and dissociative parts: A trauma-informed approach* (2nd ed.). Instituto INTRA-TP.

Moss, E., Tarabulsy, G. M., Dubois-Comtois, K., Cyr, C., Bernier, A., & St-Laurent, D. (2018). The attachment video-feedback intervention program: Development and validation. In H. Steele & M. Steele (Eds.), *Handbook of attachment-based interventions* (pp. 318–338). Guilford Press.

Muratori, P., Polidori, L., Chiodo, S. *et al.* A Pilot Study Implementing Coping Power in Italian Community Hospitals: Effect of Therapist Attachment Style on Outcomes in Children. *J Child Fam Stud* 26, 3093–3101 (2017). https://doi.org/10.1007/s10826-017-0820-7

National Institute for Health and Care Excellence (NICE). (2018, December 5). *Posttraumatic stress disorder*. NICE. https://www.nice.org.uk/guidance/ng116

Oaklander, V. (2007). *Hidden treasure: A map to the child's inner self*. Karnac Books.

Ogden, P. (2019). Acts of triumph: An interpretation of Pierre Janet and the role of the body in trauma treatment. In G. Craparo, F. Ortu, & O. van der Hart (Eds.), *Rediscovering Pierre Janet: Trauma, dissociation, and new context for psychoanalysis* (pp. 200–209). Routledge.

Ogden, P., & Fisher, J. (2015). *Sensorimotor psychotherapy: Interventions for trauma and attachment*. W. W. Norton & Company.

Ogden, P., & Gómez, A. M. (2013). EMDR therapy and sensorimotor psychotherapy with children. In A. M. Gómez (Ed.), *EMDR therapy and adjunct approaches with children: Complex trauma, attachment and dissociation* (pp. 247–271). Springer Publishing Company.

Ogden, P., Minton, K., & Pain, C. (2006). *Trauma and the body: A sensorimotor approach to psychotherapy*. W. W. Norton & Company.

Oh, A., Eun You, S., & Jin Park, B. (2013). The effect of sandplay therapy with parent–children on mother-child's attachment security and communication. *Korean Journal of Child Studies, 34*(6), 31–55. https://doi.org/10.5723/KJCS.2013.34.6.31

Olivier, E., de Roos, C., & Bexkens, A. (2022). Eye movement desensitization and reprocessing in young children (ages 4–8) with posttraumatic stress disorder: A multiple-baseline evaluation. *Child Psychiatry & Human Development, 53*(6), 1391–1404. https://doi.org./10.1007/s10578-021-01237-z

Pagani, M., Di Lorenzo, G., Verardo, A. R., Nicolais, G., Monaco, L., Lauretti, G., Russo, R., Niolu, C., Ammaniti, M., Fernandez, I., & Siracusano, A. (2012). Neurobiological correlates of EMDR monitoring–An EEG study. *PLOS ONE, 7*(9), e45753. https://doi.org/10.1371/journal.pone.0045753

Panksepp, J. (1998). *Affective neuroscience: The foundations of human and animal emotions*. Oxford University Press.

Panksepp, J., & Biven, L. (2012). *The archaeology of mind: Neuroevolutionary origins of human emotions*. W. W. Norton & Company.

Papanikolopoulos, P., Nikolaou, A., Prattos, T., & Zourna, C. (2021). In response to an emergency: Trial use of EMDR group traumatic episode protocol for humanitarian workers on Greek islands. *Hellenic Journal of Cognitive Behavioral Research and Therapy, 7*(2), 9–16.

Paulsen, S. (2009). *Looking through the eyes of trauma and dissociation: An illustrated guide for EMDR therapists and clients.* Bainbridge Institute for Integrative Psychology.

Paulsen, S. L., & Golston, J. (2014). Stabilizing the relationship among self-states. In U. F. Lanius, S. L. Paulsen, & F. M. Corrigan (Eds.), *Neurobiology and treatment of traumatic dissociation: Toward an embodied self* (pp. 321–340). Springer Publishing Company.

Perls, F. S., Hefferline, R. F., & Goodman, P. (1951). *Gestalt therapy: Excitement and growth in the human personality.* Dell Publishing.

Popky, A. J. (2009). The desensitization of triggers and urge reprocessing (DeTUR) protocol. In M. Luber (Ed.), *Eye movement desensitization and reprocessing (EMDR) scripted protocols: Special populations* (pp. 489–511). Springer Publishing Company.

Porges, S. W. (2011). *The Polyvagal Theory: Neurophysiological foundations of emotions, attachment, communication, and self-regulation.* W. W. Norton & Company.

Porges, S. W. (2017). *The pocket guide to the Polyvagal Theory: The transformative power of feeling safe.* W. W. Norton & Company.

Porges, S. W. (2021). *Polyvagal safety: Attachment, communication, self-regulation.* W. W. Norton & Company.

Porges, S. W., & Dana, D. (Eds.). (2018). *Clinical applications of the Polyvagal Theory: The emergence of polyvagal-informed therapies.* W. W. Norton & Company.

Putnam, F. W. (1997). *Dissociation in children and adolescents: A developmental perspective.* Guilford Press.

Rae, R. (2013). *Sandtray: Playing to heal, recover, and grow.* Jason Aronson.

Reynolds, M. (2020). *Coach the person, not the problem: A guide to using reflective inquiry.* Berrett-Koehler Publishers.

Ridley, C. R. (2005). *Overcoming unintentional racism in counseling and therapy: A practitioner's guide to intentional intervention* (2nd ed.). Sage Publications.

Rodenburg, R., Benjamin, A., de Roos, C., Meijer, A. M., & Stams, G. J. (2009). Efficacy of EMDR in children: A meta-analysis. *Clinical Psychology Review, 29*(7), 599–606. https://doi.org/10.1016/j.cpr.2009.06.008

Ruiz-Aranda, D., Cardoso-Álvarez, S., & Fenollar-Cortés, J. (2021). Therapist attachment and the working alliance: The moderating effect of emotional regulation. *Frontiers in Psychology, 12*, 784010. https://doi.org/10.3389/fpsyg.2021.784010

Rumball, F. (2019). A systematic review of the assessment and treatment of posttraumatic stress disorder in individuals with autism spectrum disorders. *Review Journal of Autism and Developmental Disorders, 6*(3), 294–324. https://doi.org/10.1007/s40489-018-0133-9

Schauer, M., & Elbert, T. (2010). Dissociation following traumatic stress: Etiology and treatment. *Zeitschrift für Psychologie, 218*(2), 109–127. https://doi.org/10.1027/0044-3409/a000018

Schore, A. N. (2011). *The science of the art of psychotherapy.* W. W. Norton & Company.

Schore, A. N. (2019). *Right brain psychotherapy.* W. W. Norton & Company.

Schwartz, A. (2021). *The complex PTSD treatment manual: An integrative mind-body approach to trauma recovery.* PESI Publishing.

Schwartz, A. (2024). *Applied Polyvagal Theory in yoga: Therapeutic practices for emotional health.* W. W. Norton & Company.

Schwartz, R. C. (1995). *Internal family systems therapy.* Guilford Press.

Schwartz, R. C. (2021). *No bad parts: Healing trauma & restoring wholeness with the internal family systems model.* Sounds True.

Schwartz, R. C., & Sweezy, M. (2020). *Internal family systems therapy* (2nd ed.). Guilford Press.

Shapiro, E. (2014, June 26–29). *Recent simplified individual and group applications of the EMDR R-TEP for emergency situations* [Paper presentation/Conference session]. 15th EMDR Europe Conference, Edinburgh, Scotland.

Shapiro, E. (2018, April 20–22). *The EMDR group traumatic episode protocol* (G-TEP) [Paper presentation/Conference session]. EMDR Early Intervention World Summit, Natick, MA, United States.

Shapiro, E. (2024). EMDR group traumatic episode protocol. In R. Morrow Robinson & S. Kemal Kaptan (Eds.), *EMDR group therapy: Emerging principles and protocols to treat trauma and beyond* (pp. 65–80). Springer Publishing Company.

Shapiro, E., & Laub, B. (2008). Early EMDR intervention (EEI): A summary, a theoretical model, and the recent traumatic episode protocol (R-TEP). *Journal of EMDR Practice and Research, 2*(2), 79–96. https://doi.org/10.1891/1933-3196.2.2.79

Shapiro, F. (2001). *Eye movement desensitization and reprocessing (EMDR): Basic principles, protocols and procedures* (2nd ed.). Guilford Press.

Shapiro, F. (2007). EMDR, adaptive information processing, and case conceptualization. *Journal of EMDR Practice and Research, 1*(2), 68–87. https://doi.org/10.1891/1933-3196.1.2.68

Shapiro, F. (2018). *Eye movement desensitization and reprocessing (EMDR) therapy: Basic principles, protocols, and procedures* (3rd ed.). Guilford Press.

Shapiro, R. (2016). *Easy ego state interventions: Strategies for working with parts*. W. W. Norton & Company.

Shen, Y.-P., & Armstrong, S. A. (2008). Impact of group sandtray therapy on the self-esteem of young adolescent girls. *The Journal for Specialists in Group Work, 33*(2), 118–137. https://doi.org/10.1080/01933920801977397

Siegel, D. J. (2010). *Mindsight: The new science of personal transformation*. Bantam Books.

Siegel, D. J. (2017). *Mind: A journey to the heart of being human*. W. W. Norton & Company.

Siegel, D. J. (2020). *The developing mind: How relationships and the brain interact to shape who we are* (3rd ed.). Guilford Press.

Siegel, D. J. (2023). *IntraConnected: Mwe (me + we) as the integration of self, identity, and belonging*. W. W. Norton & Company.

Silberg, J. L. (2022). *The child survivor: Healing developmental trauma and dissociation* (2nd ed.). Routledge.

Smith, S. D. (2012). *Sandtray play and storymaking: A hands-on approach to build academic, social, and emotional skills in mainstream and special education*. Jessica Kingsley Publishers.

Solomon, J., & George, C. (Eds.). (2011). *Disorganized attachment and caregiving*. Guilford Press.

Solomon, R. M. (2024). *EMDR therapy treatment for grief and mourning: Transforming the connection to the deceased loved one*. Oxford University Press.

Spinazzola, J., van der Kolk, B., & Ford, J. D. (2021). Developmental trauma disorder: A legacy of attachment trauma in victimized children. *Journal of Traumatic Stress, 34*(4), 711–720. https://doi.org/10.1002/jts.22697

Steele, H., & Steele, M. (Eds.) (2008). *Clinical applications of the adult attachment interview*. Guilford Press.

Steele, K. (2009). The road is made by walking: A quarter century of being with dissociation. *Voices: Journal of the American Academy of Psychotherapists, 45*(2), 6–12.

Steele, K. (2021). Beyond attachment: Understanding motivational systems in complex trauma and dissociation. In D. J. Siegel, A. Schore, & L. Cozolino (Eds.), *Interpersonal neurobiology and clinical practice* (pp. 85–112). W. W. Norton & Company.

Steele, K., Boon, S., & van der Hart, O. (2017). *Treating trauma-related dissociation: A practical, integrative approach*. W. W. Norton & Company.

Teke, E., & Avşaroğlu, S. (2021). Efficacy of eye movement desensitization and reprocessing (EMDR) therapy for children and adolescents with post-traumatic stress disorder. *Journal of School and Educational Psychology, 2*(1), 1–12. https://doi.org/10.47602/josep.v2i1.1

Tervalon, M., & Murray-García, J. (1998). Cultural humility versus cultural competence: A critical distinction in defining physician training outcomes in multicultural education. *Journal of Health Care for the Poor and Underserved, 9*(2), 117–125. https://doi.org/10.1353/hpu.2010.0233

Tsouvelas, G., Chondrokouki, M., Nikolaidis, G., & Shapiro, E. (2019a). A vicarious trauma preventive approach. The group traumatic episode protocol EMDR and workplace affect in professionals who work with child abuse and neglect. *Dialogues in Clinical Neuroscience & Mental Health, 2*(3), 130–138. https://doi.org/10.26386/obrela.v2i3.123

Tsouvelas, G., Liafou, V., Shapiro, E., Ventouratou, D., Sfyri, V., & Amann, B. (2019b, June 28–30). *Pilot study with G-TEP EMDR in women victims of intimate partner violence* [Paper presentation/Conference session]. 20th EMDR Europe Conference, Krakow, Poland.

Turner, B. A. (Ed.). (2017). *The Routledge international handbook of sandplay therapy.* Routledge.

UNHCR. (2022). *Global trends: Forced displacement in 2022.* https://unhcr.org/global-trends-report-2022

Urdaneta Melo, V., & Triana, V. (2024). EMDR integrative group treatment protocol-ongoing traumatic stress (EMDR IGTP-OTS). In R. M. Robinson & S. K. Kaptan (Eds.), *EMDR group therapy: Emerging principles and protocols for trauma and beyond* (pp. 51–64). Springer Publishing Company. https://doi.org/10.1891/9780826152954.0004

van den Berg, D. P. G., de Bont, P. A. J. M., van der Vleugel, B. M., de Roos, C., de Jongh, A., van Minnen, A., & van der Gaag, M. (2015). Prolonged exposure versus eye movement desensitization and reprocessing versus waiting list for posttraumatic stress disorder in patients with a psychotic disorder: A randomized clinical trial. *JAMA Psychiatry, 72*(3), 259–267. https://doi.org/10.1001/jamapsychiatry.2014.2637

van der Hart, O., Brown, P., & van der kolk, B. (2019). Pierre's Janet treatment of posttraumatic stress. In G. Craparo, F. Ortu, & O. van der Hart (Eds.), *Rediscovering Pierre Janet: Trauma, dissociation, and a new context for psychoanalysis* (pp. 163–177). Routledge.

van der Hart, O., Nijenhuis, E. R. S., & Steele, K. (2006). *The haunted self: Structural dissociation of the personality and treatment of chronic traumatization.* W. W. Norton & Company.

van der Kolk, B. A. (2014). *The body keeps the score: Brain, mind, and body in the healing of trauma.* Viking Penguin.

van der Kolk, B. (2021). Safety and reciprocity: Polyvagal Theory as a framework for understanding and treating developmental trauma. In S. W. Porges & D. Dana (Eds.), *Clinical applications of the Polyvagal Theory: The emergence of polyvagal-informed therapies* (pp. 27–33). W. W. Norton & Company.

van der Kolk, B. A., Spinazzola, J., Blaustein, M. E., Hopper, J. W., Hopper, E. K., & Simpson, W. B. (2007). A randomized clinical trial of eye movement desensitization and reprocessing (EMDR), fluoxetine, and pill placebo in the treatment of posttraumatic stress disorder: Treatment effects and long-term maintenance. *Journal of Clinical Psychiatry, 68*(1), 37–46. https://doi.org/10.4088/jcp.v68n0105

Vlieger, N., Tang, E., Midgley, N., Luyten, P., & Fonagy, P. (2023). *Therapeutic work for children with complex trauma: A three-track psychodynamic approach.* Routledge. https://doi.org/10.4324/9781003044918

Watkins, J. G., & Watkins, H. H. (1997). *Ego states: Theory and therapy.* W. W. Norton & Company.

Waters, F. S. (2013). Assessing and diagnosing dissociation in children: Beginning the recovery. In A.M. Gómez (Ed.), *EMDR therapy and adjunct approaches with children* (pp. 129–149). Springer.

Waters, F. S. (2016). *Healing the fractured child: Diagnosis and treatment of youth with dissociation.* Springer.

Webb, E., Lupattelli Gencarelli, B., Keaveney, G., & Morris, D. (2024). Is trauma research neglecting neurodiverse populations? A systematic review and meta-analysis of the prevalence ACEs in adults with autistic traits. *Advances in Autism, 10*(3), 104–119 https://doi.org/10.1108/AIA-07-2023-0037

Wiersma, J. K., Freedle, L. R., McRoberts, R., & Solberg, K. B. (2022). A meta-analysis of sandplay therapy treatment outcomes. *International Journal of Play Therapy, 31*(4), 197–215. https://doi.org/10.1037/pla0000180

Williams, S (2022). *Evaluating early EMDR G-TEP for NHS staff* [Unpublished doctoral dissertation University of Worcester].

Wilhelmus, B., Marissen, M. A., van den Berg, D., Driessen, A., Deen, M. L., & Slotema, K. (2023). Adding EMDR for PTSD at the onset of treatment of borderline personality disorder: A pilot study. *Journal of Behavior Therapy and Experimental Psychiatry, 79*, Article 101834. https://doi.org/10.1016/j.jbtep.2023.101834

World Health Organization. (2013). *WHO Guidelines for the management of conditions that are specifically related to stress.* World Health Organization. https://who.int/publications/i/item/9789241505406

Yosso, T. J. (2005). Whose culture has capital? A critical race theory discussion of community cultural wealth. *Race Ethnicity and Education, 8*(1), 69–91. https://doi.org/10.1080/1361332052000341006

Young, J. E., Zangwill, W. M., & Behary, W. E. (2002). Combining EMDR and schema-focused therapy: The whole may be greater than the sum of the parts. In F. Shapiro (Ed.), *EMDR as an integrative psychotherapy approach: Experts of diverse orientations explore the paradigm prism* (pp. 181–208). American Psychological Association. https://doi.org/10.1037/10512-007

Yunitri, N., Chu, H., Kang, X. L., Wiratama, B. S., Lee, T.-Y., Chang, L.-F., Liu, D., Kustanti, C. Y., Chiang, K.-J., Chen, R., Tseng, P., & Chou, K.-R. (2023). Comparative effectiveness of psychotherapies in adults with posttraumatic stress disorder: A network meta-analysis of randomised controlled trials. *Psychological Medicine, 53*(13), 6376–6388. https://doi.org/10.1017/S0033291722003737

Yunitri, N., Kao, C. C., Chu, H., Voss, J., Chiu, H. L., Liu, D., Shen, S. H., Chang, P. C., Kang, X. L., & Chou, K. R. (2020). The effectiveness of eye movement desensitization and reprocessing toward anxiety disorder: A meta-analysis of randomized controlled trials. *Journal of Psychiatric Research, 123*, 102–113. https://doi.org/10.1016/j.jpsychires.2020.01.005

Yurtsever, A., Konuk, E., Akyüz, T., Zat, Z., Tükel, F., Çetinkaya, M., Savran, C., & Shapiro, E. (2018). An eye movement desensitization and reprocessing (EMDR) group intervention for Syrian refugees with post-traumatic stress symptoms: Results of a randomized controlled trial. *Frontiers in Psychology, 9*, 493. https://doi.org/10.3389/fpsyg.2018.00493

INDEX

Note: Italicized page locators refer to figures.

AAI. *see* adult attachment interview (AAI)
abandonment, fear of, 68, 220, 298
abdicated caregiving system, therapeutic encounter and, 296
"absent network," 94
abstract items, in miniature figures collection, 393
abuse issues, 348–59
  attachment to the perpetrator, 348–55
  dysfunctional positive affect, 355–59
acceptance, healing of the wounded mind and, 19
accordion, in parenting wheel, 157, *322,* 325, *326,* 329
"accordion technique"
  expansion and constriction and, 284
  as powerful interweave, 230
ACEs. *see* adverse childhood experiences (ACEs)
acknowledgment, 31
  validation and, 45
  of your own humanity, uncertainty, and the unknown, 46
actions
  new, interweaves for, 227–28
  urges and, 52, 398
activated freeze, fright, and collapse responses, in defense cascade, 225–26
active pathways, reprocessing of attachment wounds and, 340
acts of triumph
  enhancing, closure phase and, 254
  in sand world, 53, 398
adaptive information and resources
  accessing or providing, interweaves for, 217–19
  co-existing presence of, 51, 398

adaptive information processing (AIP) model, xiv, xv, 19, 304, 305
  EMDR therapy and, 5–7
  IPNB constructs and concepts incorporated into, xv
  multiplicities of the mind addressed by, 23
  shared memory network and, 144–45
adaptive network, new, building, 75, 76
addictions, 364–69
  addiction-focused EMDR approach to, 367–69
  complexity of co-occurring symptomatology in, 364
  intense internal conflicts in, 368
  Phase 1 in treatment of, 365–66
  Phase 2 in, 366–67
  reprocessing phases in treatment of, 369
  roots of, 365
  trauma and, 364, 367, 369
  trauma-focused EMDR approach to, 367, 369
ADHD, 372, 374
adolescents
  effectiveness of sand-based therapies with, scientific support for, 4, 7
  EMDR-sandtray-based therapy with, 13–14
  group work and benefits for, 310
  mild to moderate dissociation in, 117
  older, timelines used with, 111
  online work with, 370
  self-administered eye movement with GTEP protocol and, 314
  young, working with defenses and, 100
adult attachment interview (AAI), 207, 298, 299

adults
  effectiveness of sand-based therapies with, scientific support for, 4
  EMDR-sandtray-based therapy with, 14–15
  mild to moderate dissociation in, 117
  sandplay for, 3
  self-administered eye movement with GTEP protocol and, 314
  timelines used with, 111
  working with defenses and, 100
adult self, working with, 129
adverse childhood experiences (ACEs), addiction and, 364
affect clarification, 42–43
affect dysregulation, complex trauma and, 1, 2
affective scans, 163
affective states, installing, TAPAS protocol Step 4, 98–99
affect regulation
  sand tray and space for, 77–81
  therapist's journey toward growth and, 300
affect scans, 111, 174
affect tolerance, 20, 181
  addiction treatment and, 366
  complex trauma and narrow threshold of, 106
  increased, sand world and, 77–81
  therapeutic process in EMDR-sandtray-based therapy and, 155, 159–60
  see also window of affect tolerance
afferent fibers, in autonomic nervous system, 301
aggression
  depictions of, watching for, 49
  lions as metaphors for, *101*
  victim–perpetrator dynamics and forms of, 349
  see also anger; rage

401

AIP model. *see* adaptive information processing (AIP) model
AIP system, in brain, 5–6
ambivalence in tray, recognizing, 43–44, *44*
amygdala, naming and calming of, 79
analogies
  from parenting wheel, incorporating into the tray, 157
  segmented psychoeducation and, 126, 127
  see also metaphors; symbols
ancestral legacy of caregiver, embracing, 178
ancestral resources, 240
  of adult client, representation of identities and assets, *360*
  of adult client, resource area for, *195*
anchors, sensory-based
  elements-based rituals, 135
  smell, 134
  sound, 134
  touch, 134–35
anchors and anchoring
  auditory, olfactory, and gustatory anchors, 187
  relational anchors, 240
  safe place protocol and, 88
  time orientation and, 186–87
  as touchstone for stability, empowerment, and regulation, 133–34
Angeles Tornero, M. D. L., 4
anger
  depictions of, watching for, 49
  exploring, generational interweaves and, 240–41
  see also aggression; rage
animal figures
  orientation to the body and, 136–37
  types of, 391–92
"animal helper," C-GTEP combined with extended preparation and, 319
animal metaphors, in representation of defenses, 101, *101*
animals as feelings, questions for, 84
anxiety, connecting with, through tray, 79
anxiety disorders, EMDR and effectiveness with, scientific support for, 7
anxious/preoccupied clinician-client dyads, 299
apps, online EMDR-sandtray therapy and, 371

arousal, modulating, interweaves for, 227–28
assessment (Phase 3) in EMDR therapy, 5*t*, 180–206
  decision-making markers, 181–83
  full entrance into traumagenic memory network and, 180–81
  information processing and, levels of, 189–99
  levels of distance from traumatic event and, 189
  staging: optimizing integrative capacities, 183–89
  titration continuum, 201–6
  working with parts, 200–201
assessment procedural steps
  assess validity of the positive cognition, 193, 197
  identify the emotions, 193, 197
  identify the image, 192, 196
  identify the location of the disturbance, 194, 197–98
  identify the negative cognition, 192, 196–97
  identify the positive cognition, 192–93, 197
  identify the subjective units of disturbance, 193–94, 197
  prepare for desensitization, 194, 198
assistive options, neurodiverse clients and, 375
associative channels
  modulated access to, 210
  unbounded access to, information processing and, 209
asynchrony, 46
attachment
  disrupted, in complex trauma, xv
  dynamics, nondirective sandtray strategies and, 149
  multimotivational systems and, 294
  patterns, defenses, trauma-related phobias, and, 70–72
attachment system, 145–46
  anxious children of preoccupied parents and, 145
  children and adults exposed to chronic traumatization and, 145
  defenses and, 146
  interweaves that work with, 216, 233–35, 288–90
attachment system: the clinician and the client, 297–300
  clinician's capacity for emotional regulation and, 300

coconstruction of relational safety and, 298
  multilayered nature of, 297–98
  overfocus on attachment system, 298
attachment tendencies and relational patterns, in the sand world, 398
attachment theory, 19, 22–23, 305, 350
attachment trauma, impact of, 2
attachment wounds, 337–41
  acts of omission and commission and, 337
  complex trauma and, 94
  Phase 1 in working with, 338–39
  Phase 2: preparation, 339–40
  reprocessing phases, 340–41
attunement, 25, 302
  with inner system of parts, 131
  psychoeducation and, 157
auditory anchors, 187
auditory dimensions, adding to client's sensory experience, 30. *see also* sounds
authentic self, "The Therapist in Me" tray and, 308
authority figures, 392
autism spectrum
  children on, building relational bridges and, 375
  struggles with metaphors/symbols and individuals on, 376–77
autism spectrum disorder, neurodiversity within context of, 372
autobiographical memory(ies), 207
  dissociative alterations in identity and, 271
  history collection and, 26
  identity formation and, 208
  of parent, boundaries in the sand tray and, 155
  resource trays and, 107
autonomic nervous system
  interweaves and, 224
  lack of safety and impact on, 68
  myelinated vagal system and, 21
  retrieving a safe place that exists in, 85
  role of, in therapeutic relationship, 301
  subsystems in, 21
autonomy *vs.* dependency, power, and powerlessness tendencies, 51, *51*

402   Index

avatars, 26, 40, 53, 215, 224, 268
  assigning to an affective experience, 79
  cognitive data and, 49, 50
  dissociative parts in sand tray and, 16
  dyadic resources and, 168
  dyadic work during reprocessing phases and, 179
  in family group work, 334
  flight response and, 225
  implicit access and, 17, 59, 60, 121
  intolerable affective states and, 78
  materialization of dorsal vagal system and, 22
  multiple, specific reevaluation and, 256
  needs and, 96, 98, 99
  perpetrator-imitating parts and, 273
  regulatory capacities and, 51
  safety cues and, 156
  seen and witnessed in the tray, 10
  states of safety and, 69
  in trays for clinicians, 306
  see also miniature figures collection; symbols
avoidance
  dysfunctional positive affect and, 358
  ostrich as metaphor for, 101, 101
avoidant and dismissive clinician-client dyads, 299
avoidant attachment, sandtray work and surfacing of, 22
avoidant parts, negotiations with, 278
"awesome four," in C-GTEP Phase 2, 317

"back of the head scale," 117, 216
Badenoch, B., 18, 39, 185
Bagamasbad, A., 269
behavioral schemas, exploring in EMDR-sandtray-based parenting protocol, 162
"being with"
  embracing the world and, 38
  world building and creation and, 87
bells, 30
betrayal
  attachment to perpetrator and, 348
  dysfunctional positive abuse and, 357
  grooming and, 359

biases
  cultural, racial, gender, religious, and ethnic, exploring, 360
  humility in the process and, 303
"bigger self," 129. see also "wiser and guiding self"
bilateral stimulation (BLS), 7
  accessing "wiser, older, and bigger self" and, 164
  anchoring or cueing and, 88
  beginning desensitization phase and, 194
  dyadic resources and, 168
  dyadic work during reprocessing phases and, 179
  EMDR-sandtray-based therapy with adolescents and, 13
  enhancing acts of triumph and, 254
  enhancing moments of knowing and expansion in the tray and, 140
  enhancing new adaptive material with, 249
  fulfilling unmet needs and, 171, 172
  future self and, 91
  future template in full session of GPEP, 330
  grief work and, 344, 345, 346
  group traumatic episode protocol and use of, 313–14, 315
  information processing in the tray and, 210–11
  installing affective states and, 98
  interweaves providing adaptive information and, 218, 219
  interweaves that modulate arousal and, 227, 228
  interweaves that work with defenses and, 238
  interweaves working with divergent states and, 223
  light-up wands for, 30
  linking positive cognition with sand world and, 249
  microprocessing and, 203
  modulated access to associative channels and, 210
  movement, sandtray-inner family, and, 132, 133
  neurodiverse clients and, 374, 375
  online EMDR-sandtray therapy and, 371
  parent's new insights and realizations and, 158

part carrying unintegrated fight-or-flight response and, 281, 282, 283
  pendulation and, 82, 83–84
  polarization and internal conflict and use of, 126
  in procedural steps for desensitization phase, 246, 247
  RDI protocol and, 91
  reparative and restorative interweaves and, 177
  resource pendulation and, 206
  resources, capacities, and realizations installed with, 53–54
  resourcing parts and, 133
  sandtray work and, 28
  Socratic method and, 220
  "this was me then, and this is me now" interweave and, 222
  "this was me then, and this is me now" pendulation protocol and, 204, 205
  video microanalysis and, 151
  wiser/guiding selves in parenting wheel and, 324
  worry world and, 109
bilateral stimulation (BLS), introducing EMDR therapy and
  eye movements, 73, 73
  light bar, 74, 74
  tactile stimulation, brushes used with, 74, 74
  tactile stimulation, movement-based, 74
  tactile stimulation, self-administered, 74
binary and rigid states
  formation of, 289–90
  interweaves that work with, 222–23
  trauma and, 21
binding and differentiating, 139–40
binoculars, 217, 267
  sense of distance created with, 232
  visual contact with trauma tray and, 187
biological states, dyadic and shared, 300–303
bipersonal field
  dance of autonomic states and, 301
  in therapeutic encounter, 300
bipolar disorder, EMDR and effectiveness with, scientific support for, 7
Biven, L., 35, 146
blocked processing, 212

Index   **403**

BLS. *see* bilateral stimulation (BLS)

body
identifying location of disturbance in, 194, 197–98
orientation to, 136–39
sensorimotor system and, interweaves that work with, 216, 224, 281–83

body-based data, nondirective sandtray strategies and, 149

body language, assessment of dissociation and, 116

body-mind connection, EMDR-sandtray work and, 23

body scan (Phase 6) in EMDR therapy, 5*t*, 202, 250–52, 291
going from object to self in, 251–52
inviting movement in, 252
release of embodied trauma and somatic holding patterns and, 18
tracking sensations in, 252

body sensations
psychoeducation about, 287
wiser/guiding selves in parenting wheel and, 323
see also emotions; movement

borderline personality disorder, EMDR and effectiveness with, scientific support for, 7

"bothering spot," in C-GTEP Phase 2, 317

bottles and jars, need-fulfillment, 235, *235*

bottom-up information processing, EMDR-sandtray-based therapy and, 9

boundaries, 277
group traumatic episode protocol and, 313
online EMDR-sandtray therapy and, 371–72
in parenting wheel, *322*, 327–28, *329*
in resource trays, 185–86
types of, in miniature figures collection, 394
world creation and, 36, 37
see also containers; coverings; dividers; doors; fences; rocks

Bowlby, J., 239, 341

brain
AIP system in, 5–6
divided, recognizing, 20
right and left hemispheres of, 20, 38, 157
symbol-based, 35

breathing patterns, 47, 49, 58

bridges, 393
building, with neurodiverse clients, 375
parenting wheel and, *326*
in sand world of woman with autoimmune disease, 346, *346*
in the tray, parental awareness of son's needs and, 167

brushes
paint or makeup, 211
for sand, 30
tactile BLS/DAS and use of, 74, *74*, 211

brushing hands, 211

bugs phobia, adolescent on the autism spectrum and, 376–77

bullying, neurodivergent individuals and, 372

butterfly hugs, 74, 314, 326, 329, 371

buzzers, self-administered eye movement with GTEP protocol and, 314

California Evidence-Based Clearinghouse for Child Welfare, EMDR for PTSD treatment recommendation, 7

calmness, clients unable to tolerate states of, 86

calm-safe or "okay" place, physicalization of, 10. *see also* safe and healing place

Capella, C., 4

care, innate motivational system and, 294

caregivers
attachment wound reprocessing and, 341
complex duality embodied in, 146–47
full session of GPEP, sand tray representing, *330*
GPEP combined with parenting wheel and inclusion of, 321–22, 323, 324, 325, 326, 327, 328
group EMDR-sandtray-based therapy for, 309, 311, 320–21
interweaves for working with, 235–36
online EMDR-sandtray therapy and, 371
potential interweaves for, 177–78
as powerful bioemotional regulators and healing agents, 147

reparative and restorative interweaves with, 177–78
reprocessing session and presence of, 183–84
working individually with, 153–54
see also children; families; parents; parents and children, systemic work with

caregivers, target identification and reprocessing phases with, 172–76
connect to the moment of activation, 173–74
reflective communication for consolidation, 174–76
trace back to the origin of the story, 174

caregiver's inner representations, working with, 154–68
accessing caregiver's inner representational world, 160–68
creating plan and road map for, 154
dyadic work and repair, 155
emotion regulation, affect tolerance, and mentalization, 155, 159–60
memory processing and integration, 155
psychoeducation, 155, 157–58
safety, 155–56

caregiving, multimotivational systems and, 294

caregiving system, 146–47

cerebral blood flow (CBF), 20

C-GTEP. *see* Children Group Traumatic Episode Protocol (C-GTEP)

chair technique, 290

character-driven story, implicit access and first level of distance and, 189–91

child-centered play therapy, 373

child–parent affective dialogue, early disruption in, dissociation and, 113–14

child parts, working with inner system of, in the sand, 272–73

children
cognitions in the tray and, 199
defense and self-protective system of, 172
EMDR-sandtray-based therapy with, 11–13, *12*
EMDR therapy and effectiveness with, scientific support for, 7

404   Index

generational interweaves and, cautionary note, 243
gifted, 376
group work and benefits for, 310
implicit, nondirective information processing and, 268–70
implicit access and first level of distance for, 59
information processing in the tray and, 210
inviting the guiding and wiser self with, 129
mild to moderate dissociation in, 117
neurodivergent, literature review on, 373
online work with, 370
sand-based therapies and effectiveness with, scientific support for, 4
self-administered eye movement with GTEP protocol and, 314
working with defenses and, 100
younger, deeper trays for, 27
see also caregivers; dyadic resources with child and parent, in preparation phase; families; group protocol for children (GPC); parents; parents and children, systemic work with
Children Group Traumatic Episode Protocol (C-GTEP), 316–20
combined with extended preparation, 319–20
goal of, 316
group size limits in, 320
Phase 1: history collection and evaluation steps, 316–17
Phase 2: preparation phase, 317–18
sand world from a complete session, *318*
termination of session in, 317–18
chimes, 30
clarifications, new information and, 42. *see also* curiosity
cleaning the tray, 255
clients
most challenging and easy-to-work-with, 307–8
seen and witnessed in the tray, 10
see also attachment system: the clinician and the client

clinicians
abuse issues and courageousness of, 348
GTEP protocols training for, 312
invited into the tray, crocodile and fly example, 79–81, *80*
privileges of, acknowledging, 360, *360*
as sandtray witnesses, 292
therapeutic capacities embodied in, 292
with unresolved attachment wounds, 293
see also attachment system: the clinician and the client; therapeutic home: learning about the clinician's mind
clinicians, sandtray strategies and exercises for, 305–8
defenses, 306–7
meeting the therapist in you, 308
mindfulness, 305–6
my most challenging and easy-to-work-with clients, 307–8
nondirective and implicit trays, 306
your companions, 306
your refuge, 306
closeness, inner system of parts and, 131
closure at end of session, 33, 54–57
container exercise and, 55–56
dismantling the tray and, 54–55
fabric coverings for tray and, 56–57
closure (Phase 7) in EMDR therapy, 5t, 252–55
allow enough time for dismantling and cleaning up (Step 6), 255
announce that it is time to end the session (Step 1), 253
bring parts of the self to safety and containment (Step 4), 255
close the tray (Step 2), 253–54
dismantle the tray (Step 5), 255
enhance acts of triumph (Step 3), 254
stability and safety of client and, 252
cloth coverings, for miniature figures collection, 29
clothing, in miniature figures collection, 394
cognitions in the tray, assessment phase and, 199

cognitive–behavioral frameworks, 4
cognitive behavioral therapy, 304
cognitive data, in exploration of the sand world, 48, 398
cognitive level of information processing, addressing in the tray, 214
cognitive needs, 396
cognitive processing therapy, scientific support for effectiveness of, 7
cognitive schemas, exploring in EMDR-sandtray-based parenting protocol, 162
cognitive system, interweaves that work with, 216, 217
coherence, 292
cohomeostatic capacities, within caregiver–child dynamic, 329
collaboration/cooperation, multimotivational systems and, 294
collapse, areas of, in the tray, 50, 398
colonization histories, generational interweaves and, 242
color palette strips, for identifying level of disturbance associated with a memory, 194
color(s)
emotional experience, sand tray, and, 10
emotion tolerance protocol with pendulation and, questions for, 83
green, yellow, and red trays, exploration of trauma memories and, 141–42
multiple, in GTEP work tray, 314
of sand, 29, 279
segmented psychoeducation and, 126–27
combat trauma, sandtray therapy and effectiveness with, 4
combination group EMDR treatment, for clients across the lifespan, 310
communication
learning to be open to layers of, xiii
with neurodiverse clients, 376
see also interpersonal communication; intrapersonal communication; nonverbal communication; reflective communication

Index **405**

companions, 329
  adult client's team of, *92*
  caregivers as, in reprocessing
    session, 183–84
  in C-GTEP Phase 2, 317
  for clinicians, creating team
    of, 306
  GPEP protocol and, *328,*
    328–29
  repair in reprocessing sessions
    and, 185
  therapists as, in EMDR-
    sandtray-based therapy,
    8, 18
  types of, 92
  see also defenders; help-
    ers; protectors; team of
    companions
companionship, EMDR-based
  groups and, 320
compartmentalization
  educating client about, 126
  lack of realization and level
    of, 136
  selection of interweaves and,
    216
compartmentalized identities,
  children presenting with,
  cautionary note, 268
compassion, 17, 37, 106, 167,
  168, 285
  children and concept of, 103
  perpetrator-imitating parts
    and, 274–75
  "The Therapist in Me" tray
    and, 308
"compassion soup," 103
complex trauma, 48, 87
  attachment system of both
    client and clinician and,
    297
  caregiving deficiencies and,
    233–34
  disrupted attachment in, xv
  extended miniature inventory
    in treatment of, 29
  grief and, 341
  increased affect tolerance and
    healing in, 77
  invisible, 2
  menus and, 169
  multifaceted nature of, 1
  narrow threshold of affect tol-
    erance and, 106
  need for more inclusive defi-
    nition of, 2
  neuroception of danger and,
    55, 112, 134, 156
  nonlinear nature of, 8
  phase-oriented, circular
    approach to, 26

preparation phase and work-
    ing with, 67
  significant attachment wounds
    and, 94
  unfulfilled, missed develop-
    mental milestones and, 2
  see also developmental
    trauma; trauma
conflict resolution, nondirective
  sandtray strategies and,
  148–49
conflict(s), 46
  areas of relational dynamics
    and, in the tray, 50
  implicit portal and, 120
  inner, polarizations and, 123–
    26, *125*
  internal, 48
  team of companions and, 93
  in tray, recognizing, 43–44, *44*
  see also polarities and
    polarizations
container exercise
  for clients of all ages, 55–56
  GTEP work tray and, 316
  meeting the therapist in you
    and, 308
containers, 141, 394
  creating before hand, 125
  for disturbing/activating mate-
    rial emerging in the sand
    world, *187*
  inside sandtrays, 28
  for miniature figures collec-
    tion, 29
containment and refuge
  bringing parts of the self to, in
    closure phase, 255
  sandtray-inner family and, 127
  sand tray work and, 100
contingency, 292
control, lion or dragon as metaphors for, 101, *101*
coregulation
  within caregiver–child
    dynamic, 329
  in the tray, 81
corrective network, psychoeducation and building of, 75–77
Corrigan, F. M., 224
Courtois, C. A., 1
coverings, 116, 277
  in C-GTEP Phase 2, 317
  fabric, 56–57
  interweaves that modulate
    emotions and, 231, 233
  in trauma tray, *187,* 187–88, *188*
COVID-19 pandemic
  C-GTEP developed during, 316
  mental health crisis in wake
    of, 309

telehealth used during and
    after, 369
  Cozolino, L., 300
  craving reduction protocol,
    reprocessing "addiction
    memory" and, 368
  crocodile and fly world, clinician
    invited into the tray in, 79
  cuing, safe place protocol and, 88
  cultural humility, 347, 360
  culturally affirming resources,
    154
  cultural sensitivity, intersection-
    ality and, 24
  cultural traditions, exploring and
    identifying, 362
  culture
    diversity, antioppressive prac-
      tices, and, 359–61, *360*
    grief and loss issues and,
      347–48
    intersectionality of identities
      and, 363–64
    reprocessing phases and influ-
      ence of, 362–63
  Cundy, L., 299
  curiosity, 40, 42, 87
    adaptive network building
      and, 75
    assessment of dissociation
      and, 116
    explicit portal and, 122
    genuine, healing of the
      wounded mind and, 19
    inviting, in wondering about
      needs, 97
    "parts as storytellers" and, 136
    polarizations and inner con-
      flict and, 123–24
    showing, 45
    working individually with the
      caregiver and, 153
    world creation and, 37

  Dalenberg, C. J., 269
  dancing, bilateral, present aware-
    ness and, 238
  danger
    check inside invitation and, 239
    developmental trauma and
      challenges in assessing, 68
    fight response and, 224
    trauma and faulty neurocep-
      tion of, 55, 112, 134, 156
  DAS. *see* dual attention stimuli
    (DAS)
  data collection
    cognitive data, 48
    emotional data, 48–49
    as primary goal, in Phase 1, 49
    sensorimotor data, 49

daydreaming, 32
decision-making, nondirective
    sandtray strategies and,
    148–49
decision-making markers
    blocked information process-
        ing and use of, 280
    readiness for assessment and
        processing phases and,
        181–83
deconstruction of created world,
    ephemeral and intangible
    dimensions of memory
    and, 55
defenders, developing relation-
    ship with, 103. *see also* com-
    panions; helpers; protectors
defense cascade, 224–26
    activated freeze, fright, and
        collapse responses, 225–26
    fight response, 224
    flight response, 224–25
defenses, 208, 216
    attachment patterns, trauma-re-
        lated phobias and, 70–72
    blocked access of dissociative
        parts and, 122
    clinician, reflecting on, 306–7
    common, animal metaphors
        for, 101, *101*
    decision-making markers and,
        182
    directive approach to working
        with, 100–104
    interweaves that work with,
        237–38
    looping and, 212
    multimotivational systems
        and, 294
    nondirective approach to
        working with, 100, 104–5
    self-protection and, 51, 398
    self-protective system and,
        189
defense system, overactive,
    therapeutic encounter and,
    296–97
defensive strategies, trauma-re-
    lated, 15
denied feelings in the tray,
    reflecting on and wonder-
    ing about, 288
depersonalization, 67, 112, 226
depression, EMDR and effective-
    ness with, scientific support
    for, 7
derealization, 67, 112
desensitization (Phase 4) in
    EMDR therapy, 5*t*, 207–47
    cocreation of self-narratives
        and meanings in, 208

complexity of, 207
deepening of inner journey
    and, 208–9
EMDR interweave and, 212–45
fluid processing *vs.* rigid pro-
    cessing and, 207
information processing and
    the titration continuum,
    209–10
information processing in the
    tray, 210–12
preparing for, 194, 198
desensitization (Phase 4) in
    EMDR therapy, general pro-
    cedural steps of, 246–47
    breath and notice (Step 1),
        246
    check the SUD (Step 5), 247
    end of a channel (Step 3),
        246–47
    physicalize (Step 2), 246
    return to target (Step 4), 247
"detective work," in C-GTEP
    Phase 2, 317
developmental stages
    of client, levels of directive-
        ness and, 64
    missed, making up for in
        sandplay, 3
developmental trauma
    attachment disruptions and,
        233
    challenges with safety and
        danger assessments and,
        68
    grief and, 341
    preparation phase and work-
        ing with, 67
    self-betrayal and, 71
    team of companions and cli-
        ents with, 92–93
    see also complex trauma;
        trauma
*Diagnostic and Statistical Manual
    of Mental Disorders*, Fifth
    Edition, trauma perspective
    in, 1–2
DID. *see* dissociative identity
    disorder (DID)
directive access of targets, 106–11
    resource trays, 106–7
    timelines, *109*, 109–11
    tracing and affect scan, 111
    worry world, 107–9, *108*
directive approach to working
    with defenses, 100–104
    closure, 104
    exploration of the system, 103
    invitation to uncover the
        self-protective system, 102
    negotiation, 103–4

psychoeducation and physical-
    ization, options for, 100–101,
    101
recognition and gratitude, 103
directiveness, switching between
    levels of, 63–64
directive sandtray strategies,
    152–53
    "a story about us," 152
    closure, 152–53
directive tactics, in EMDR-
    sandtray-based therapy, 11,
    13, 63, 64
discrete behavioral states theory
    (Putnam), 16
dismissiveness, sandtray work
    and surfacing of, 22
dismissive state of mind, AAI
    characterization of, 299
disorganized and unresolved cli-
    nician-client dyads, 299
disorganized attachment
    development of dissociative
        processes and, 113–14
    dissociative symptomatology
        and, 67–68
    macro- and microruptures in, 2
    sandtray work and surfacing
        of, 22–23
displaced populations, global,
    treatment delivery chal-
    lenges and, 309
dissociation
    addiction and, 369
    assessment of, multidimen-
        sional approach to, 112,
        113–14
    attachment wounds and, 94
    bird metaphors for, 101
    complex trauma and, 1, 2
    core dynamics of, 352
    depathologizing approach to,
        16–17, 114, 115, 140
    educating client about, 126
    EMDR-sandtray-based therapy
        and, 16–17, 114–17
    fantasy proneness and, 269
    mild to moderate, working
        with, 117–18
    moderate, "observant charac-
        ters" and, 112–13
    multidimensional assessment
        of, 112, 113–14
    peritraumatic, emergence
        of, 113
    preparation phase and, 67–68,
        72
    severe: absence of a unified
        sense of self in, 118–19
    structural, multiple levels
        of, 23

Index   407

dissociation (*continued*)
  utilizing tray in assessment and exploration of, *115,* 115–17
  working with parents who experience, 173
dissociation theory, 19
dissociative identity disorder (DID), 23
dissociative matrix, 215, 263, 357
dissociative processes, sandtray work and, 32
dissociative table technique, adapted for EMDR therapy, 126
distance, 100
  binoculars and sense of, 232
  decreasing level of, TAPAS protocol Step 5, 99
  explicit access and second level of, *61,* 61–62
  explicit access and second level of, story about worry or difficulty, 194–95
  explicit access and third level of, 62–63
  implicit access and first level of, 59–60, *60*
  implicit access and first level of: a character-driven story, 189–91
  inner system of parts and, 131
  levels of, in EMDR-sandtray work, 32–33
  maintaining, sandtray therapy and, 40
  reprocessing trauma memories and, 267
  in setting up the landscape, 277
  TAPAS protocol and levels of, 95, 96, 98
  titration continuum and, 58
  in trauma tray, 187, *188*
  in world building and creation, 87
distancing *vs.* approach, 51
divergent states, interweaves working with, 222–23
diversity, culture, antioppressive practices, and, 359–61, *360*
divided brain, recognizing, 20
dividers, 277, 323, 393
  adding to C-GTEP sand tray, 317, *318*
  in GTEP work tray, 313, *313*
  in the sand: binding and differentiating and, 139
divisions in the personality, 67
dolls, nesting, 78

doors, 277
  in sand world, of woman with autoimmune disease, 346, *346*
dorsal vagal system
  immobility, EMDR-sandtray and, 33
  materialization of, in sandtray worlds, 22
DPA. *see* dysfunctional positive affect (DPA)
dresser
  in parenting wheel, *322,* 325–26, 329
  in the tray, 157
droppers/dropper bottles, 78, 286
  for checking the SUD, 247
  for identifying level of disturbance associated with a memory, 194
  for identifying positive cognition's validity, 248
  interweaves that modulate emotions and, 231
drumming, 74, 326, 329
  online EMDR-sandtray therapy and, 371
  self-administered eye movement with GTEP protocol and, 314
DSM-5. *see Diagnostic and Statistical Manual of Mental Disorders,* Fifth Edition (DSM-5)
dual attention
  as fundamental in trauma processing, 114
  restoring, interweaves for, 238–40
dual attention stimuli (DAS), 7
  accessing "wiser, older, and bigger self" and, 164
  anchoring or cuing and, 88
  beginning desensitization phase and, 194
  dyadic resources and, 168
  dyadic work during reprocessing phases and, 179
  EMDR-sandtray-based therapy with adolescents and, 13
  enhancing acts of triumph and, 254
  enhancing moments of knowing and expansion in the tray and, 140
  enhancing new adaptive material with, 249
  fulfilling unmet needs and, 171, 172
  future self and, 91
  future template in full session of GPEP and, 330
  grief work and, 344, 345, 346

group traumatic episode protocol and use of, 313–14, 315
  information processing in the tray and, 210–11
  installing affective states and, 98
  interweaves providing adaptive information and, 218, 219
  interweaves that modulate arousal and, 227, 228
  interweaves that work with defenses and, 238
  interweaves working with divergent states and, 223
  light-up wands for, 30
  linking positive cognition with sand world and, 249
  microprocessing and, 203
  modulated access to associative channels and, 210
  movement, sandtray-inner family, and, 132, 133
  neurodiverse clients and, 374, 375
  online EMDR-sandtray therapy and, 371
  parent's new insights and realizations and, 158
  part carrying unintegrated fight-or-flight response and, 281, 282, 283
  pendulation and, 82, 83–84
  polarization and internal conflict and use of, 126
  in procedural steps for desensitization phase, 246, 247
  RDI protocol and, 91
  reparative and restorative interweaves and, 177
  resource pendulation and, 206
  resources, capacities, and realizations installed with, 53–54
  resourcing parts and, 133
  sandtray work and, 28
  Socratic method and, 220
  "this was me then, and this is me now" interweave and, 222
  "this was me then, and this is me now" pendulation protocol and, 204, 205
  video microanalysis and, 151
  wiser/guiding selves in parenting wheel and, 324
  worry world and, 109
dual attention stimuli (DAS), introducing EMDR therapy and, 73–74
  eye movements, 73, *73*
  light bar, 74, *74*

408   Index

tactile stimulation, brushes used with, 74, *74*
tactile stimulation, movement-based, 74
tactile stimulation, self-administered, 74
dyadic and shared biological states
  attuned clinician and, 301–2
  clinician's assets and resources, acknowledging, 302–3
  clinician's personal ideology and belief system and, 300–301
  Polyvagal Theory and, 301
  same defense systems used by clients and clinicians, 302
dyadic regulating system, flow of adaptive information processing and, 292
dyadic resources with child and parent, in preparation phase, 168–72
  defense and self-protective system of parents and children, 172
  guessing and meeting unmet needs, 169–72, *171*
  menus and, 169
  sacred space in sandtray work, 168
dyadic work and repair, therapeutic process in EMDR-sandtray-based therapy and, 155
dysfunctional positive affect (DPA), 355–59
  addictions and, 367, 368
  definition of, 355
  sexual abuse and, 355–59

educational interweaves, 228
efferent fibers, in autonomic nervous system, 301
ego states, 121–22, 305
ego states therapy
  multiplicity of the mind and, 23
  questions from, connection to inner system and, 123
Elbert, T., 225, 226
element-based rituals, 135
EM. *see* eye movement (EM)
embodiment
  healing after trauma and, 250
  somatic intelligence and, 162
embracing the world: "being with" and "sitting with," in EMDR-sandtray-based therapy, 33, 38

EMDR and Adjunct Approaches with Children: Complex Trauma, Attachment, and Dissociation (Gómez), 56
EMDR interweaves. *see* interweaves
EMDR-sandtray-based group work with families, xvi, 330–36
  adapting, 331
  case example, 335–36
  eight phases of EMDR treatment and use of, 332
  increasing relational safety in, 331–32
  nondirective worlds and, 333
  processing with families, 334–35
  single tray cocreated during a family session, *332*
  treatment goal in, 330–31
EMDR-sandtray-based parenting protocol
  access additional resources (Step 5), 165–68
  access and physicalize the "wiser, older, and bigger self" (Step 4), 163–65, *166*
  accessing caregiver's inner representational world with, 160–68
  closure (Step 6), 168
  create space in the tray (Step 1), 160
  explore cognitive, emotional, behavioral, and somatic schemas and temporal orientation (Step 3), 162–63
  physicalize internal representation of the self and of the child (Step 2), 160–62, *161*
EMDR-sandtray-based therapy
  with adolescents, 13–14
  with adults, 14–15
  aligning research efforts with observed clinical practice in, 378
  with children, 11–13, *12*
  client as storyteller in, 8
  continuum of directive-nondirective tactics used in, 11
  dissociation and, 16–17, 114–17
  EMDR phases and unique uses for sandtray and figures in, 10–11
  engagement of multiple levels of information processing in, 9–10
  explaining, for children and young adolescents, 72–73

explaining for older adolescents and adults, 73
explicit access, 61–64
healing the parent–child bond with, 143
implicit access and first level of distance, 59–60
multimodal approach to, xv, 18–19
physicalization invited into the tray in, 10
portals into the mind in, 58–64
restoration of caregiver–child relationship in, 147
roots and origins of, xiv–xv
therapist as active companion in, 8
transformative principles of, honoring, 377–78
transtheoretical and multimodal use of, 305
tray work as pathway to the psyche and unconscious in, 8
union, enrichment, and honoring of two models in, 8
utilization of AIP model in, 8
vertical and horizontal integration in, 20
see also EMDR-sandtray-based group work with families; group EMDR-sandtray-based therapy; special populations and considerations, in EMDR-sandtray-based therapy
EMDR-sandtray-based therapy, procedural steps and protocol, 33–58
  closure, 33, 54–57
  embracing the world: being with and sitting with, 33, 38
  introduction and invitation, 33–36
  note-taking and case conceptualization, 33, 57–58
  resource identification, 33, 53–54
  world creation, 33, 36–38
  world exploration, 33, 39–48
EMDR-sandtray session summary, 399–400
EMDR-sandtray work, levels of distance and levels of reprocessing in, 32–33
EMDR Systems Model, categories of interweaves in, 213
EMDR therapy
  adaptive information processing system (AIP) model and, 5–7

Index   **409**

EMDR therapy (*continued*)
bilateral stimulation or dual attention stimuli in, 7
clinician training in, 304
comprehensive support for, xv
development of, 5
distinction between group traumatic episode protocol and, 311
eight phases of treatment in organization of, 5*t*, 7, 19
goal of, 32
integrating sandplay therapy with, 3, 4
multiple delivery formats for, xvi
scientific support for, 7–8
significant therapeutic benefits of, 8
transformative nature of, xiv–xv
as a unifying theory and model, 18
union of sandtray therapy and, lack of research on, 8
see also EMDR-sandtray-based therapy
emotional data, in exploration of the sand world, 48–49, 398
emotional field of awareness, enriching, 89–90
emotional figures, 391
emotional level of information processing, addressing in the tray, 214
emotional needs, 397
emotional safety domain, 69
emotional schemas, exploring in EMDR-sandtray-based parenting protocol, 162
emotional shifts, noticing without interpretation, 43
emotional system, interweaves that work with, 216, 231–33, 285–87
emotion regulation, therapeutic process in EMDR-sandtray-based therapy and, 155, 159–60
emotions
attachment injuries and, 339, 340
identifying, 193, 197
inviting, interweaves for, 233, 287–88
locating in the body, 88
modulating, interweaves for, 231–33
world building and creation and, 87–88

see also feelings
emotion tolerance protocols, pendulation and, 81–84
empathy, 168
empowerment, 7
empowering metaperceptions, 329
intersectionality of identities and, 363
see also group parenting empowerment protocol (GPEP)
engagement, healing of the wounded mind and, 19
enmeshment, adults with attachment preoccupation and, 299
expansion and constriction, clients with complex trauma and, 284–85
explicit access, 61–64
level of directiveness and, 63–64
to perpetrator loyalty, 354–55
second level of distance and, *61*, 61–62
second level of distance and: a story about a worry or difficulty, 194–95
third level of distance and, 62–63
third level of information processing and: a story about the actual traumatic event, 198–99
explicit information processing, setting up the landscape and, 276–80
explicit memories, sandtray work and, 17
explicit memory networks, frozen in time, traumagenic material and, 3
explicit mind
sandtray work as vehicle for, 4
symbols and, 70
explicit portal or road
into accessing the inner system, 121–22
into defensive systems, 100–101
into memory networks, 264
extended group treatment, 310
external safety domain, 69
eye movement (EM)
BLS/DAS forms and, introducing EMDR therapy, 73, *73*, 74, *74*
self-administered, group traumatic episode protocol and, 314

fabric coverings, 56–57
facial expressions, 301
assessment of dissociation and, 116
family group work and, 334
modulating, 42
viscera linked to, 300
families
coconstruction of family "trees" and, 333
EMDR-sandtray-based group work with, xvi, 309, 311, 330–36
see also caregivers; children; parents; parents and children, systemic work with
fanometer, 117
fantasy figures, 392
fantasy proneness, dissociation and, 269
fear
innate motivational system and, 294
love and, 223
"feeling carnivals," 78
"feeling finder" or "feeling detector," 194, 198, 251
"feeling guests," 78
"feeling parties," 78, 319
feelings
emotion tolerance protocol with pendulation and, questions for, 84
taming by naming, 79
see also emotions
fences, 277, 323, 393
adding to C-GTEP sand tray, 317
in family group work trays, 331, 332
in GTEP work tray, 313, *313*
in sand world for inner system of parts, 131, *131*
"fertile void," in gestalt therapy, 124
fidgeting, 224
fight-or-flight responses, 49
sympathetic nervous system and, 21
unintegrated, complex internal systems and, 281–83
fight response, in defense cascade, 224
first responders, GTEP protocol effectively administered to, 311
Fisher, J., 224
flag and faint response, 226
flexibility, 34, 72
flight response, in defense cascade, 224–25

410   Index

Floor Games (Wells), 2
fluid processing, rigid processing *vs.,* 207
Fonagy, P., 41, 268, 269, 293
food and drink, in miniature figures collection, 393
Ford, J. D., 1
four elements
  GTEP work tray and use of, 314, 316
  self-regulation and, 329
fragmentation, absence of a unified sense of self and, 118–19
Fraser, G. A., 126
"free and protected space," 3
Fried, K., 371
frontal neocortex, 20
furniture, in miniature figures collection, 392
future template, 90–91, 259–62, *262*
  bringing challenges into the tray (Step 4), 261–62
  GPEP protocol and, 329, 330, *330*
  identity themes and, 363
  install the positive cognition (Step 3), 261
  invite client to connect to a future challenge (Step 1), 260
  invite client to create a future world (Step 2), 260–61, *262*
  mastery, empowerment, and personal agency in, 262
  as vital prong in EMDR treatment, 260

gems, in GTEP work tray, 314, 315
gender-affirmative and gender-fluid figures, 394
gender identity, 360, 361
general reevaluation, 255–56
general treatment authorization, 57
generational healing, caretaker's profound journey of, 177–78
generational trauma. *see* intergenerational trauma
generational wounds
  children's symptoms and, 320
  interweaves that work with, 240–44, *244*
genocide histories, generational interweaves and, 242
genograms
  generational wounds underneath addictions and, 366

in shared family trays, 333
gestalt theory, 305
gestalt therapy, 4, 20–21
  chair technique in, 290
  polarities concept and "fertile void" in, 124
gestures, 47, 49
"get-together," preparing tray for, 128
gifted children, EMDR-sandtray-based therapy for, 376
giftedness, 372
Gilson, G., 213
glitter, adding to sand, 29
goals, physicalizing, 65–66
Gómez, A. M., 101, 312, 316, 317, 321
"good thoughts," in C-GTEP Phase 2, 317
Google search/scan
  GPEP protocol and, 329
  GTEP and use of, 315
gorilla beats, self-administered eye movement with GTEP protocol and, 314
GPEP. *see* group parenting empowerment protocol (GPEP)
grains, adding to sand, 29
Grant, R. J., 372, 374, 375, 377
gratitude, 132, 167
  dismantling the tray and, 55
  recognition and, 103
Greenwald, R., 92
grief and loss issues, 341–48
  attachment system and, 341–42
  attachment wounds and, 94
  autoimmune disease (Case 3), 346, *346*
  brother's death (Case 2), 345
  culture and, 347–48
  father's death (Case 1), 344–45
  implicit information processing and, 347
  multifaceted nature of grief, 341, 345
  reprocessing phases and, 342–44
  in sand world, 52, 398
  scenes of, in the sand world, 52, *52*, 342
  treatment goal with, 341
grooming process in sexual abuse, dysfunctional positive affect and, 355, 356, 359
grounding and groundedness
  grounding ritual, 134
  increasing engagement and relational presence with, 239

promotion of, EMDR-sandtray work and, 112
sandtray-inner family work and, 128
group EMDR-sandtray-based therapy, 309–36
  for caregivers, 309, 311, 320–21
  C-GTEP combined with extended preparation, 319–20
  Children Group Traumatic Episode Protocol, 316–18
  delivery of, organizational formats for, 310
  with families, 309, 311, 330–36
  group parenting empowerment protocol and the parenting wheel, 321–30, *322*
  group traumatic episode protocol in the tray, 311–16
  multiple studies supporting effectiveness of, 310–11
  offering, benefits of, 309–10
  protocols for, 310–11
  various forms of, 309
group parenting empowerment protocol (GPEP)
  adapting, expanding access to relational resources and, 331
  approach used with, 321
group parenting empowerment protocol and parenting wheel
  GPEP sessions: steps in, 328–30
  GPEP Step 2: relational resources, *328*
  GTEP and RDI protocols and, 321
  inclusion of caregivers with, 321–22
  Phase 1, 322–28
  symbolic richness with GPEP protocol, 330
  tray as mirror with, 321
group protocol for children (GPC), 310
group release, generational interweaves and, 242
group traumatic episode protocol (GTEP), 310
  BLS/DAS forms used with, 313–14
  clients and appropriateness levels for, 312
  clinician training and, 312
  delivering in the tray, 312–16
  development and basis of, 311
  distinction between conventional EMDR therapy and, 311
  intake meeting and screening, 313

Index   **411**

group traumatic episode protocol (GTEP) (*continued*)
preparation for, 313–14
readiness for EMDR reprocessing and, 312
rules and boundaries, 313
sandtray version of the GTEP work tray, *313*
size of group and, 312
as stand-alone or more comprehensive treatment, 311
state change procedure, 312
therapeutic contract and, 312
worksheet for, 313
GTEP worktray, steps in, 314–16
accessing beginning of the traumatic episode (Step 2), 314
accessing traumatic episode (Step 5), 315
bring group back to homeostasis (Step 7), 316
bring up entire episode and rate distress and disturbance level (Step 6), 315
follow-up (Step 8), 316
guide members to a memory associated with positive affect (Step 3), 314
identify/represent positive metaperceptions (Step 4), 315
installation of positive cognition, 316
invite group members to practice the four elements (Step 1), 314
"guiding self"
assessing readiness and, 266
hostile and aggressive parts and, 276
inviting, sandtray-inner family and, 129
see also "wiser and guiding self"
gustatory anchors, 187

healing
depth of therapeutic work needed for, 18
EMDR-sandtray therapy and movement toward, 9
of parent–child bond, 143
play and, 112
of the wounded mind, IPNB and, 19–20
healing ceremonies in the tray, caregivers and, 178
healing place. *see* safe and healing place; safe place protocol, sandtray strategies and

heat and activation, noticing areas of, 49, *49*, 398
helpers
in resource tray, modulating emotions and, 232
in the tray, noticing, 51
see also companions; defenders; protectors; team of companions
here-and-now consciousness, assessing, 117
Herman, J. L., 1
hidden trauma, 2
high-intensity mentalization interventions, 41, 42
highly activated competition and ranking system, therapeutic encounter and, 295–96
historical trauma, 360, *360,* 363
history and treatment planning (Phase 1), in EMDR-sandtray therapy, 5*t*
aim of, 48
overview of, 25–26
homeostasis, 142, 340
closure and, 54, 252
defenses, self-protective system, and, 189
reestablishing, five safety domains and, 69
unmyelinated vagal pathway and, 21
visceral efferent (motor) pathways and, 301
Homeyer, L. E., 3, 26, 33, 40, 303
hope, future self and, 90
horizontal integration, 20, 214
horror figures, 392
hostile and aggressive parts, 276, *277*
house analogy, for memory system harboring traumatic event, 180
houses and buildings figures, 392
human figures, 391
humanitarian workers, GTEP protocol effectively administered to, 311
human suffering, attachment injuries at core of, 337
humility, 18, 24, 34
cultural, 347, 360
in the process, 303
"The Therapist in Me" tray and, 308
hyperactivation state, selection of interweave and, 214–15
hypervigilance, 68
hypervigilance, prairie dog as metaphor for, *101*

hypoactivation state, selection of interweave and, 214–15

I am curious or confused interweave, 221
identity(ies)
elements of, inquiring about, 361
intersectionality of, empowerment and, 363
memories and formation of, 208
IGTP. *see* integrative group treatment protocol (IGTP)
illness and loss, generational interweaving and, 243–44
images, of the safe place, 85
immigration status, 360
immobility areas, in the tray, 50, 398
implicit access
attachment to the perpetrator and, 350–54, *351*
characteristics of, 17
first level of distance and, 59–60, *60*
first level of distance and, a character-driven story, 189–91
implicit emotions, labeling, 43
implicit information processing, grief and, 347
implicit memories, cognitions in the tray and, 199
implicit memory networks, frozen in time, traumagenic material and, 3
implicit mind
sandtray work as vehicle for, 4
symbols and, 70, 71
implicit portal or road
to accessing the inner system, *120,* 120–21
into defensive systems, 100
into memory networks, 264
implicit stories, sandtray work and, 17
implicit trays, for clinicians, 306
in-and-out strategies, exploration of trauma and, 142
inclusivity, culturally affirming practices of, 24
individuation in children, sandplay work and, 3
infants, identity formation in, 16
information processing
blocked, 212
emotional arousal and stalling of, 231

412 Index

implicit and nondirective, with complex clients, 268–71
multiple levels of, EMDR-sandtray therapy and, 9–10
plateaus of, 213–14
restarting flow of, interweaves and, 213
stalled, returning to the target and, 247
titration continuum and, 209–10
in the tray, 210–12
see also specific reevaluation, targeting
information processing levels, in assessment phase, 189–99
cognitions in the tray, 199
creating the reprocessing platform, procedural steps for, 195–96
explicit access and the second level of distance: story about worry or difficulty, 194–95
explicit access and third level of information processing, story about actual traumatic event, 198–99
implicit access and the first level of distance: a character-driven story, 189–91
implicit and nondirective world creation and exploration, 192–94
procedural steps for the assessment phase, 196–98
world creation and exploration, procedural steps for, 196
information processing system, BLS/DAS and activation of, 7
information processing with complex internal systems, 280–90
importance of interweaves in, 280
interweaves that invite emotions, 287–88
interweaves that titrate, 283–85
interweaves that work the attachment system, 288–90
interweaves that work with the body and sensorimotor system, 281–83
interweaves that work with the emotional system, 285–87

inner child of caregiver, inviting visits to, 177
inner conflict, polarizations and, 123–26, *125*
inner implicit maps, caregiver responses and, 159
inner journey, deepening of, during desensitization phase, 208
inner representations
    mirror neurons and, 300
    in parents' minds, 143
    see also caregiver's inner representations, working with
inner system, accessing, 120–22
    explicit portal in, 121–22
    implicit portal in, 120–21
insecure attachment, macro- and microruptures in, 2
"inside check-ins" or "inside visits," building safe place in th tray and, 133
installation (Phase 5) in EMDR therapy, 5t, 202, 248–50, 291
    check if the positive cognition still fits (Step 1), 248
    check the VoC (Step 2), 248–49
    enhance new adaptive material with BLS/DAS (Step 4), 249
    explicit and implicit access and, 18
    initiate BLS/DAS to link positive cognition with the sand world (Step 3), 249
    invite playfulness (Step 5), 250
intangible spaces, 31
integration
    EMDR-sandtray therapy and movement toward, 9
    reflective statements and, 41
    synthesis and, 139
    see also staging: optimizing integrative capacities; wholeness
integrative group treatment protocol (IGTP), 310
intergenerational trauma, 360, *360*
    addressing, generational interweaves and, 240–44, *244*
    group work and healing of, 320
    parental involvement in breaking cycle of, 147
intergenerational wounds, systemic work with parents and children and, 144
internal family systems

developing a part-self relationship and, 129
    questions from, connection to inner system and, 123
internal safety domain, 69
internal working models, 292, 298, 340, 350
    in depth of EMDR-sandtray work, 53
    of parents, actively addressing, 154
International Society for the Study of Dissociation, 26
    EMDR recommended by, for PTSD treatment, 7–8
interoceptive awareness, interweaves using mindfulness and, 229–31
interoceptive intelligence, 112, 123
interpersonal communication
    implicit information processing and, 268
    in reprocessing phases with complex clients, 263
interpersonal competencies, complex and relational trauma and, 144
interpersonal neurobiology (IPNB), xiv, xv, 19–20, 305
interpretation, discouragement of, 40
intersectionality
    cultural sensitivity and, 24
    of identities, culture and, 363–64
intersubjective congruency, getting to know inner system of parts and, 131
intersubjective field
    intangible spaces and, 31
    in the sand world, 52–53, 398
interweaves, 208, 270
    accompanying caregivers with, 176
    blocked processing and need for, 212
    categories of, in EMDR Systems Model, 213
    children exposed to chronic traumatization and, 268
    definition of, 212
    design of, 213
    differentiation from perpetrator and, 274
    dysfunctional positive affect and, 355–56, 358
    educational, 228
    generational, 240–44, *244*
    grief work and, 343, 344, 346

Index   413

interweaves (*continued*)
  I am curious or confused type, 221
  for inviting emotions, 233
  multiple, attachment wounds and, 340
  online EMDR-sandtray therapy and, 371
  potential, for caregivers, 177–78
  preparing in advance, 213
  reflective techniques used as, 46
  reparative and restorative, 177–78
  safety checks, 216, 226
  that access or provide adaptive information, 217–19
  that go from object to self, 228–29, 230
  that invite emotions, 233, 287–88
  that modulate arousal, 227–28
  that provide temporal orientation, 221–22
  that repair, paying attention to, 184
  that titrate, 283–85
  that use mindfulness and interoceptive awareness, 229–31
  that work with attachment system, 216, 233–35, 288–90
  that work with defenses and self-protective system, 237–38
  that work with higher cognitive system, 216, 217
  that work with polarizations and binary states, 222–23
  that work with self-protective system, 216
  that work with sensorimotor system and the body, 216, 224, 281–83
  that work with the emotional system, 216, 231–33, 285–87
  two-hand, 290
  types of, 217–44
  utilizing Socratic method, 219–21
  for working with parents and caregivers, 235–36
  for working with polarizations and binary states, 222–23
  for working with significant others, 236–37
  zoom-in and zoom-out, 217
Interweave Systems model in EMDR-sandtray, 212, 213–16
  design of, 213

five categories of interweaves in, 213
Interweave Systems model in EMDR-sandtray, markers in decision-making process, 213–16
  five systems where processing blockages may occur, 216
  hyperactivation and hypoactivation, 214–15
  levels of information processing: cognitive, emotional, and sensorimotor, 214
  plateaus of information processing, 213–14
  presence and compartmentalization, 215–16
intimate partner violence victims, GTEP protocol effectively administered to, 311
intrapersonal capacities, complex and relational trauma and, 144
intrapersonal communication
  implicit information processing and, 268
  in reprocessing phases with complex clients, 263
introduction and invitation step, in EMDR-sandtray-based therapy, 33–36
  adult and adolescent clients and, 35
  uniqueness of each client and, 33–34
  working with children and, 34, 35
invisible complex trauma, 2
IPNB. *see* interpersonal neurobiology (IPNB)

Jacobvitz, D., 2
Janet, P., phase-oriented model of, 25
Jang, M., 4
Jarero, I., 310
jealousy, 49
Jung, C., 2, 3
Jungian psychology
  expansion of sand-based therapy field and, 4
  tray in, 26

Kalff, D. M., 2, 3, 8, 27, 31, 70
Kalisch, L. A., 373
Kaplan, S., 213
kindness, 103. *see also* compassion; love
Knipe, J., 216, 357, 368
"knowing" and "not knowing" conflict, 290

Korkmazlar, Ü., 310
Korn, D. L., 321

landscape setup, explicit information processing and, 276–80
learning and cognitive disabilities, 372
Leeds, A. M., 321
left hemisphere of the brain
  EMDR-sandtray therapy and, 20
  explanation and, 38
  psychoeducation, representation in the tray, and, 157
Levin, R., 269
Levine, P. A., 81, 300
Liberman, M. D., 75
life experiences, miniature figures collection and, 391
life stories
  reclaiming agency and authorship over, 18
  shared memory network and, 143
light bar, eye movements and, 74, *74*
light-up wand
  eye movements and, 73, *73*
  for providing BLS/DAS, 30, 222
little self story keeper, working with parts in assessment phase and, 200–201
lobster part in internal system, orientation to the body and, 137
looping, 212, 217, 224, 290
loss. *see* grief and loss issues
love, 98, 103, 170, 285
  belongingness and, 395
  fear and, 223
  grief and, 341
  rainbow and sun in parenting wheel and, 327
Lowenfeld, M., 2, 27, 31
Lowenfeld method, expansion of sand-based therapy field and, 4
low-intensity mentalization interventions, 41, 42
loyalty and idealization of wounding figure, dogs and puppies as metaphors for, 101, *101*
lust, innate motivational system and, 294
Lyles, M., 31, 32, 303, 323
Lyons-Ruth, K., 2

magical figures, 392
major depressive disorder, EMDR and effectiveness with, scientific support for, 7

Manfield, P., 95
manipulation, spiders and snakes as metaphors for, 101, *101*
Mann, D., 124
marching, 74, 326, 329
  "marching in" experiences, 171
  online EMDR-sandtray therapy and, 371
  present awareness and, 238
  sand story and, 74
  self-administered eye movement with GTEP protocol and, 314
marginalization, institutional, reprocessing phases and, 363
Marich, J., 352
Martin, K. M., 126
Maslow's hierarchy of needs
  EMDR-sandtray-based therapy context and, 75–76
  expansion of, for fuller understanding of needs, 395–97
Maté, G., 364
Maxfield, L., 309
mean farmer and the bull session, with 13-year-old, 11–12, *12*
meaning, new, EMDR work and emergence of, 7
meaning-making system, interweaves that work with, 216
measuring spoons, 78, 286
  for checking the SUD, 247
  for identifying level of disturbance associated with a memory, 194
  for identifying positive cognition's validity, 248
  interweaves that modulate emotions and, 231
  presence in the here and now and use of, 117
medical figures, 393
medical personnel, GTEP protocol effectively administered to, 311
memory(ies)
  "absent network" and, 94
  of actual traumatic event, explicit access and story about, 198–99
  assimilation of, EMDR therapy and, 32
  autobiographical, 26, 107, 155, 207, 208, 271
  dual attention and integration of, 238
  identity formation and, 208

implicit, cognitions in the tray and, 199
  reprocessing, related to caregiver's actual child, 177
  segmentation of, trays in assessment phase and, 202
  "sorting out," brushes used for, 74, *74*
  traumatic, biological imprints of, 6
memory networks, inner system and two access routes into, 264
memory processing and integration, therapeutic process in EMDR-sandtray-based therapy and, 155
memory systems, in depth of EMDR-sandtray work, 53
mentalization, 25
  affective, early trauma and deficits in, 293
  interventions, high-intensity and low-intensity, 41, 42
  therapeutic process in EMDR-sandtray-based therapy and, 155, 159–60
  unmet needs and, 170
  "wiser and guiding self" and, 167–68
mentalization theory, 305
menus, 169, 287
  identification of embodied needs and, 171
  for "needless" clients, 234
  polarizations and, 169
Merckelbach, H., 269
metaphors, 34, 98, 141, 268
  analogies and metaphors from, incorporating into the tray, 157
  distance and, 40
  in family group work, 334
  fantasy-prone dissociative children and, 269
  implicit access and, 59, 60
  individuals on the autism spectrum and, 376
  within metaphors, reflecting on, 45
  parenting wheel and, 323
  in sandtray therapy, 32
  segmented psychoeducation and, 126
  see also analogies; miniature figures collection; symbols
microadjustments, in EMDR-sandtray-based therapy, 9
microprocessing, 202–3, 210
migration histories, generational interweaves and, 242

mind
  complexity of, 24
  models of multiplicity of, 23
  Siegel's definition of, 19–20
mindfulness, 19
  for clinicians, 305–6
  interweaves that use interoceptive awareness and, 229–31
  titrated, 283–84
miniature figures collection, 3, 29–31
  addiction treatment and, 368
  C-GTEP and use of, 317, 318
  comprehensive, 29–30
  connecting to the moment of activation and, 173
  culturally affirming and inclusive, 30
  display of, 31
  family group work and, 331–32, 333
  group traumatic episode protocol and, 312, 314
  identity themes and representation in, 361
  introducing, 34
  levels of presence and, 216
  materials used in, 30
  multiple figures showcasing multiplicity in, *30*
  number of figures in, 29
  organizing in the sandtray, 30–31
  orientation to the body and, 136
  picking figures from, 35–36
  polarized self-states and, 290
  as potent anchor, 134
  RDI protocol and, 91
  recommended classifications and miniature groups in, 391–94
  search for figures in, 29
  self-discovery and, 9
  sizes of figures in, 30
  story about actual traumatic event and, 198
  therapeutic spaces and, 31
  touching figures with open and closed eyes, 87
  unique relationships with, 210
  see also avatars; metaphors; symbols
minor disturbance in the tray, creating, 88
mirroring, 31, 38, 43, 171, 292–93, 326
  complex trauma clients and, 279
  in exploring the tray, 41

Index   415

mirroring (*continued*)
grief work and, 343
somatic consciousness and, 47
working individually with the
caregiver and, 153
working with mild to moderate dissociation and, 118
mirror neurons, inner representations and, 300
mobility
neurodiverse clients and
issues with, 375
in therapy room, creating, 32
see also movement
moment-to-moment deci-
sion-making, sequencing in
the tray, 159–60
mother–child attachment security, assessed effect of sandplay therapy on, 5
motivational systems
of client and therapist, interplay between, 295
growth and maturation of, 294
innate, categories of, 294
origination of, 293
of perpetrator, 349–50
motivational systems and therapeutic relationship, 293–97
highly activated ranking/com-
petition system, 295–96
overactive defense system,
296–97
overactive or abdicated caregiving system, 296
overactive sexuality/lust system, 297
mourners
pendulation and, 343
safe and sacred space for, in
EMDR-sandtray, 341
see also grief and loss issues
movement
building of trauma tray and,
187
C-GTEP combined with
extended preparation and,
319
creating minor disturbance
and 88
dyadic work during reprocessing phases and, 179
emotional experience, sand
tray, and, 10
emotion tolerance protocol
with pendulation and, questions for, 84
inviting body scan and, 252
inviting into the tray, 47–48
for keeping client engaged
and connected, 238, 239

neurodiverse clients and, 375
resource trays and, 106–7
in sandtray, social engagement and, 32–33
sandtray-inner family and,
132–33
segmented psychoeducation
and, 126
see also marching; mobility
multifactor model of preparation
phase, 72–81
affect tolerance and affect regulation, 77–81
coregulation in the tray, 81
customizing to client's unique
needs and circumstances,
72
explaining EMDR-sandtray-
based therapy, 72–73
introducing EMDR therapy
and dual attention stimulus,
73–74
psychoeduation and the building of the corrective network, 75–77
multimodal approach to EMDR-
sandtray-based therapy,
18–19
attachment theory, 22–23
gestalt therapy, 20–21
interpersonal neurobiology,
19–20
intersectionality and cultural
sensitivity, 24
limitations of, recognizing, 24
models of multiplicity of the
mind, 23
Polyvagal Theory, 21–22
recognizing the divided brain,
20
somatic therapies, 23–24
multimotivational systems, nine
categories of, 294
music
auditory anchoring with, 187
C-GTEP termination of session
and, 317
dyadic work during reprocessing phases and, 179
musical boxes, 30
my bigger, wiser self, inner
guide, in parenting wheel,
322, 323–24, 324, 329
my dresser, in parenting wheel,
322, 325–26, 329
myelinated vagal system (parasympathetic ventral vagal),
21
My Goals activity, initial phases
of EMDR-sandtray-based
therapy and use of, 65–66

my mirror, in parenting wheel,
322, 326, 329
my playful self, in parenting
wheel, 322, 327, 329
my shield and my boundaries,
in parenting wheel, 322,
327–28, 329
my inner sun, in parenting
wheel, 322, 327, 329
my thermostat and my accordion, in parenting wheel,
322, 324–25, 326, 329

National Institute for Health and
Care Excellence, EMDR
PTSD treatment recommen-
dation, 7
natural elements, in miniature
figures collection, 393
"navigational capital," 361
need-fulfillment bottles and jars,
235, 235
"needless" clients, menus for, 234
needs
accessing, TAPAS protocol
Step 2, 96–97
acknowledging, 289
attachment injuries and, 339,
340
cognitive, 396
comprehensive list of, 234
embodied, menus and, 171
emotional, 397
grief and, 343
love and belongingness, 395
meeting, TAPAS protocol Step
3, 97–98, 98
physiological, 396
play, 397
psychoeducational sand tray,
TAPAS protocol Step 1, 95–96
psychoeducational sand tray
focused on, 95
safety and security, 396
self-actualization, 396
self-worth, 396
unmet, guessing and meeting,
169–72, 171
unmet, meeting with TAPAS
protocol, 94–99
and wants in the tray, reflecting on and differentiating,
44
negative cognition
assessing validity of, 193
identifying in assessment procedural steps, 192, 196
neglect, unmet needs and, 94,
169
negotiation with protectors,
103–4

416 Index

nervous system patterns, nondirective sandtray strategies and, 149
nesting dolls, 78
neural tendencies, preparation phase informed by, 69, 72
neuroception, faulty, resetting of, 112
neurochemicals, caregiving system and, 146
neurocognitive capacities, complex and relational trauma and, 144
neurodivergence, definition of, 372
neurodivergent individuals, trauma and, 372, 373–74
neurodiverse clients
  building relational bridges with, 375
  communication with, 376
  connecting to themselves and their inner world, 375–76
  EMDR-sandplay therapy for, 373–77
  mobility issues with, 375
  reprocessing phases and, 376–77
  sensory engagement with, 374
neurodiversity, complexity in and diverse range of, 372
nonbinary clients, preferred pronouns and, 362
nondirective approach to working with defenses, 100, 104–5
nondirective sandtray strategies, 148–52
  attachment dynamics, 149
  body-based data and nervous system patterns, 149
  coherence of the tray world, 149
  conflict within family dynamic and, 151–52
  creation of the worlds, 149
  decision-making and conflict resolution, 148–49
  end of session, 150–51
  interaction with the clinician, 150
  inviting parent and child to play in the sand, 148
  organization of the world, 148
  parent–child interaction, 149
  in raccoon stuck in a storm story, 150
nondirective tactics, in EMDR-sandtray-based therapy, 11, 63, 64
nondirective trays, for clinicians, 306

nonverbal communication, family group work and, 334. *see also* body language; facial expressions; gestures; pauses and silence; vocal prosody and tone
note-taking step, in EMDR-sandtray-based therapy, 33, 57–58
  connections to macro- and micro-treatment perspectives and, 58
  picture-taking and, 57
  timing of session and, 57
"not me, not mine, not self" state of consciousness, 78, 189
numbers, GTEP work tray and use of, 314, 315
nurturing figures, 232, 394

Oaklander, V., 289
"observant characters," moderate dissociation and, 112–13
obsessive-compulsive disorder, EMDR and effectiveness with, scientific support for, 7
obstruction, being attentive to moments of, in the tray, 213
Ogden, P., 224
olfactory anchors, 187. *see also* scents; smell
online EMDR-sandtray therapy
  advance preparation for, areas to note, 371–72
  advantages and challenges with, 370
openness, healing of the wounded mind and, 19
oppression and marginalization, honoring protective stance of clients facing, 362
oppressive cognitions, being mindful about presence of, 363
over-accessing, 41
overactive caregiving system, therapeutic encounter and, 296
overworking, ant as metaphor for, *101*
"owl self," 129
ownership and realization, sandtray work and, 78

pain, EMDR and effectiveness with, scientific support for, 7
paint brushes, 211
"painting in" experiences, 171

panic, EMDR and effectiveness with, scientific support for, 7
panic/grief, innate motivational system and, 294
panic/loss, multimotivational systems and, 294
Panksepp, J., 35, 146
parasympathetic shutdown and collapse, 225
parenting episodes, reprocessing of, EMDR-sandtray-based group therapy for caregivers and, 321
parenting wheel (PW)
  analogies and metaphors from, incorporating into the tray, 157
  approach used with, 321
  delivery of, 323
  my bigger, wiser self, inner guide, self in, *322*, 323–24, *324*, 329
  my dresser in, *322*, 325–26, 329
  my mirror in, *322*, 326, 329
  my playful self in, *322*, 327, 329
  my shield and my boundaries in, *322*, 327–28, 329
  my inner sun in, *322*, 327, 329
  my thermostat and my accordion in, *322*, 324–25, *326*, 329
  seven elements of, *322*
parents
  defense and self-protective system of, 172
  deshaming and depathologizing, 176
  with dissociative tendencies, working with, 173
  interweaves for working with, 235–36
  timeline creation and, 109, 110–11
  see also children; dyadic resources with child and parent, in preparation phase; EMDR-sandtray-based parenting protocol; group parenting empowerment protocol and parenting wheel
parents and children, systemic work with, 143–79
  attachment system and, 145–46
  caregiver's inner representation and, 154–76
  caregiving system and, 146–47

Index   **417**

parents and children, systemic
work with (*continued*)
  gathering history and explor-
    ing relationship through
    sandtray strategies, 147–54
  importance and necessity of,
    143–44
  intergenerational trauma and,
    143, 144
  investigate resourcing and
    process triggers, 176–79
  shared memory network and,
    144–45
parts
  assessment phase and work-
    ing with, 200–201
  challenging, questions related
    to, 137–38
  consensus among, readiness
    for assessment and, 181–82
  defining, 23
  dissociated, emergence in the
    tray, 113
  implicit access and, 60
  implicit portal and communi-
    cation among, 121
  inviting to join sandtray-inner
    family, 129–30
  locked up or imprisoned, 130
  meaning behind actions of,
    138–39
  resourcing, 133
  severe dissociation and,
    118–19
  as "storytellers" and "story
    holders," 119, 140
  symbolic nature of sandtray
    work and, 121
  temporal and spatial orienta-
    tion in the tray and, 135–36
  trauma-bound compartmental-
    ized life experiences in, 123
  "tucked in," homeostasis and,
    132
parts in the sand, working with
  inner system of, 271–76
  complexity of, 271
  hostile and aggressive parts,
    276, 277
  perpetrator-imitating parts,
    273–76
  young and child parts, 272–73
passive pathways, reprocessing
  of attachment wounds and,
    340
pathways and bridges, 393
pauses and silence, using, 45–46
pendulation, 210
  addiction treatment and, 369
  complex trauma clients and,
    278

emotion tolerance protocols
  and, 81–84
exploration of trauma and, 142
gradual entrance into memory
  and, 267
gradual entrance into trauma
  tray and, 188
implicit access and, 121
mourners and, 343
neurodiverse clients and, 377
resource, *205*, 205–6, *206*
resource trays and, 107
in the sand world, 288
somatic experiencing and
  importance of, 284
somatic therapies and, 203
team of companions and, 93
"this was me then, and this is
  me now" protocol, 204–5
pendulation interweaves, modulation of emotions and, 232
perfectionism, bee as metaphor
  for, 101
peripheral reprocessing, 194
peritraumatic dissociation, emergence of, 113
perpetrator, attachment to,
  348–55
  complex dynamics behind,
    349
  explicit access, 348, 354–55
  implicit access, 348, 350–54,
    351
  multidimensional conse-
    quences of abuse and,
    348–49
perpetrator-imitating parts,
  273–76
  binding and differentiating
    with, 139–40
  compassion and, 274–75
  differentiation and, 274
  emergence of, 273
  reenactments during repro-
    cessing and realization and,
    275
  temporal orientation and, 275
  validation and reflections and,
    275–76
persons with disabilities, EMDR-
  sandtray-based therapy
  with adults and, 14
phantom echoes of the past,
  confronting, assessment
  phase of EMDR treatment
  and, 180
phobias, trauma-related, 183
  attachment patterns, defenses,
    and, 70–72
  double bind around unmet
    needs and, 94

EMDR and effectiveness with,
  scientific support for, 7
implicit access and, 59
unmet needs and, 170
physical distance, reprocessing
  of trauma memories and,
  267
physicalization
  binding and differentiating
    and, 139–40
  of communication between
    dissociative parts, *132*
  in directive approach to work-
    ing with defenses, 100–101
  fulfilling unmet needs and,
    171–72
  interweaves working with
    polarizations and, 222
  inviting into the sand tray, 9
  orientation to the body and,
    137
  of protectors, 102
physical sensations, 47. *see also*
  body sensations
physical/somatic safety domain,
  69
physiological activation, trauma
  and constant state of, xiii
physiological needs, 396
picture-taking
  note-taking and, 57
  before tray is dismantled, 55
plastic bins, for miniature figures
  collection, 31
play
  benefits of, xv
  healing and, 2, 112
  innate motivational system
    and, 294
  multimotivational systems
    and, 294
  as primary need of children,
    327
  symbolic, dissociative children
    and, 269
playfulness, inviting, in installation phase, 250
play items, 393
play needs, 397
play system
  EMDR-sandtray-based therapy
    with adolescents and, 13
  EMDR-sandtray-based therapy
    with adults and, 14
  inhibited, 35
play therapy, xv, 304, 305
pleasing, chameleon as metaphor for, 101
points of disturbance (PoDs),
  reprocessing in GTEP work
  tray, 315

418   Index

polarities and polarizations, 50
  implicit access and, 60
  inner conflict and, 123–26, *125*
  interweaves that work with, 222–23
  inviting into the tray, 46
  menus and, 169
  polarized self-states, 289–90
  team of companions and, 93
  unveiling, drawing distinctions and, 44, *44*
  young and child parts and, 272, 273, *273*
polytraumatization, multifaceted nature of, 1
polyvagal-based interventions, enhanced power of EMDR and sandtray therapies and, xv
Polyvagal Theory, xiv, 19, 226, 304, 305
  as a matrix for eight phases of treatment, 21–22
  understanding of therapeutic relationship and, 301
Porges, S. W., 21, 134, 228, 230, 283, 301
portals, levels of titration and, 266–67. *see also* explicit portal or road; implicit portal or road
positive affect, addiction and processing dysfunctional level of, 368
positive cognition
  assessing validity of, 193, 197
  checking fit of, in installation phase, 248
  identifying in assessment procedural steps, 192–93, 196
  installation of, future template and, 261
  installation of, in GTEP work tray, 316
  linking with sand world, 249
positive memory, in C-GTEP Phase 2, 317
positivism, 70, 71
post-traumatic stress disorder (PTSD), xvi
  addiction and, 369
  EMDR and effectiveness with, scientific support for, 7–8
posture, 47
potentialities, new, sandtray work and, 158
power imbalances, fixing, 360
prayer, 362
predation, multimotivational systems and, 294

predatory aggression, victim–perpetrator dynamics and, 349
prefrontal cortex, passive and active defense responses and, 224
preparation (Phase 2) in EMDR therapy, 5t, 67–111
  acknowledging unique qualities of each client in, 67
  attachment patterns, defenses, and trauma-related phobias, 70–72
  core overarching areas in, 67–72
  directive approach in working with defenses, 100–104
  dissociation and organization of, 67–68, 114
  enriching client's emotional and somatic field of awareness, 89–91
  identifying and exploring targets during, 105–11
  inner-systemic work pivotal during, 123
  length and organization of, 67
  level of safety in five domains and, 68–69
  multifactor model of, 72–81
  my team of companions and, 92–93
  neural tendencies and, 69
  nondirective approach in working with defenses, 104–5
  pendulation and emotion tolerance protocols, 81–84
  resource development and installation protocol, 91
  sandtray strategies and the safe place protocol, 84–88
  TAPAS protocol and, 94–99
presence, 292
  miniature figures collection and levels of, 216
  promotion of, EMDR-sandtray work and, 112
  selection of interweave and, 215
  template for bridge into, 118
presence checks, 117
present awareness, interweaves for restoring, 238–40
pretend play, dissociative children and, 270
procedural memory, challenging, interweaves for, 227–28
professions, miniature figures in groups of, 391

progress note format, elements in, 57–58
pronouns, preferred, inquiring about, 362
prosocial systems, promotion of regulation and, 294
protectors, 208
  clinician, reflecting on, 306–7
  inviting into resource tray, 189
  negotiation with, 103–4
  nondirective approach in working with defenses and, 104
  physicalization of, 102
  in the tray, noticing, 51
  see also companions; defenders; helpers; self-protective system; team of companions
psychoeducation, 154
  about emotions and body sensations, 287
  accessing "wiser, older, and bigger self" and, 164
  building of corrective network and, 75–77
  delivery of the parenting wheel and, 323
  in directive approach to working with defenses, 100–101, *101*
  EMDR-sandtray-based group therapy for caregivers and, 321
  EMDR-sandtray-based group treatment and, 310
  "feeling guests" and, 78
  segmented, family group work and, 331
  segmented, integrating adaptive information and, 157
  segmented, sandtray-inner family and, 126–27
  segmented, working individually with the caregiver and, 154
  TAPAS protocol Step 1, *95,* 95–96
  therapeutic process in EMDR-sandtray-based therapy and, 155, 157–58
  unmet needs and, 170
psychoeducational tray, with representations of defenses, 100, 101, *101*
psychosis, EMDR and effectiveness with, scientific support for, 7
psychosocial history, gathering, sandtray work and, 10
PTSD. *see* post-traumatic stress disorder (PTSD)

Index   **419**

pupil, variations in eye and, 49
Putnam, F. W., 16, 271
PW. *see* parenting wheel (PW)

questions
  asking about the present and, 238
  general and specific, in world exploration, 39–41
  for getting to know inner system of parts, 130
  pair, reflect, and summarize with, 45
  pendulation and, 82, 83
  related to dissociative experiences, 116
  sadness in sand world and, 77, 78
  somatic consciousness and, 47
  for working implicitly with a character, 171

racial disparities, interweaves in work with children and, 243
racial identity, representations of, 360, *360*
Rae, R., 33, 36
rage
  innate motivational system and, 294
  victim–perpetrator dynamics and, 349
  see also aggression; anger
RDI protocol. *see* resource development and installation (RDI) protocol
reaccessing of sand world from previous session, client opposition to, reasons for, 258–59
readiness
  assessing, for complex clients, 266
  markers for complex and dissociative clients, 264–65
reality of client, acknowledging, importance of, 361–62
Recent Traumatic Episode Protocol (R-TEP), GTEP protocol based on, 311
reciprocity, 25
recognition, gratitude and, 103. *see also* validation
reenactments
  children, implicit access, and, 59
  in the tray, 53
  of unresolved and unhealed trauma, 293
reevaluation (Phase 8) in EMDR therapy, 5*t*, 255–59

case: closure and reevaluation with implicit and first level of information processing, 257–58
  fundamental importance of, 255
  general reevaluation, 255–56
  specific reevaluation, targeting: explicit information processing, 258–59
  specific reevaluation, targeting: implicit and first level of information processing, 256–58
reflective communication, 25, 38, 99, 239, 241, 326
  consolidation and use of, 174–76
  explicit portal and, 122
  in exploring the tray, 40
  interventions and approaches with, 42–46
  nondirective approach in working with defenses and, 105
  perpetrator loyalty issues and, 352, 353, 354
  psychoeducation and, 157
  working individually with the caregiver and, 153
  working with mild to moderate dissociation and, 118
  world creation and use of, 36
reflective statements, 41–42
  hostile and aggressive parts and use of, 276
  widening of client's consciousness field and, 90
refugees
  C-GTEP and, 318
  GTEP protocol and, 311
refuge for clinicians, creating, 306
regulatory capacities, 51–52, 398
relapses, addiction treatment and, 366
relational anchors, 240
relational bonding, healing power of, 147
relational bridges, building with neurodiverse clients, 375
relational choreographies in the tray, dissociative parts and, 119, 121
relational dynamics, conflict areas in the tray and, 50, 398
relational misattunement, chronic, hidden complex trauma and, 2
relational resources, in GPEP Step 2, *328*, 328–29

relational safety domain, 69
relational templates, 48
relational trauma, caregiving system and, 146
relational tray, my team of companions and, 92–93
religious figures and spiritual symbols figures, 392
religious identity, representations of, 360, *360*
religious traditions, exploring and identifying, 362
repair, interweaves delivered by caregivers and, 184. *see also* rupture(s)
reparative and restorative interweaves for caregivers, potential, 177–78
reprocessing
  of generational wounds, 244
  levels of, in EMDR-sandtray work, 32–33
  of peripheral targets, assessing readiness for, 194–95
reprocessing phases
  dyadic work during, 178–79
  following rhythm of client's mind in, 183
  target identification and, with caregivers, 172–76
  ultimate goal in, 209
reprocessing phases with complex clients, advanced strategies during, 263–91
  assessing readiness, 263, 266
  explicit information processing: setting up the landscape, 276–80
  implicit and nondirective information processing, 268–71
  information processing with complex internal systems, 280–90
  navigating through the reprocessing phases, 290–91
  portals and levels of titration, 266–67
  readiness markers, 264–65
  two levels of communication and, exploring and assessing, 263–64
  working with the inner system of parts in the sand, 271–76, *277*
reprocessing platform, procedural steps for creating, 195–96
  resources, 196
  staging, 195
reprocessing sessions
  caregiver invited to, 183–84

420 Index

enhancing acts of triumph
and, 254
phases 4, 5, and 6, 176
in the tray, *244–45*
resilience, 106
future self and, 90
intersectionality of identities
and, 363
traumatized individuals and,
xiii
resistance, EMDR-sandtray-based
therapy with adolescents
and, 13
resonance, 292
healing of the wounded mind
and, 19
with inner system of parts
and, 131
resource areas, for reprocessing
session in sand tray, *244*
resource development and installation (RDI) protocol, 84,
91, 321, 333
EMDR-sandtray-based group
therapy for caregivers and,
320
resourcing parts and, 133
resource identification step, in
EMDR-sandtray-based ther-
apy, 33, 53–54
resource pendulation, *205,* 205–
6, *206*
resources
adaptive information and,
bringing into client's field
of consciousness, 43
addiction treatment and, 369
ancestral, *360*
built-in, C-GTEP and, 317
capacities, realizations and, in
sand world, 53–54, 398
C-GTEP combined with
extended preparation and,
319
creating platform for reprocessing and, 185
examples of, in resource areas
or resource tray, 186
internal/external, symbols
and images in tray and,
10–11
"painting in," brushes used for,
74, *74*
pendulation from memory/
trauma tray to, 267
resource trays, 141
of an adult and her inner dissociative system, *274*
building, 82
completed, taking notice of,
278

connecting to moment of activation and, 173–74
coverings in, *187*
directive access and, 106–7
entire system of parts invited
into, 290–91
of older adolescent, platform
to support processing, *195*
"resource areas" created in,
185
resources included in, examples of, 186
sandtray-inner family and,
127–28
timelines and, 110
working with parts in assessment phase and, 200, 201
"rest area" space, 131
retraumatization, minimizing
risk of, 128
right hemisphere of the brain
description and, 38
EMDR-sandtray therapy and,
20
psychoeducation, representation in the tray, and, 157
rigid and binary states, formation
of, 289–90
rigid processing, fluid processing
vs., 207
rituals, generational interweaves
and, 242
rocks, 277
adding to C-GTEP sand tray,
317, *318*
in family group work trays,
332
in GTEP work tray, 313, *313,*
314, 315
in sand world for inner system
of parts, 131, *131*
R-TEP. *see* Recent Traumatic Episode Protocol (R-TEP)
rumination, children's play in
the sand and, 270
rupture(s)
acknowledging and recognizing, 46
being attentive to moments of,
in the tray, 213
repair and, trauma-formed
relational templates and,
295
repairing, in the sand tray, 170

sadness in the sand world, questions for, 77, 78
safe and healing place, 329
complex clients and, 266, 267
creation of trauma tray and
safe refuge of, 277

in miniature figures collection, 394
physicalizing, in GTEP work
tray, 314
resource areas in reprocessing
session in the tray and, *244*
safe place protocol, sandtray
strategies and, 84–88
anchoring or cuing, 88
being with and sitting with, 87
clients who do not tolerate
safety or calm states, 86
clients who have had adaptive
experiences of safety and
protection, 85
clients who have not had
adaptive experiences of
safety and protection, 85
emotions, 87–88
image of safe place, 85
location in the body, 88
minor disturbance, 88
resourcing parts and, 133
words used for safe place,
84–85
world building and creation,
86–87
safety
addictions and temporary
sense of, 364
anchoring and, 186
assessment phase and, 201
bringing parts of the self to, in
closure phase, 255
chronic trauma and faulty
neuroception of, 55, 112,
134, 156
clients unable to tolerate
states of, 86
closure phase and, 252
cues of, therapeutic process in
EMDR-sandtray-based ther-
apy and, 155–56
defenses, self-protective system, and, 189
distance and coverings in
trauma tray and, 187
level of, in five domains,
68–69
mentalization and state of, 25
microprocessing and, 202
as a precursor of treatment,
134
prioritizing, sandtray collection and, 30
readiness for assessment and
processing and, 182
relational, attachment wound
reprocessing and, 340
relational, in addiction treatment, 365

Index **421**

safety (*continued*)
  relational, increasing in family group work, 331–32, 334
  sandtray collection and, 30
  team of companions and, 92, 93
  therapeutic moment and unique need for, 32
  of therapeutic relationship, challenges to, 293
  therapist's life story and creation of, 298
  "this was me then, and this is me now" pendulation protocol and, 204
  world creation and sense of, 37
safety agreements, safety of parts and, 130
safety and protection
  clients who have had adaptive experiences of, 85
  clients who have not had adaptive experiences of, 85
safety and security needs, 396
safety checks, 117–18, 142, 216, 226
sand
  colors or textures of, 29, 279
  introducing, 34
  playing with, 87
  as potent anchor, 134
sand-based therapies
  homeostasis and wholeness supported in, 8
  scientific support for effectiveness of, 4–5
sand-based therapy field, expansion of, 4
sandplay
  definition of, 2
  description of, 2–3
  "free and protected space" in, 3
  meta-analysis, multiple studies of, 4–5
  missed developmental stages made up for in, 3
sandplay therapy
  assessment of mother–child attachment security in, 5
  integrating EMDR therapy with, 3, 4
sandtray-based therapies
  clinician training and, 304
  origins of, 2
sandtray equipment and collection, creating, 26–32
  miniature figures collection, 29–31, *30*
  sand, 29

sandtray, 26–28, *27*
  therapeutic spaces, 31–32
sandtray-inner family, 126–33
  closure, 132–33
  getting to know the system, 130–32, *131, 132*
  inviting other parts of the system to join, 129–30
  inviting the guiding and wiser self, 129
  preparing the tray for the "get-together," 128
  relational environment of safety and trust and, 126
  resource tray, 127–28
  segmented psychoeducation, 126–27
sandtray pictures, printing on T-shirts, pillowcases, and napkins, 91
sandtrays, 26–28
  assessment and visible capacities of client in, case examples, 182–83
  as bridge between child's inner and outer worlds, 2
  burying hands in, 87
  closing, 253–54
  cocreation of, in family group work, *332*, 332–33
  coregulation in, 81
  dismantling and cleaning up, 255
  fabric coverings for, 56–57
  homeostasis and wholeness supported in, 8
  ideal height for, 28
  introducing, 34
  mapping and sequencing in injurious interactions in, 159
  materials used in, 27–28
  multiple, pendulation and, 81–82
  multiple angles of access to, 31
  octagonal, *27*
  organizing space in, multiple ways of doing, 31
  as potent anchor, 134
  RDI protocol and, 91
  recommended number, sizes, and shapes of, 27
  rectangular, 27, *27*
  reprocessing session in, *244–45*
  round and square, 27
  as a sacred space, 26
  self-discovery and, 9
  stands or tables with wheels for, 28, 31

temporal and spatial orientation in, 135–36, 142
  tray measurement in, 26
  as vehicle for restoring safety and social engagement, 69
  waterproof, 28
  working with parts in assessment phase and, 200, 201
sandtray strategies, exploring parent–child relationship through, 147–54
  directive sandtray strategies, 152–53
  nondirective sandtray strategies, 148–52
  working individually with the caregiver, 153–54
sandtray strategies, incorporating, overview of, 25
sandtray theory, 305
sandtray therapy
  definition of, 3
  flexibility of, 3
  multiple delivery formats for, xvi
  roots and origins of, xv
  six-step protocol in, 33
  union of EMDR and, lack of research on, 8
sandtray work
  assessment and exploration of dissociation in, *115*, 115–17
  trauma-related defensive strategies and, 15
sand world
  consistently positive, trauma-related defensive strategies and, 15
  as a field of possibilities, 263, 272
  landscape of, multiple topographies and territories in, 232
  obedience and defiance depicted in, *249*
  pendulating in, 288
sand world, areas of exploration in, 48–53
  actions and urges, 52, 398
  approach *vs.* distancing, 51, 398
  areas of collapse, immobility, and shutdown, 50, 398
  areas of conflict and relational dynamics, 50, 398
  areas of heat and activation, 49, 398
  areas where adaptive information and resources exist, 51, 398
  autonomy *vs.* dependency, power, and powerlessness tendencies, 51, 398

422   Index

cognitive data, 48, 398
defenses and self-protection, 51, 398
emotional data, 48–49, 398
grief and loss, 52, 398
intersubjective field, 52–53, 398
regulatory capacities, 51–52, 398
sensorimotor data, 49, 398
summary, 398
scents
emotion tolerance protocol with pendulation and, questions for, 84
olfactory anchoring with, 187
Schauer, M., 225, 226
Schore, A. N., 52
seasons
emotion tolerance protocol with pendulation and, questions for, 84
feelings related to, questions about, 286
secure attachment
absence of, diminished capacity to mentalize and, 293
of clients to their psychotherapists, 299
seeking, innate motivational system and, 294
selective focusing, dysfunctional positive affect and, 358
self
EMDR work and renewed connection to, 6–7
interweaves that go from object to, 228–29
interweaves that go from object to, body scan and, 251–52
self-acceptance, 106
self-actualization needs, 396
self-awareness, 124, 298
self-betrayal, developmental trauma and, 71
self-compassion, 7, 103, 129, 305
self-determination, 7
self-discovery, 105, 106, 123
self-harming behaviors, 279
self-knowing, 124
self-narratives, 207
cocreation of, during desensitization phase, 208
reorganization of, 293
self-organization, getting to know, 130
self-protection
defenses and, in sand world, 51
defenses and, in staging process, 189

trauma and mastering art of, 100
self-protective system
of adult client, sand world depicting, 102
defenses and, 189
interweaves that work with, 216, 237–38
recognition and gratitude and, 103
uncovering, invitation for, 102
self-recognition, 124
self-regulation, diminished, complex trauma and, 81
self-states
polarized, 289–90
vertical and horizontal integration and, 20
self-sufficiency, cats as metaphors for, 101, 101
self-system, resource creation and, 128
self-worth needs, 396
sensations, tracking, body scan and, 252
sensorimotor data, in exploration of the sand world, 49, 398
sensorimotor level of information processing, addressing in the tray, 214
sensorimotor psychotherapy, 23, 304
sensorimotor system, interweaves that work with the body and, 216, 224, 281–83
sensory engagement, with neurodiverse clients, 374
sensory modalities, multiple, sandtray work and, 16
sexual abuse, 109, 349
dysfunctional positive affect and, 355
effectiveness of sandplay and sandtray therapies for children with history of, 4
profound anguish attached to, 354
sexuality, multimotivational systems and, 294
sexuality/lust system, overactive, therapeutic encounter and, 297
sexual orientation, 360
shadow figures, 392
shame, 68
Shapiro, E., 3, 310, 311, 313, 321
Shapiro, F., xiv, xv, 5–6, 7, 18, 23, 26, 40, 75, 114, 212, 213, 214, 219, 238, 248, 271

shared memory network
AIP model and, 144–45
description of, 143
"we territory" and, 144
short-term group treatment, 310
shutdown, areas of, in the tray, 50, 398
Siegel, D. J., xiii, 19, 20, 38, 79, 145, 199
significant others, interweaves for working with, 236–37
signs, in miniature figures collection, 394
Silberg, J. L., 269
silence
active, using pauses and, 45–46
figure selection and, 36
single photon emission computed tomography (SPECT), 20
"sitting with"
embracing the world and, 38
world building and creation and, 87
skin color changes, 49
slowing down
as powerful interweave, 230
what is happening in the tray, 42, 173
smell, as sensory-based anchor, 134. see also scents
social dominance aggression, victim–perpetrator dynamics and, 349
social engagement, 292
active pathways and, 156
movement and play in the tray and, 32–33
passive pathways and, 340
resource trays and, 106–7
restoring, interweaves for, 238–40
safety cues conveyed by therapist and, 301–2
Socrates, 219
Socratic method, 219–21
somatic experiencing, 23
somatic field of awareness, enriching, 89–90
somatic intelligence, embodiment and, 162
somatic methodologies, 4
somatic paradigms, 19
somatic processing and consciousness
healing after trauma and, 250
representing in the tray, 47
somatic schemas, exploring, in EMDR-sandtray-based parenting protocol, 162

Index   **423**

somatic therapies, 23–24

somatization, complex trauma and, 1

songs, C-GTEP termination of session and, 317

sounds
creating, objects for, 30
dyadic work during reprocessing phases and, 179
emotional experience, sand tray, and, 10
as sensory-based anchor, 134

spatial orientation in the sand tray, 135–36

special populations and considerations, in EMDR-sandtray-based therapy, 337–78
abuse issues, 348–61
addictions, 364–69
attachment wounds, 337–41
grief and loss issues, 341–48
neurodiversity, 372–77
special considerations in delivery of EMDR-sandtray therapy, 361–64
virtual EMDR-sandtray-based therapy, 369–72

specific reevaluation, targeting
explicit information processing, 258–59
implicit and first level of information processing, 256–58

SPECT see single photon emission computed tomography (SPECT)

spray bottles, 78, 286
for checking the SUD, 247
for identifying level of disturbance associated with a memory, 194
for identifying positive cognition's validity, 248
interweaves that modulate emotions and, 231

spring toys, for identifying positive cognition's validity, 248–49

staging: optimizing integrative capacities, 183–89
anchors and anchoring, 186–87
companions, 185
defenses and the self-protective system, 189
distance and coverings, 187, 187–88, 188
inviting caregiver and, 183–84
resources, 185–86, 188

stagnation in the tray, being attentive to moments of, 213

Steele, K., 129, 271, 273, 294, 295, 348

steppingstones, colored, resource pendulation and use of, 206, 206. see also rocks

stop or slowdown signals, 111

stories
dissociative parts in sand tray and, 16
helping clients stay connected to, 211
within, EMDR-sandtray therapeutic work as portal to, 9

story holders, parts as, 119, 140

Story of the Weeping Camel, The (movie), 147

storytellers
clients as, in EMDR-sandtray-based therapy, 8, 18
parts as, 119, 140

storytellers: the mind, the heart, and the body
introducing, 34, 72–73
This Is Me protocol and, 65
visiting, after container creation and, 56

storytelling
age of children and types of, 13
sensory, awakening, 24

structural dissociation
EMDR-sandtray work and, 113
vertical and horizontal integration and, 20

structural dissociation theory, 23, 304, 305

structured interventions, 97

subjective units of disturbance (SUD), 57–58
C-GTEP Phase 1 and, 317
checking, in desensitization phase, 247
dysfunctional positive affect and, 355, 357
GTEP work tray and, 315
identifying and assessing, 193–94, 197
of zero, reprocessing down to, 202

submit state, 224

substance use disorder, EMDR and effectiveness with, scientific support for, 7. see also addictions

SUD. see subjective units of disturbance (SUD)

suicidal ideations, 279

suicide attempts, locked up parts and, 130

summarizing, 43

survival mode, dyadic and shared biological states and, 301

Sweeney, D. S., 3, 26, 33, 40

symbol-based brain, 35

symbolic distance, reprocessing trauma memories and, 267

symbolic nature of sandtray work, explicit and implicit access and, 17–18

symbolic play, dissociative children and, 269

symbols, 35, 141, 215
assigning to an affective experience, 79
caregiver–child dyads and, 146
dignity of, 70
distance and, 40
explicit access and, 62
in family group work, 334
in GTEP work tray, 314, 315
helping clients stay connected to, 211
individuals on the autism spectrum and, 376
in sandtray therapy, 32
signs and, 394
spiritual, figures for, 392
targets and, 106
see also analogies; metaphors; miniature figures collection

sympathetic nervous system
in EMDR-sandtray, 33
fight/flight defensive responses and, 21

synchronicity, 25, 292

synergetic play therapy, up- and down-regulation of emotions and, 76

systemic delivery, of EMDR-sandtray-based group treatment, 310

systemic discrimination histories, generational interweaves and, 242

systemic EMDR-sandtray-based therapy, healing of generational wounds and, xvi

tactile stimulation
movement-based, 74
reprocessing in the tray with brushes, 74, 74
self-administered, 74

tangible spaces, 31

TAPAS. see tolerance and amplification of positive affective states protocol (TAPAS)

target identification
with caregivers, 172–76
exploration of trauma and, 140–42

424   Index

targets, identifying and exploring
during preparation phase,
105–11
directive access, 105, 106–11
nondirective access, 105, 106
tastes, emotion tolerance protocol with pendulation and,
questions for, 84
team of companions
for adult client, *92*
relational trays and, 92–93
resource trays and, 107
telehealth, 369
temporal biases, 186
temporal orientation
exploring, in EMDR-sandtray-
based parenting protocol,
162–63
future template and three-
pronged approach to, 259–60
interweaves providing sense
of, 221–22
perpetrator-imitating parts
and, 275
restoring dual attention and,
285
rigid, traumatic memory systems and, 6
in the sand tray, 135–36, 142
"this was me then, and this is
me now" pendulation protocol and, 204
young and child parts and, 272
termination, premature, 296
textured miniatures, 30
therapeutic alliance, co-creation
of, 53
therapeutic choices, knowing
one's "home," and, 305
therapeutic dance, slowing down
and speeding up in, 124
therapeutic home: learning about
the clinician's mind, 303–5
basement, 304
first floor, 304
second floor, 304–5
therapeutic relationship
attuned companionship and,
in EMDR-sandtray-based
therapy, 9
importance of, as agent of
change, 292
motivational systems and,
293–97
Polyvagal Theory and, 301
therapeutic spaces, for sandtray
work, 31–32
Theraplay, 373
thermostat, 157. *see also* my thermostat and my accordion,
in the parenting wheel

"The Therapist in Me" tray, 308
This Is Me protocol, initial
phases of EMDR-sandtray-
based therapy and use of,
64–65
this was me then, and this is me
now
complex trauma client and,
280
interweave, 221–22
pendulation protocol, 204–5
thought scale, 193, 197
timelines, *109*, 109–11
generational wounds underneath addictions and, 366
neurodiverse clients and,
375–76, 377
time orientation, anchors and,
186–87. *see also* temporal
orientation
titrated mindfulness, 283–84
titration
complex trauma clients and,
278
interweaves, complex clients,
and, 283–85
portals and levels of, complex
clients and, 266–67
titration continuum, 46, 141,
201–6, 240, 271
distance and, 58
getting to know inner system
of parts and, 132
identifying and exploring targets and, 105–6
information processing and,
209–10
microprocessing and, 202–3
neurodiverse clients and, 377
pendulation and, 203–6
psychoeducation: TAPAS protocol Step 1 and, 95
segmentation of the memory
and, 202
selection of entry road and,
201
unbounded access to multiple channels of association
in, 202
tolerance and amplification of
positive affective states protocol (TAPAS)
accessing needs (Step 2),
96–97
decreasing the level of distance, 99
focus of, 94
installing affective states (Step
4), 98–99
meeting the needs (Step 3),
97–98, *98*

meeting unmet needs and,
94–99
psychoeducation (Step 1), *95,*
95–96
tone of voice. *see* vocal prosody
and tone
tools and instruments, in miniature figures collection, 394
top-down information processing, EMDR-sandtray-based
therapy and, 9
touch, as sensory-based anchor,
134–35. *see also* tactile
stimulation
trace backs, 111, 163, 174
transgender clients, preferred
pronouns and, 362
transparent fabrics, interweaves
that modulate emotions
and, 231, 287
transportation vehicles, in miniature figures collection, 392
trauma
addictions and, 364, 367, 369
AIP system imbalances and, 6
definition of, 209
dissociation as heart of, 113
generational, 360, *360*
hidden, 2
historical, 360, *360,* 363
narrowed field of affective
states and, 89
neurodivergent individuals
and, 372, 373–74
oscillation between opposites
and, 222
physical and somatic manifestation of, 250
target identification and exploration of, 140–42
unresolved and unhealed,
reenactments and, 293
voices silenced by, xiii
see also complex trauma;
developmental trauma;
historical trauma; intergenerational trauma
traumagenic memories
EMDR-sandtray as road
into, 8
self-protection and, 100
traumagenic memory networks,
209
assessment and portals for
access route into, 180, 183
entrance into, assessment
phase questions and, 180
gradual approaches to accessing, 201
trauma-related defensive strategies, 15

Index   **425**

trauma-related phobias, 7, 59, 170, 183
   attachment patterns, defenses, and, 70–72
   double bind around unmet needs and, 94
"traumatic play," complex clients and, 265
traumatized mind, polarities and, 124
trauma trays
   building, 187
   coverings in, *187,* 188, *188*
   entire system of parts invited into, 290
trays
   exploration of, working individually with the caregiver, 153–54
   representing your most challenging and easy-to-work-with clients, 307–8
   see also resource trays; sandtrays; trauma trays
tray world, coherence of, 149
triggers, reprocessing, parent–child relational dynamics and, 176
trust
   EMDR-sandtray-based therapy with adolescents and, 14
   healing of the wounded mind and, 19
   readiness for assessment and processing and, 182
   world creation and sense of, 27
tunnels, resource pendulation and use of, 206, *206*
Turner B. A., 2, 3
12-step groups, 366
two-hand interweave, 290

Uganda, effectiveness of sandplay therapy for children with history of homelessness in, 4
uncertainty, sitting with, 239
unified sense of self, absence of, 118–19
unmet needs
   blocked processing and, 216
   caregiving deficiencies and, 234
   guessing and meeting, 169–72, *171*
   recognizing and validating, during reprocessing phases, 288–89

unmyelinated vagal pathway (parasympathetic dorsal nervous system), 21
unspoken experiences, weight of, xiii
urge reduction protocols, 369
urges, actions and, 52, 398
U.S. Department of Defense, EMDR for PTSD recommendations, 8
U.S. Department of Veterans Affairs, EMDR for PTSD recommendations, 8

vagus nerve, 21
validation, 31, 94
   acknowledgment and, 45
   addiction treatment and, 366–67
   EMDR-based groups and, 320
   generational interweaves and, 242
   grief work and, 343
   low-intensity interventions and, 42
   reflections and, perpetrator-imitating parts and, 275–76
   of unmet needs, 170
   working individually with the caregiver and, 153
validity of the positive cognition (VoC) scale, 57
van der Hart, O., 113, 209
van der Kolk, B. A., 68
ventral vagal state, 156
ventral vagal system
   EMDR-sandtray and, 33
   manifestation of, in sandtray worlds, 22
vertical integration
   actively promoting, 214
   Siegel's definition of, 20
victim–perpetrator dynamics, motivational systems and, 349–50
victims and perpetrators figures, 392
victory, bringing up moments of, 53–54
video microanalysis, goal of and value of, 151
virtual EMDR-sandtray-based therapy, 369–72
visibility, offering multiple levels of, 46
visiting emotions, acknowledging, 99
visiting figures bucket, anchoring or cuing and, 88

VoC, checking, Step 2 in installation phase, 248–49
vocal prosody and tone, 33, 42, 47, 116, 301
VoC scale. *see* validity of the positive cognition (VoC) scale

waiting times, group work and reduction in, 309
war-themed items, in miniature figures collection, 394
water in sandtrays, multiple embodied encounters with, 28
weapons, in miniature figures collection, 393
weather, emotion tolerance protocol with pendulation and, questions for, 83
Wells, H. G., 2
"we-space"
   dance of autonomic states and, 301
   entry into, 19
wet sandbox, possibilities for sensory and kinesthetic stimulation in, 28
wholeness
   EMDR-sandtray-based therapy and movement toward, 9, 19
   inherent, reconnecting to, 352
   realizing, painful journey to, xiii
window of affect tolerance
   anchoring and, 186
   distance levels and, 58
   expansion of, 81
   "feeling carnivals" and "feeling parties"and, 78
   microprocessing and, 202–3, 210
   neurodiverse clients and, 377
   resource pendulation and, 206
wise characters in the tray, noticing, 51
"wiser and guiding self"
   assessing readiness and, 266
   in EMDR-sandtray-based parenting protocol, 160, 163–65, *166*
   inviting, sandtray-inner family and, 129
   reflective communication for consolidation and, 175
withdrawal symptoms, 365
"wonder box," in World Technique, 2
workplace trauma survivors, GTEP protocol effectively administered to, 311

world building and creation,
86–88
anchoring or cuing and, 88
being with and sitting with
and, 87
emotions and, 87–88
location of feelings in the
body and, 88
minor disturbance and, 88
sensory modulation strategies
and, 87
world creation and exploration
implicit and nondirective
steps in, 191–92
procedural steps for, 196
world creation step, in EMDR-
sandtray-based therapy, 33,
36–38
awareness of client's space
in, 36
placing figures in the tray in,
36–37
reflective communication
in, 36
sense of completion and, 38
world exploration step, in EMDR-
sandtray-based therapy, 33,
39–48
areas of exploration of sand
world, 48–53
conflicts and, 46
distance and, 40
general and specific questions
in, 39–41
reflective communication and
mentalizing strategies for,
42–46
somatic consciousness and,
47–48
title for world and, 39
titration continuum and, 46
World Health Organization,
EMDR PTSD recommenda-
tion, 7

World Technique, creation of, 2
World War I, Lowenfeld's
sandtray and children
impacted by, 2
worry or difficulty, current,
explicit access and story
about, 194–95
worry world
directive protocol and, 107–9
numerous surgeries and, *108*
written authorization, picture-taking and, 57

Yosso T. J., 361
young parts, working with inner
system of, in the sand,
272–73
Yunitri, N., 7

zoom-in and zoom-out
interweaves, 217
strategies, using, 45

Index   **427**

ABOUT THE AUTHOR

Ana M. Gómez is a leading expert in the field of complex trauma, dissociation, and intergenerational trauma, with a particular focus on children and adolescents. She is the founder and director of the AGATE Institute in Phoenix, AZ and a psychotherapist, author, and international speaker who has trained thousands of clinicians worldwide through workshops and keynote presentations. A recognized authority in EMDR therapy, she is a fellow of the International Society for the Study of Trauma and Dissociation (ISSTD) and the author of *EMDR Therapy and Adjunct Approaches with Children: Complex Trauma, Attachment, and Dissociation*. She is also the coeditor of *The Handbook of Complex Trauma and Dissociation in Children: Theory, Research, and Clinical Applications* and has written multiple book chapters on EMDR therapy, complex trauma, and intergenerational trauma. Her groundbreaking contributions to the field have earned her prestigious awards, including the *Francine Shapiro Award* (EMDRIA, 2023), the *Hope Award* (Sierra Tucson, 2012), and the *Distinguished Service Award* (Arizona Play Therapy Association, 2011).